President
David Baldwin

Executive Director
Mary Warlick

Interactive & Marketing Director/Editor
Kevin Swanepoel

Editor
Audrey N. Carpio

Contributing Editors
Emily Isovitsch
Maiko Shiratori

Designer
Danielle Macagney

Cover and Divider Page Design
Faile/Brooklyn

Published by
One Club Publishing LLC
21 E. 26th Street, 5th Floor
New York, NY 10010
Tel: +1 (212) 979 1900
Fax: +1 (212) 979 5006
Email: publishing@oneclub.org
Web: www.oneclub.org
In Association with The One Club

First Printing
ISBN: 0-929837-30-4

Distribution (USA and International)
Rockport Publishers, Inc.,
a member of
Quayside Publishing Group
33 Commercial Street
Gloucester, MA 01930, USA
Web: www.rockpub.com
www.quaysidepublishinggroup.com

Copyright © 2006 as a collection by The One Club. All Rights Reserved. No part of this book or DVD may be reproduced in any way by any means whatsoever without the expressed written consent of the publisher.

INTRODUCTION // CREDITS

Introduction

002 The One Club
003 President
004 Interactive and Marketing Director
005 One Show Interactive Judges
008 Judges' Choice

Pencil Winners

024 Banners: Fixed Space
036 Banners: Dynamic
046 Beyond the Banner
056 Web Sites
096 Brand Gaming
098 Viral & Email
110 Online Movies
120 Innovation & Development
126 Other Digital Media
146 Integrated Branding
160 College Competition

Merit Winners

168 Banners: Fixed Space
177 Banners: Dynamic
184 Beyond the Banner
204 Web Sites
238 Brand Gaming
242 Wireless
243 Online Movies / Viral & Email
253 Other Digital Media
255 Innovation & Development
260 Integrated Branding
264 College Competition

Index

268

The One Club

THE ONE CLUB

Based in New York City, The One Club was founded in 1975 and is a non-profit organization dedicated to maintaining the highest standards of creativity in advertising. Its 1,000 members include many of advertising's most respected art directors and copywriters, as well as students of advertising.

MISSION

As part of its mission to promote high standards of creative excellence, The One Club produces the advertising industry's most prestigious awards program, The One Show. Judged by a panel of the advertising industry's elite creative directors, this annual event acknowledges excellence in art direction, design, and copywriting in a variety of categories, including television, radio, newspapers, magazines, billboards and public service. The coveted One Show "Gold Pencils" are regarded as the zenith of achievement in the advertising world.

In 1998, The One Club launched One Show Interactive, the first awards show dedicated exclusively to advertising in new media. With the One Show Interactive awards, The One Club extended its mission of recognizing creative excellence to the field of new media.

PROGRAMS

The One Club regularly produces a variety of events, programs and publications that encourage aspiring advertising professionals to hone their craft. These programs include:

- "Gold on Gold" Lecture Series—award-winning industry professionals discussing the creative process

- Student Portfolio Reviews

- One Show College Competition

- Creative Workshops

- one.a magazine—a quarterly publication by and for advertising creatives

- One Club Gallery Exhibitions

- Traveling One Show Exhibitions

- The One Show Annual, the indispensable hard cover reference showcasing the best advertising worldwide

- The One Show Interactive Annual, the first book of its kind, highlighting the best new media advertising

EDUCATION

In 1995, The One Club established an education department, dedicated to fostering the creative talents of advertising students nationwide. The department sponsors educational programs and events, and administers scholarships to outstanding students in advertising programs at selected colleges and advertising schools throughout the country.

DAVID BALDWIN
President // The One Club

It's time to admit it: interactive is now good old-fashioned traditional marketing. Okay, maybe it's good new-fashioned traditional marketing, but you know what I mean.

Remember all the delineations between traditional marketing and interactive marketing? Interactive was this world where many clients and agencies were just making the step into, some boldly, some rather timidly. Well, I wish I was talking about five years ago, but I'm talking about six months ago and in some instances, right now.

A funny thing has happened in the world. Interactive is now plain old traditional marketing. It's just another tool in the toolbox, often at the center, but just another tool. It is, however, one of the best ways to facilitate a conversation between a brand and its customers. It's often the glue.

The question now isn't whether interactive is brave or bold or something a brand should be doing. The question is whether your interactive is any good. Is it inspiring and engaging and moving people to act and do all the things traditional advertising is supposed to do?

Look through the work here and tell me you don't find all of that and more, because this is the best in the world, my friends. Created by the best people and judged by the best judges.

Humble congratulations to all of this year's winners.

Kevin Swanepoel
Marketing & Interactive Director // The One Club

A mere five years after the Internet was pronounced dead, it has staged a remarkable comeback. But it isn't just back, it's now even better than we imagined.

Interactive advertising continues to experience tremendous growth. Internet advertising revenues in the U.S. totaled $12.5 billion in 2005, a new annual record exceeding the previous year by 30 percent. And high-speed Internet access in U.S. homes now reaches 73 million.

Agencies and clients are discovering the effectiveness of building brands online and creating one-on-one brand experiences with their consumers using this engaging medium.

The Internet is also fulfilling many of the visions that were bandied about in the late '90s—legal music, TV and movie downloads, Internet phones, high-speed wireless access and the proliferation of real, online communities.

This year, One Show Interactive reflects these trends: entries were up by a record 40 percent, and the work tested the boundaries between innovation and creativity.

And for the first time, six of the 35 creative directors who judged this year's award show came from predominantly traditional agencies.

One Show Interactive, like the One Show, is about rewarding great creative advertising; it's always been about the Idea. I look forward to the time when it is not about the technology, or whatever new channel or medium, or whether the concept came from an account guy, media person or a creative—but rather when we can look through One Show annuals and marvel at simply great creative advertising, period.

We at the One Club most sincerely thank our jury of 35 interactive judges who traveled from nine countries, and who spent many intensive hours viewing banners, clicking through Web sites, and yes, playing games, to decide this year's best interactive advertising. Moreover, we appreciate the discussion they brought, and the occasional verbal brawls—this ongoing debate only furthers our understanding of what interactivity means to the industry, what direction it's heading, and where creativity will emerge from next.

Interactive Judges

JEFF BENJAMIN (CHAIR)
Crispin Porter + Bogusky / Miami

DAVE BEDWOOD
Lean Mean Fighting Machine / London

NICKE BERGSTROM
Farfar / Stockholm

RASMUS BLAESBJERG
Saatchi & Saatchi / Los Angeles

JOAKIM BORGSTRÖM
DoubleYou / Barcelona

JOHN BUTLER
Butler, Shine, Stern & Partners / Sausalito

MARK CHALMERS
Strawberry Frog / Amsterdam

PAUL COLLINS
Framfab / Stockholm

CRYSTAL ENGLISH
Venable, Bell & Partners / San Francisco

PETE FAVAT
Arnold / Boston

DAN FEDERMAN
Big Spaceship / New York

PIERO FRESCOBALDI
Unit 9 / London

DOMINIC GOLDMAN
Publicis & Hal Riney / San Francisco

JULIANE HADEM
Tribal DDB / New York

FLORIAN HEISS
Dare Digital / London

REI INAMOTO
AKQA / San Francisco

DOUG JAEGER
The Happy Corp / New York

KRIS KIGER
R/GA / New York

THORSTEN KRAUS
Scholz & Volkmer / Wiesbaden

MAURICIO MAZZARIOL
DM9DDB / São Paulo

PETTER RINGBOM
Flat / New York

SEB ROYCE
Glue / London

YASUHARU SASAKI
Dentsu / Tokyo

MICHAEL SCHMIDT
Cuban Council / San Francisco

GLEN SHEEHAN
Wunderman / Irvine

FRED SIQUEIRA
AgenciaClick / São Paulo

YOSHI SODEOKA
Project C505 / New York

NIKO STUMPO
Hanazuki / Amsterdam

IAIN TAIT
Poke / London

KISHIMOTO TAKAYOSHI
Unit9 / London

MARK TAYLOR
Crispin Porter + Bogusky / Miami

REMON TIJSSEN
Fluid / Tilburg

JOHNNY VULKAN
Anomaly / New York

VICKI WONG
Meomi / Vancouver

JÖRG WALDSCHÜTZ
Neue Digitale / Frankfurt

Counterfeit Mini Integrated

AGENCY // Crispin Porter + Bogusky . CLIENT // MINI
ANNUAL ID // 06057N

NICKE BERGSTROM
Farfar / Stockholm

I must say that I had a hard time finding my one favorite because two pieces had a strong impact on me. They are very different yet they both show how outstanding interactive communication can be.

The UK Pavilion shows how great it is to physically interact with things on a screen. Interaction beyond the browser is awesome and it's definitely something I want to see a lot more of in the future. But I never got the chance to experience the Pavilion live and therefore my personal favorite is The Counterfeit MINI campaign. It has so many angles to it. It's integrated. It's entertaining. It's relevant and it feels fresh and unique. I'm impressed by all the content and the balance between feeling low-key home-made and at the same time being a full blown campaign in many different medias with amazing quality in the details.

JUDGES' CHOICE // NICKE BERGSTROM / DAVE BEDWOOD / SEB ROYCE

Mini Convertible-izer-ometer

AGENCY // Taxi . **CLIENT //** MINI Canada
ANNUAL ID // 06012N

DAVE BEDWOOD
Lean Mean Fighting Machine / London

When you look to great examples of advertising you rarely look to online. Why? Because the great writers and art directors usually work in the big ATL agencies. Online has traditionally been more about design and technology, and quite often the award juries galvanize this. Hence why I like this bit of work so much. It isn't a newfangled bit of technology, it isn't even a new idea, it's an online questionnaire, how boring. But it is written so well, the humor is spot on and perfect for MINI. This quality of writing is the skill and expertise we need to see more of in online. Marry this with the already brilliant design and technology practitioners and we will start to see more great advertising.

SEB ROYCE
Glue / London

I love the MINI work coming out of Canada. The thing that really sets it apart for me is the tone and the quality of the writing, something that is almost a forgotten art on the web and these days. This piece for the MINI convertible hasn't had money thrown at it but has been beautifully written with a tone and art direction that is bang on the MINI brand—engaging, fun, tongue-in-cheek, leftfield. It made the whole jury laugh and survives repeat visits unlike much web content where design is the main attraction. Go MINI go.

Judges' Choice
9

Dream Kitchens for Everyone

AGENCY // Forsman & Bodenfors. CLIENT // IKEA Sweden
ANNUAL ID // 06024N

JOAKIM BORGSTRÖM
DoubleYou / Barceclona

This is a great example of the combination of a simple idea and great production. Turning the *Matrix* effect into an interactive experience makes this piece unique. It's like visiting the Ikea showrooms, when you go around and explore the kitchens. 100 percent viral. Turn up the volume and enjoy!

KRIS KIGER
R/GA / New York

Perfect, beautiful execution. This site was so simple in what it did, but it did that one thing very well. Its smooth animation of a 360 degree view of one frozen moment in time seamlessly transformed from space to space. Married with an amazing soundtrack, each vignette had a tone and style appropriate to the type of kitchen it was showing. Fabulous, perfect way for people to experience how dynamic and different each of the IKEA are.

PETTER RINGBOM
Flat / New York

IKEA's "Dream Kitchens For All" has got to be my pick. It's simple, engaging and has an incredible wow-factor. The first time I saw the site, I was simply blown away, which doesn't happen very often. You could argue that it's lacking in technological innovation and having a big concept, but with its simple interaction, flawless execution and very satisfying payoff, it really doesn't matter.

JUDGES' CHOICE // JOAKIM BORGSTRÖM / KRIS KIGER / PETTER RINGBOM / MARK CHALMERS

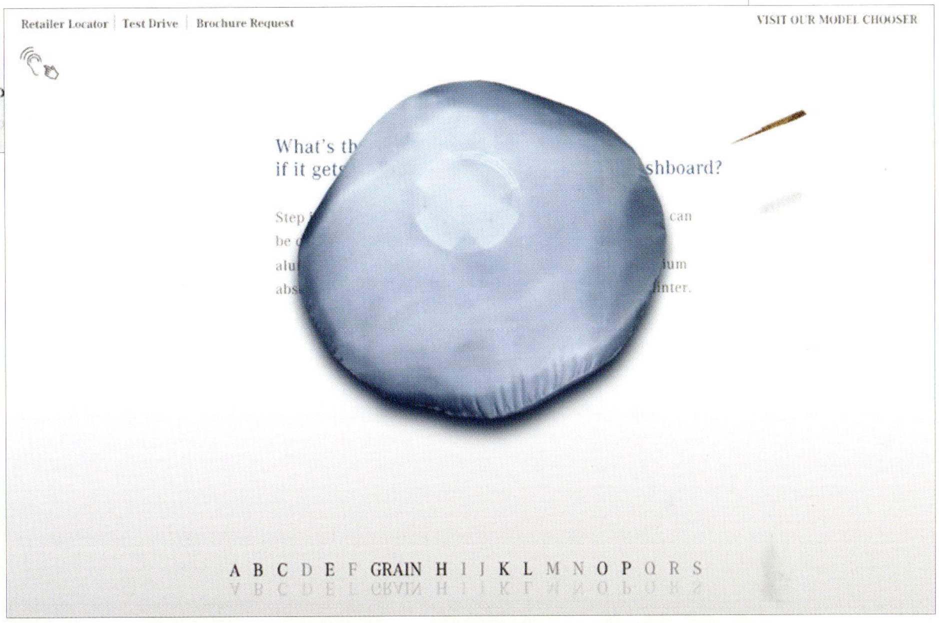

From A-Class to S-Class

AGENCY // Agency Republic . CLIENT // Mercedes Benz Passenger Cars UK
ANNUAL ID // 06027N

MARK CHALMERS
Strawberry Frog / Amsterdam

MINI work and W+K's Honda work for redefining the category of car advertising in general, but I hand it to Agency Republic for redefining car advertising online. We've all seen the simulations and the perfect 3D journeys around the perfect product, but "from A-Class to S-Class" is the only work that has translated the ever-progressive Mercedes Benz technologies into textural and emotional values online. It's so good it's like popping bubble wrap. I'd better shut up about this one. I'm continually singing its praises. Take your award, get drunk.

Judges' Choice
11

Featured Logo

AGENCY // Daddy . CLIENT // Volksvagen Sverige

PAUL COLLINS
Framfab Sweden and Paregos / Stockholm

Standards are forever being raised in the different interactive categories, but it's still the simple, clever ideas, based on traditional advertising techniques, that catch my eye. After going through numerous entries in the rich media ads category, I found one piece of work that stood out and really grabbed my attention. It was a cool banner ad for VW, produced by the Gothenburg-based agency Daddy. They did a great job of exposing the user to multi USPs by simply using the company's logotype in a context of animation.

This ad hit the right balance between multi-messaging communication and branding; a truly great piece of work.

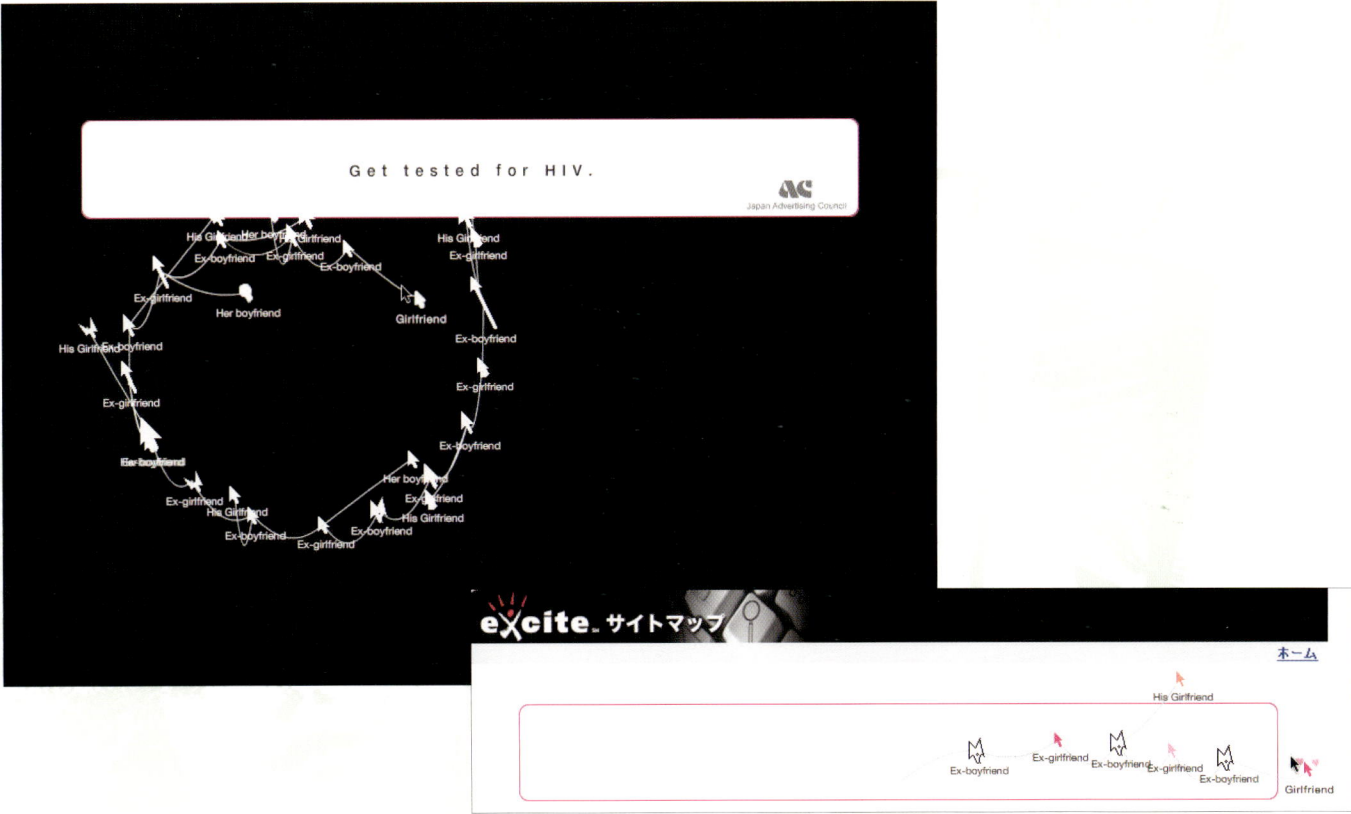

Her Past

AGENCY // Dentsu . **CLIENT //** Japan Advertising Council
ANNUAL ID // 06011N

CRYSTAL ENGLISH
Venable Bell and Partners / San Francisco

There were so many great entries this year, both big and small, but for me it was one of the little guys that stood out. These days it's difficult to do something fresh in the banner category, but the Japan Advertising Council's banner, "Her Past," surprised a rather jaded jury with a banner to raise HIV awareness in Japan. It used a simple medium, one often taken for granted, in a smart and powerful way. An interactive cursor pulls from a woman's name an endless history of boyfriends, their girlfriends, their boyfriend's girlfriends, and so on and on—creating this endless web of possible infection points. The design, interactivity and idea were seamless in communicating a message we're all familiar with, but with such intelligence and creativity that it created a visceral reaction. A perfect example of how a simple, smart execution can have a big impact.

VICKI WONG
Meomi / Vancouver

This piece stands out to me as a truly creative way to communicate a very difficult and delicate message within tight technological restraints. The visual aesthetics are elegant and clever, complimenting the approach without being preachingly pedantic (as often happens with social messages when they are translated into 'advertisements'). The interactivity is subtle and appropriately witty. I commend the designers on an excellent piece of problem solving.

Comcastic.com

AGENCY // Goodby Silverstein & Partners . CLIENT // Comcast
ANNUAL ID // 06028N

DAN FEDERMAN
Big Spaceship / New York

Who wants to hear marketing yada yada about the benefits of high-speed Internet or On Demand entertainment? Comcastic gives the gist using simple metaphors. On Demand? Command this puppet right here. High speed? See how fast you can control your mouse. Animation blazes, sound is great, design is super-clean, puppets have some of the best IK I've seen in Flash and the voice functionality is truly amazing. Overall, a truly outstanding interactive experience.

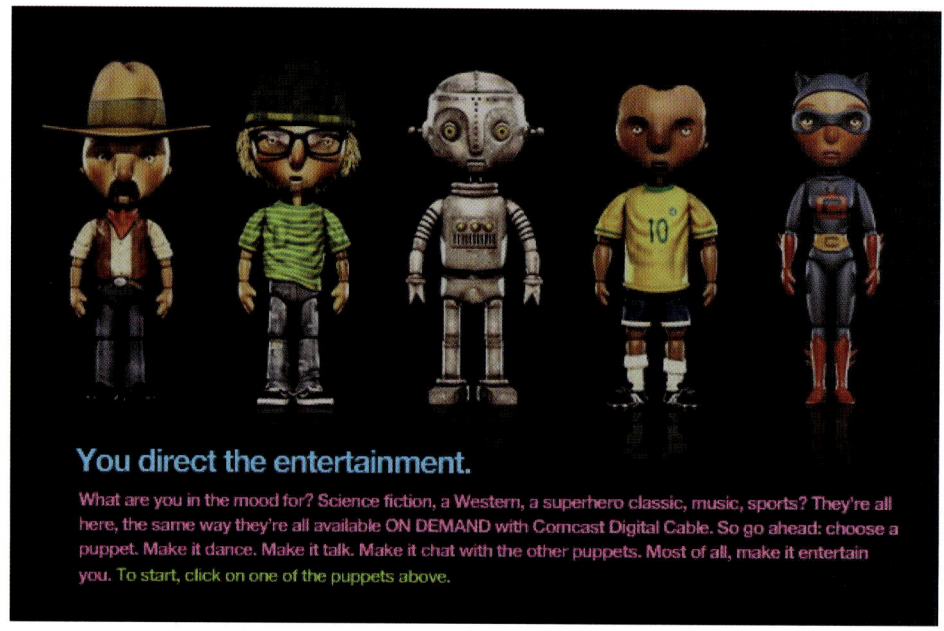

Animal Vision

AGENCY // Lowe Tesch . CLIENT // Saab Automobile
ANNUAL ID // 06023N

FLO HEISS
Dare Digital / London

There were some heated discussions in the interactive jury over what should get Gold and what shouldn't. Most of the time we concurred, but not always.

I am therefore delighted to get the opportunity here to pick out my favorite piece this year which only got Bronze: Lowe Tesch's Animal Vision site for Saab.

On this site one jumps into the skins of different Swedish forest animals allowing one to marvel at the car from different angles. There is a moose, an owl and a red fox amongst others. Once you have found the lynx the car drives off and leaves you with the line "Not all Swedish animals live in the forest."

I love this site for it's simple idea and beautiful horror-movie-esque execution.

And yes, it did make me want to buy the car.

JÖRG WALDSCHÜTZ
Neue Digitale / Frankfurt

From the outset I was fascinated with the site, which immediately captivates the user. Like an exciting thriller, the user is sent on an interactive tour of discovery around the vehicle. This simple idea of placing the car in a snowy forest at night, seen from the view of various wild animals, positions it without fail at the centre of an assumed drama.

Even though hardly any further content on the Saab 9-5 Sedan and 9-5 Sport-Combi can be found on closer inspection, the site remains both visually and audibly a genuine experience that increases product awareness and desire for the new Saab.

UK Pavilion

AGENCY // Land Design Studio . CLIENT // UK Government,
Foreign & Commonwealth Office . ANNUAL ID // 06055N

JULIANE HADEM
Tribal DDB Worldwide / New York

I was encouraged by the body of work submitted this year. While the majority of the work continues to be tactical in nature, it's clear that agencies and clients are finally realizing that big, multi-channel ideas are needed to truly engage the consumer.

My personal favorite was the UK Pavilion at the Aichi Expo 05 in Japan. The pavilion interior contained seven original interactive installations that were inspired by nature and approached environmental challenges with new technologies in a very dynamic and innovative way.

KRIS KIGER
R/GA / New York

This was a beautiful example of a completely immersive experience. The combination of elegant visuals, simple animation and sound made you feel like you were entering into another place all together. The interactions seem to play with type and design in such a smart and effective way. It was truly memorable, and that was just from experiencing it from a video! I can only imagine how it would feel to actually be in the space.

I loved this piece because it represents an immersive transformative experience, and is what I could imagine all interactions being in this medium. It becomes something much more encompassing and moving beyond the simple bounds of the screen.

VON NULL AUF HUNDERT IN 6,5 SEKUNDEN:
DER MEGANE RENAULT SPORT.

HIER ERFAHREN SIE MEHR ▸

Renault Megane Sport

AGENCY // Nordpol+ Hamburg . CLIENT // Renault Germany
ANNUAL ID // 06035N

REI INAMOTO
AKQA / San Francisco

The interactive category is a really difficult category to judge because of its very nature: One has to interacte with it and spend some time with the work in order to get the full effect. Often times, the work that wins in award shows is the one that's easy to judge and quick to get. For that reason, I don't believe any award show is a good representation of the best work being done by creatives around the world today.

Having said, this piece stood out of me for a few simple reasons:

- The work had a clear idea behind it.
- The idea was based on the truth about the product it's advertising.
- It was executed well and interactive (after all, this is the interactive category. The work should be representative of that word.)

Above all, what struck me so strongly was its simplicity. The idea was so pure and so was the execution. The people who did this work restrained themselves from putting any frills. It's so elegantly subtractive and the message shines through so clearly.

FRED SIQUEIRA
AgênciaClick / São Paulo

F.ck! How come I didn't think about it before?

Amid huge productions, media innovations, the omnipresence of viral concepts and so on, what always most impressed me is a simple and powerful idea like this one. A clear and direct message with a perfect use of the media, allowing the user to experience, with an ordinary day-by-day tool (the scroll bar), the true essence of the ad: acceleration. This is about clever simplicity.

Judges' Choice
17

SithSense

AGENCY // Crispin Porter + Bogusky . CLIENT // Burger King
ANNUAL ID // 06021N

MAURICIO MAZZARIOL
DMB9DDB / São Paulo

2005 was a great year for interactive and for the industry in general, so it was hard to choose among so many brilliant works, but in my opinion there's one that deserves special attention. Burger King's SithSense.

The ad gives the user, through a simple but amazing engine, a rich and entertaining experience. It's a once-in-a-life-time chance to challenge Darth Vader himself, one of the biggest pop culture characters, in a mind guessing game.

Relevant, conceptual, entertaining and beautifully art directed.

Communication Evolved

AGENCY // THA LTD . CLIENT // Amana
ANNUAL ID // 06029N

KISHIMOTO TAKAYOSHI
Unit 9 / London

I have chosen "Communication Evolved" as my Judge's Choice because I feel the project has achieved the "ideal model" in terms of using the Internet as a passive medium.

The simplicity of the approach, digitally displaying a different image every second, accompanied by beautiful music, emphasizes the sheer vastness of the product, and creates a strong emotional engagement with the brand.

By gathering together a large number of photos, classifying and editing them, then displaying them on the screen as a continuous experience, the project is analogous to the Internet itself. The Internet has the same structure, collecting vast amounts of information that are later classified by various technologies (like search engines, etc.), in an attempt to grasp at the truth.

I'm giving it a huge round of applause for the creators' deep insight and its beautiful execution.

Nike Run London Integrated

AGENCY // AKQA . CLIENT // Nike
ANNUAL ID // 06058N

IAIN TAIT
Poke / London

From my point of view the work for Nike's Run London campaign truly represents from start-to-finish what an integrated campaign should be all about. Starting from the insight that runners are human, and things get in the way of our desire to keep running. The campaign asked people to pledge to "Run a Year" then supported them with a series of events, emails and web content (including probably the best brand Google Maps mash-up I've seen—allowing runners to plot and share their running routes of London).

The highlight of the campaign was a 10k run where chips attached to runners' shoes enabled Nike to email (or send to their mobile) a video clip of them crossing the finish line just hours after the event.

In a world of glossy, overproduced, sportswear campaigns, Run London had purpose, deep engagement, and surprisingly for a brand site, a real reason to exist.

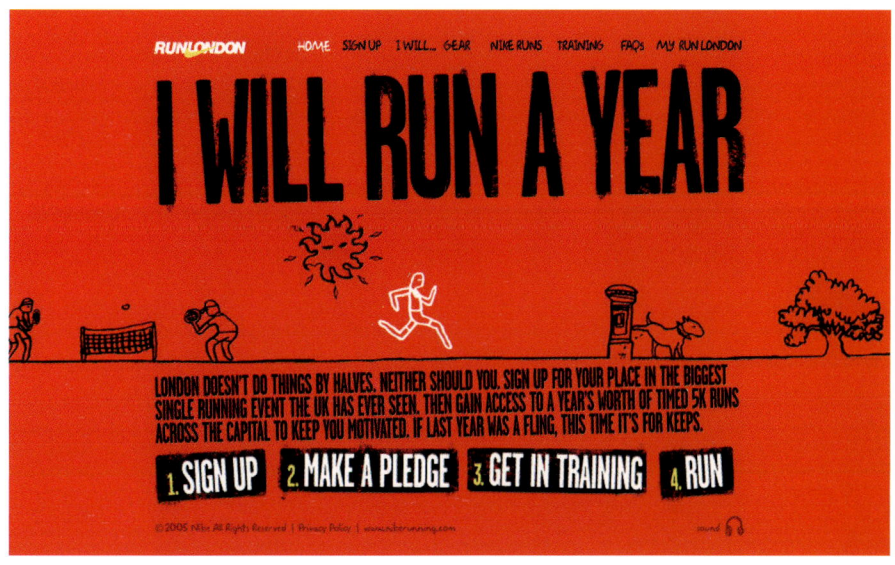

20 JUDGES' CHOICE // IAIN TAIT / KISHIMOTO TAKAYOSHI

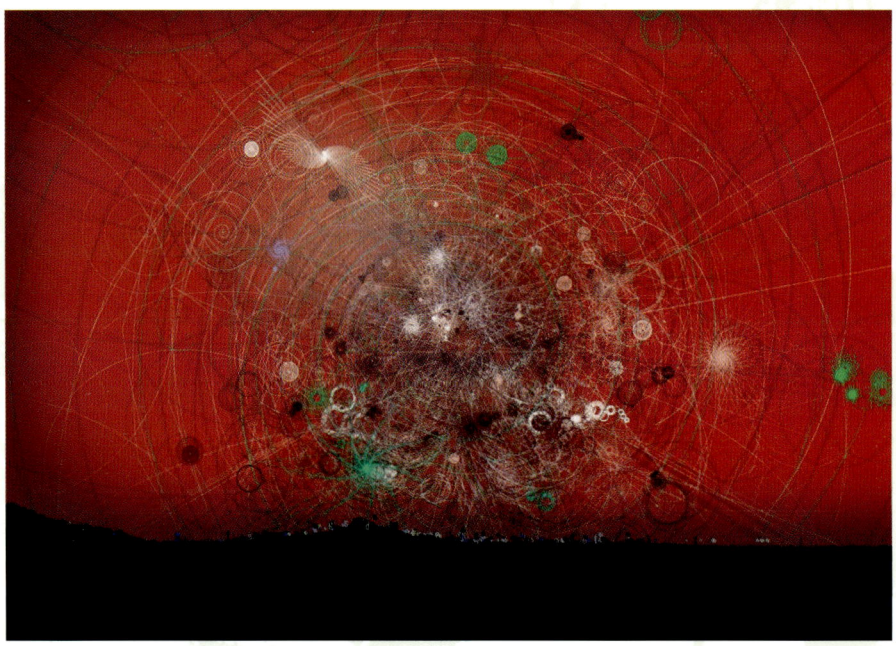

Spam Recycling

AGENCY // Jung von Matt . CLIENT // EnBW
ANNUAL ID // 06025N

YASUHARU SASAKI
Dentsu / Tokyo

One day, I got a short email from a lady.
It was an email notifying me of a change in our meeting time.
However, I had no clue about this meeting and even about this lady.
This email must be addressed to someone else by mistake. So I didn't reply to it.
The following day, I got an email from her apologizing that she sent the email by mistake.
That was what I expected.

From that day on, she began to email me about nothing, just small talk.
She's 27 years old, works as a secretary but makes a lot of mistakes at work so her boss often scolds her. Her hobby is Japanese flower arrangement and now she is into yoga.
168 cm height.

Over the past two weeks, that lady had emailed me more than ten times.
Still, I never replied to her. Then one day, she got out of touch for a while.
I wonder what has happened to her and it bugged me a little.

Few days later, I got an email from her.
She told me that she made a big mistake at work and that she was really upset, and that she wanted to be comforted by someone. And she said that she wanted to see me if possible.
Finally, for the first time, she gave me an address where to meet her.
It was a link to SPAM.

Spam mail in Japan is evolving.
I think the Spam Recycling site contributes to global peace. It is just fabulous. Beautiful.
Hope this will support Japanese Kanji characters soon.

A Clockwork Arrange

DDB Brasil's ingenious banner tells the exact time and sends the message that your package is well taken care of, to the minutest detail.

AWARD:
SILVER

CATEGORY:
Banners . Fixed Space:
Business To Consumer . Single

AGENCY:
DDB Brasil / São Paulo

CLIENT:
FedEx

ART DIRECTOR:
Pedro Gravena

WRITER:
Keke Toledo

PRODUCTION COMPANIES:
Heloisa Lima, Roberta Padilla
Renata Oliveira, Sandra Zimb
Helena Bordon

CREATIVE DIRECTORS:
Sergio Valente, Wilson Mateos
Marcos Medeiros, Fernanda Romano

ANNUAL ID:
06001N

URL:
http://www.dm9ddb.com.br/
awards/oneshow/justintime.html

How did you synchronize the clock with the real time? It is a very simple flash action script that synchronizes animations with the computer's clock. Every number in Fedex's clock is an animation of the boxes arriving to build the number and then leaving. This animation is controlled by the computer's clock, thus they can last one second, one minute or one hour, according to the clock's time.

Where did you get the idea for the clock, and is that a factory line? There was no intention to relate the ad with a production line. The proposal was to show the deliveries arriving and leaving accurately in the instant that they would, and that was the insight for the clock. I know that is a current relationship, and that there are many greats works using clocks on the Web*, so I tried to make it as simple as possible. Then came the idea of using the boxes. They are a strong FedEx icon and represent all kinds of stuff, so I thought that a clock made by FedEx boxes could be the best way to express the idea.

* Human Clock (www.humanclock.com)
  A dot for every second in the day
  (www.vendian.org/envelope/dir2/day_of_dots_clock/?do=11:48:12#topofclock)
  Clockblock, Clocksphere and Industrious clock (www.yugop.com)

Pencil Winners
25

The Sound of Her Voice

Now here is a banner that gives good aural. An advertisement for an adult shop starts off quite innocently with a woman recounting the time she ran into an old flame. The cursor starts to vibrate as the narrator's speech, still uninterrupted, explodes with intriguing sighs.

AWARD:
BRONZE
CATEGORY:
Banners . Fixed Space:
Business To Consumer . Single
AGENCY:
ant / Tokyo
CLIENT:
Lovely Pop
ART DIRECTORS:
Norikazu Yamashita
Takanori Yamada
WRITER:
Takayuki Hino
DESIGNER:
Norikazu Yamashita
DIGITAL ARTIST/MULTIMEDIA:
Yukihiro Sasae
CREATIVE DIRECTOR:
Takayuki Hino
ID:
06002N
URL:
http://www.a-n-t.jp/
06awards/pop/voice_e.html

My Name is Roy G Biv

Want individuality and the name brand without the messy adventure of spray-painting a pair of sneakers? Framfab's glossy banner commands you to identify yourself, and through the power of naming, your own uniquely hued shoe is born.

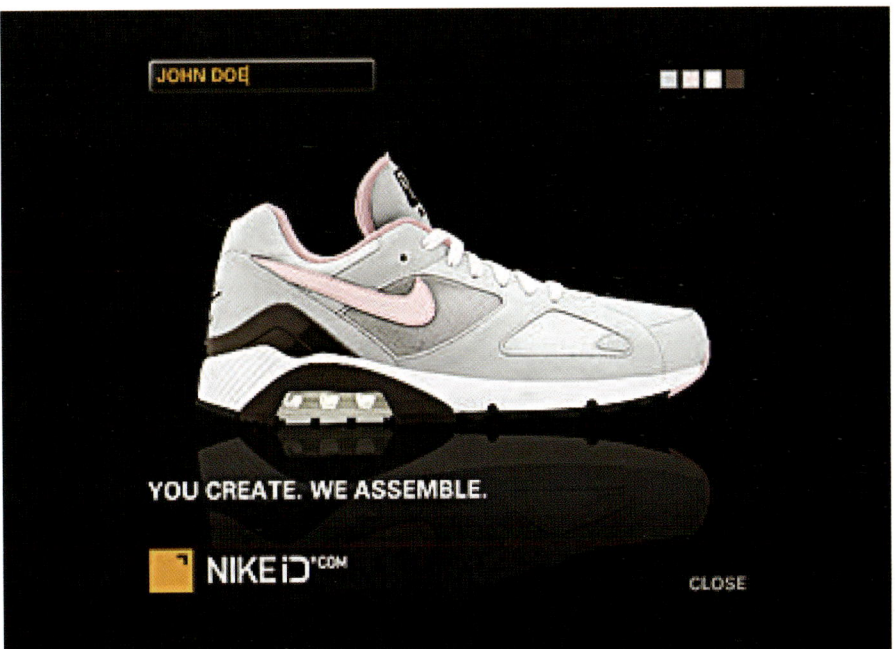

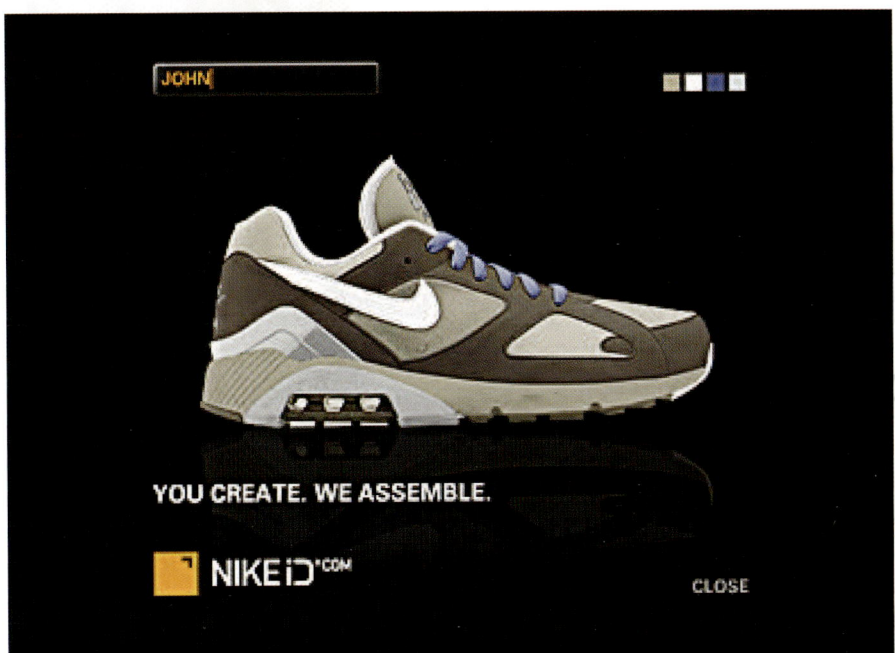

AWARD:
BRONZE
CATEGORY:
Banners . Fixed Space:
Business To Consumer . Single
AGENCY:
Framfab / Copenhagen
CLIENT:
Nike
DESIGNER:
Patrik Danielsson
PROGRAMMER:
Jesper Weiss
CREATIVE DIRECTOR:
Lars Cortsen
CONTENT STRATEGIST:
Martin Kristensen
ID:
06003N
URL:
http://nikeid-europe.nike.com/nikeid
-europe/banner/identify_yourself

Mean Streets

It's high noon and there's a crazed sniper in the clocktower. He's shooting from all directions and you think maybe it's not just one lone gunman. Where to hide? Where to run? Mayhem, madness, and indeed, funny interactive killing ensue on the sidewalks of this black-and-white charmer evocative of classic gangster films.

This is not your typical athletic ad. What inspired you to use this kind of imagery for a gym? The inspiration was taken from old-time movies, in which giant threats and surreal catastrophes spread panic through big cities. That was a fun way to express the concept "Run and Live Longer."

One of the judges, Joakim Borgstrom, described the banner as 100 percent Brazilian. What do you think he means? The most accurate answer to this question comes from Joakim himself: "Maybe the best example of what a juror wants to see after several hours of judging. You don't need to explain anything. Just one minute of simple interactive funny killing. What a pleasure. Great sound ambient. One shot." Thanks Joakim.

AWARD:
GOLD
CATEGORY:
Banners . Fixed Space:
Business To Consumer .
Campaign
AGENCY:
DDB Brasil / São Paulo
ART DIRECTOR:
Mauricio Mazzariol
WRITER:
Mauricio Mazzariol
PRODUCTION COMPANIES:
Heloisa Lima, Roberta Padilla
Renata Oliveira, Helena Bordon
Sandra Zimb
CREATIVE DIRECTORS:
Sergio Valente, Ricardo Chester
Felipe Cama, Fernanda Romano
CLIENT:
Companhia Athletica
ID:
06004N
URL:
http://www.dm9ddb.com.br/
awards/oneshow/run01.html

Erasing the Roof

The low-slung roof of a MINI is a great place to show off one's creative stylings and mad personalization skills without involving fuzzy dice. Using artful tools appropriated from childhood, like spin-painting and Lite-Brite pegs, you can create abstract or pointillist masterpieces that loudly announce you wherever you go (as well conveniently disguise bird crap).

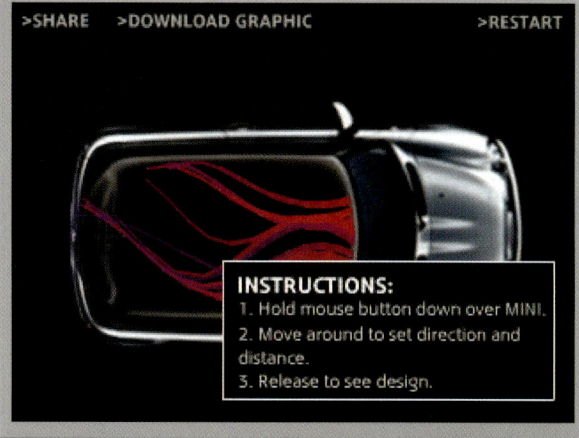

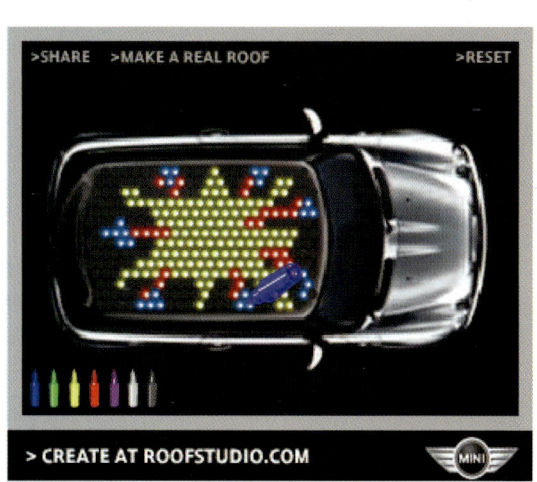

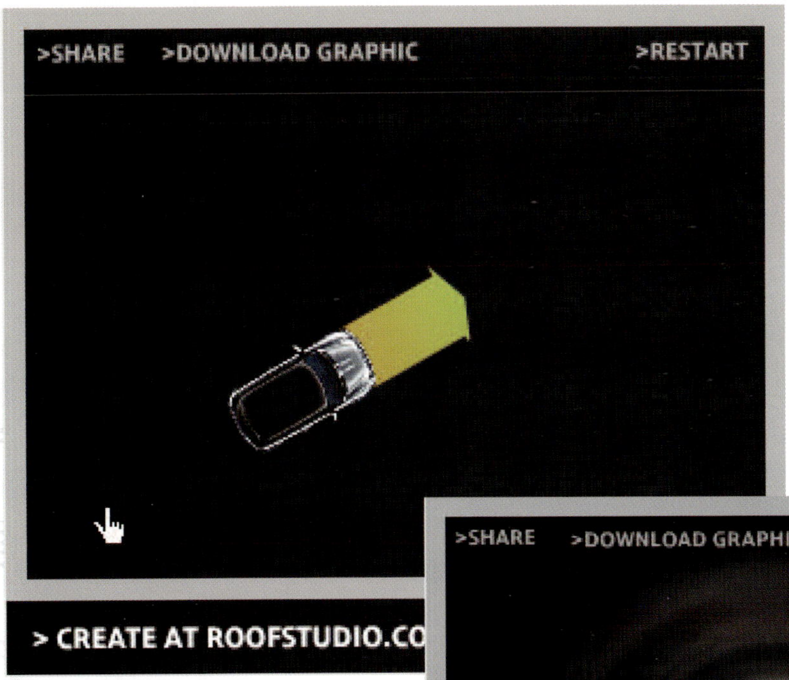

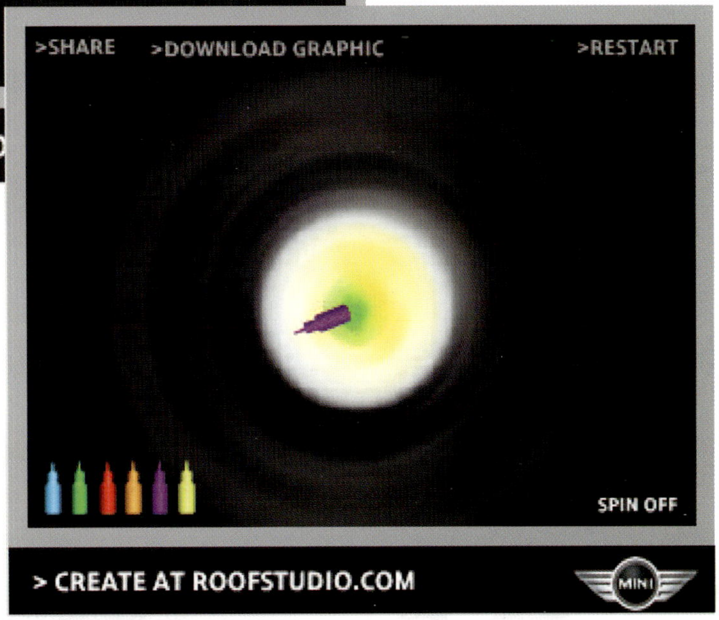

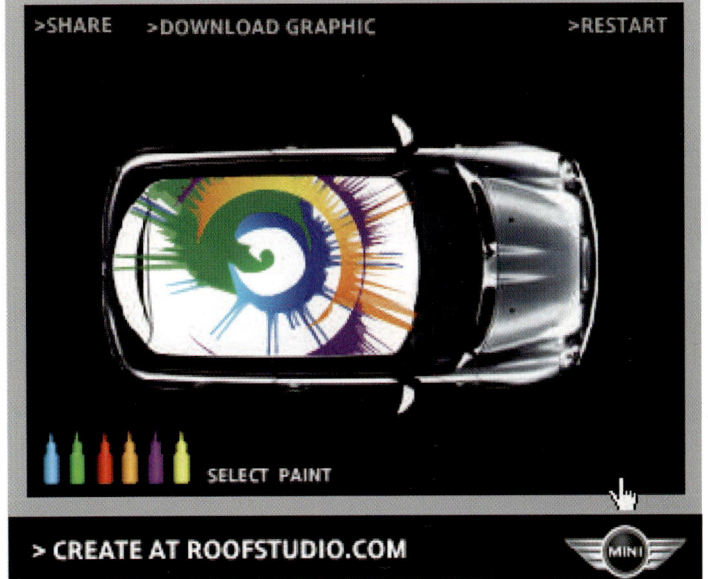

AWARD:
SILVER
CATEGORY:
Banners . Fixed Space:
Business To Consumer .
Campaign
AGENCY:
Crispin Porter + Bogusky / Miami
CLIENT:
MINI
ART DIRECTOR:
Rahul Panchal
WRITER:
Brian Tierney
DESIGNER:
Chean Wei Law
PRODUCTION COMPANY:
Dev Impact
CREATIVE DIRECTORS:
Alex Bogusky, Andrew Keller
Rob Strasberg, Jeff Benjamin
ID:
06005N
URL:
http://www.cpbgroup.com/awards
/roofstudiobanners.html

A Hard-hitting Message

A child is not a punching bag. Agency.com addresses an important social problem with sensitivity, using simple but stark visuals.

AWARD:
SILVER

CATEGORY:
Banners . Fixed Space:
Public Service / Non-Profit /
Educational . Single

AGENCY:
Agency.com / London

CLIENT:
NSPCC

ART DIRECTOR:
Scott Bedford

WRITER:
Jon Mackness

DESIGNERS:
Wil Bevan, Rob Mills
Paul Collins

CREATIVE DIRECTOR:
Paul Banham

ID:
06006N

URL:
http://awards.london.agency.com
/nspcc/july_05/index_01.html

Childhood bruises aren't always accidental.

Help us stop it. Donate now.

NSPCC
Cruelty to children must stop. FULL STOP.

What was the brief from the client? The objective of this campaign was to encourage a predominately male target audience to donate £10 a month to the National Society for the Prevention of Cruelty to Children (NSPCC). This was a new audience for NSPCC—normally activity focuses on £2 a month donation targets.

Describe your creative approach. The creative deliberately took an emotive route in order to grab the attention of the audience and give them a clear reason to donate £10 a month. This execution powerfully focuses on the physical abuse of children, depicting a child swinging, before a punchbag swings across the unit. The creative simply invites the user to think about the abuse from a child's point of view.

Rev and Run

This expanding banner provides several unbeatable minutes of time-wasting fun, as you race against the computer or challenge friends in a slot car rally race.

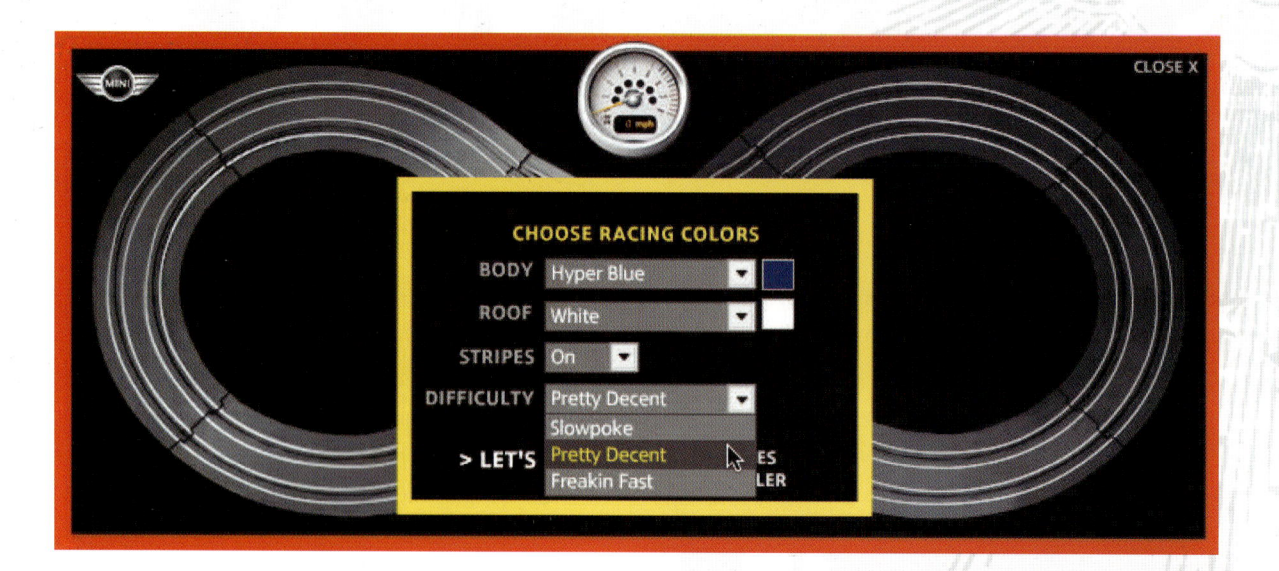

AWARD:
SILVER

CATEGORY:
Banners . Dynamic: Business To Consumer . Single

AGENCY:
Crispin Porter + Bogusky / Miami

CLIENT:
MINI

WRITER:
Brian Tierney

DESIGNER:
Chean Wei Law

PROGRAMMER:
Domani Studios

CREATIVE DIRECTORS:
Alex Bogusky, Andrew Keller
Jeff Benjamin

ID:
06007N

URL:
http://www.cpbgroup.com/awards/rallyrace.html

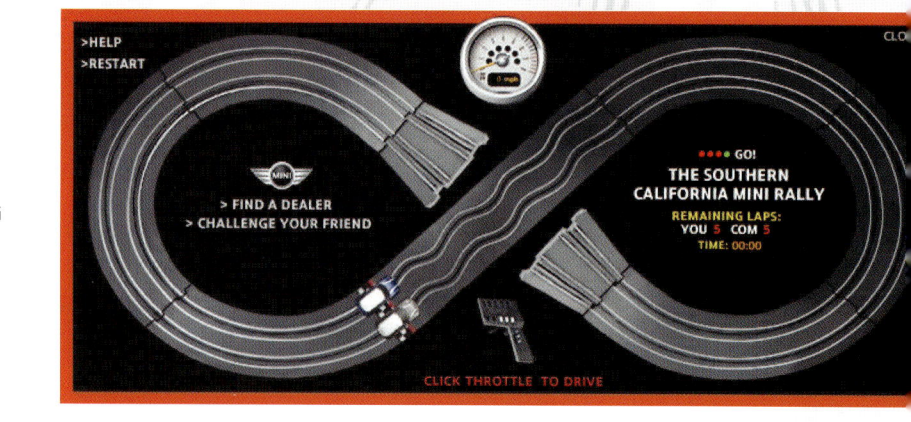

SILVER WINNER // CRISPIN PORTER + BOGUSKY

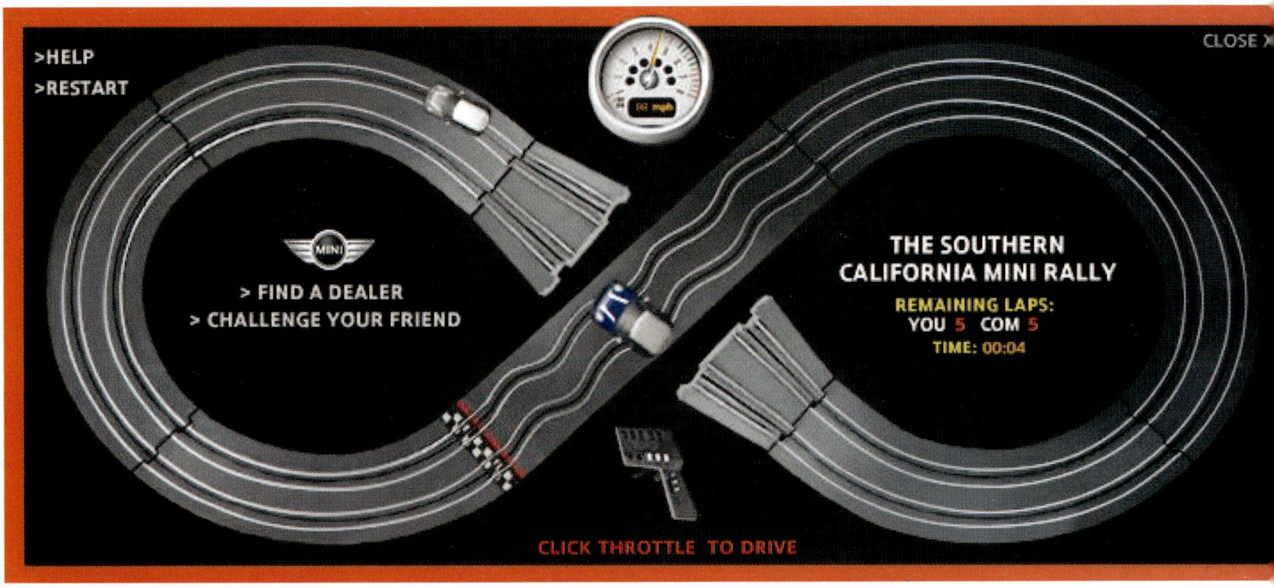
>HELP
>RESTART
CLOSE X
MINI
> FIND A DEALER
> CHALLENGE YOUR FRIEND
THE SOUTHERN CALIFORNIA MINI RALLY
REMAINING LAPS:
YOU 5 COM 5
TIME: 00:04
CLICK THROTTLE TO DRIVE

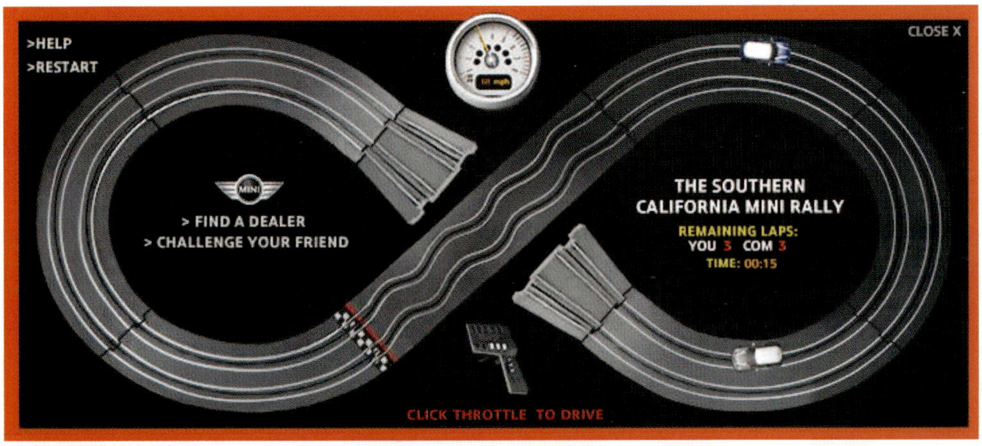
>HELP
>RESTART
CLOSE X
MINI
> FIND A DEALER
> CHALLENGE YOUR FRIEND
THE SOUTHERN CALIFORNIA MINI RALLY
REMAINING LAPS:
YOU 3 COM 3
TIME: 00:15
CLICK THROTTLE TO DRIVE

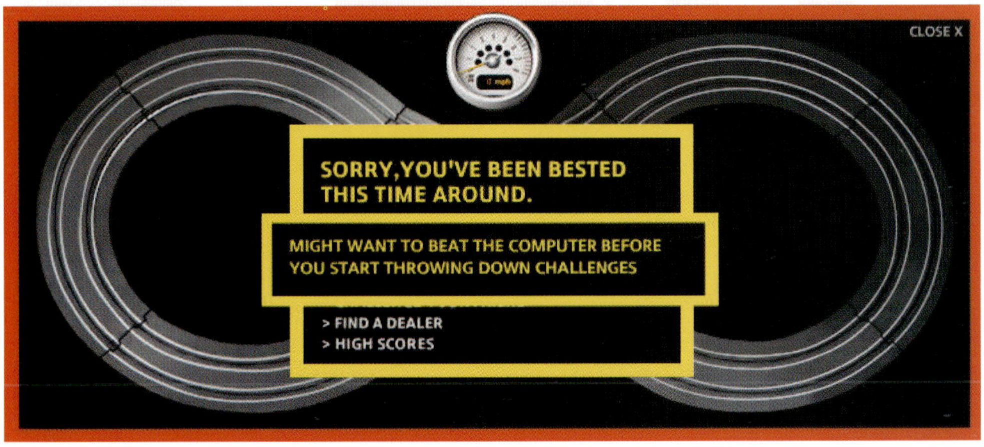
CLOSE X
SORRY,YOU'VE BEEN BESTED THIS TIME AROUND.
MIGHT WANT TO BEAT THE COMPUTER BEFORE YOU START THROWING DOWN CHALLENGES
> FIND A DEALER
> HIGH SCORES

Smooth Operators

What can WD-40 do? Practically everything, from shining diamonds to lubricating pinball machine flippers and removing Play-Doh from hair. This all-purpose spray is given a techie twist in a highly amusing banner created by Proximity Singapore.

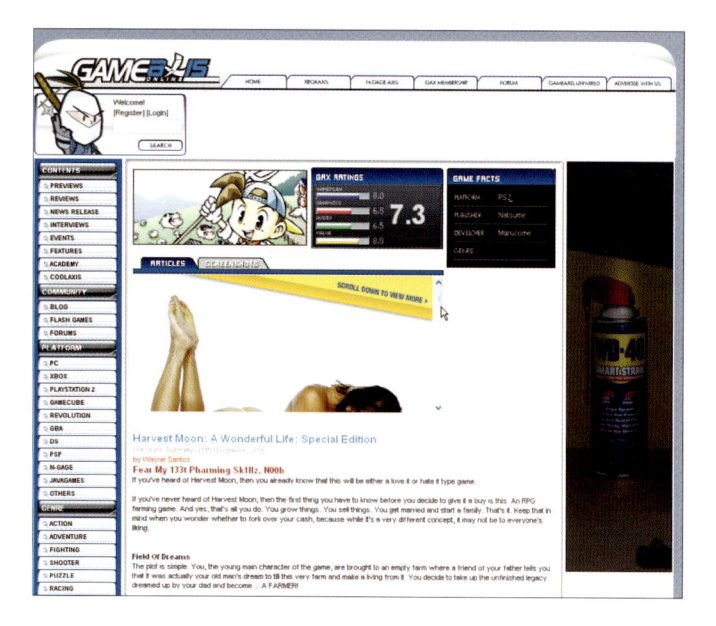

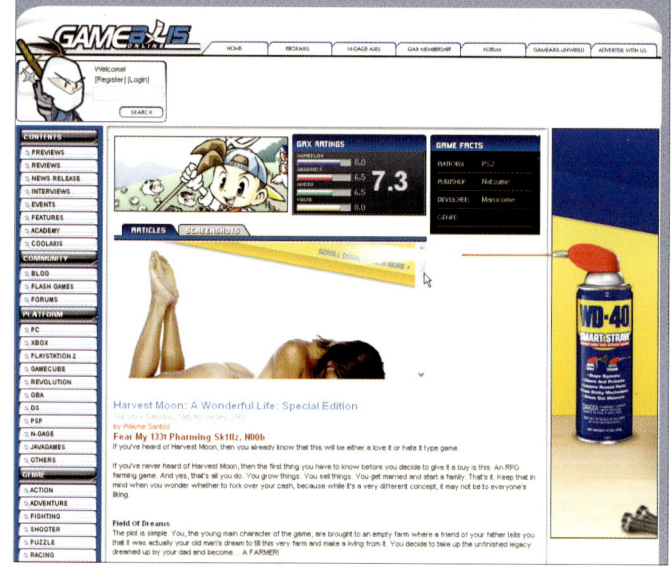

What was the creative rationale behind the idea? Engaging executions using online interaction with consumers were created to demonstrate the many uses of WD-40. The executions were relevant to both site content and web functions, making use of familiar user interface elements such as scroll bars, buttons and pre-loaders. Consumers are thus reminded that things usually taken for granted to work can fail, making WD-40 a handy product to always have around.

Who were you aiming for and where did you place the banners? Targeting mainly males, male-skewed web sites such as gaming and hardware sites were chosen for the execution.

It's quite a tease. Describe what happens. A suggestive picture was placed strategically on the site, teasing users to scroll down in order to see what it would reveal. The scroll bar is designed to get jammed when the user attempts to scroll for more. The WD-40 can, lying unobtrusively at the side of the page, then springs into action, lubricating the scroll bar. The scroll bar then glides with ease.

38 BRONZE WINNER // PROXIMITY

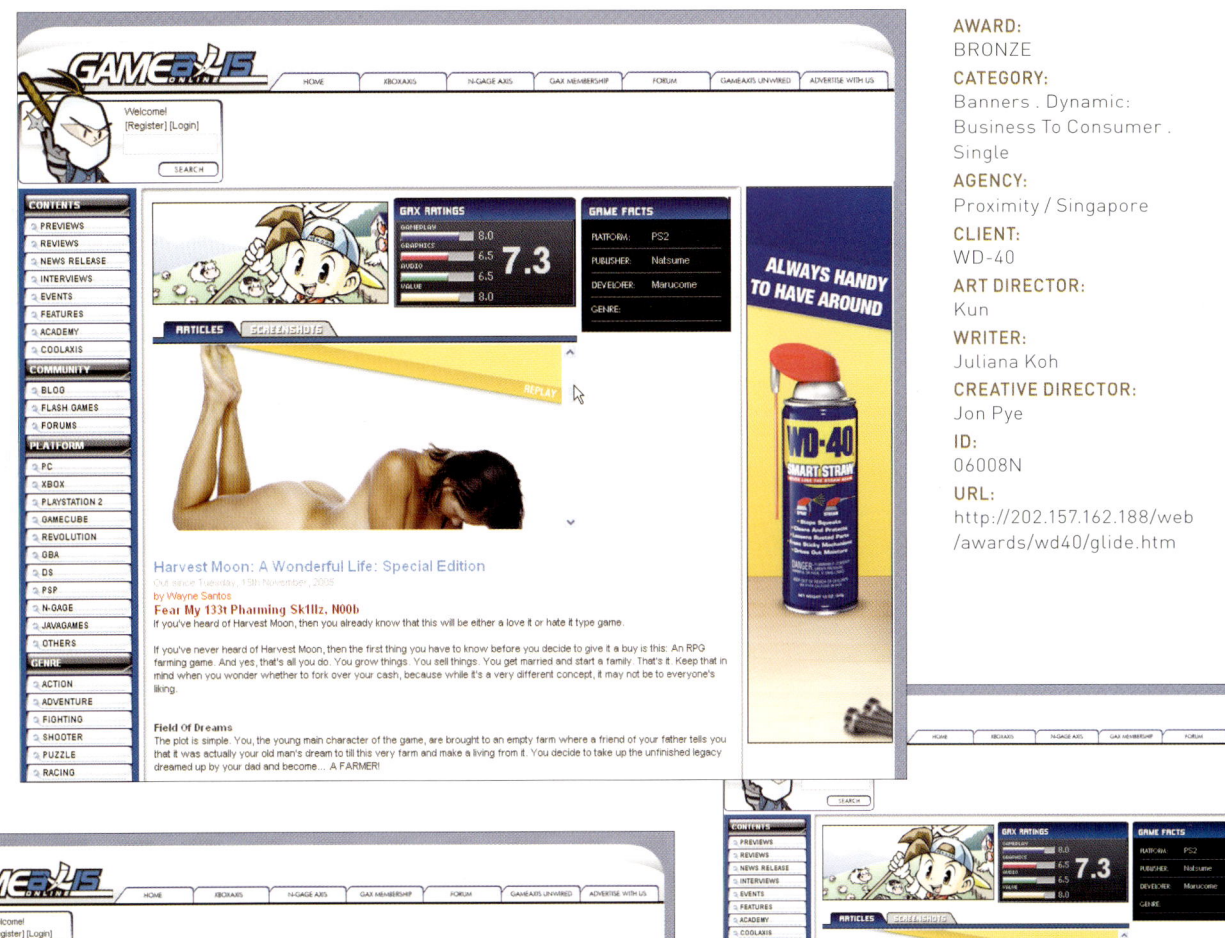

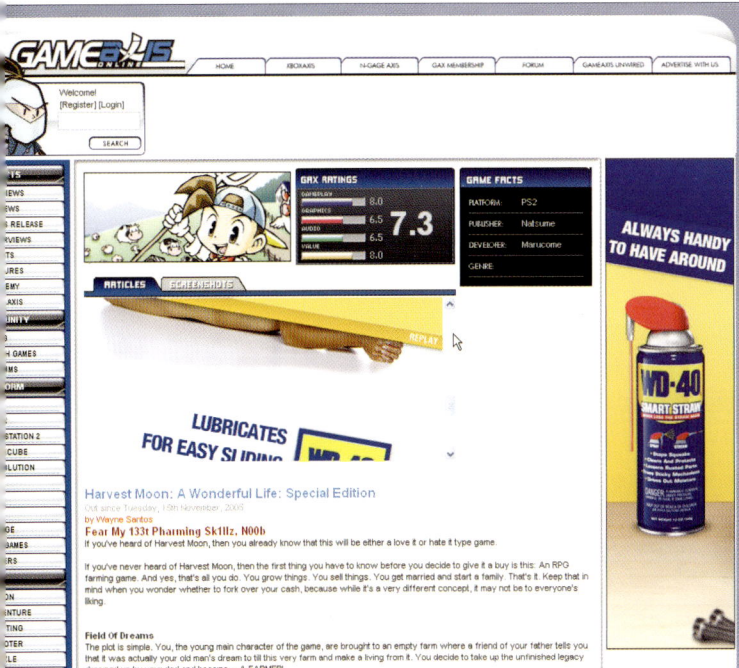

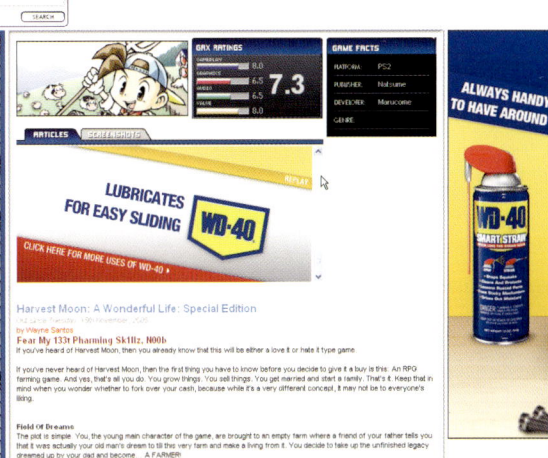

AWARD:
BRONZE
CATEGORY:
Banners . Dynamic:
Business To Consumer .
Single
AGENCY:
Proximity / Singapore
CLIENT:
WD-40
ART DIRECTOR:
Kun
WRITER:
Juliana Koh
CREATIVE DIRECTOR:
Jon Pye
ID:
06008N
URL:
http://202.157.162.188/web/awards/wd40/glide.htm

The Language of Play

The irrepressible fragments of PlayStation's four elemental icons reconstruct into familiar figures from the entertainment world, signifying that the PSP is more than just a handheld gaming machine.

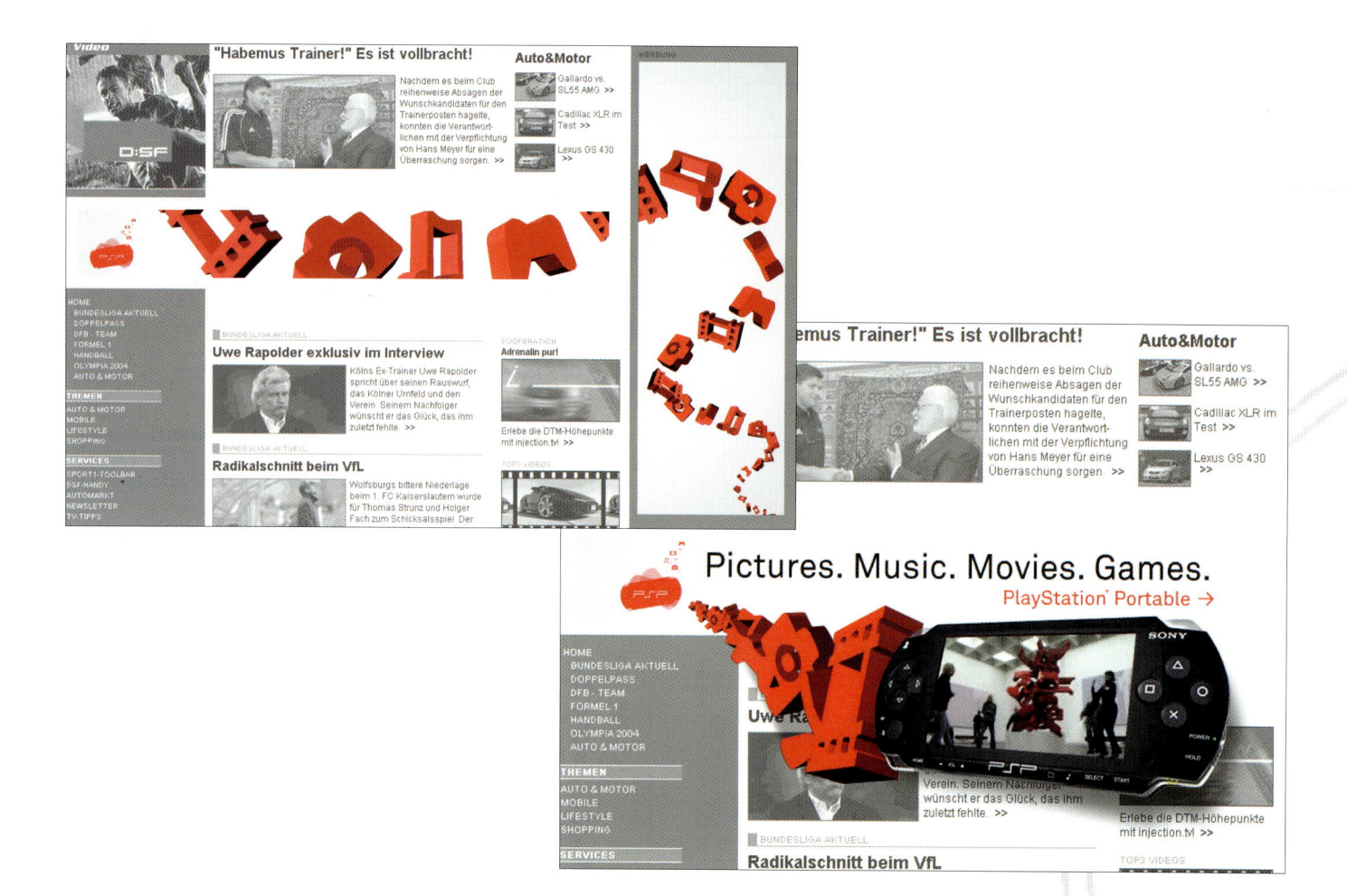

What was the concept behind the banners? PlayStation Portable is a mobile entertainment system that provides multimedia fun wherever you are. The online campaign aimed to show that with PlayStation Portable, you could do more than just play. You can enjoy music, browse pictures, even watch a movie—anytime and anyplace you want.

In the "Transformer" online campaign, the four icons—pictures, music, movies and games—represent the unlimited possibilities of the PlayStation Portable. The icons respond to the user's movement on the site and rearrange to create characters from the worlds of music, movies or games.

The banners show all the possibilities the PSP offers by just moving the cursor. It transforms by interactivity. By rollover we included the TV commercial to flesh out this benefit.

All together it was also a technical challenge. Dynamic Flash with streaming video and the combination of different banners on one website.

How we got the idea? Easy, by using our client's product.

40 BRONZE WINNER // OGILVYINTERACTIVE

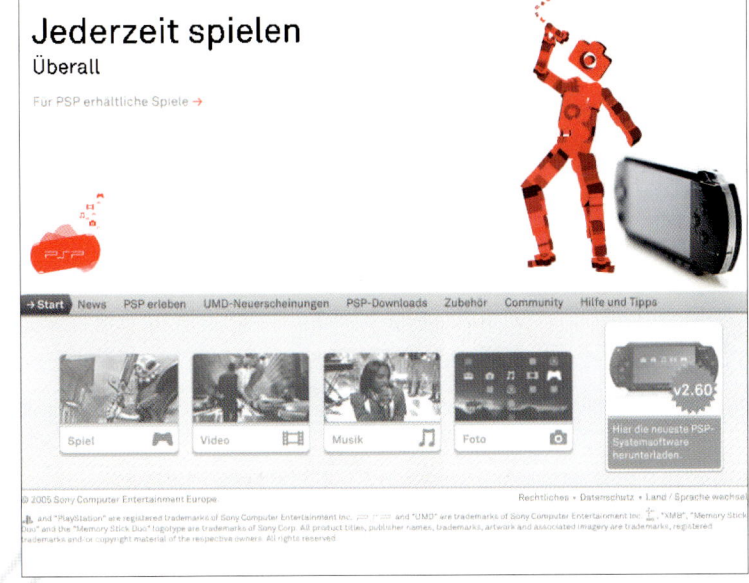

AWARD:
BRONZE
CATEGORY:
Banners . Dynamic: Business To Consumer . Campaign
AGENCY:
OgilvyInteractive / Frankfurt
CLIENT:
PlayStation Portable
ART DIRECTORS:
Melanie Bott
Thorsten Voigt
PROGRAMMERS:
Uwe Holland
Thorsten Voigt
CREATIVE DIRECTOR:
Michael Kutschinski
ID:
06009N
URL:
http://www.ourwork.de/oneshow/psp/transformer/

Pulling Some Strings

DoubleYou managed to have all the images and text of Elle's homepage in black and white, so the only colors seen were from the shoestrings that dangle delightfully, and the candy-kissed Nike sneakers that spring when you twist and tug on the loose lace.

AWARD:
SILVER

CATEGORY:
Banners . Dynamic: Promotional Advertising . Single

AGENCY:
DoubleYou / Barcelona

CLIENT:
American Nike

ART DIRECTOR:
Blanca Piera

WRITER:
Esther Pino

DESIGNER:
Natalie Long

PROGRAMMER:
Joakim Borgström

DIGITAL ARTIST/MULTIMEDIA:
Nacho Guijarro

CREATIVE DIRECTORS:
Edu Pou, Joakim Borgström

CONTENT STRATEGIST:
Jordi Pont

ID:
06010N

URL:
http://festivals.doubleyou.com/2006/nikesprintsister/oneshow.html

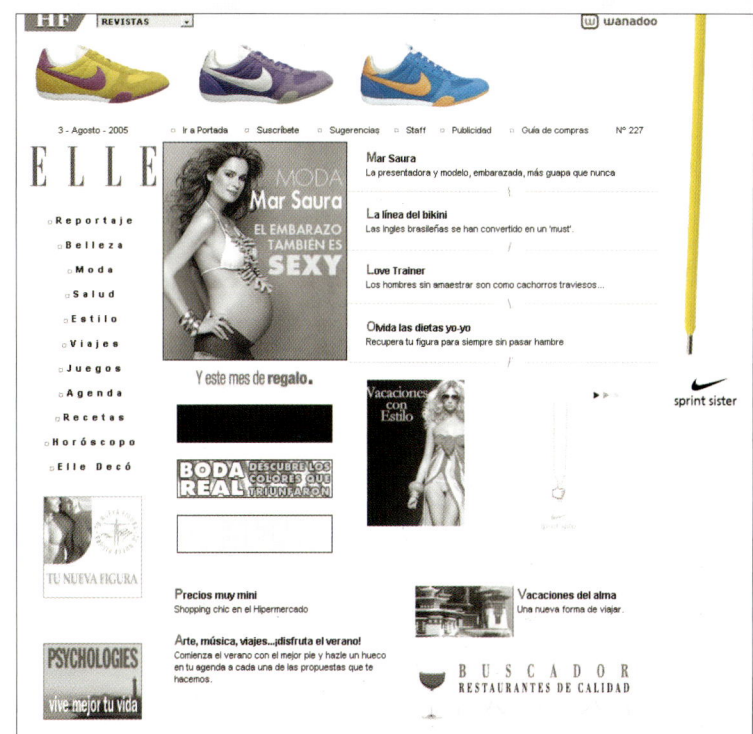

Pencil Winners
43

You Never Sleep Alone

Trailing cursors were just another pretty effect until this banner came along with its potent "come-on." Dentsu unfolds a meaningful message in its HIV-awareness ad with a simple but powerful analogy about sexual partners and the invisible network people create when they start to date.

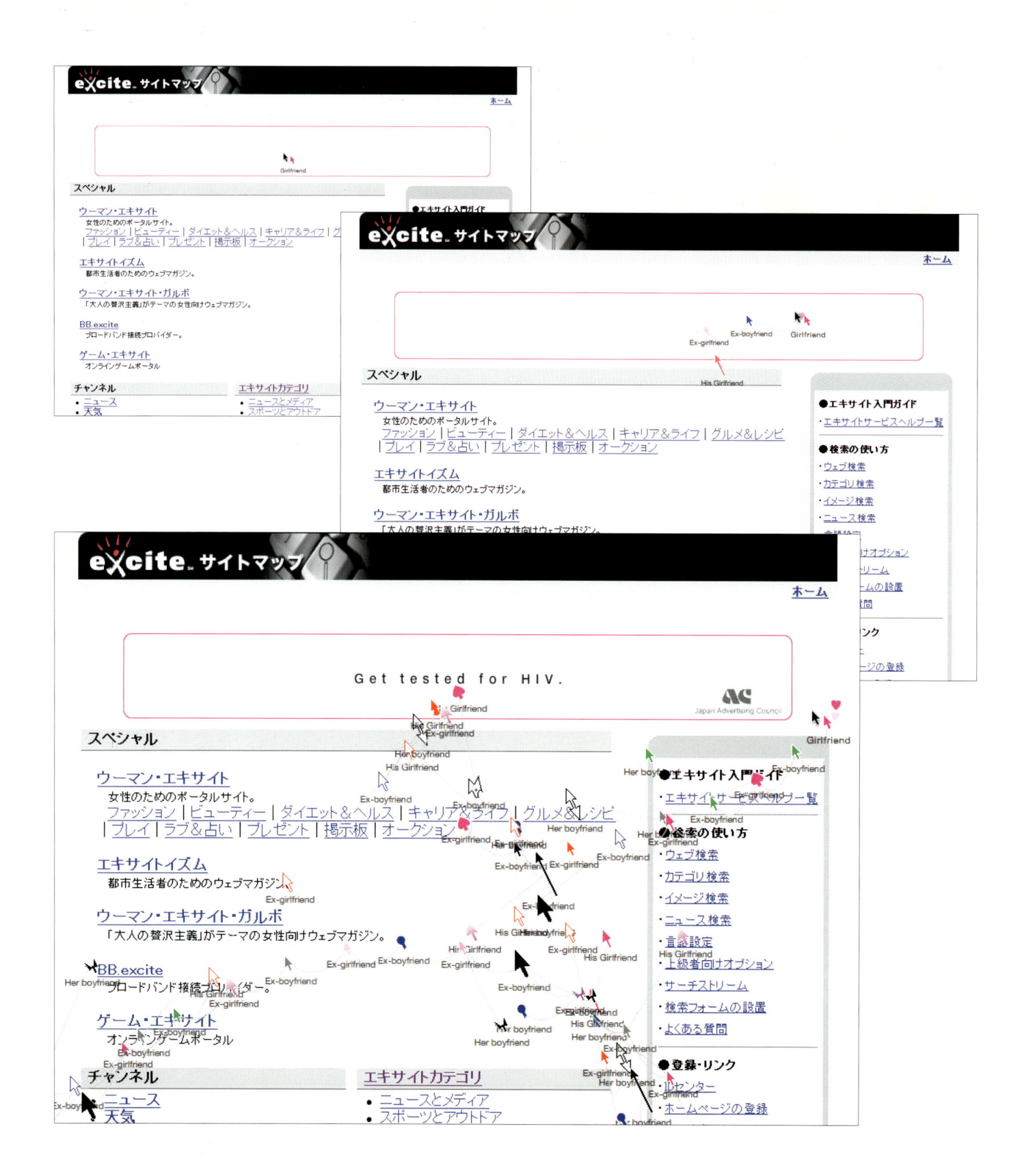

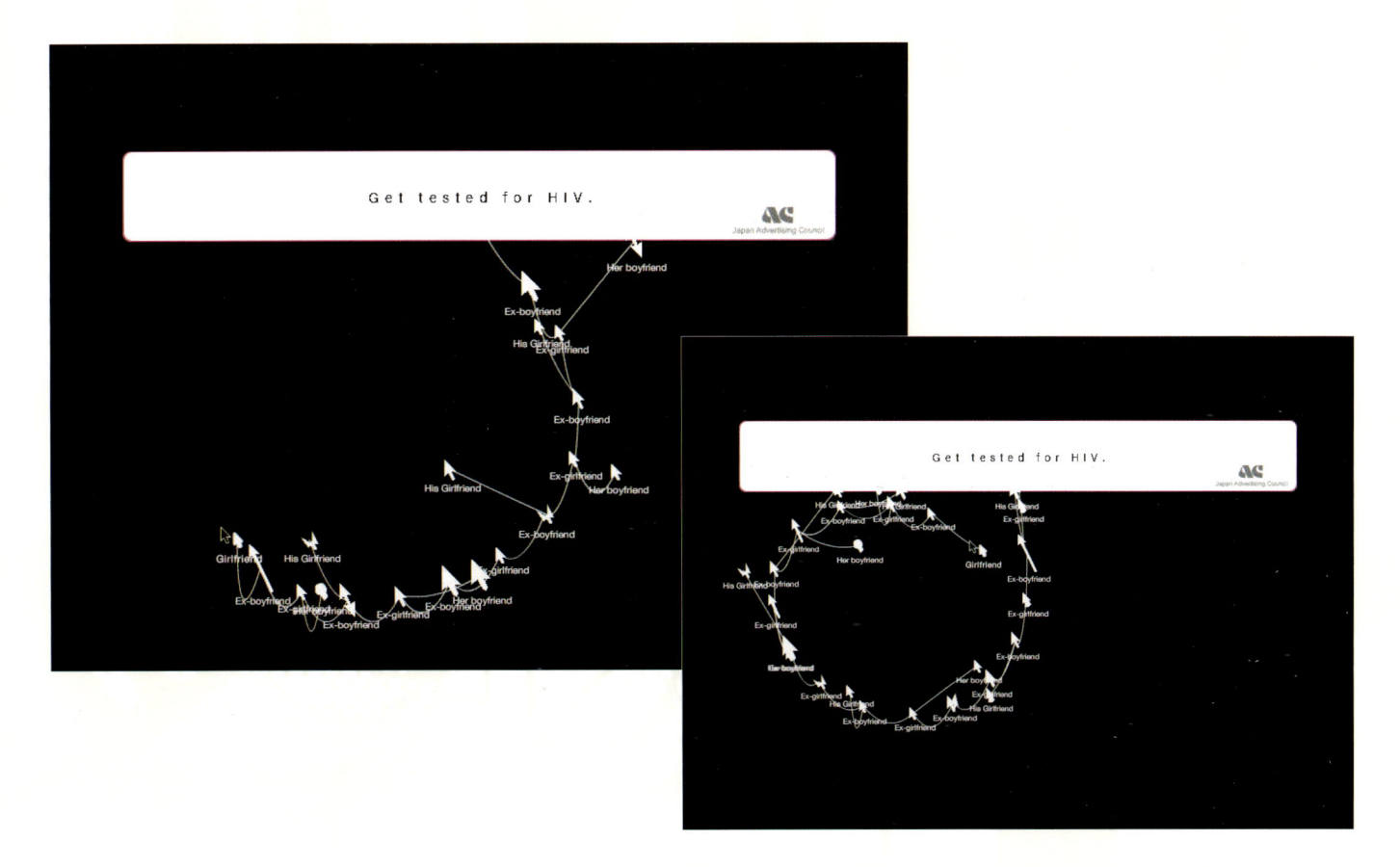

AWARD:
GOLD

CATEGORY:
Banners . Dynamic:
Public Service /Non-Profit /
Educational . Single

AGENCY:
Dentsu / Tokyo

CLIENT:
Japan Advertising Council

ART DIRECTORS:
Yusuke Kitani
Hiroki Nakamura

WRITER:
Satoshi Nakajima

DIGITAL ARTIST/MULTIMEDIA:
Hiroki Nakamura

CREATIVE DIRECTOR:
Satoshi Nakajima

ID:
06011N

URL:
http://www.interactive-salaryman.com/pieces/past_e/

For a society that is not yet very aware or concerned about the rise of HIV, how did you approach the topic? This campaign's target audience was young people who are unconcerned about HIV. It is not effective to simply tell them the importance of taking HIV tests. As a solution, we used a familiar sound, a sexy female voice, to make the audience experience a realistic seduction. We tried to send out a powerful message and importance of HIV tests.

Why did the Japan Advertising Council choose to address this issue? Japan Advertising Council has been promoting campaigns to raise awareness of social issues in Japan. Japan is the only developed country where the number of HIV cases is increasing. They say indifferent young people are the cause for this state. Therefore, we decided to set this campaign's theme as "Stress the importance of HIV tests to young people, and encourage them to take the tests."

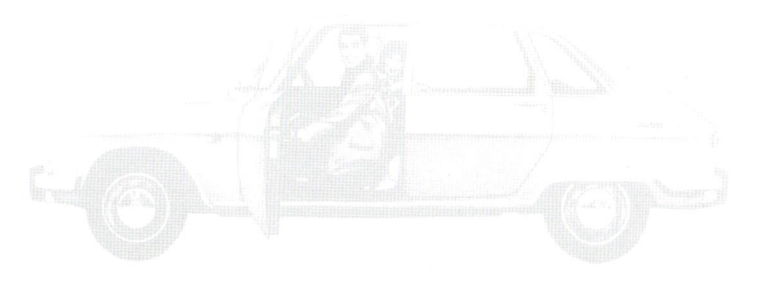

MINI Mash-ups

For one of the quizzes, TAXI needed to come up with the most bizarre passenger to be seen with in a MINI Convertible. Their first choice was a C.H.U.D., but unless you're a B-horror movie nerd, the reference is rather obscure. "We argued back and forth until we mutually agreed on a Chupacabra. It's nice to be in an industry where that kind of debate is rewarded," say the creatives of TAXI.

AWARD:
GOLD
CATEGORY:
Beyond The Banner:
Business To Consumer.
Single
AGENCY:
TAXI / Toronto
CLIENT:
MINI Canada
ART DIRECTOR:
Alison Hladkji
WRITER:
Jason McCann
DESIGNER:
Alison Hladkji
PROGRAMMER:
pixelpusher.ca
CREATIVE DIRECTOR:
Steve Mykolyn
ID:
06012N
URL:
http://www.neverinneutral.com/convertible/

WEATHER
LOW PRESSURE SYSTEM

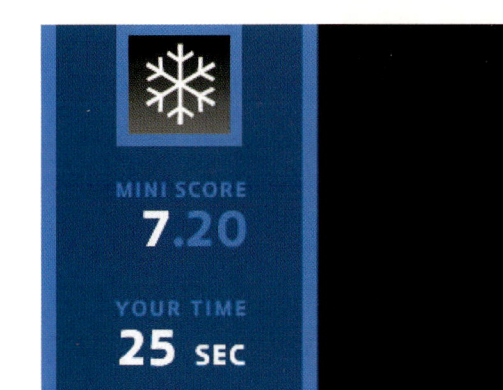

MINI SCORE 1.20
YOUR TIME 15 SEC

MINI SCORE 7.20
YOUR TIME 25 SEC

YOUR CONVERTIBLE-ILZER-OMETER SCORE IS 7

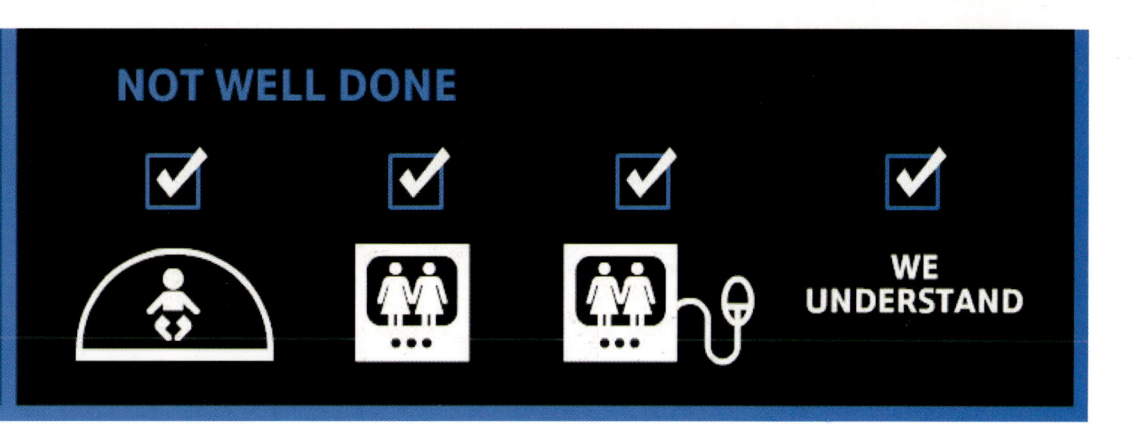

MINI SCORE 7.20
YOUR TIME 25 SEC

NOT WELL DONE

WE UNDERSTAND

Pencil Winners
47

Tough Glove

He may not be subservient, but this victim of Crispin's MINI Counterfeit banner will have to put up with much of your slapping and smacking. With an oversized palm, users practice "tough love" on a senseless sucker who falls for an obviously inauthentic MINI Cooper. Just don't let it get out of hand.

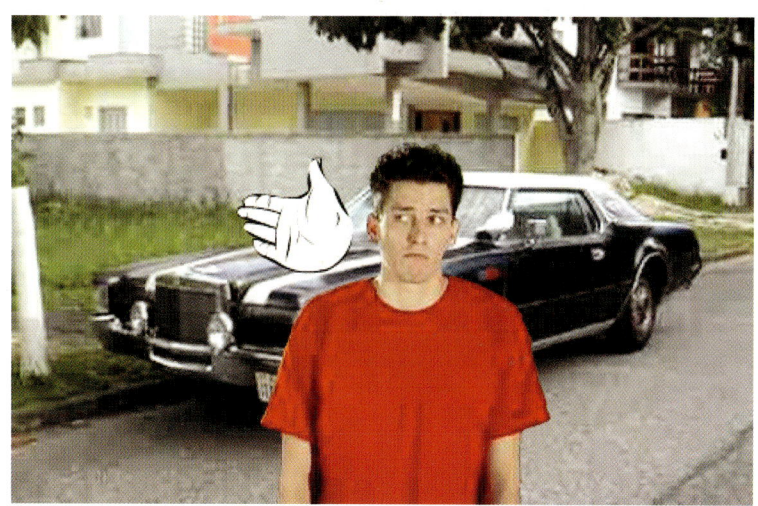

AWARD:
BRONZE
CATEGORY:
Beyond The Banner:
Business To Consumer .
Single
AGENCY:
Crispin Porter + Bogusky /
Miami
CLIENT:
MINI
ART DIRECTORS:
Paul Stechschulte
Tiffany Kosel
Rahul Panchal
WRITERS:
Franklin Tipton, Rob Reilly
Steve O'Connell
PROGRAMMER:
Luis Santi
CREATIVE DIRECTORS:
Alex Bogusky, Andrew Keller
Jeff Benjamin
ID:
06013N
URL:
http://www.cpbgroup.com
/awards/slapsomesense.html

The Holiday's Mischief of Staff

It's cute, it's tiny, and it's got all the submissive fun without the servility! "Send an Elf" is a plucky puck-o-gram of pure delight, and invites recipients to uncover a myriad of ways to prod and provoke the little fellow. Once you've gotten him snuggled up in your heart all wrapped up with a bow, you pass him along. To someone you just can't say no to.

What were the technical challenges in creating the animation? Were there any hidden goodies that one might have missed? Some people might not have known that you can actually pick him up with your mouse (and fling him around if you feel so inclined). Also, you can make him float way up into heavenly clouds by holding down the "a" key. And take him in his heli-pack all the way up to the moon. It's ripe for exploration; we didn't want to add a ton of directions.

The elf is quite adorable compared to the other elves out there. How did his design come about? We passed the character back and forth with Unit 9 in sketch form until we landed on the right look. We wanted him to be irresistible, but not entirely cutesy. That's why he breathes fire and roars like a beast—to keep him from getting too precious.

Why do you think people really dig manipulating puppets and elves and other strange creatures? There are no elves in the real world (that you can get your hands on, anyway) so we wanted to create one that felt like a real little pet. We wanted to give that feeling of opening up a new toy, but it's alive. That's intriguing to people—to interact with lifelike characters and "see what happens when I do this." You can't get that in any other medium.

YOU'RE NOW THE PROUD OWNER OF
ELF #0,117,278

Why an elf?

Well, he's loads of fun. But most important, he's a symbol of our commitment to helping you out – at the holidays and beyond.

Discover Card offers unlimited cash rewards, tip-top security, and service designed around you. All to make your life a little easier.

Enjoy, and play nice.

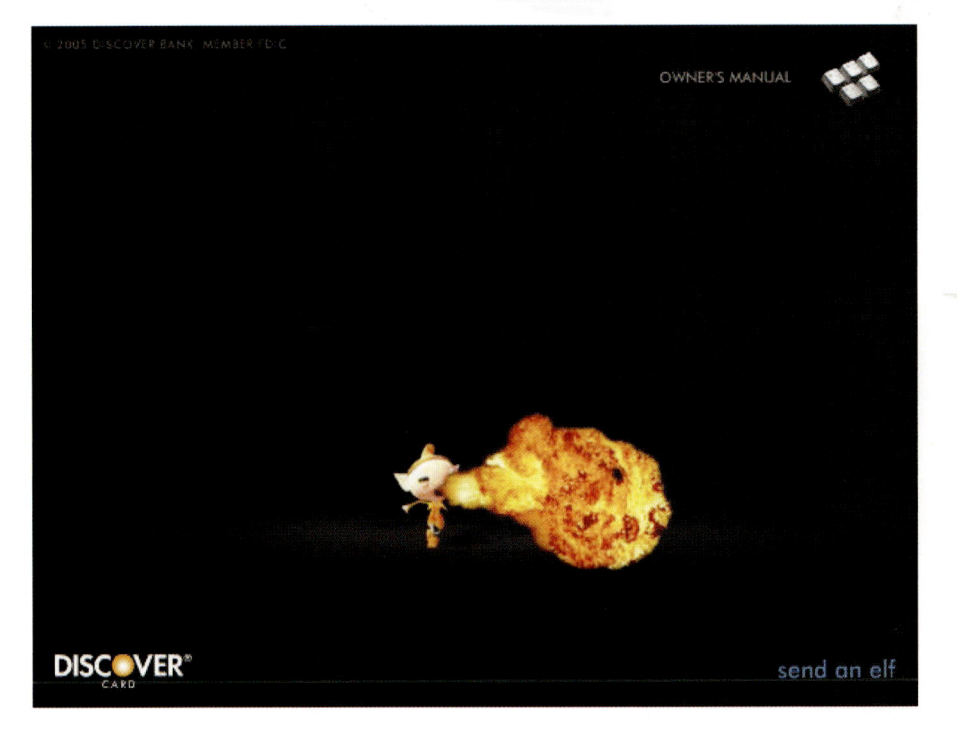

DISCOVER CARD

OWNER'S MANUAL

send an elf

AWARD:
BRONZE
CATEGORY:
Beyond The Banner:
Business To Consumer.
Single
AGENCY:
Goodby, Silverstein & Partners /
San Francisco
CLIENT:
Discover Card
ART DIRECTOR:
Aaron Dietz
WRITER:
Mandy Dietz
PRODUCTION COMPANY:
unit9.creative.production
CREATIVE DIRECTORS:
Keith Anderson
Will McGinness
CONTENT STRATEGISTS:
Dora Lee, Mike Geiger
ID:
06014N
URL:
http://www.goodbysilverstein.com/awards/oneshow_2006/discover_elf_site/

Pencil Winners
51

Anatomy Lesson

The human body gets a graphic dissection in a website made by Goodby, Silverstein & Partners for cycling gear brand Specialized. Peeled and revealed in all its squishy splendor, it's even better than biking naked.

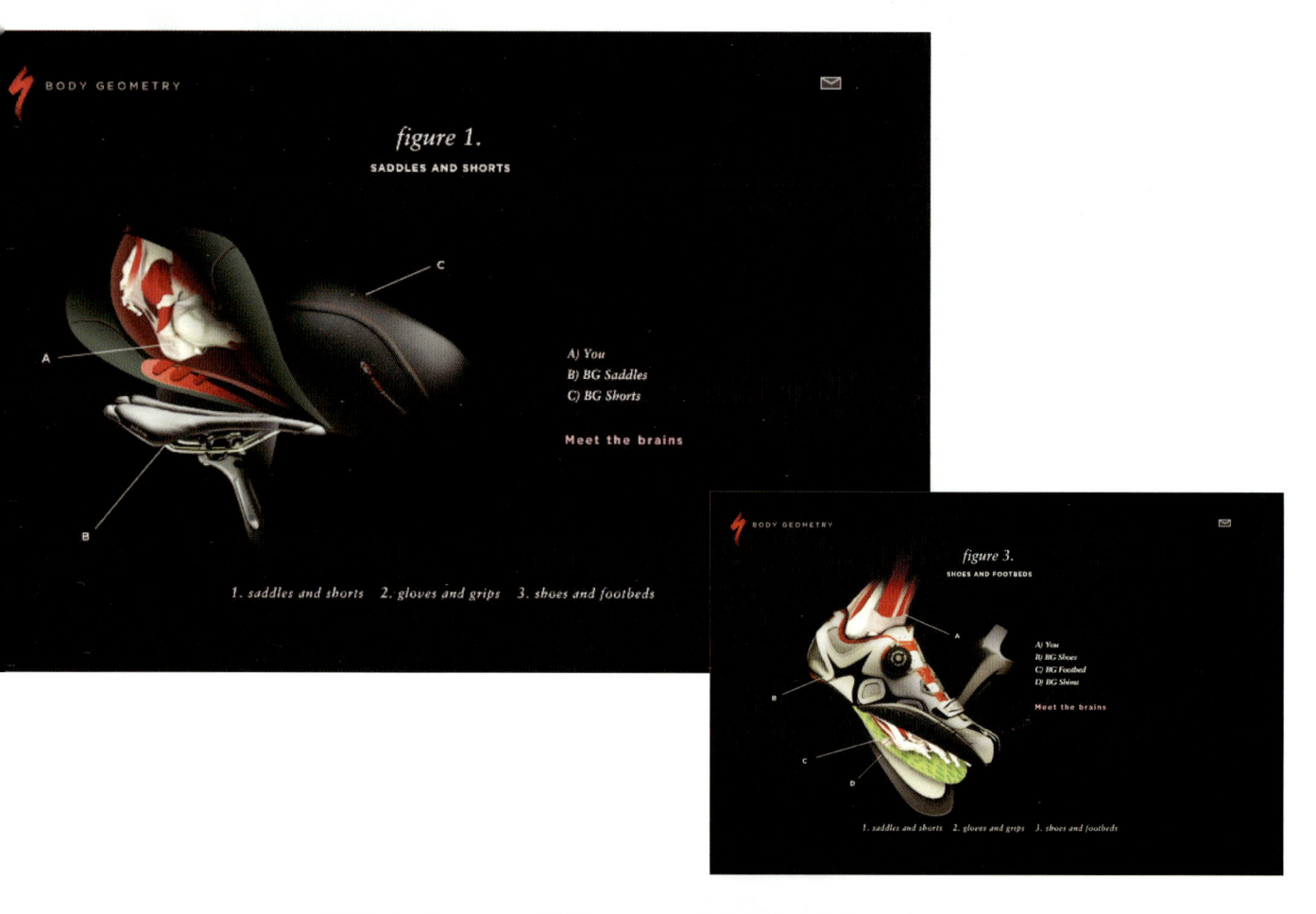

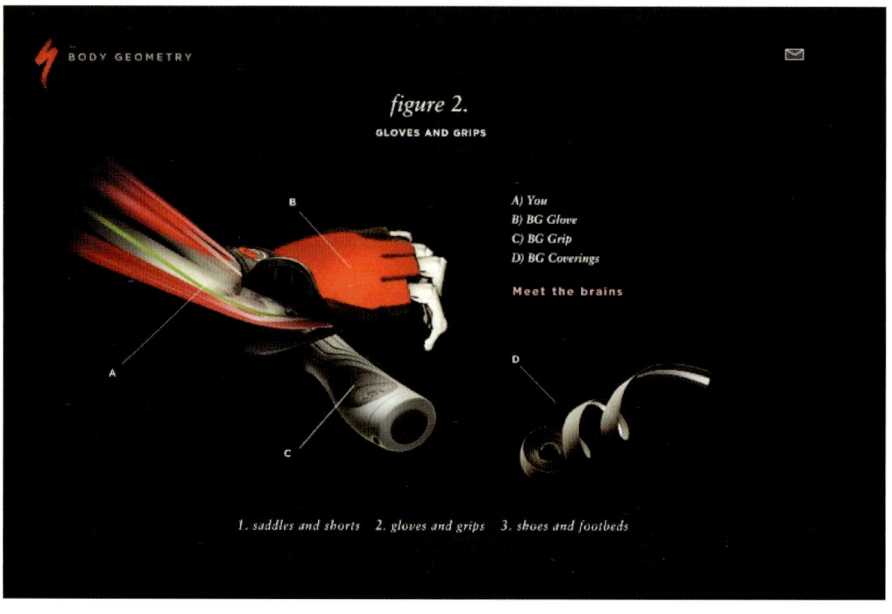

52 BRONZE WINNER // GOODBY, SILVERSTEIN & PARTNERS

AWARD:
BRONZE
CATEGORY:
Beyond The Banner:
Business To Consumer .
Single
AGENCY:
Goodby, Silverstein & Partners /
San Francisco
CLIENT:
Specialized
ART DIRECTOR:
Aaron Dietz
WRITER:
Mandy Dietz
CONTENT STRATEGISTS:
Carey Head, Mike Geiger
PRODUCTION COMPANY:
Enjoy Greener Grass
CREATIVE DIRECTORS:
Steve Mapp, Albert Kelly
Keith Anderson
ID:
06015N
URL:
http://www.goodbysilverstein.com
/awards/oneshow_2006/specialized
_body_geometry/

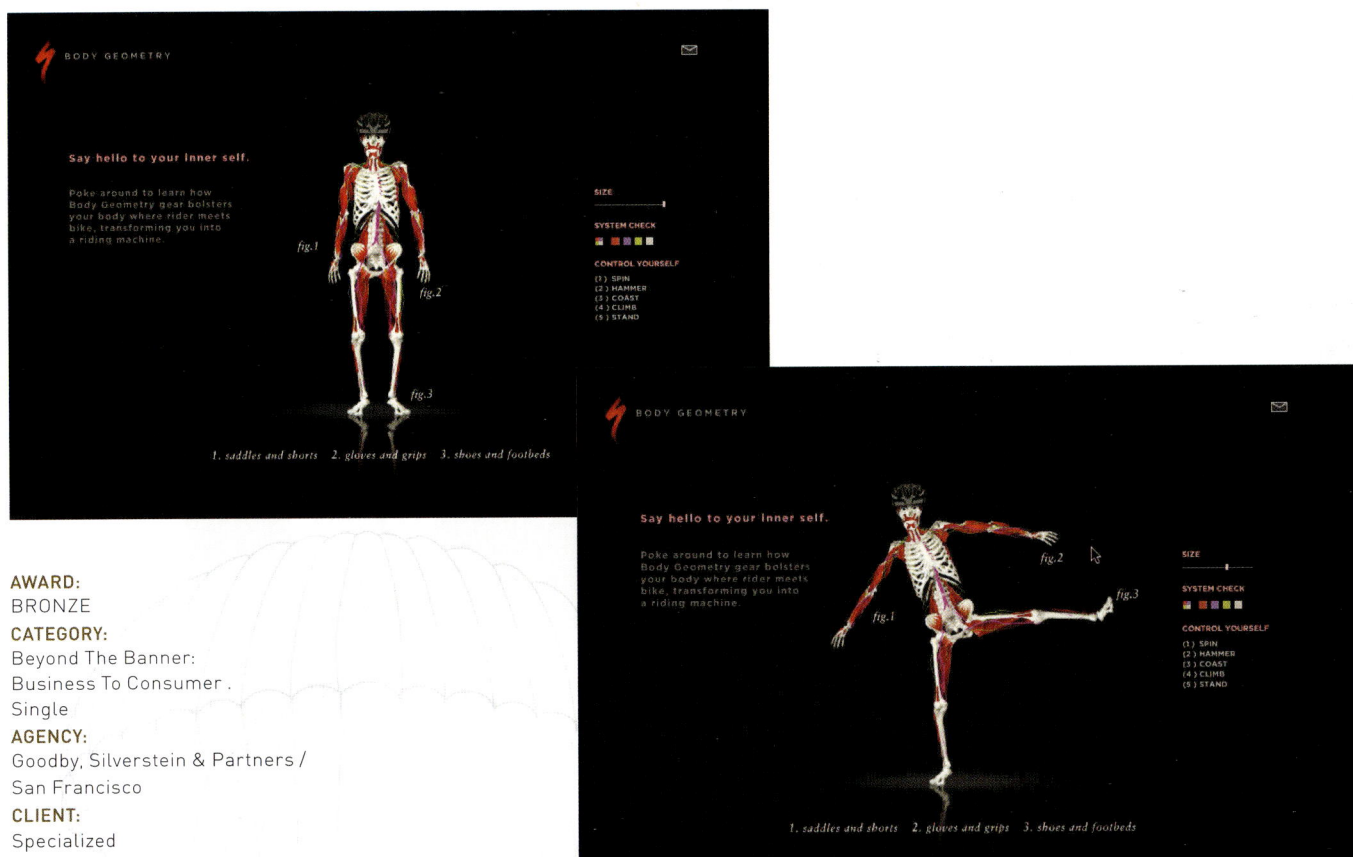

It's kind of gory in a scientific-realist way. Why did you choose this particular approach? It felt natural to go down that path, since the products were all scientifically developed. Using the gory inner workings of the body is fun – seeing a skeleton ride in on a bike is good stuff. But it's not just for shock value. It actually helps you understand the products.

How did you model the body in its various system states? We got our hands on some great 3-D renderings of human anatomy – detailed reference materials used by med students. We illustrated the rider based on that, working closely with Specialized to get the riding poses accurate.

What were the reactions to the site from its intended audience of serious bikers? The Body Geometry site tripled traffic to specialized.com. Feedback from site visitors and Specialized customers was overwhelmingly positive, and confirmed that the site resonated with both advanced and casual cyclists.

2054

Self-promotion can be a tough brief. Lean Mean Fighting Machine sidesteps the pat-yourself-on-the-back routine by focusing on the future—that is, their grisly deaths by hovercraft. This funny and ultimately optimistic banner/microsite/film campaign looks back at their lives as yet unlived.

AWARD:
SILVER

CATEGORY:
Beyond The Banner:
Self-Promotion . Campaign

AGENCY:
Lean Mean Fighting Machine /
London

CLIENT:
Lean Mean Fighting Machine

WRITERS:
Jim Field-Smith, Ben Willbond
Sam Ball, Dave Bedwood

DESIGNER:
Mark Beacock

PROGRAMMER:
Dave Cox

PRODUCTION COMPANY:
Idiotlamp

CREATIVE DIRECTORS:
Sam Ball, Dave Bedwood

CONTENT STRATEGIST:
Tom Bazeley

ID:
06016N

URL:
www.leanmeanfightingmachine.co.uk/2054campaign

There is definitely a sense of morbid humor to this piece. How did it feel writing your own obituaries? True, I suppose looking at it now, it is morbid isn't it. Your own death. At the time, we just thought it was funny and a good way to create a bit more of a context and story to surround the mock documentary we had already shot.

How did you go about picking the actors who played the geriatric, near-death future you? Well the temptation at first was to pick people who looked vaguely like us, but to get that and good actors was a bit of a long shot. So we just opted for good actors. As they don't look like us it sort of made it a bit funnier.

What was the most difficult part of creating the piece? Actually doing it, it was one of those ideas we had in the office and thought that would be great, but usually you just never get off your backside and do them. Once we did, we had a friend who runs a production company and a comedy writer so once he was onboard it was a breeze.

On what kind of sites did you place the Self-Promotional banner? The banner went onto Brand Republic, which is *Campaign* magazine's website. Our target audience for this, our peers and marketing directors, can be found on this site. It didn't need to be a big media spend, and our industry is so small that it got sent around pretty quick—we didn't need 15 billion hits like a certain chicken got.

Pencil Winners
55

Tokyo Babylon

A 40-year-old woman who dresses up in baby clothes. A special-effects artist obsessed with The Fifth Element. Clubheads who will spend more money on fashion than they ever will on food and rent. These people make lifestyles and careers out of looking at things differently and looking very, very different, yet also belong to style tribes where the followers are fanatics. Welcome to Japanese street-style, where pop culture is devoured, identity is exploded, and the image reigns supreme.

AWARD:
Silver

CATEGORY:
Web Sites: Business To Consumer

AGENCY:
Great Works / Stockholm

CLIENT:
V&S Absolut Spirits

ART DIRECTORS:
Max Larsson
Von Reybekiel

WRITER:
Kristoffer Triumf

DESIGNERS:
Fredrik Karlsson
Jens Eriksson

PROGRAMMERS:
Fredrik Karlsson
Oskar Sundberg
Jocke Wissing

CREATIVE DIRECTOR:
Ted Persson

CONTENT STRATEGISTS:
Magnus Wålsten
Patrik Persson

ID:
06017N

URL:
http://absolut.com/metropolis

ABSOLUT advertising is an industry unto itself, and its print campaigns are legendary. As ABSOLUT's interactive arm, how do you integrate with the brand's offline identity? How is it different? ABSOLUT has been running one of the world's most famous print campaigns based on the same concept for more than 25 years. From the launch of the first ABSOLUT website in 1996 until three to four years ago, we considered the Internet as a somewhat more niche medium.

But not so any more. As media consumption behaviors change, the brand has to change as well. When developing an updated ABSOLUT brand identity which also features definitions of how the brand behaves in digital environments, we made a clear distinction between the actual brand and the executions in different media. Instead of basing the digital identity on the look and feel of a print ad, we looked to the different aspects of the brand and found the best way to communicate that in digital environments.

Talk about the idea of mapping the Tokyo underground creative. Who did you collaborate with? ABSOLUT has collaborated with artists within the fields of art, fashion and music since the famous ad painted by Andy Warhol in 1985. The ABSOLUT METROPOLIS campaign is the first ABSOLUT project where non-professional creatives' view on the brand was expressed, from a street-style perspective. We not only thought that their interpretations of the brand were interesting, but also the personalities behind them.

All of the people featured in the campaign live in Tokyo, so in one way the website invites you on a trip to their city to see their work and the things that inspire them. And subway maps are a pretty common way of traveling in metropolitan areas, so we gave every person his/her own subway line.

The creative direction and art direction were done by us in Stockholm, but the movies were shot in Tokyo by our partner agency TYO-ID. We also collaborated with TBWA\PARIS who were in charge of the offline components of the campaign. Photographer Nadav Kander shot the images. Sabina Hägglund and Sebastian Billing at ABSOLUT also played an very important role in the definition and development of the project.

The artists featured are hyper-trendy club kids and fashion extremists who seem to be rejected by mainstream Japanese (and perhaps Western) society. Who was your target audience? How did you find the right eleven people? The target group for the campaign was culturally curious people interested in art and fashion. The print campaign was a collaboration with TRACE Magazine. In digital channels we did tailor-made advertising on fashion and design blogs such as coolhunting and mocoloco.

The people were scouted through talent agencies, street casting and recommendations from the creative leader of the campaign, Pyuupiru.

Pencil Winners
57

58 SILVER WINNER // GREAT WORKS

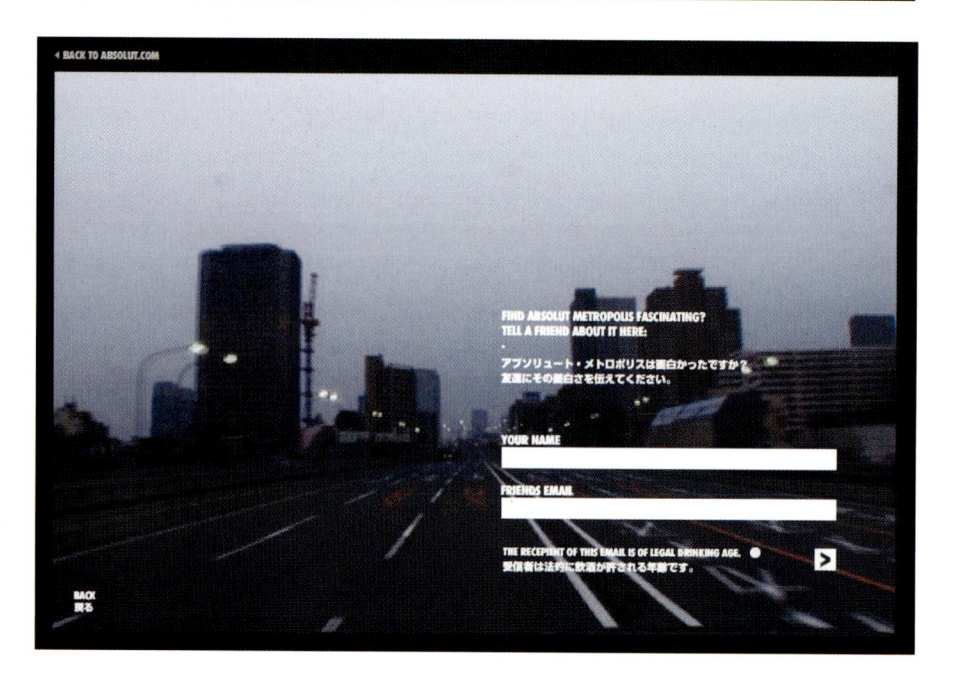

Pencil Winners
59

Walk This Way

Adidas Originals references the brand's old school aesthetic—relaxed, funky and sporty, but slouching towards Run DMC more than long-distance running. NEUE DIGITALE's website keeps it real with an interactive video that shifts from black-and-white to full Krylon color—the landscape of the streets.

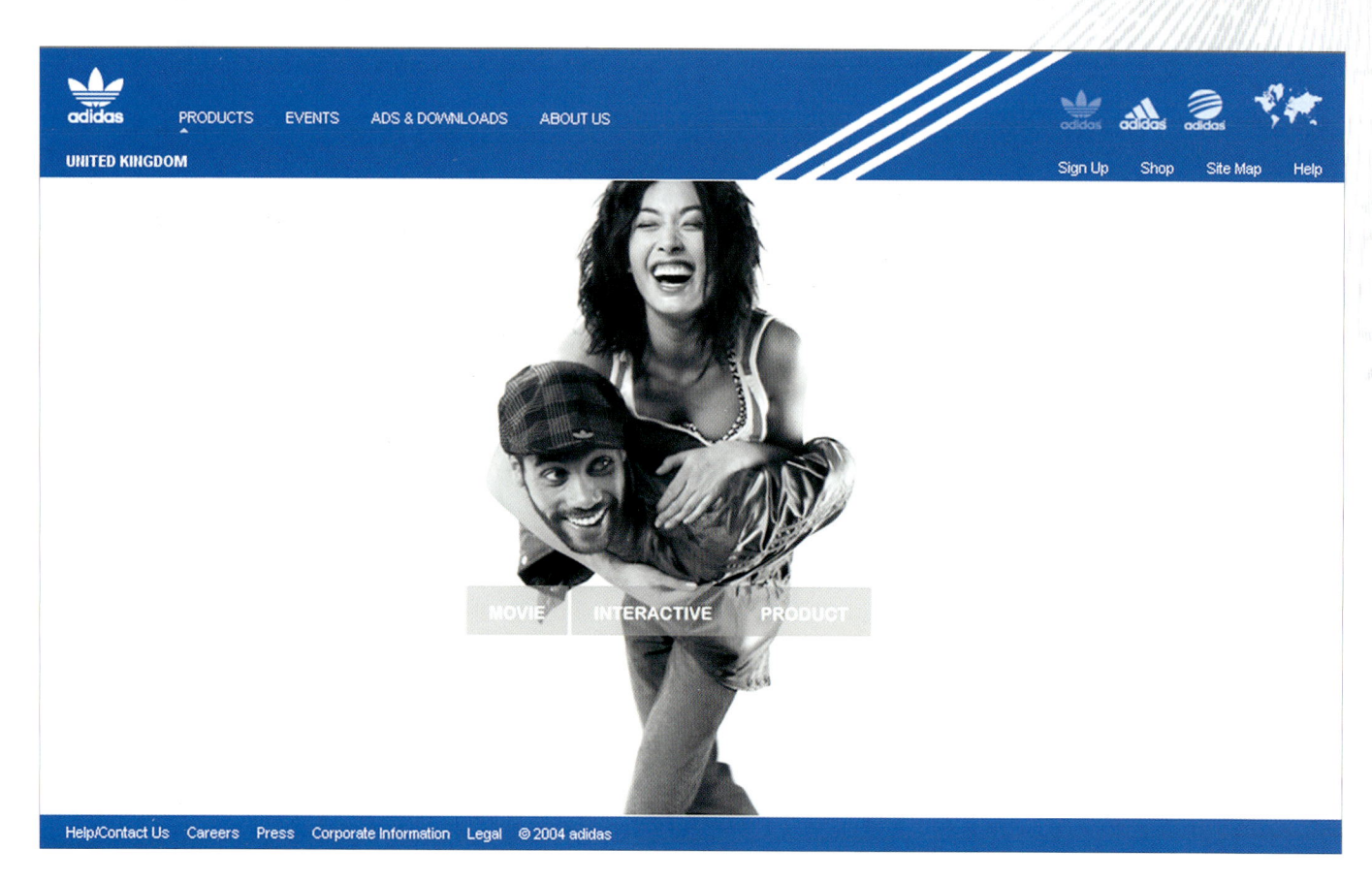

AWARD:
SILVER
CATEGORY:
Web Sites:
Business To Consumer
AGENCY:
NEUE DIGITALE /
Frankfurt
CLIENT:
adidas
ART DIRECTOR:
Bejadin Selimi
PROGRAMMER:
Jens Steffen
CREATIVE DIRECTOR:
Olaf Czeschner
ID:
06018N
URL:
www.neue-digitale.de/projects/originals_ss2005

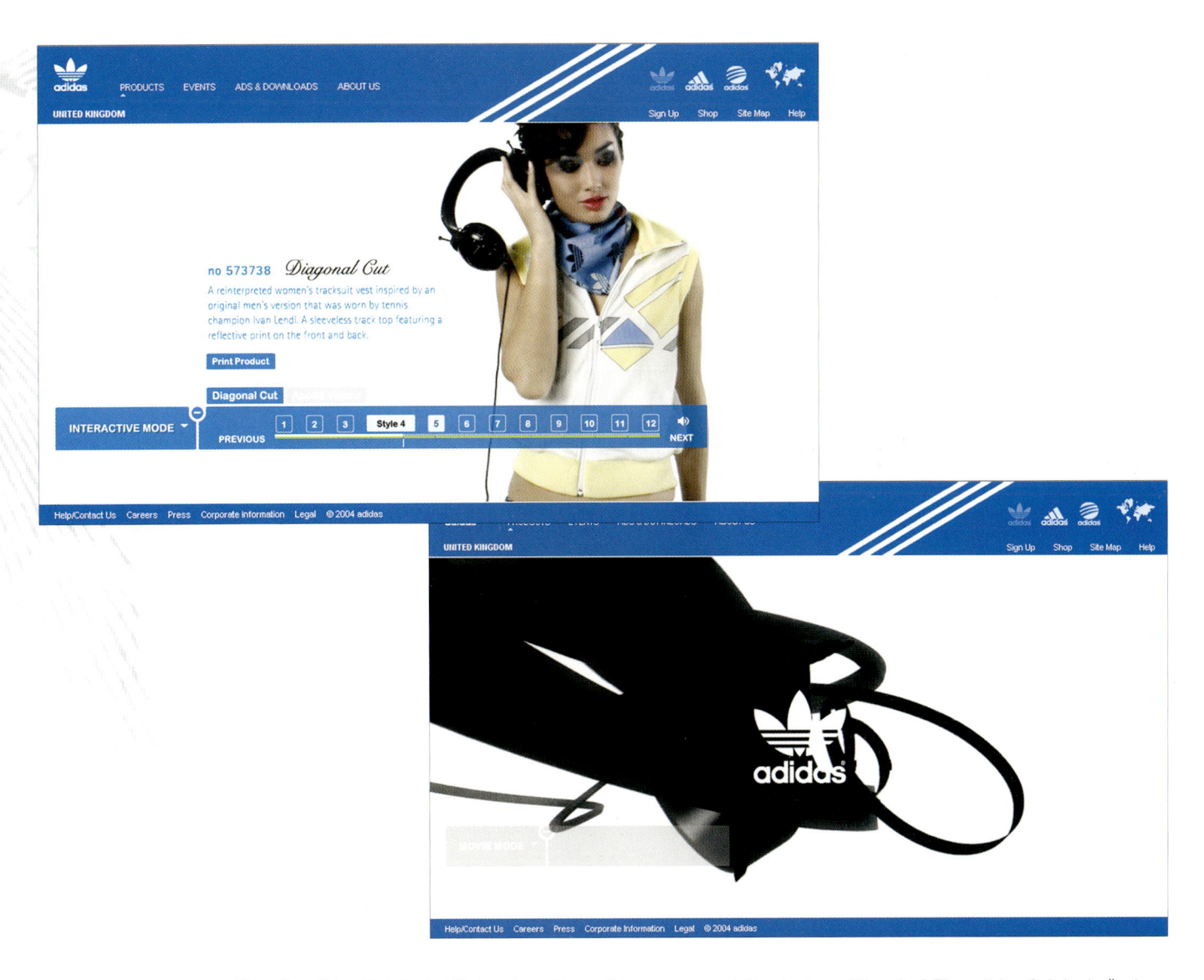

What is adidas Originals all about and how did you approach the design of the site? The adidas Originals "celebrate originality" website is an innovative product showcase that introduced the spring/summer 2005 collection. This website was the world's first full-screen web-based interactive video on the web. However, the main goal of the art direction was to pursue the three key values of the adidas Originals brand: authenticity, innovation, and originality.

What makes the video innovative? The video runs extremely slick at an even higher resolution than the common television formats like PAL or NTSC. This required extensive technical research in bandwidth consumption, performance and video-encoding. Ease of use, in particular, was a key factor as well, because average Internet users won't be spending much time trying to figure out how the interface works so we build a convenient multi-mode navigation-system to accommodate their needs.

The project was implemented for a global audience. What creative considerations did you take to make it appeal to many different countries? Cross-cultural web design is always a huge challenge because it goes beyond just managing different character sets and content for localization. For instance, we study first the international target group to examine design elements prevalent in the different cultures; this provides a useful guideline containing a wide range of crucial country-specific and cultural issues. This helps us to determine the key factors and to avoid potential obstacles on the path to a successful multilingual customization.

SILVER WINNER // NEUE DIGITALE

Pencil Winners
63

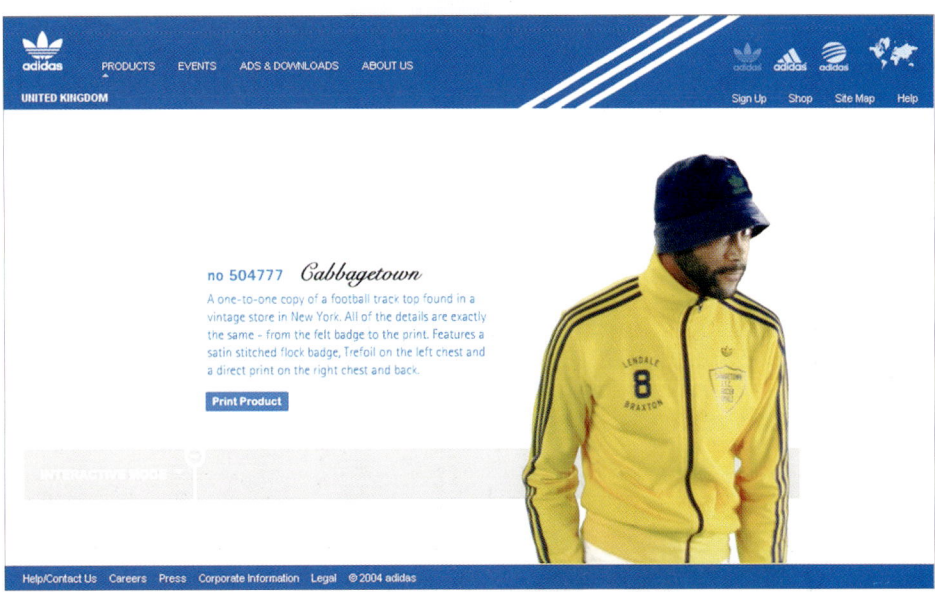

Nice Cubes

Three is the magic number, but cube is the divine function. This year, NEUE DIGITALE's cutting edge website for the Yohji Yamamto-designed adidas label Y-3 gives us gravity-free futuristic fashion.

AWARD:
SILVER

CATEGORY:
Web Sites: Business To Consumer

AGENCY:
NEUE DIGITALE / Frankfurt

CLIENT:
adidas

ART DIRECTOR:
Jörg Waldschütz

PROGRAMMER:
Jens Steffen

DESIGNERS:
Antje Thomsen
Peter Kirsch
André Bourguignon
Stefan Schuster

CREATIVE DIRECTOR:
Olaf Czeschner

ID:
06019N

URL:
http://www.neue-digitale.de/projects/y-3_fw2005

Your work for Y-3 has been regularly awarded, each year innovativing the design as it relates to the motif, which has evolved from kaleidoscopes to catwalks, and now cubes. Discuss the ideas behind its latest reincarnation. The idea was to create a new view of the fashion exhibition. The success of this project lies with the strong ideas and advanced technical and visual demands which were implemented by NEUE DIGITALE. The product is always the focus. Moving away from traditional techniques, in this case the Brand User Experience rotates completely around the product—a positive brand experience also provokes long-term customer loyalty to a product.

What challenges did you face in technical execution? The technology serves primarily as an aid to the implementation of the idea. The implementation of a three-dimensional area to display the fashion was difficult to do. An interactive fashion experience should be created that links virtual space and real fashion photography.

The spinning model is actually the loading time. How were the effects achieved seamlessly? Firstly, the models were photographed in 24 separate pictures on a rotating platform and then animated in Flash. It was important that the turn always began exactly from the last pose of the model. Only in this way could both a vertical and a horizontal 360-degree turn be achieved.

Deliverance

Hybrid cards are the latest in correspondence technology! With this half-email, half-snail mail wonder, why mosey to the mailbox when you can mouse it, but why send an intangible "thinking of you" when you can send a handholdable hardcopy? No need to get postal with Åkestam.Holst's real handwritten postcards.

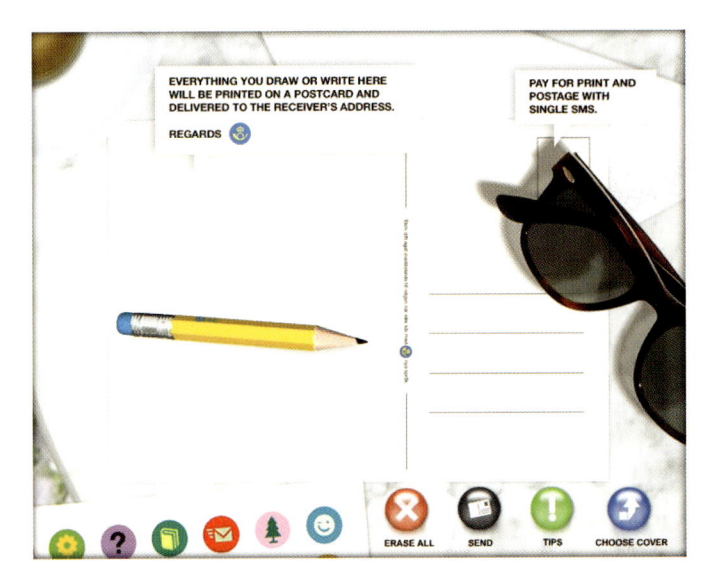

AWARD:
BRONZE
CATEGORY:
Web Sites:
Business To Consumer
AGENCY:
Åkestam.Holst / Stockholm
CLIENT:
Posten (Swedish Post Office)
ART DIRECTOR:
Fredrik Josefsson
PROGRAMMER:
Bengt Sjölén
PRODUCTION COMPANY:
B-Reel
INFORMATION ARCHITECT:
Magnus Hamberg
ID:
06020N
URL:
http://www.b-reel.com/submit/oneshow06/posten/

There's something ironic yet clever about using the Internet to send out snail mail. What was the brief from the client and what were they trying to achieve? Surveys show that people still love to get physical mail, especially private mail. The obstacle is actually sending them. That's why we invented the hybrid postcard about a year ago. In this campaign the brief was about integrating The Swedish Post's new graphic identity with the hybrid card.

How do the pictograms work as part of Posten's new identity? All pictograms are based on the original Posten logo which is an icon with a blue circle and a yellow blow horn. With the symbols we try to do two things. First we create a communication language that is impossible to miss. Second we show hundreds of things that hide behind the Posten logo, up to now well known only for letters and parcels. All campaigns for Posten are based on simple pictogram puzzles using just text and icons. There is no limited set of icons, we keep inventing new icons along the way. Today we have about 350 icons and we create new nearly every day.

What was the most difficult part about creating the site? In the application, you can mix your own uploaded jpg image with drawings and icons. The most difficult part of the production was converting all the graphics into one printable image. Just using the http protocol we send a string with the position of the icons and all the mouse coordinates of the drawing together with the location of the uploaded image to the server. We then put it all together again to recreate a printable image of what the user created in the application. I was surprised that the production went very smooth overall, and we have not experienced any downtime or lost cards as far as I know.

How many postcards have been mailed out so far? Is this going to be a permanent feature for the Post Office? The Handwritten Postcards campaign was just meant to run during the campaign period, but the response was so good that the client decided to keep the application as a permanent feature. When this was decided we produced three new special versions for Christmas, Easter and Valentine's Day. So far approx 100,000 postcards have been printed and sent out.

The Empire Strikes BK

Using the Darth side of the Force, Lord Vader attempts to read your mind in a little game of deductive guessing. Does it have wings? Does it burrow in small holes? Does it want fries with that? With each visit to the site, Vader gets a little smarter. But he does get some psychic help from his fellow caped madman, the King. The website tied in with Burger King's Star Wars Episode III: Revenge of the Sith in-store promotion, "Choose Your Destiny."

AWARD:
BRONZE
CATEGORY:
Web Sites:
Business To Consumer
AGENCY:
Crispin Porter + Bogusky /
Miami
CLIENT:
Burger King
WRITERS:
Paul Johnson
David Povill, Larry Corwin
DESIGNER:
Rahul Panchal
PRODUCTION COMPANIES:
Firstborn Multimedia, 20Q
CREATIVE DIRECTORS:
Alex Bogusky, Andrew Keller
Rob Reilly, Jeff Benjamin
ID:
06021N
URL:
http://www.cpbgroup.com
/awards/sithsenseone.html

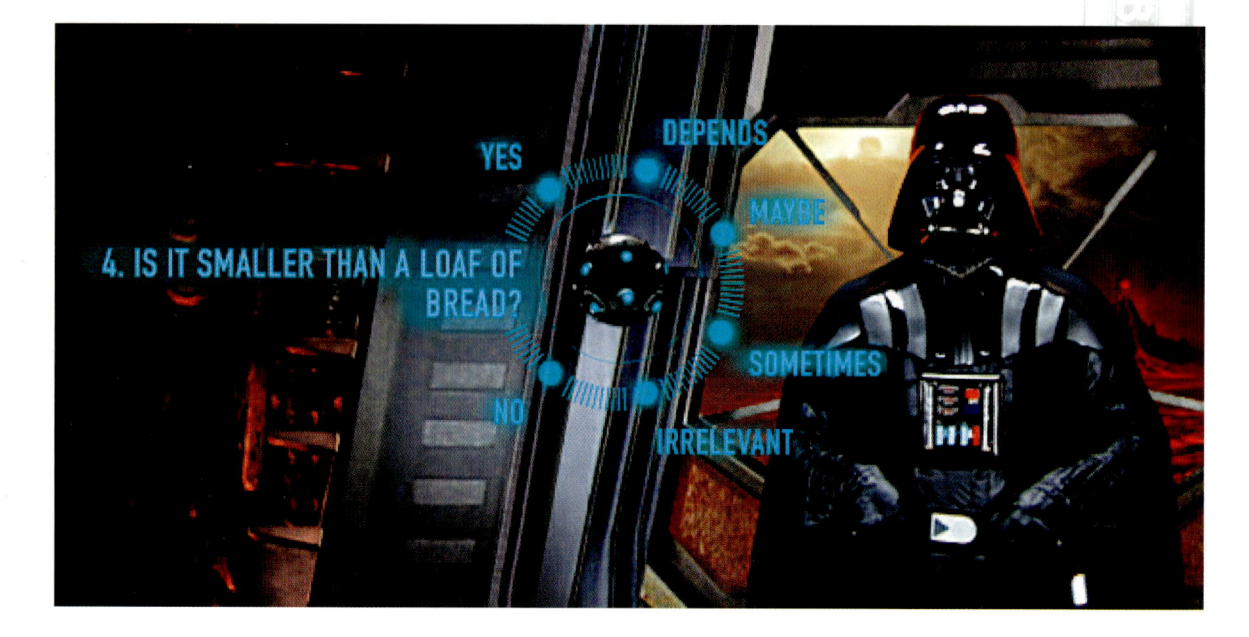

LORD VADER HAS READ YOUR MIND

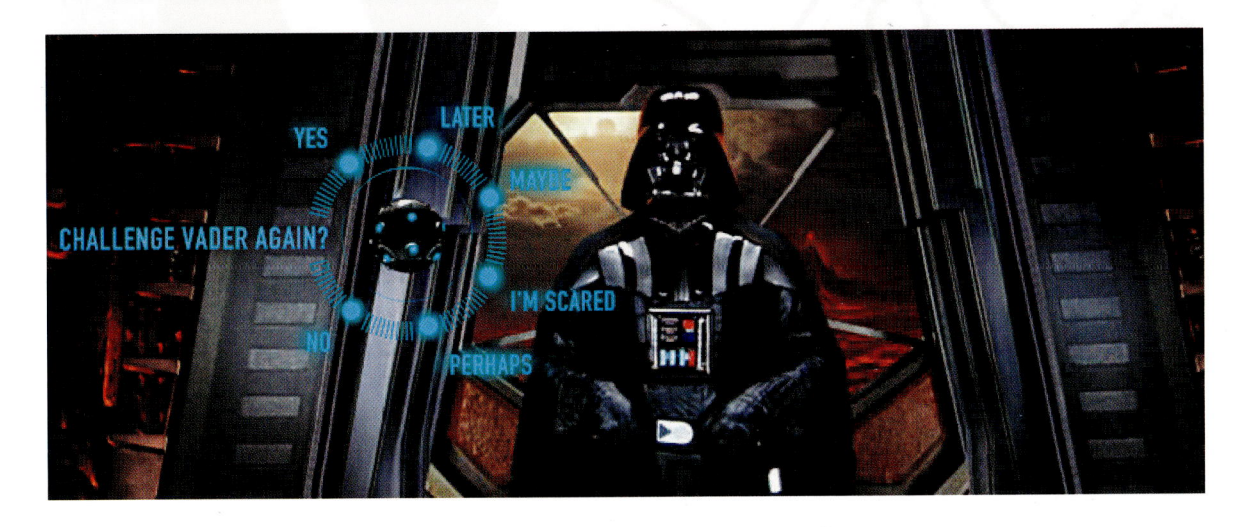

CHALLENGE VADER AGAIN?
YES
NO
LATER
MAYBE
I'M SCARED
PERHAPS

Pencil Winners
69

Top Heavy

Roofstudio.com is a gallery where MINI aficionados who refuse to drive with a clean slate can submit their rooftop Rembrandts, their crazy Pi-car-ssos. Hardcore enthusiasts have the option to download a graphic and turn them into a real vinyl appliqué for their cars. Rims and hydraulics may be passé, but the roof is on fire!

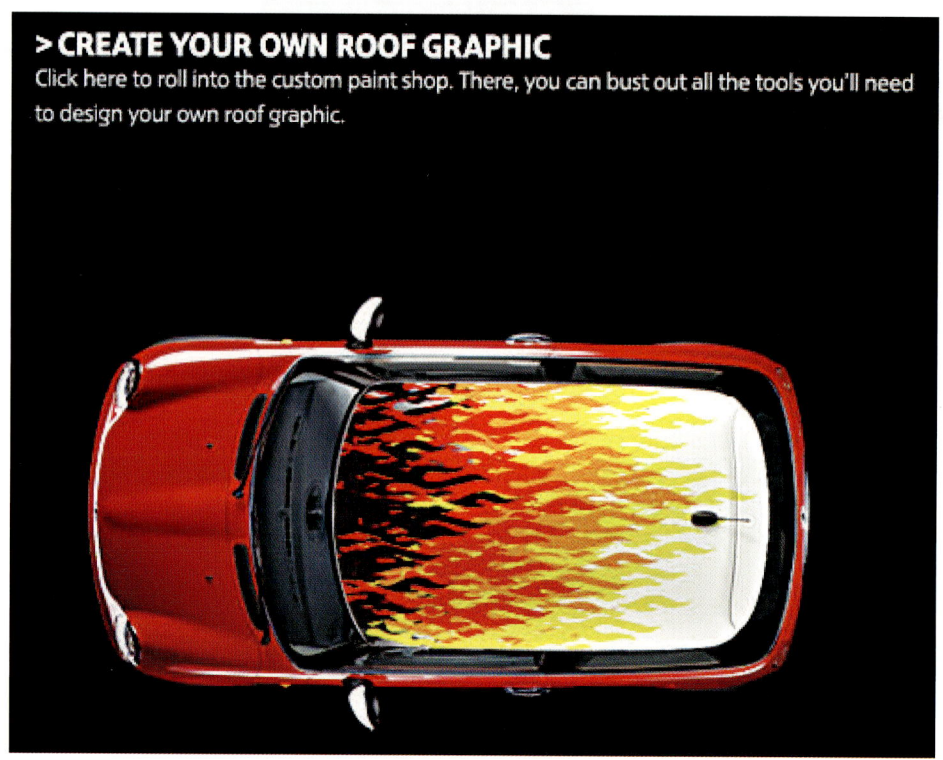

> **CREATE YOUR OWN ROOF GRAPHIC**
> Click here to roll into the custom paint shop. There, you can bust out all the tools you'll need to design your own roof graphic.

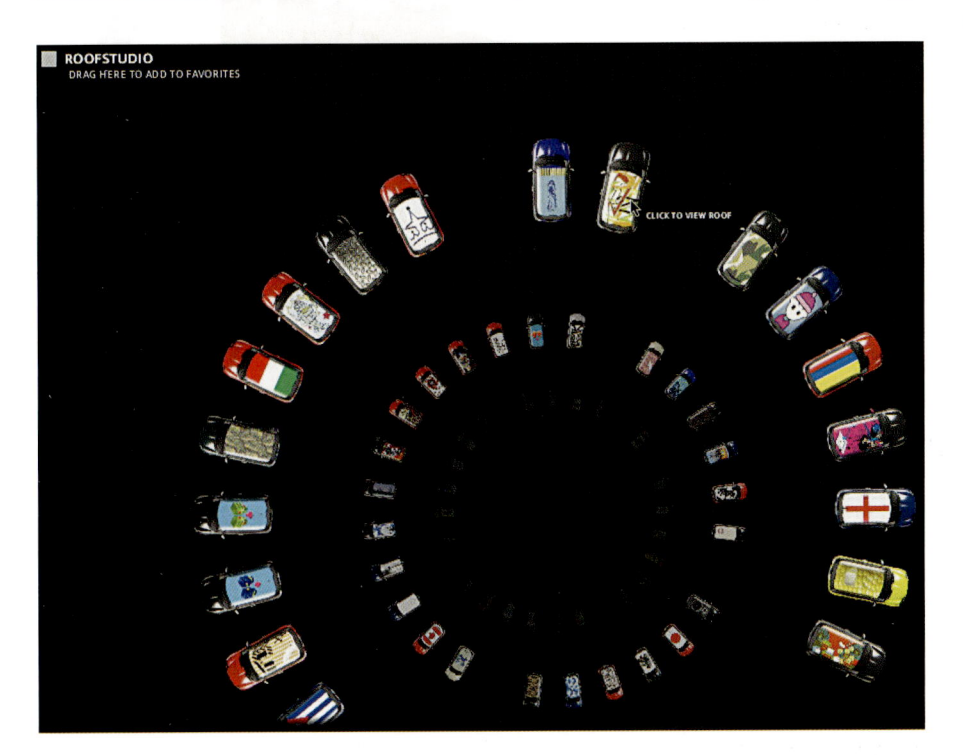

AWARD:
BRONZE
CATEGORY:
Web Sites: Business
To Consumer
AGENCY:
Crispin Porter + Bogusky /
Miami
CLIENT:
MINI
ART DIRECTOR:
Rahul Panchal
Trisha Ting
WRITERS:
Brian Tierney
Jackie Hathiramani
PROGRAMMER:
EVB
PRODUCTION COMPANY:
Beam Interactive
CREATIVE DIRECTORS:
Alex Bogusky, Andrew Keller
Jeff Benjamin
ID:
06022N
URL:
http://www.cpbgroup.com/awards/roofstudio.html

Woodland Nocturne

Machine and animal meet in the night's silvery forest in this film-like website from Lowe Tesch, interspersed with spooky videos of lynxes and foxes running through the trees. Whether they be prey or predator is left to the imagination.

The eyes of an animal

Only when you come face to face with the new Saab 9-5 can you fully appreciate its most striking feature. The front has been radically redesigned. A new grille and distinctive wraparound headlights give the car a unique expression. Behind the beauty there's plenty of brawn, with a powerful turbo engine that makes driving even more exhilarating.

READ MORE AT SAAB.COM
TAKE A TEST DRIVE
FIND A SAAB DEALER
VIEW FILMS
TELL A FRIEND

The eyes of an animal

Only when you come face to face with the new Saab 9-5 can you fully appreciate its most striking feature. The front has been radically redesigned. A new grille and distinctive wraparound headlights give the car a unique expression. Behind the beauty there's plenty of brawn, with a powerful turbo engine that makes driving even more exhilarating.

READ MORE AT SAAB.COM
TAKE A TEST DRIVE
FIND A SAAB DEALER
VIEW FILMS
TELL A FRIEND

AWARD:
BRONZE
CATEGORY:
Web Sites:
Business To Consumer
AGENCY:
Lowe Tesch / Stockholm
CLIENT:
Saab Automobile
ART DIRECTORS:
Tim Scheibel, Johan Tesch
WRITER:
Stephen Whitlock
DIGITAL ARTIST/MULTIMEDIA:
Daniel Isaksson
CREATIVE DIRECTOR:
Niklas Wallberg
ANNUAL ID:
06023N
URL:
http://www.lowetesch.com/showroom/saab/animalvision/GLOBAL/en/index.html

The Kitchen Counter Revolution

Visitors to this online showroom swing their way through gorgeously rendered three-dimensional kitchens built for every taste and style. Frozen in happy accidents, the models and their model kitchen provide a cinematic canvas for exploring IKEA products while a soundtrack from the golden age of domesticity plays. Carouse around again and you'll find yourself crashing a party, or surely suffering from shiny appliance envy.

The Matrix is often referred to when this site is viewed. What were the challenges in bringing this effect to a website? How long did it take to complete? The freeze-frame effect was a way of showing spectacular kitchens and at the same time bringing the warmth and entertainment of everyday people to the scene. The greatest challenge in terms of production was the complexity of a film shoot that took place in six large-scale and detailed constructed environments in parallel, including a slew of special effects. The scenes are actually shot in real time, with the people holding absolutely still during the whole sequence. The extensive post process in order to maximize the effect of the film sequences in a web site was another challenge to be overcome. From brief to site release, it took about four months to complete.

AWARD:
GOLD

CATEGORY:
Web Sites:
Promotional Advertising

AGENCY:
Forsman & Bodenfors /
Gothenburg

CLIENT:
IKEA Sweden

ART DIRECTORS:
Anders Eklind
John Bergdahl
Mathias Appelblad
Andreas Malm
Karin Frisell

WRITERS:
Fredrik Jansson
Anders Hegerfors

DESIGNERS:
Mikko Timonen
Nina Andersson
Jerry Wass
Viktor Larsson

PRODUCTION COMPANIES:
Sammarco Productions
Kaka Entertainment

ANNUAL ID:
06024N

URL:
http://demo.fb.se/e/ikea/dreamkitchen2/

ALSO AWARDED:
SILVER New Media Innovation + Development: Web Sites

There's a very cinematic and voyeuristic quality to the site. It's like peering into a stranger's life at just the right moment of human expression. Where did you draw inspiration from? Wanting to show completely different kitchens and the different people living in them, we were inspired by episode films like *Short Cuts* and *Magnolia*. The voyeuristic aspect you mention was an emotion we specifically wanted to create in order to differentiate very personal Ikea kitchens from the competitor's often very clinical and anonymous communications.

Sound is quite important to the user's experience. How did you go about choosing the music for each set? The challenge was to create music that helps set the mood of each scene and build the characters' emotional context. The whole team was involved in the process of trying out a plethora of soundtracks over the course of four weeks.

76   GOLD WINNER // FORSMAN & BODENFORS

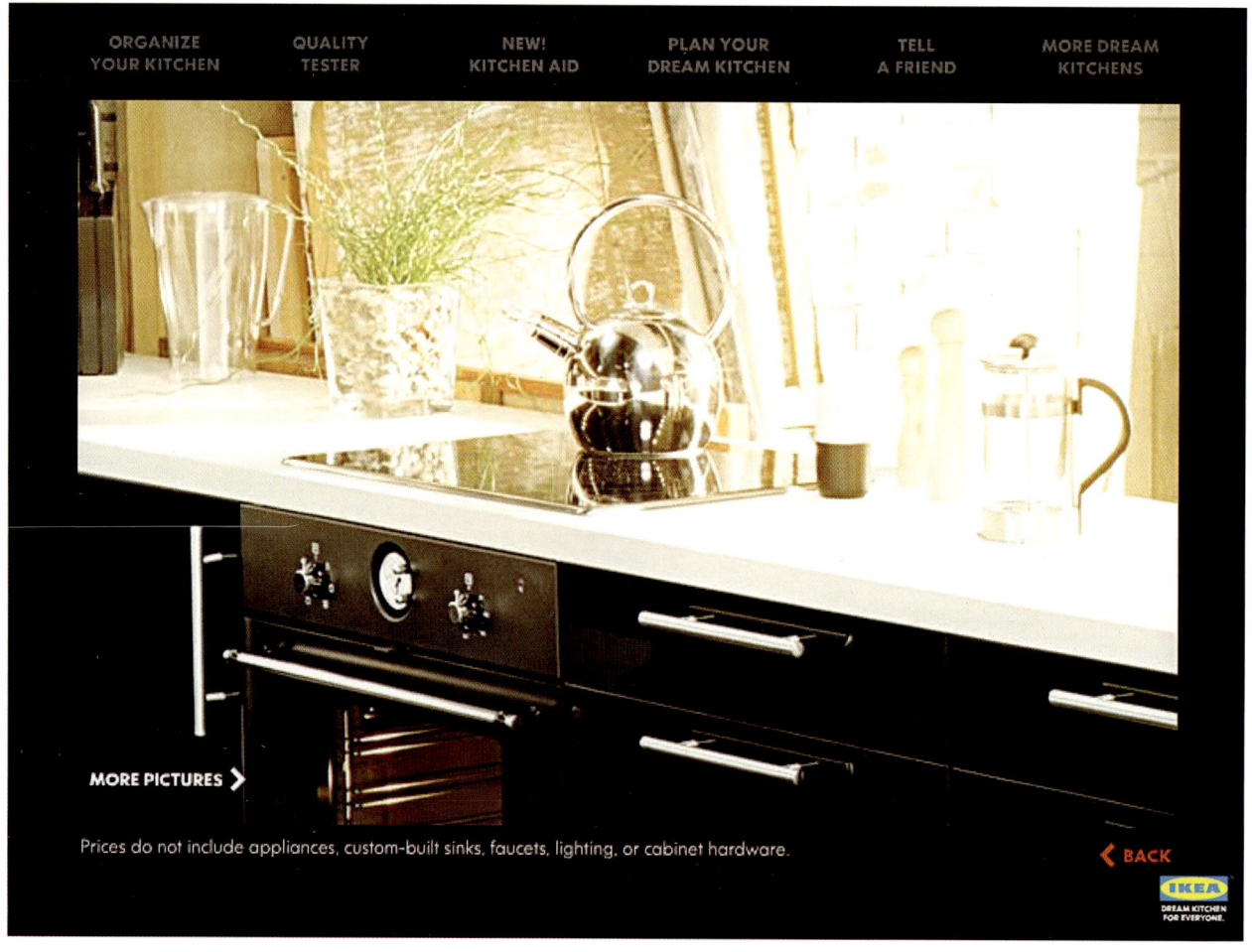

WASTE SORTING. RATIONELL waste-sorting bins and pull-out trays keep the often rather neglected space under the sink clean and tidy. Hide your plastic bags away in a RATIONELL dispenser on the inside of the door.

BACK

ORGANIZE YOUR KITCHEN

BACK

Pencil Winners
77

Dislocating the Humerus

The online component of Mother's campaign for TBS brought its "Humor Study" into an interactive laboratory that analyses visitor's responses to puerile challenges like "deface this face," and identifying the funniest part of a man to hit a ball with. Breaking comedy down to its particles, you realize that everything, really, is quite ridiculous.

78 SILVER WINNER // MOTHER NEW YORK

AWARD:
SILVER

CATEGORY:
Web Sites:
Promotional Advertising

AGENCY:
Mother / New York

CLIENT:
Turner Broadcasting
System (TBS)

ART DIRECTOR:
Rory Hanrahan

WRITER:
Dave Clark

PRODUCTION COMPANY:
Big Spaceship

CREATIVE DIRECTORS:
Linus Karlsson
Paul Malmstrom

ANNUAL ID:
06026N

URL:
www.tbshumorstudy.com

How do you make funny? To help TBS steer clear of common pitfalls in this cut-throat, dog-eat-dog, rabbit-outwit-duck, duck-shoot-pig, anvil-smush-coyote, Chico-trip-Zeppo field of funny business, Big Spaceship joined forces with the good folks at Mother to turn their very silly printed questionnaire into an addictive, fully interactive site. In this clinically antiseptic, digital environment, vulnerable specimens such as cheap puns, sausages, and paleontologists undergo grueling and methodical prodding by an advisory board of blasé professionals, a.k.a. the site visitors.

We assembled our own team to analyze, interpret, decipher, re-analyze and redact the printed survey into a combination of multiple choice and fully interactive questions. But the forty or so questions in the survey were clearly too many for a web audience. So we built a framework to intelligently serve this content, alternating between fully interactive questions and copy-based questions, in more manageable chunks (five, based on our own limited attention spans) with each user visit.

Next, in a creative collaboration with Mother, we moved on to some new, original features to be housed in the Humor Lab, allowing users to create their own comedic content, such as future sitcoms, short films with flatulence-filled soundtracks, a pun translated around the world...and back again, and the Mother-produced and aptly titled "Funny Shorts."

Our Art Director on the project ran into the poor actor who got nailed with the ball (in the name of science, of course) at a local Borders in LA. He pretended not to know him...
-Big Spaceship

80 SILVER WINNER // MOTHER NEW YORK

Play in the Humor Lab

tbs Dept. of Humor Analysis
Comprehensive Study of Humor & Humorousness

MUSIC ON / OFF

Wallpaper Generator

Instructions

Click on backgrounds and objects to add them to your custom desktop. Once they are on the canvas you can move and resize them. When you are done, click *I'M DONE*.

BACKGROUNDS | OBJECTS

→ Clear Canvas   → I'm Done   → Send to a friend!

tbs very funny. | © 2005 Turner Broadcasting System, Inc. A Time Warner Company. All Rights Reserved. | TERMS OF USE | PRIVACY POLICY

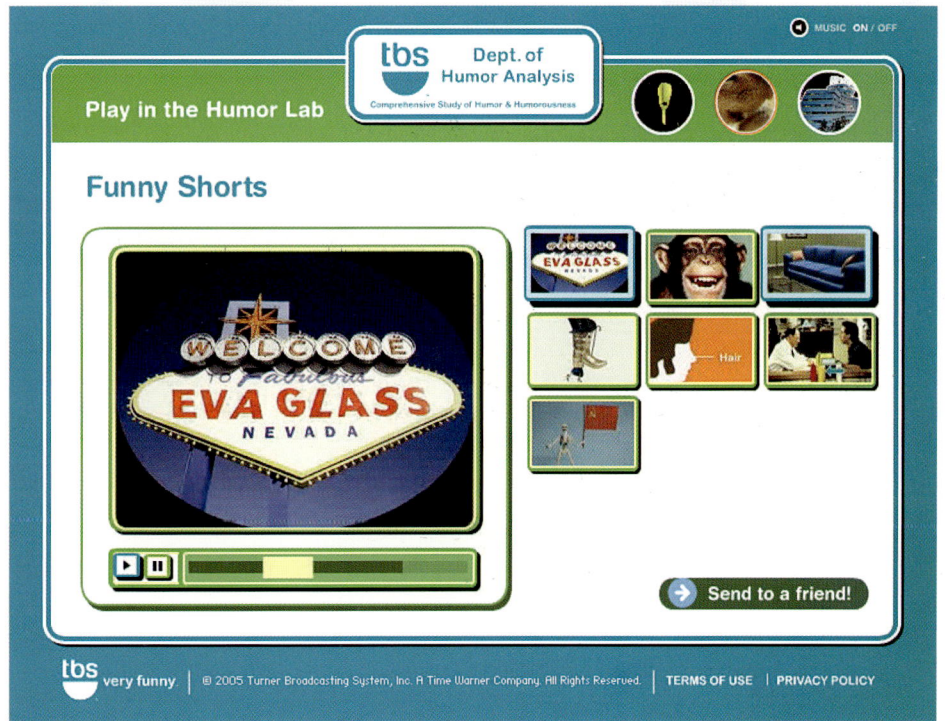

Play in the Humor Lab

tbs Dept. of Humor Analysis
Comprehensive Study of Humor & Humorousness

MUSIC ON / OFF

Funny Shorts

→ Send to a friend!

tbs very funny. | © 2005 Turner Broadcasting System, Inc. A Time Warner Company. All Rights Reserved. | TERMS OF USE | PRIVACY POLICY

Pencil Winners
81

Class Culture

Agency Republic takes us on a stellar road trip of the senses in this smooth A-Z device. Along the way, interesting nibblets about Mercedes-Benz are fed to you as a sumptuous 19-course meal. And you never have to look at a car.

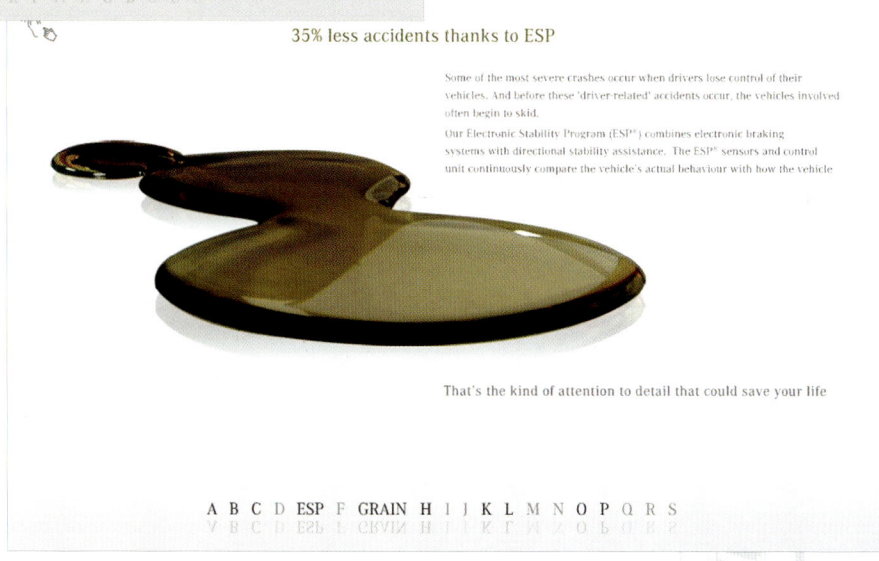

AWARD:
BRONZE
CATEGORY:
Web Sites:
Promotional Advertising
AGENCY:
Agency Republic / London
CLIENT:
Mercedes-Benz
Passenger Cars UK
ART DIRECTORS:
Gavin Gordon-Rogers
Gemma Butler
WRITERS:
Gavin Gordon-Rogers
Gemma Butler
DESIGNER:
Marga Arrom-Bibiloni
CREATIVE DIRECTOR:
Andy Sandoz
ANNUAL ID:
06027N
URL:
www.a-to-s.co.uk

82 BRONZE WINNER // AGENCY REPUBLIC

This was your first work for a new client. Where did you come up with the idea of going through the alphabet? We had a lot of different amazing facts and pieces of information which we were free to talk about. The aim of the site was to illustrate whether a potential buyer might be interested in the cheapest A-Class model or the most luxurious S-Class. Every Mercedes-Benz shares a vast array of truly exceptional inventions and little touches. The alphabet seemed a natural way to order all these disparate pieces of information and of course we made it run from 'A' to 'S' as those are the Mercedes car classes.

There's a very tactile quality to the site without it having to showcase 3D models and high-tech simulations. Talk about the creative process behind the project. We wanted to avoid showing any cars. First of all, because every car site, every TV commercial, every press ad and on and on shows the car. Auto manufacturers are obsessed about showing their product rather than talking about it. Luckily, because it was a new client who wanted something different, and also because we were talking about every Mercedes-Benz passenger car rather than one in particular, we were able to avoid the usual clichés. We focused on trying to convey the essential experience of each benefit we were communicating. We were trying to make a user feel as though they'd been as close as possible to actually sitting in the car and checking it out in the real world.

Touching the leather seat was delicious, and the emu feather was also loads of fun to play with. Was it a challenge translating some of the quirkier facts about Mercedes-Benz into an interactive experience? The entire process was a lot of fun. In fact it was exhilarating—we felt like we were pushing the boundaries. We came up with ideas about how to convey each fact in an interactive way and then spoke to our Flash gurus about how we could make them happen. Some ideas had to be dropped, but we're very happy with the outcome—especially as we weren't allowed to use Flash 8 (which would have made a lot of potential ideas possible). The quirky facts were the easy ones. Something like "Recyclable" sounded so normal, but was harder to make interesting.

Higher Language

A stock photo agency flashes through images in a random manner, a free-floating movie. But these seemingly unconnected pictures are assembled together to convey the 12 concepts of their company. An image only means what you confer on it, and so the website fittingly embodies the word amana—"the source of creation."

AWARD:
SILVER

CATEGORY:
Web Sites:
Business To Business

AGENCY:
Tha Ltd. / Tokyo

CLIENT:
Amana

ART DIRECTOR:
Yosuke Abe

DESIGNER:
Yosuke Abe

PROGRAMMER:
Yugo Nakamura

DIGITAL ARTIST/MULTIMEDIA:
Suguru Yamaguchi

CREATIVE DIRECTOR:
Yugo Nakamura

ID:
06029N

URL:
http://amana.jp/company/tsutawaru/

Pencil Winners
85

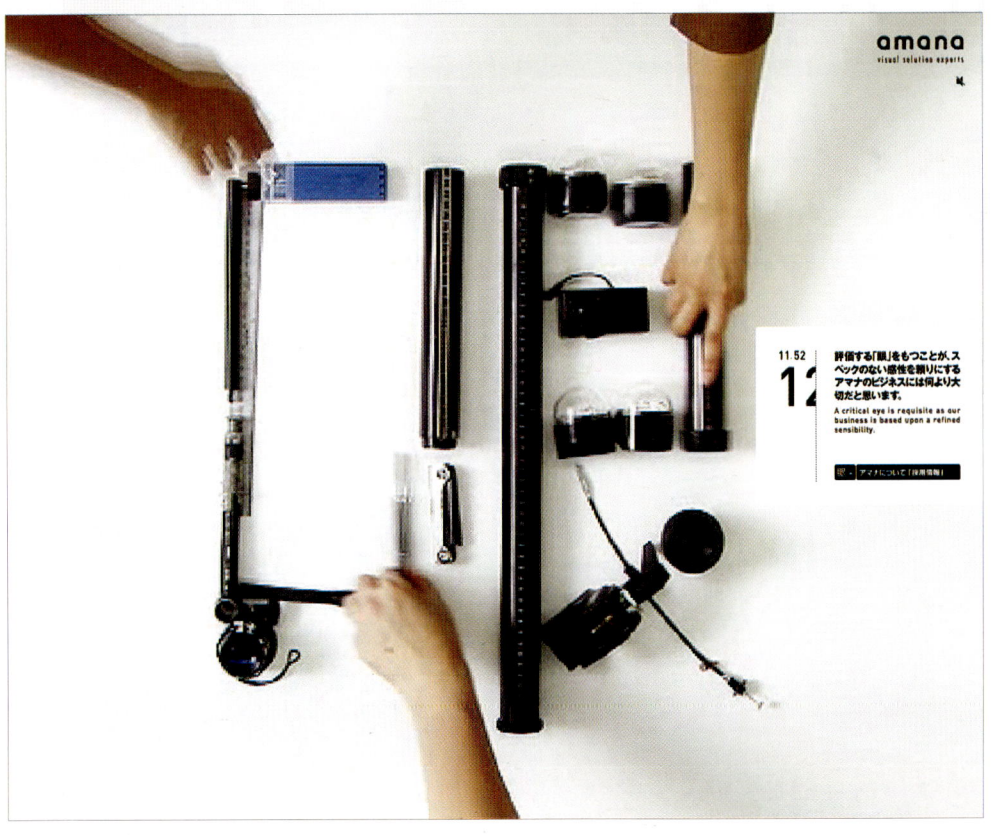

Swing Out, Sister

Nike Women's intensely groovy website will leave you sweating, if not drooling over the workout clothes and the fit bodies that rock them. Celebrityism is stamped all over the videos, with choreography from Jamie King and a bumping soundtrack from Rihanna. Despite the graphics-heavy content, navigation—and the tricky-looking dance steps—feel totally carb-free.

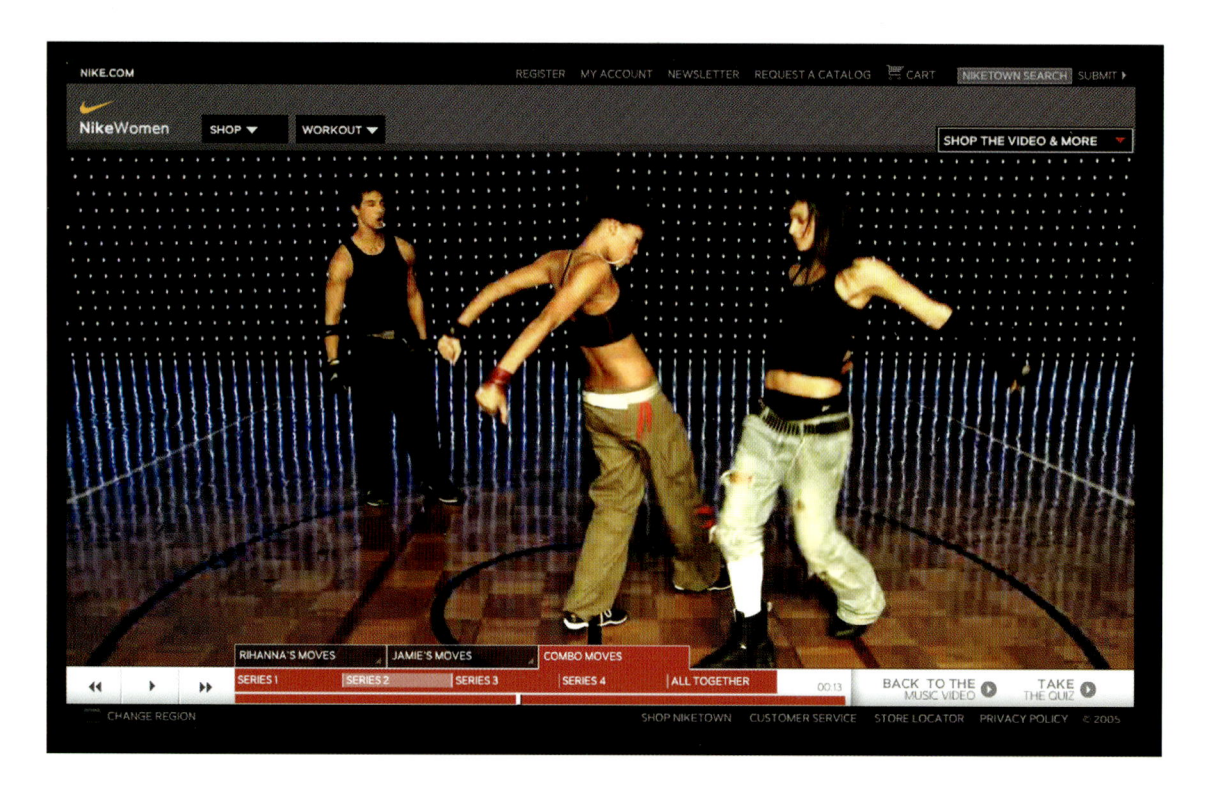

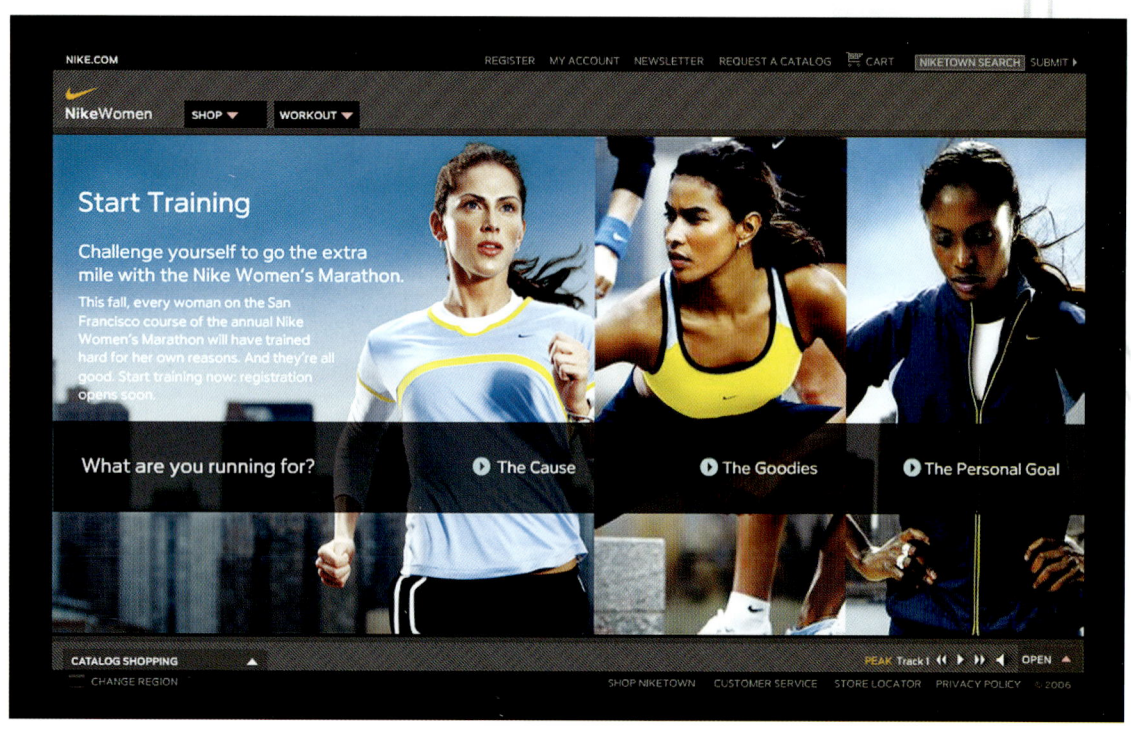

RD:
NZE

GORY:
Sites: E-commerce

NCY:
/ New York

NT:

DIRECTOR:
me Austria

GNERS:
nrongphut Korad
Lubliner, Kenji Shimonura

ER:
ael Spiegel

GRAMMERS:
Billig, Kumi Tominaga
ael McLoughlin

AL ARTIST/MULTIMEDIA:
Johannesdottir

NCY PRODUCER:
ifer Allen

RMATION ARCHITECT:
ust Yang

ON

//www.nike.com/nikewomen
ndex.jhtml

It's a very content-rich site. How did you approach the design of the interface? Well, we wanted to satisfy the two sides of our target consumer. In this case, the nikewomen.com consumer is very shopping-centric, but also very fitness-oriented so we decided to create two very unique environments. When you visit the site, all of the content is bucketed either in a shop section or a workout section. Our main philosophy behind the interface design was to simplify, simplify, simplify. We wanted everything to be easy to navigate. When a consumer is in the shop environment, she shouldn't be overly distracted with non-shopping content. Great product imagery was also key in making the shopping experience feel premium and more like a boutique shopping experience.

Women shop differently from men. How was this taken into consideration when designing the online store? Two key insights we had before we started designing the online store was that women love to shop by outfit and also love to see outfits within the context of their use. Given those insights we created the 'shop by outfit' feature, the e-stylist feature, and we tried to integrate products into the Rihanna music video workout.

The workout videos are awesome, however they seem to be more aspirational and entertaining than practical. How are they being used? I would beg to differ—I thought the instructional videos were very practical. Users could consume the videos on-line or download them to their iPod, PSP, or post them to their blog/myspace environment. In my opinion, the instructional videos were a huge success, just go to youtube.com and type in 'Rihanna SOS' into the search field. You will get pages upon pages of videos of kids dancing to the Rihanna SOS instructional videos. That type of cultural following speaks volumes to the success of those instructional videos.

Pencil Winners
87

Big Pencils Get Big Pencils

This site is map to the land of Leoburnettians, a multi-dimensional view of a terrain guided by black squiggly lines and landmark logos. Plunge into the vistas of Visa and sands of Samsung—a landscape of big ideas and the great campaigns they generated. Leo's ghostly specter comes up every now and then to hand you an apple of advice.

AWARD:
SILVER

CATEGORY:
Web Sites: Self-Promotion

AGENCY:
Leo Burnett and Arc Worldwide / Toronto

CLIENT:
Leo Burnett Canada

ART DIRECTORS:
Ian Kay, Israel Diaz
Peter Gomes

WRITERS:
Arthur Shah, Len Preskow

DESIGNER:
Peter Gomes

PROGRAMMERS:
Mike Findlay, Dan Purdy

CREATIVE DIRECTORS:
Judy John, Shirley Ward-Taggart

ANNUAL ID:
06031N

URL:
www.leoburnett.ca

88   SILVER WINNER // LEO BURNETT AND ARC WORLDWIDE CANADA

What does "Big Ideas Come From Big Pencils" actually mean? Way back in the 1930s, Leo Burnett saw the big Alpha 245 pencil as a metaphor for the kind of big and bold ideas he was pioneering for his clients.

In every Leo Burnett office around the world you'll find big pencils with Leo Burnett's signature. They have become part of Burnett's iconography and culture.

Why are our pencils big? They are a constant reminder of the size of our ambition. We challenge ourselves to create ideas big enough to change people's minds, touch people's hearts and, when we're at our very best, move entire categories.

Was it necessary to include "Navigation for Linear Thinkers"?
We added the linear nav out of respect for different user needs.

Some site visitors, like creative and potential employees, will get right into the site and take the time to explore it fully. Others, like clients or potential clients, may just want a contact name or a quick look at a specific brand's creative.

What was the thought process behind the "unstructured" structure of the site? The big idea was to use our Leo Burnett's symbols (his signature, the pencil, apples and stars) in a very unique space, driven and defined by experiential navigation, not architecture. We envisioned a site with a multi-layered, multi-dimensional space – a kind of 3-D, minimalist, black & white canvas, where you are drawn in explore the content randomly instead of by going down a linear path. So, as you interact with the site, you become an integral part of its creativity.

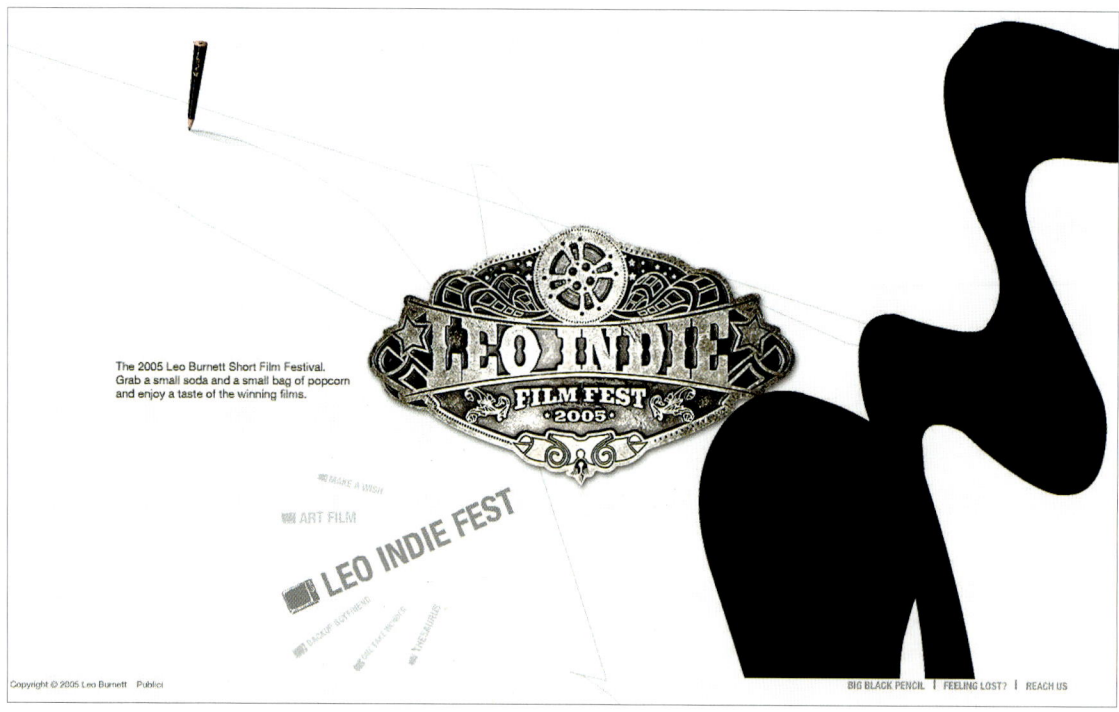

90   SILVER WINNER // LEO BURNETT AND ARC WORLDWIDE CANADA

Pencil Winners
91

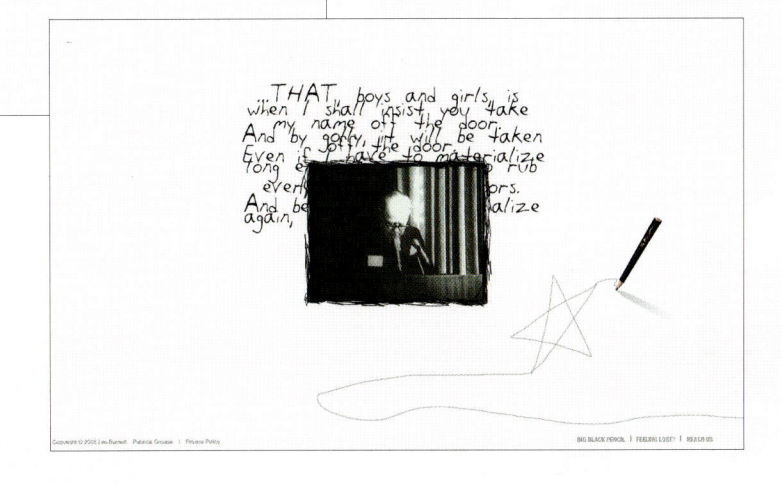

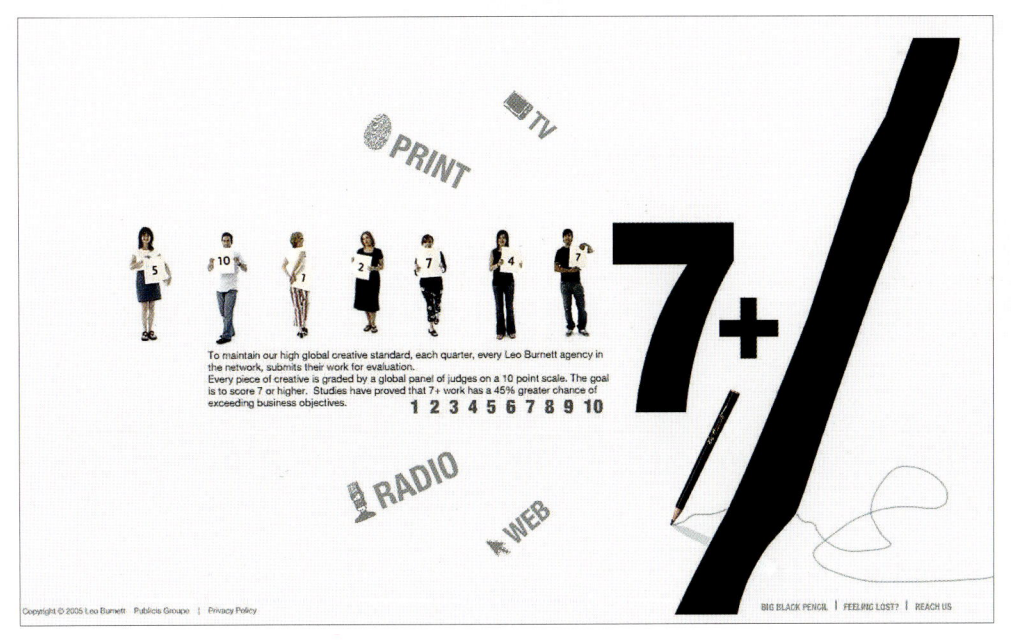

String Theory

In an elegant universe, everything disparate is actually made of the same vibrating loops of energy. With the form and function of lines of filigree, Hakuhodo and Hakuhodo DY's self-promotional website shows how everybody is connected.

AWARD:
BRONZE
CATEGORY:
Web Sites:
Self-Promotion
AGENCY:
HAKUHODO i-studio /
Tokyo
CLIENT:
Hakuhodo
ART DIRECTORS:
Katsuhiko Sano
Hironobu Tsuchiya
WRITER:
Mariko Ogata
DESIGNERS:
Katsuhiko Sano
Tatsuro Ooe
Ryuhei Nakadai
PRODUCTION COMPANIES:
Hakuhodo i-studio
Hakuhodo
CONTENT STRATEGISTS:
Teruaki Tomikawa
Hiroyuki Murayama
Kyoko Kochi
CREATIVE DIRECTOR:
Yutaka Sugiyama
ANNUAL ID:
06032N
URL:
http://award.i-studio.co.jp/2005_musubi/en/

Please explain the concept of musubu and how this was embodied in the design of the website. *Musubu* (tie), as a key word for the connection between the public and corporate, is visualized throughout the site. Specifically, we built an interface wherein the components all connect along one line. Hakuhodo and Hakuhodo DY media partners are the content of this website and also the line in which to connect to all other elements. The site map, commanding the entire interface, represents the intricately intertwined elements of the site.

How did the new recruits participate in the creation of the section "Freshman's Day?" They are the junior employees with a few years of experience. We asked them to document their daily schedule with pictures and presented their voice in the copy. To highlight their originality, we recorded their voices and used them for the voiceover.

The Case Study section shows the relationships between the different members of the agency and the process of creating ads. How do the new recruits respond to the orientation? Does it prepare them for the office culture at Hakuhodo? It did. It's primary object is to let people who don't know anything about advertising understand the work flow at Hakuhodo and Hakuhodo DY media partners. Although we haven't got the specific response to this content, we'll be happy if this section interests many people.

Pencil Winners
93

Smart Mobs

Wave your placard high—the revolution has been digitized. Street protests and warm bodies still have relevance as live spectacle, but it's the virtual rallies, sit-ins, and shut downs that can have a wider, global reach. Agency Republic, teaming up with Glue London and AKQA, staged a peaceful but powerful online demonstration in support of the Make Poverty History campaign.

The virtual rally won first place in response to one of the "World's Toughest Briefs." How did you get involved with this cause (Make Poverty History)? Our agency has a division called Social Republic which specifically handles charities. They brought the brief to our attention and we, along with a few of our colleagues, were keen to respond. Little did they know at the time what a massive amount of work the entire project was going to be! We were very happy because a fellow team from Republic came runner up in the competition and it was just great to see two digital ideas come first and second when the brief was open to any media.

There's no automatic screening of offensive messages people might submit. Did that become a problem? We thought that this could be a problem, so we decided to include the option for users to report offensive messages. In the end we really needn't have bothered. We were astounded by how few negative or offensive messages were written. It really must have been only two or three out of 50,000. I think it goes to show that when people go to a website they go there for a reason, not just to surf and make trouble. It also made the whole site feel really positive—even the joke messages were received well—there was no animosity on that site at all.

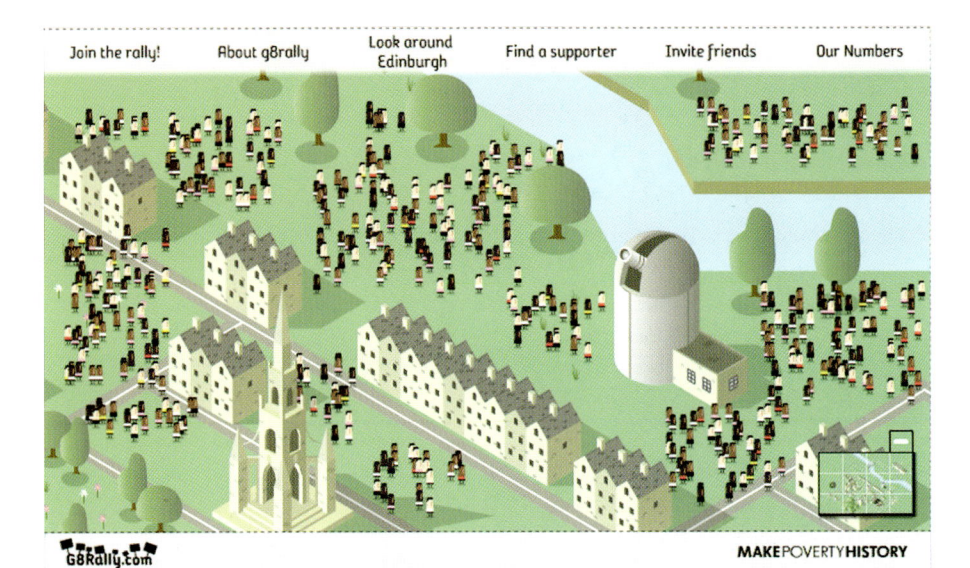

The site enlisted 53,000 campaigners whose average age is 27. What did you learn from this experience? At first we thought "53,000 is not an amazingly huge number" and we were kind of disappointed. But our Creative Director put it in perspective when he reminded us that the site had launched just two days before the real event; that the AOL site which we had no knowledge of was effectively doing the same thing; and that our site had virtually no promotion at all. When we look back at the site now, we see campaigners from all over the world, of all ages, and although it could have been bigger, it still feels like we made a big, big contribution to the cause. Imagine 53,000 people marching along a road—it's actually a hell of a lot of people. Never underestimate the power of online!

AWARD:
BRONZE
CATEGORY:
Web Sites: Public Service /Non-Profit / Educational
AGENCY:
Agency Republic / London
CLIENT:
Comic Relief
ART DIRECTORS:
Gemma Butler
Gavin Gordon-Rogers
WRITERS:
Gavin Gordon-Rogers
Gemma Butler
DESIGNER:
Oli Laruelle
PROGRAMMER:
Andy Hood
ANNUAL ID:
06033N
URL:
http://www.agencyrepublic.com/awards/mph/

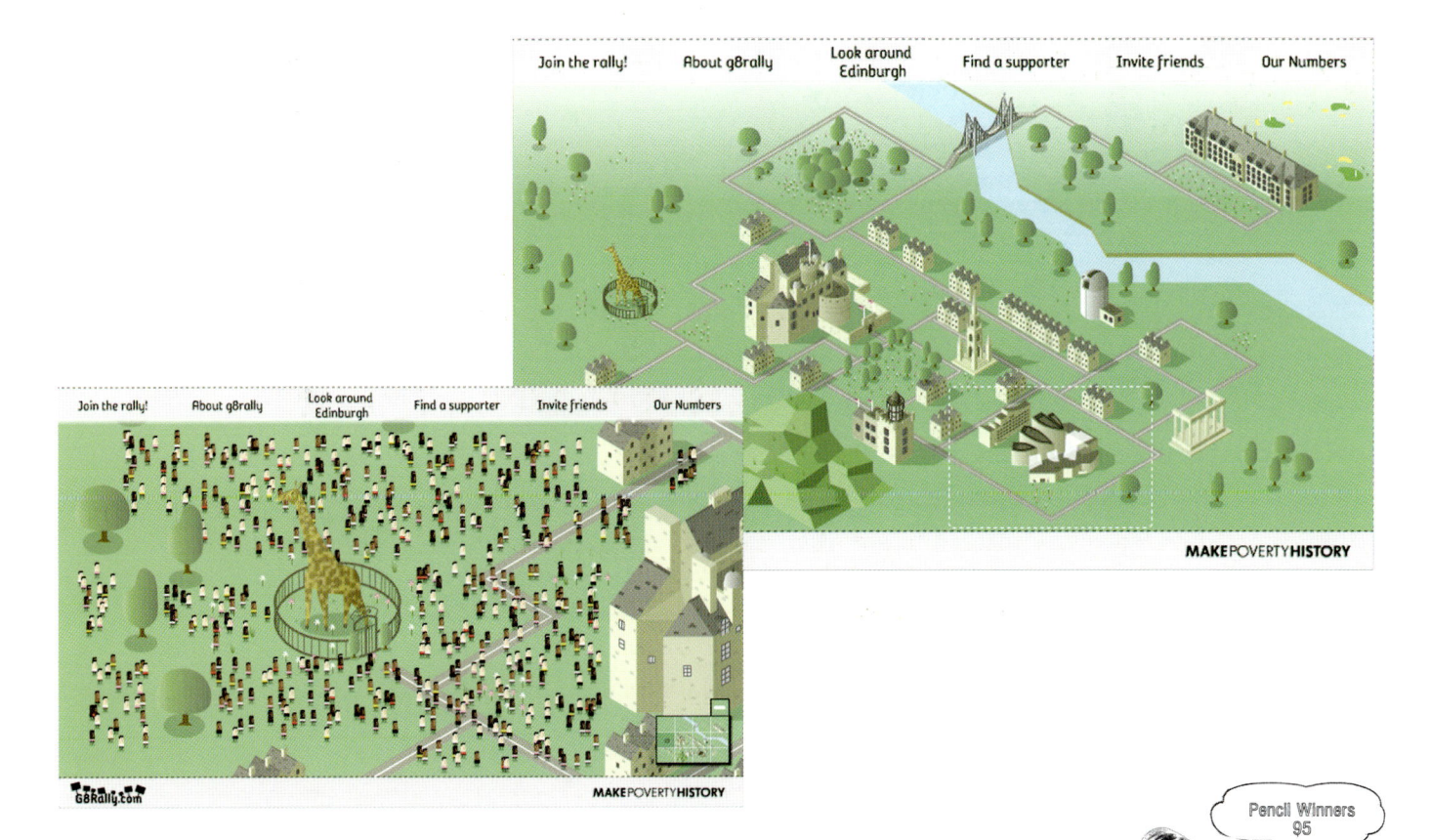

In the Bluff

The only brand-gaming winner this year combines the best of the web: Poker and softcore pornography. Kidding aside, Panty Poker is hot and campy and reminds you of those daring college days when you were drunk but not too drunk to hope you were wearing your best skivvies.

AWARD:
BRONZE
CATEGORY:
Brand Gaming:
Business To Consumer
AGENCY:
Crispin Porter + Bogusky /
Miami
CLIENT:
PINK
ART DIRECTOR:
Tiffany Kosel
WRITER:
Scott Linnen
PROGRAMMERS:
Luis Santi, North Kingdom
PRODUCTION COMPANY:
North Kingdom
CREATIVE DIRECTORS:
Alex Bogusky, Scott Linnen
Jeff Benjamin
ANNUAL ID:
06034N
URL:
http://www.cpbgroup.com/awards/poker.html

Pencil Winners
97

Accelerate, Exhilarate

Can you get a speeding ticket from opening email? This one from Nordpol+ is just like one of those letters where you have to scroll all the way to the bottom to see the punchline—only here, the way down is whizzing in a car, with the scenery stripping by as the odometer gets crunked. Woo!

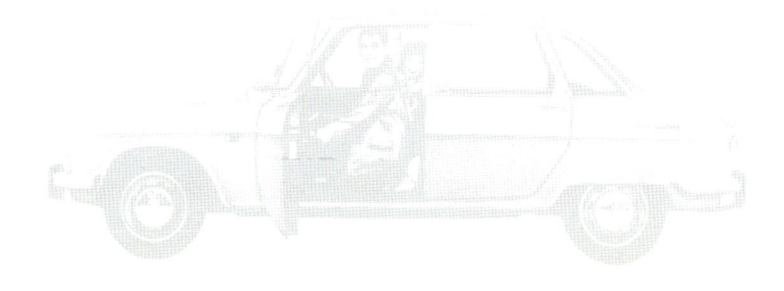

AWARD:
GOLD

CATEGORY:
Viral And Email:
Business To Consumer

AGENCY:
Nordpol+ Hamburg

CLIENT:
Renault Germany

DESIGNER:
Mark Höfler

ART DIRECTORS:
Dominik Anweiler
Gunther Schreiber

WRITER:
Ingmar Bartels

CREATIVE DIRECTOR:
Ingo Fritz

ANNUAL ID:
06035N

URL:
http://www.nordpol.com/2005/renault/meganesport/en/

Pencil Winners
99

Sphere Factor

Each webisode starts off with a song: "The true adventures of Chad, the guy who was so into Super Monkey Ball Deluxe that he decided to live in a ball." Everything after is a riot of satisfyingly silly humor, as we track Chad's all-but-normal attempts at attending class, making the soccer team, cutting up the dance floor, and finally finding someone special to ball—Super Monkey Ball, that is.

AWARD:
SILVER

CATEGORY:
Viral And Email:
Business To Consumer

AGENCY:
Mekanism /
San Francisco

CLIENT:
Sega

CREATIVE DIRECTORS:
Tommy Means
Ian Kovalik

ANNUAL ID:
06036N

URL:
www.mybigball.com

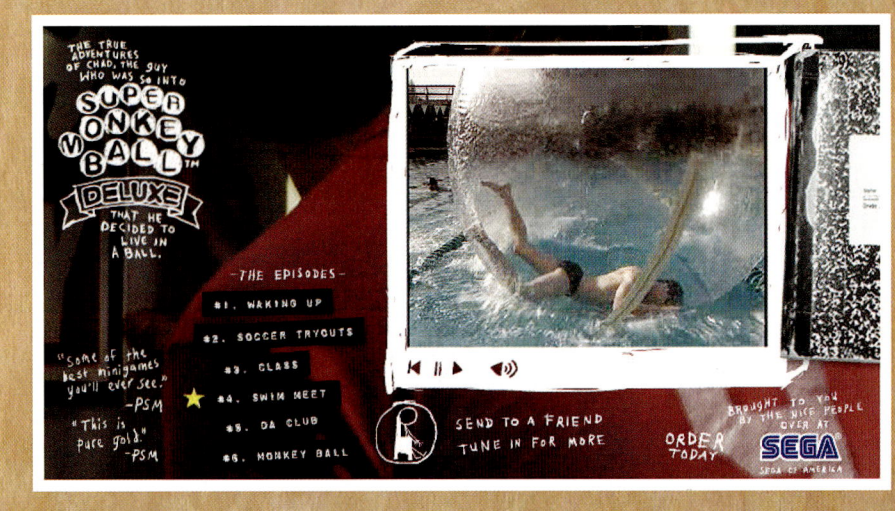

Which "Bubble Boy" inspired you more, the one from the Seinfeld episode or the one Jake Gyllenhaal played? Neither. The only true bubble boy is Todd Lubitch, played by John Travolta of course in the *The Boy in the Plastic Bubble*. Many peope don't know that Buzz Aldrin appeared in that movie and presented Travolta with his sterile space suit.

The aim was to promote Monkey Ball to gamers older than the 10-14 year old demographic. How did you go about targeting them? We made the Chad character a college student. The logic was high school, college students, and twentysomethings can all relate to the daily challenges of personal hygiene, sports, relationships, and trying to get some luvin'...while living inside a six-foot ball. We also persuaded Sega to ease up on showing game footage and really make humor the hero. The gamble paid off huge when we tracked the viral "pass-along" metrics.

"The True Adventures of Chad" was one of the more successfully funny campaigns of the year. There's a lot of physical comedy while staying in tune with the outsider-ness of the classic geek. Where did you draw the humor and story ideas from? The idea of a guy inside a giant rubber ball was so riduculous that I wanted "Chad" and everyone around him to be completely oblivious of his situation. If he was self aware in any way, the humor would have misfired.

The physical humor of *It's a Mad Mad Mad World* was great inspiration...especially when Jonathon Winters destroys the gas station with his bare hands. We also watched a few Buster Keaton flicks for inspiration. His physical comedy with a completely straight face is pure genius.

Story ideas were drawn from one premise. How much bubble boy stupidity can you shoot in one day?

Khaki Tease

Gap wants you to watch it change. In promoting its renovation special, this viral from Crispin Porter + Bogusky allows you to fashion an avatar of your changeling self. Bursting from a dressing room, you dance all the funny dance moves and then strip—for a sexy, socks-on moment—before shimmying into your more sedate Gap threads.

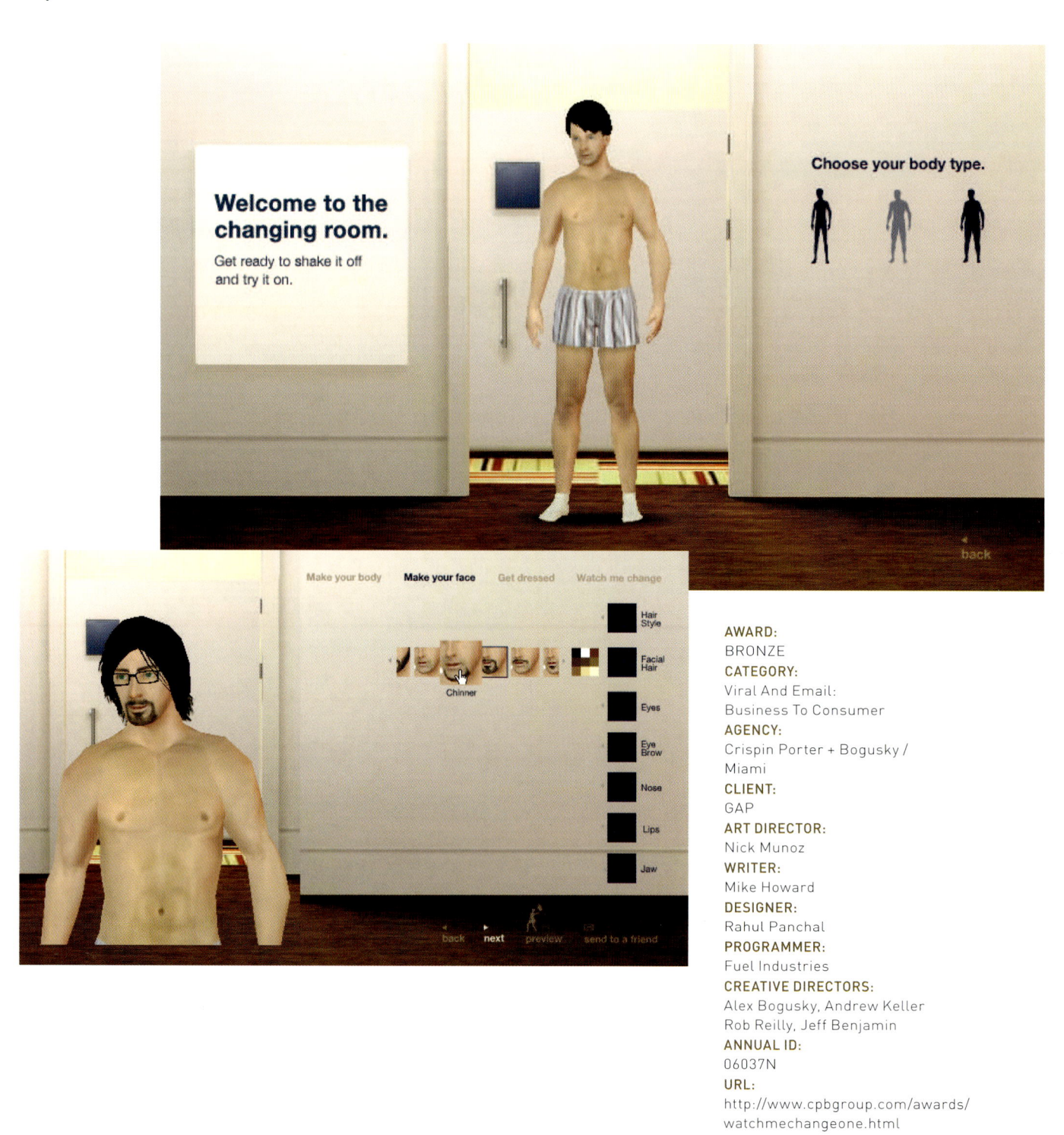

AWARD:
BRONZE
CATEGORY:
Viral And Email:
Business To Consumer
AGENCY:
Crispin Porter + Bogusky /
Miami
CLIENT:
GAP
ART DIRECTOR:
Nick Munoz
WRITER:
Mike Howard
DESIGNER:
Rahul Panchal
PROGRAMMER:
Fuel Industries
CREATIVE DIRECTORS:
Alex Bogusky, Andrew Keller
Rob Reilly, Jeff Benjamin
ANNUAL ID:
06037N
URL:
http://www.cpbgroup.com/awards/watchmechangeone.html

Pencil Winners
103

Becoming Behemoth

Featuring vast, dreamy plains guarded by creatures of epic proportions, an unusual video game such as Shadow of the Colossus requires a launch that is just as unique. The drop from Tequila spread another layer into the popular consciousness, a middle reality where giants once roamed the earth, and bloggers followed.

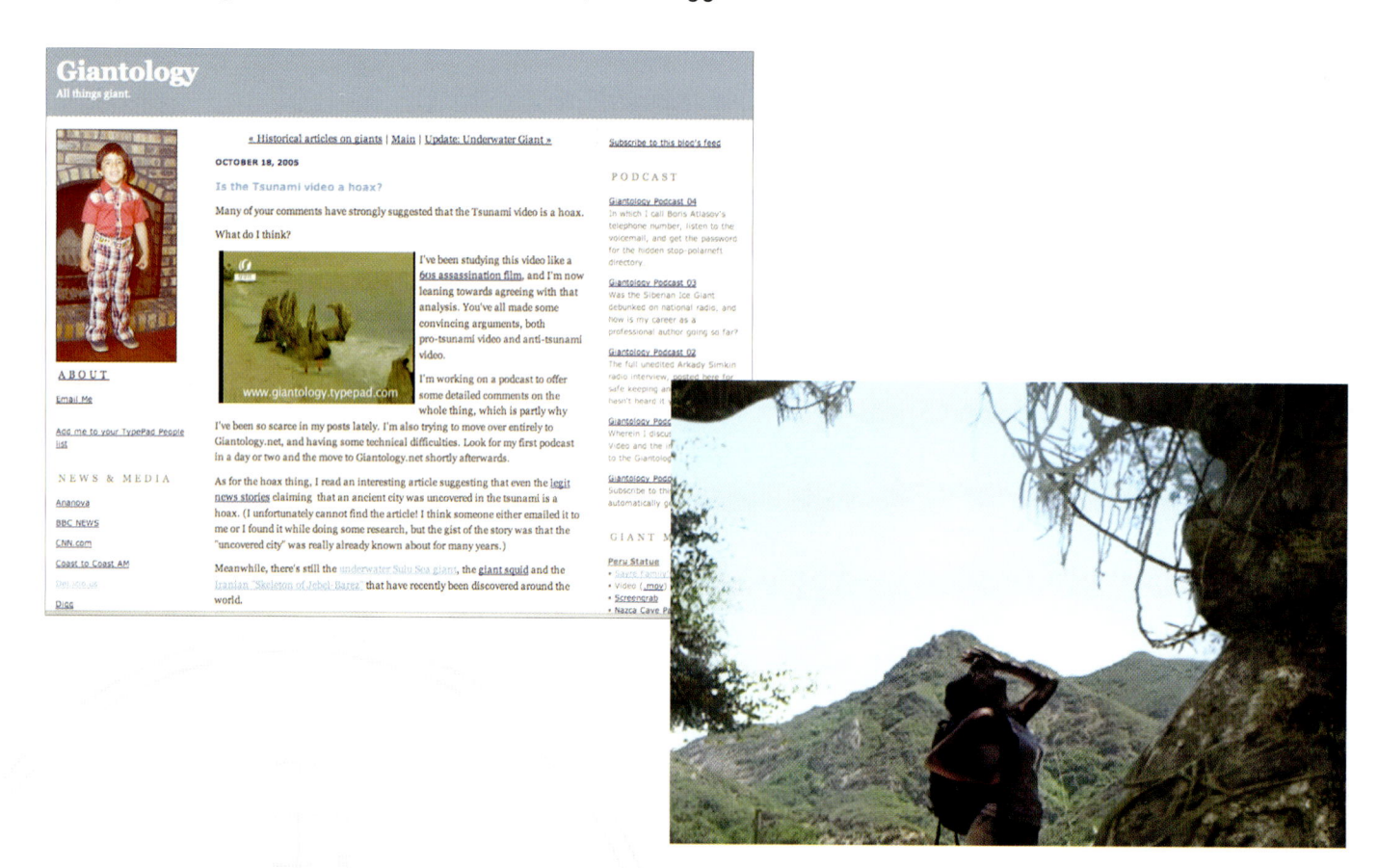

How did the game itself, designed by Fumito Ueda, inspire the viral marketing campaign? When we saw the game footage, the colossi were clearly the stars. These creatures are so bizarre, we knew people would react to them. We had to use them as the centerpiece of our campaign. So we asked ourselves the question, what if these giants started getting discovered around the world?

That led us to the idea of creating videos and photos—if we saw footage of some enormous creature washed up onshore, we'd be hooked even if we thought it was a hoax. So it all started with these strange, beautiful monsters.

Many of the recent sprawling ad campaigns revolve around hoaxes and setting up fake websites. To what extent did this one go "down the rabbit hole?" We talked a lot about how to make this campaign so complex and believable that it'd be very hard to pull apart. And it was important to us that even when people knew it was advertising, they'd stick around because the journey was so interesting. Which is why we researched everything and pinned each of the colossi to real locations and events, like the tsunami or melting arctic ice. We had our websites reference other sites, news stories, scientific theories. We wrote a year's worth of content for the Giantology blog. We had the IP addresses registered under different names. Most people just assumed that no one would go to so much trouble for an ad campaign. For us, it was a staggering amount of work over a much longer period of time than most campaigns and we all went a little mad in the process.

During the course of the campaign, did you ever have to alter the script due to unforeseen circumstances? We planned from the start to use the blog to help us manage the public's reaction as much as possible. But we didn't expect such a huge response so quickly, and we found ourselves scrambling to stay ahead of the audience, who were very involved in the campaign early on.

Every day, we read dozens of public message boards and blogs, plus all the comments that were sent to our fictional characters. This really helped us stay ahead of the audience when we were writing new blog posts.

At one point, we discovered that someone had hijacked an email address we'd posted to a site, and was sending emails in character! Rather than panic, we upped the game and created a new site that incorporated this development. To get the password, you had to dig into the HTML code, call a number in England and listen to a voicemail in Russian. We loved that people knew we were playing with them, but went along for the ride anyway.

AWARD:
BRONZE
CATEGORY:
Viral And Email:
Business To Consumer
AGENCY:
TEQUILA / Los Angeles
CLIENT:
Sony PlayStation
ART DIRECTOR:
Mako Miyasato
WRITERS:
Glenn Sanders, Eric Haugen
Rob Ingall
PROGRAMMERS:
Todd Resudek, Malik Jones
CREATIVE DIRECTORS:
Doug Speidel, Nathan Hackstock
Nick Davidge, Gerry Gentile
ANNUAL ID:
06038N
URL:
http://showcase.tequila.com/sites/sotc_campaign

Friendly Fire

In a perfectly dimmed room, confronted with the vengeful assassin Joanna Dark, you will give anything up, even your best friend. Said poor chum soon receives chilling email evidence of his or her slaying. Joanna confirms the kill with a cell phone call back to you, completing the triumvirate of web video usage and ensuring the hit is passed along.

AWARD:
BRONZE
CATEGORY:
Viral And Email:
Promotional Advertising
AGENCY:
AKQA / San Francisco
CLIENT:
Xbox
ART DIRECTOR:
Thiago Zanato
WRITER:
Justin Kramm
DIGITAL ARTISTS/MULTIMEDIA:
Jason Gatt, Garth Williams
CREATIVE DIRECTORS:
Mauro Alencar, Rei Inamoto
PJ Pereira
ANNUAL ID:
06039N
URL:
http://awards.sf.akqa.com
/creative/pdzdemo/index.html

How important is viral marketing to the gaming industry, and how was it in particular to this game? Viral marketing is extremely important, not only to the gaming industry, because when done right, it essentially represents a willingness from the users part to pass along something that they considered compelling and interesting enough to share with people in their social circle. That gives the brand or product in question a level of credibility and endorsement that would take a lot more money/effort to achieve with a non-viral approach.

The important thing to understand though is, contrary to what a lot of people think, viral is a consequence, not a mechanic. The work we created for Perfect Dark Zero wasn't designed to be a viral marketing piece. It was created to be a fun one-to-one experience, and it became viral because people really enjoyed passing it along to more and more friends.

The crux of this campaign was that you got to put a hit on your friend who in turn will pass it on. Why did you decide to include the cell phone call to the original sender? To close the loop and make the whole experience feel more real and immersive. We imagined if you hire someone to do a job for you, you would like to be informed when it's done. It was also a way to keep the relationship between the experience and the user alive for longer by providing a fun and unusual reason to go back and check the additional content.

The exploratory microsite contained teasers from the game. Would non-gamers experience the room in a different way from gamers or those familiar with the routine? Not really. This was a very specific assignment that had a very specific target audience. This experience was designed for a group of people that expect to be challenged and entertained while they look for a deeper insight into the fantasy world created by the game itself. We didn't want to compromise the experience by making it more accessible for people that would never even buy the game anyway.

Pencil Winners
107

Master of Puppets and Pop-up Boxes

Comcastic.com's one-two punch delivers genre-inspired puppets rigged to your own voice, and nifty games that let you wage war on your desktop. Show those rogue spreadsheets who's boss!

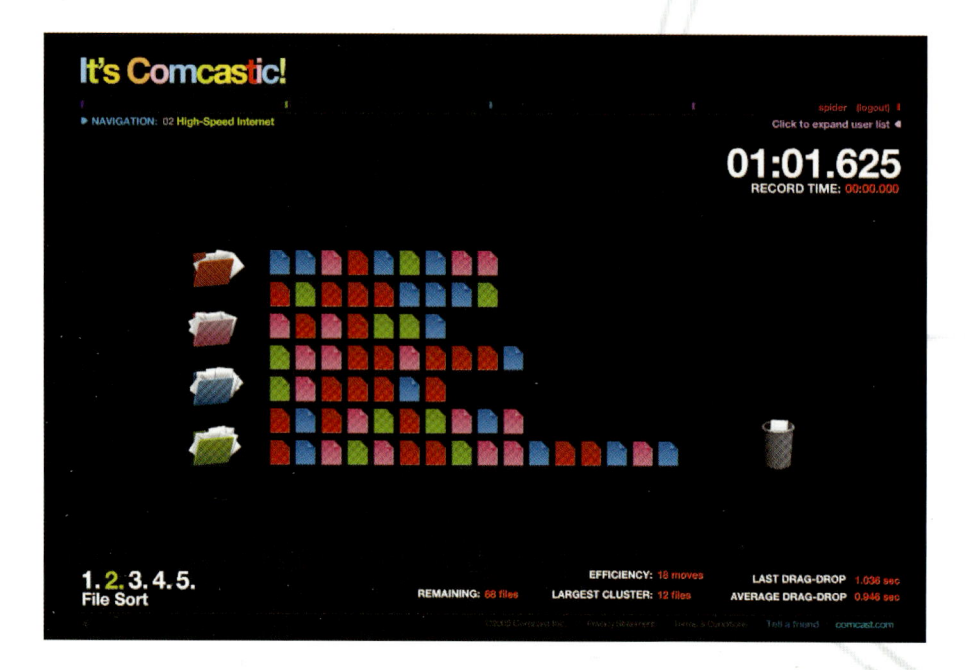

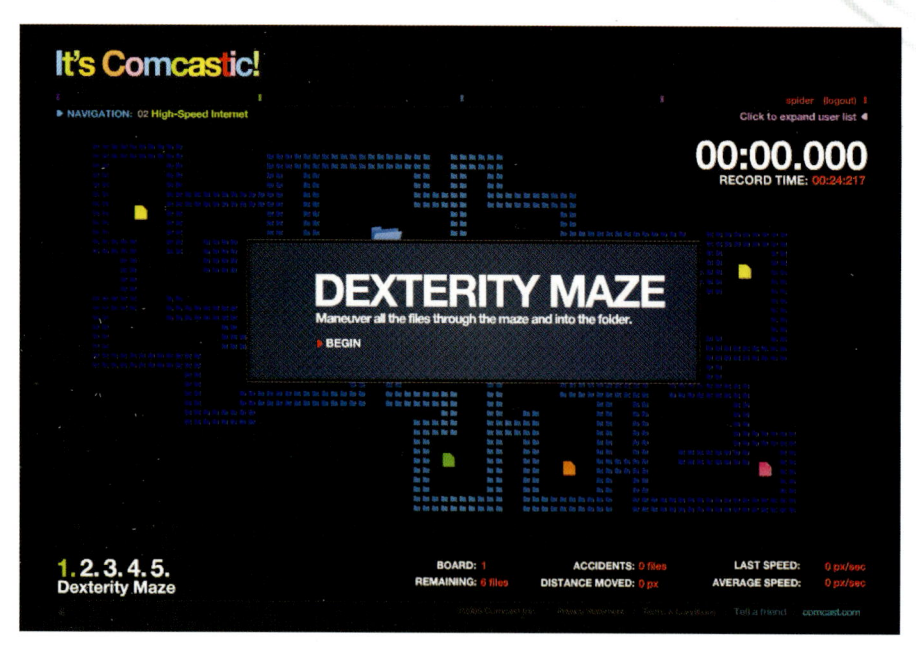

AWARD:
BRONZE
CATEGORY:
Viral And Email:
Promotional Advertising
AGENCY:
Goodby, Silverstein & Partners /
San Francisco
CLIENT:
Comcast
DESIGNER:
Devin Sharkey
ART DIRECTOR:
Will McGinness
WRITER:
Toria Emery
DIGITAL ARTISTS/MULTIMEDIA:
Brian Taylor, Keytoon Animation Studio, Gino Nave
Chris Ewen, Sean Drinkwater
PRODUCTION COMPANIES:
Natzke Design, Branden Hall
Number 9, The Barbarian Group
CONTENT STRATEGISTS:
Dora Lee, Amanda Kelso
Mike Geiger
CREATIVE DIRECTORS:
Toria Emery, Keith Anderson
Will McGinness
ANNUAL ID:
06040N
URL:
http://www.goodbysilverstein.com/awards/oneshow_2006/comcastic/
ALSO AWARDED:
BRONZE Websites:
Promotional Advertising

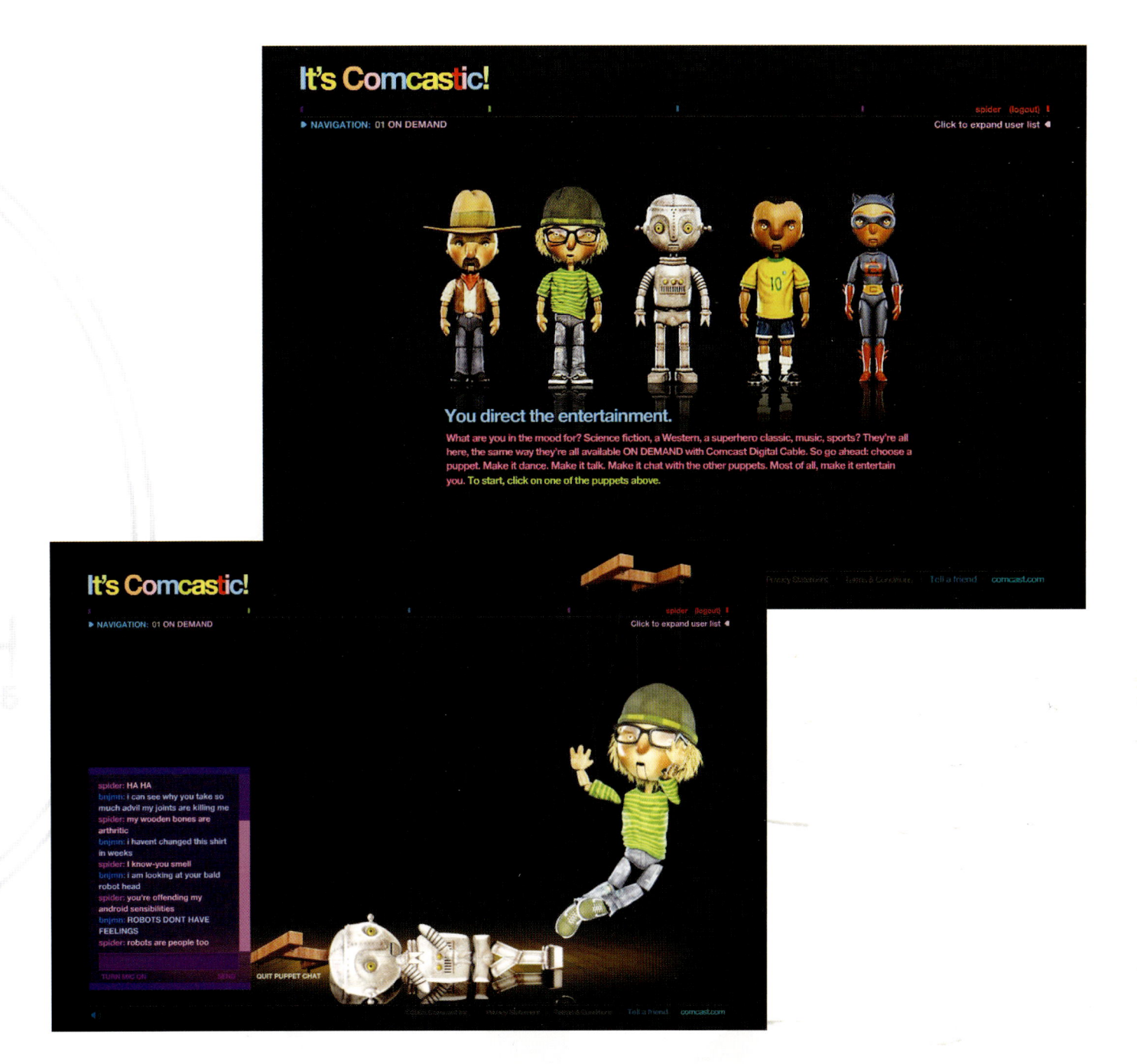

The skill tests that promoted Comcast's high speed Internet were a great representation of our daily use and frustrations with our desktop. Talk about the idea behind the games.
From a strategic standpoint, the overarching idea behind the games was: High-Speed. From a design and user experience standpoint, the idea was to engage and amuse people, and get them to come back again and again. We felt that the overall experience had to be more stylish than the usual desktop games—the graphics have a sense of dimension and depth; the music is kind of cool, but also kind of ironic. The challenges themselves were designed to play off the kinds of things people do on their desktop every day—there's something satisfying about overcoming the ubiquitous pop-up box in Precision Click, or neatly filing everything away in File Sort.

Pencil Winners
109

Many Films

A martini, a gun, and a pair of lacy undies. These recurring elements make up multiple wholes, little slivers of movies that you create by restructuring a grid. The only way to solve the mystery, or find out what the mystery is, for that matter, is to keep mixing them up. A gun, a martini, a suitcase of nuclear weapons? The possibilities are quite addictive.

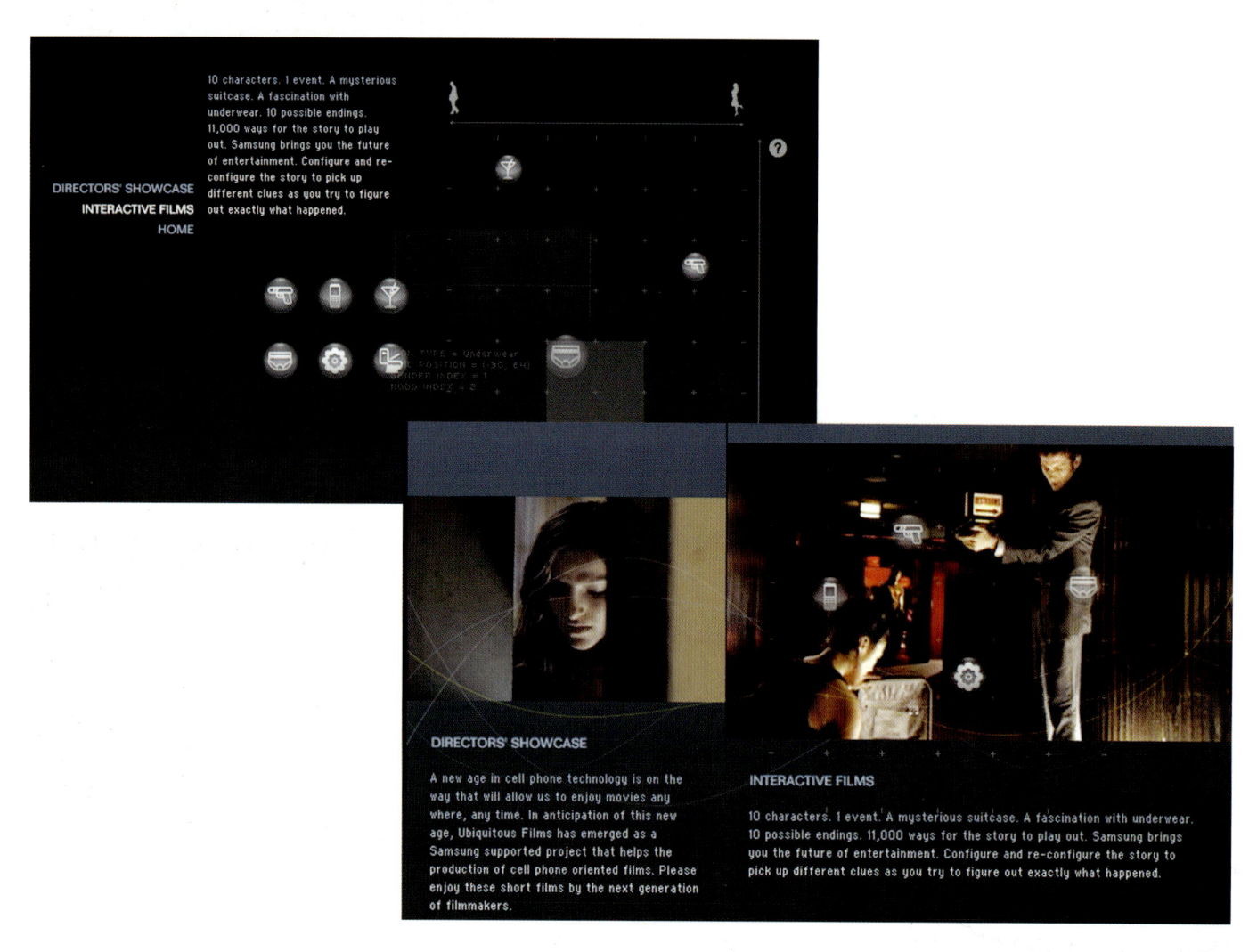

AWARD:
BRONZE
CATEGORY:
Online Movies:
Business To Consumer
AGENCY:
MargeotesFertittaPowell /
New York
CLIENT:
Samsung
WRITERS:
Josh Rogers, Neil Powell
Dan Shefelman, Jenny Lee
DESIGNERS:
Mark Sloan
The Barbarian Group
PRODUCTION COMPANIES:
The Barbarian Group
Outside Editorial
CREATIVE DIRECTORS:
Neil Powell, Chris Bradley
Josh Rogers, Morihiro Harano
CONTENT STRATEGIST:
Morihiro Harano
MUSIC & SOUND:
Berwyn
ANNUAL ID:
06041N
URL:
www.anyfilms.net
ALSO AWARDED:
BRONZE Website:
Business to Consumer
MERIT New Media
Innovation: Movies

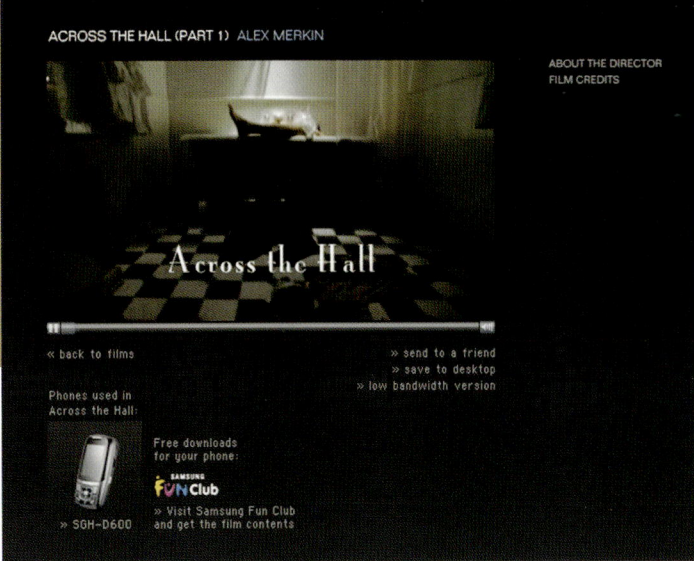

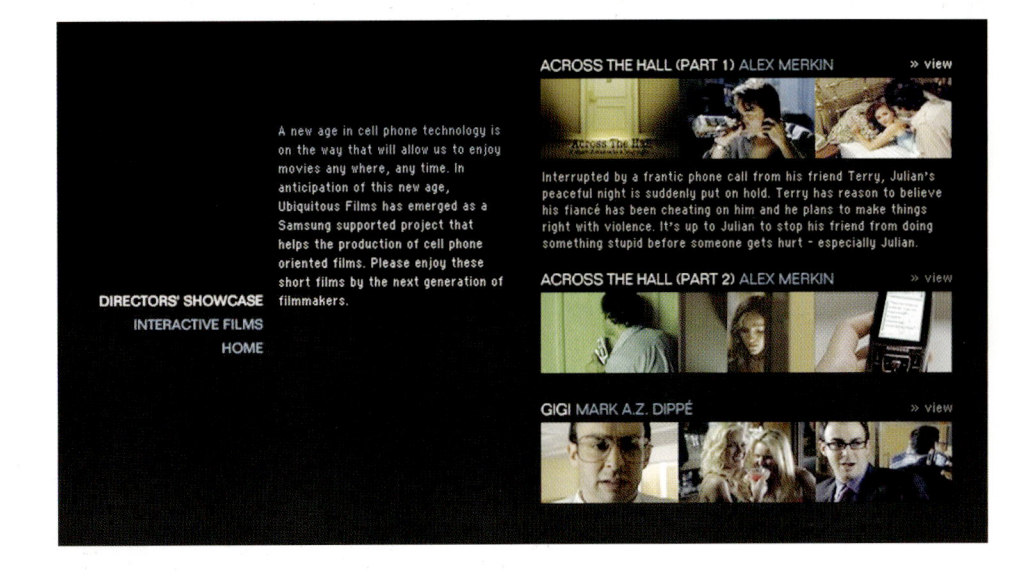

You Otter be in Movies

Miller Auditions bring the ridiculous and the sublime under one URL. Directed by prankster Spike Jonze, these webfilms are the outtakes of down-on-their-luck show animals trying out for TV parts. A gentle stab at all the creatures that have been featured in other beer ads, we presume.

AWARD:
BRONZE
CATEGORY:
Online Movies:
Business To Consumer
AGENCY:
Young & Rubicam / Chicago
CLIENT:
Miller Brewing Company
ART DIRECTORS:
Mark Figliulo
Corey Ciszek
WRITERS:
Ken Erke, Pete Figel
PROGRAMMER:
Michael Brumm
DIGITAL ARTIST/MULTIMEDIA:
Chris Von Ende
PRODUCTION COMPANY:
MJZ
DIRECTOR:
Spike Jonze
CREATIVE DIRECTORS:
Dave Loew, Jon Wyville
Mark Figliulo
MUSIC & SOUND:
Tyrell LLC
ANNUAL ID:
06042N
URL:
www.millerauditions.com
/otter.php

The Foot of God?

With the World Cup looming, there was never a better time to release a mysterious viral of Ronaldinho, two-time FIFA World Player of the Year, doing remarkable things with a football and the crossbar that make it look like Brazilian ping pong. Whether or not the footage is "real," we'll suspend our belief, just because it's beautiful.

AWARD:
GOLD
CATEGORY:
Online Movies: Promotional Advertising
AGENCY:
Framfab / Copenhagen
CLIENT:
Nike
ART DIRECTOR:
Rasmus Frandsen
PRODUCTION COMPANY:
Niels Kau
DIRECTOR:
Christian Lyngbye
CREATIVE DIRECTOR:
Lars Cortsen
CONTENT STRATEGIST:
Caroline Bendixen
ANNUAL ID:
06043N
URL:
http://www.nikefootball.com/tiempo/viral/
ALSO AWARDED:
MERIT Viral and Email: Promotional Advertising

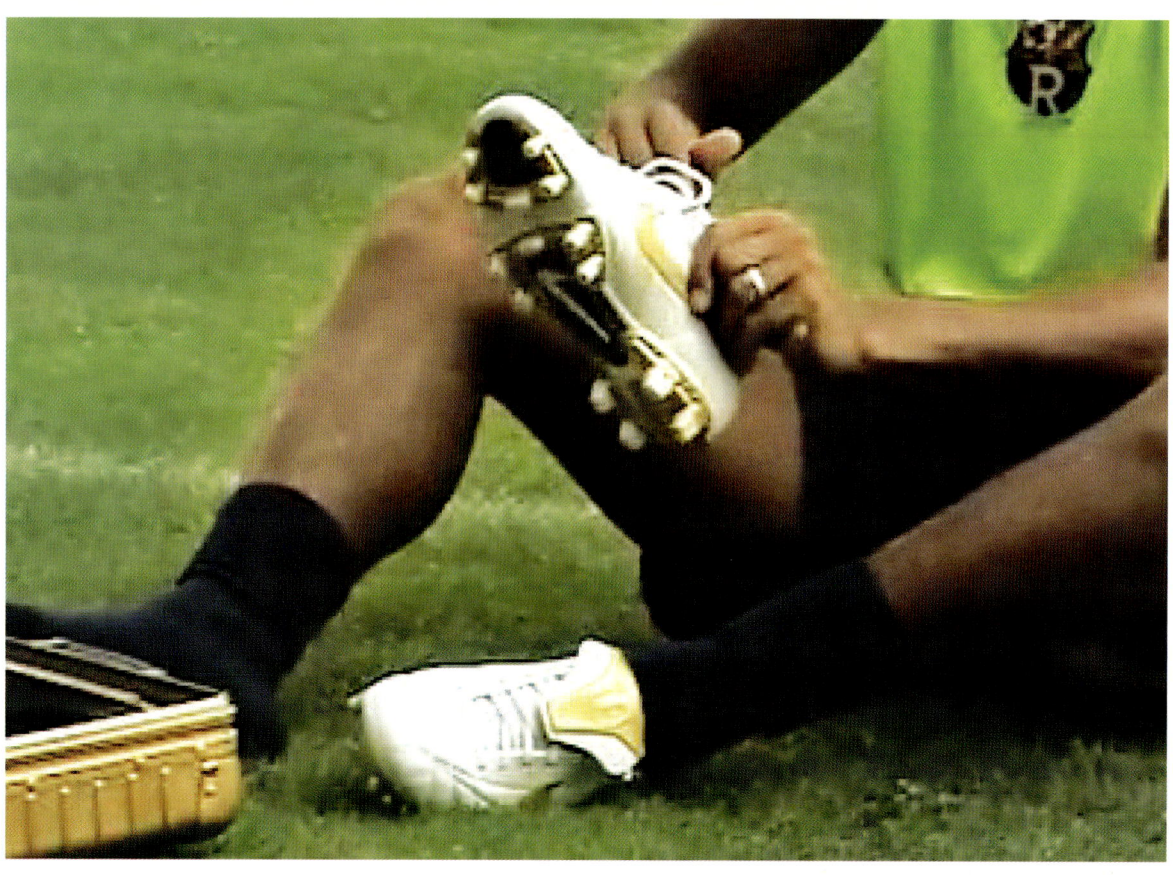

So is it real or not? Ronaldinho said in an interview that it was real, Juventus player Zlatan Ibrahimovic argued in another that this trick could not be done. This question still splits the world of football.

What was the idea behind the viral? For the global launch of the Ronaldinho Tiempo legend Limited Edition boot, Nike wanted a campaign that didn't use traditional media. We shot a viral piece starring Ronaldinho that was "almost too good to be true". Then we posted the exclusive footage on relevant peer-to-peer networks for download and distribution. Labeling the content "secret" and "Ronaldinho" maximized curiosity and made the football fans distribute the spot like wildfire.

The idea was to surprise Ronaldinho on the training pitch, presenting him with his new tailor-made boots and asking him to give them a field test. The result was one amazing, almost 3 minutes long sequence, showing the world's greatest player in action. The highlight, where he plays ping-pong with the crossbar several times, made this not only a highly distributed, but also a very debated viral all over the net, on TV, in newspapers, on pitches all around the world, and anywhere else football is talked about. Real or not?

The campaign has been highly successful and the viral has been viewed and distributed millions of times around the world, free of charge. We can't give the exact download numbers, but on youtube.com alone, the spot has been viewed more than 8 million times and still counting. Just to name one channel.

Ladies Love a Man with an Axe Scent

So in this woman-forsaken town, the proverbial bungheap called Ravevsntoke Alaska, a concerted effort was made by the local male citizenry to make their town more attractive to the opposite sex. Using methods such as crop-dusting and plane-spraying, the men filled the town with Axe. This mock-news report from The Viral Factory documents Ravenstoke's brief but glorious moment when the women arrived in droves, proving that if you spray it, they will come.

AWARD:
SILVER
CATEGORY:
Online Movies:
Promotional Advertising
AGENCY:
The Viral Factory / London
CLIENT:
Unilever
WRITER:
The Viral Factory
PRODUCTION COMPANY:
The Viral Factory
DIRECTOR:
The Viral Factory
with James Rouse
ANNUAL ID:
06044N

Pencil Winners
117

Sound Bites Back

Saatchi & Saatchi takes an aural pun to painful new heights with this clip about a day in the life of a sound engineering studio.

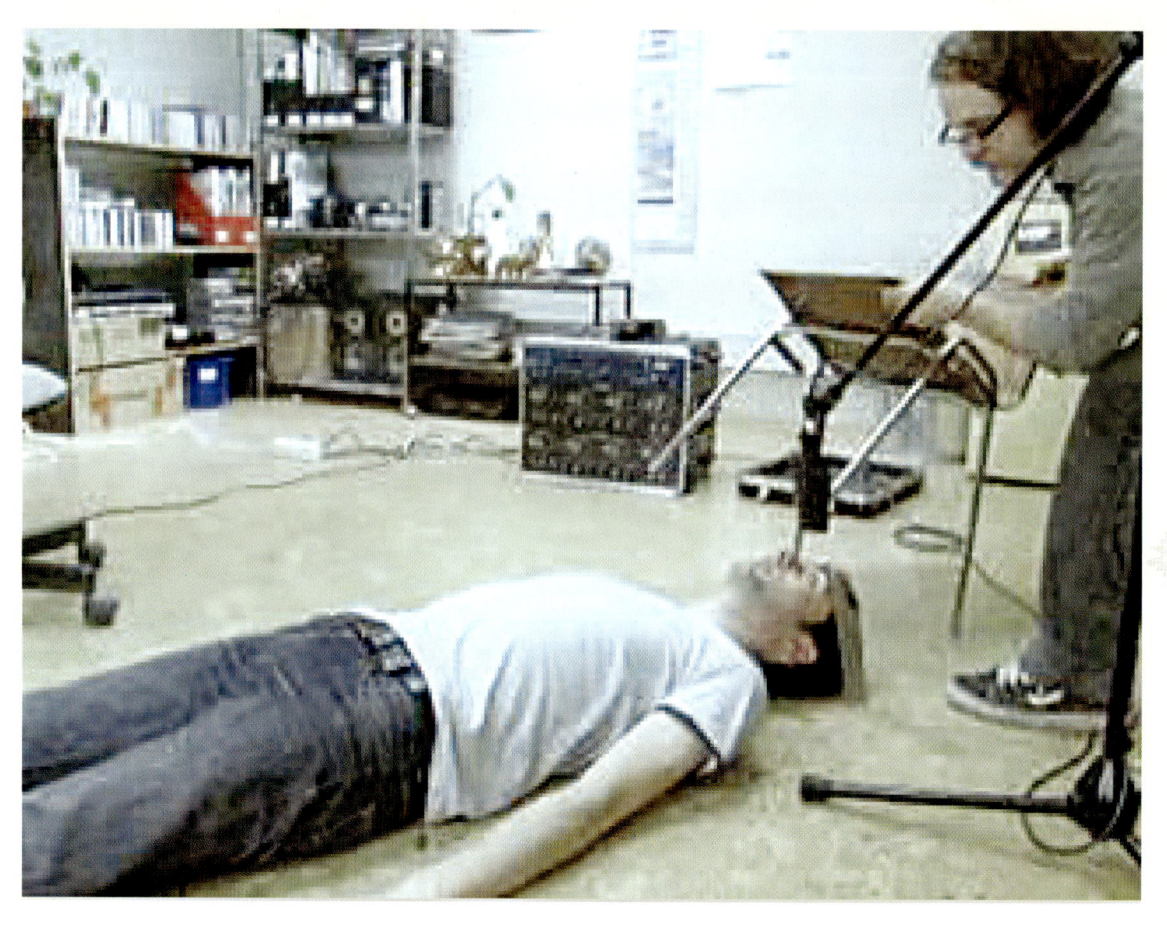

AWARD:
GOLD
CATEGORY:
Online Movies:
Business To Business
AGENCY:
Saatchi & Saatchi /
Frankfurt
CLIENT:
A.R.T. Studios
ART DIRECTOR:
Nicole Groezinger
WRITER:
Alex Priebs-Macpherson
PRODUCTION COMPANY:
Schulten Film
DIRECTOR:
Alex Feil
CREATIVE DIRECTORS:
Eberhard Kirchhoff
Thomas Kanofsky
ANNUAL ID:
06045N
URL:
www.art-studios.de

FÜR DEN BESTEN TON GEBEN WIR ALLES.

A.R.T. STUDIOS
AUDIOPRODUKTION FÜR WERBUNG

Breaking the Barrier

The sound of speed, the speed of style: everything is propelled to full force once you hit 170 mph. With animation that literally blazes, racing with one arrow key has never been this thrilling.

The site integrates very well with the racing game, by letting users drive and speed up to levels which showcase the game's different elements. Talk about the innovative aspect of this acceleration mechanism used to unlock content. The working line for the game when we started developing the work was "Style begins at 170 miles per hour" so we thought, why not make the site change and become cooler and more exciting after you reach 170 mph? That's where it all came from. I believe the reason users reacted so well to the experience was because it was a fresh way of showcasing the content. Something that they were definitely not expecting to see. Yes, they were expecting to see cars racing, but not on the navigation mechanic itself.

The user really feels like he or she is racing furiously (while miraculously never crashing into anything). What feats did you have to pull to achieve this effect? It was a combination of beautiful art direction and a Flash development work that was nothing short of amazing. Our guys pulled a few all-nighters just to fine-tune the animations and transitions between all the cars/sections of the site. The great 3D work done by our friends at Palma FX was also key to the quality of the final product.

AWARD:
SILVER
CATEGORY:
New Media Innovation
& Development: Web Sites
AGENCY:
AKQA / San Francisco
CLIENT:
Xbox
ART DIRECTOR:
David Lee
WRITER:
Steve Tornello
DESIGNER:
Matthew Law
DIGITAL ARTISTS/MULTIMEDIA:
Hoj Jomehri, Sam Bouguerra
Guillermo Torres
CREATIVE DIRECTORS:
Mauro Alencar, PJ Pereira
Rei Inamoto
ANNUAL ID:
06046N
URL:
http://awards.sf.akqa.com
/creative/pgr3/index.html
ALSO AWARDED:
MERIT Websites:
Promotional Advertising

Interactive ads for video games are the closest way people can actually get a taste of what it would be like to play. Was using a simulation the obvious choice when you were conceptualizing for this product? Not necessarily an obvious choice, but one we thought would make sense in this specific case. The way we see the site, you don't really race other cars. You race the site itself. To be honest, the last thing we want when we create any digital experience for Xbox games is for people to think they'll come to the site to play the game itself. That's the console's job and it wouldn't even be practical to try to showcase the amazing next-generation gaming experience a console like the Xbox360 brings you to it's full glory on a website.

Spam Alchemy

It's a post-pomo phenomenon, turning the excess of things that are useless, discarded and disgusting into practical home furnishings, edible nourishment, even high art. In the digital realm, we get barraged and garbaged with a ton of virtual junk. What to do with those silly pharma ads, gramatically incorrect porn links, and money-donating cons from "businessmen" in Nigeria? Jung von Matt helps fight back by turning scam art into spam art.

How did you come up with the idea? The client, an energy company with 20,000 employees, has a big recycling program. He said: "Our company can turn all kinds of waste into new energy." And we said: "Sorry Sir—and digital waste?" That's how it all started.

How does it work? As the first SPAM RECYCLER of the world works with exactly the same formula Coca-Cola uses, we unfortunately cannot reveal too much. But the basics are: send your spam to spam@spamrecycling.com, grab an orange juice, and watch how they are recycled into something new. The spam recycler breaks them apart and changes them into a beautiful piece of art—each one being an original, since none of the patterns created are ever the same.

AWARD:
SILVER
CATEGORY:
New Media
Innovation + Development:
Websites
AGENCY:
Jung von Matt / Stuttgart
CLIENT:
EnBW
WRITER/CONCEPT:
Paul Fleig
DESIGNER:
Fabian Buergy
PROGRAMMERS:
Marko Ritter, Joerg DiTerlizzi
DIGITAL ARTIST/MULTIMEDIA:
Fabian Roser
CREATIVE DIRECTOR:
Stefan Walz
ANNUAL ID:
06025N
URL:
www.spamrecycling.com
ALSO AWARDED:
SILVER Web Sites:
Promotional Advertising

How does it work exactly? (NERDS ONLY) The creation of the artwork may look fractal, but in fact, it is not. Its generation can be described as behavioral tracing of existing spam particles. A major inspiration for these algorithms were resulting images of collider experiments in modern physics—every particle leaves a characteristic trace, only depending on its type and individual kinetic energy. The process starts with breaking the spam mail down into its very particles and accelerating them. Once this is accomplished each particle starts a trace with its individual predetermination on what shape to draw—from there on it follows its course, depending solely on its momentum. Sometimes, however, user input can shape the spam particle's fate in a completely different direction....

What about the Laotse thing? Every mail we receive is preprocessed. Attached pictures are resized and a starting configuration of the recycler is calculated by comparing the mail to our reference text: "Some wise words by Laotse." That's true.

Can I send anything to spam@spamrecycling.com? Yes, of course. We had good results with briefings, too. And rumors say that speeches of George W. Bush have produced beauty no human has seen on planet earth.

Why did you make it so arty? Because unlike in 1999, being a screen designer doesn't impress the girls anymore. So now we are artists. Please refer to our account people as "A&R managers" from now on, too.

How did people react? We got positive feedback from all over the world. And one complaint from DEV8 Email Marketing LLC Inc, Ramon Arias Ave., Maheli Building Office 12E, Panama City, 5535 PA.

Can you also turn waste into money? Yes, but only $3,000 a month.

Pencil Winners
125

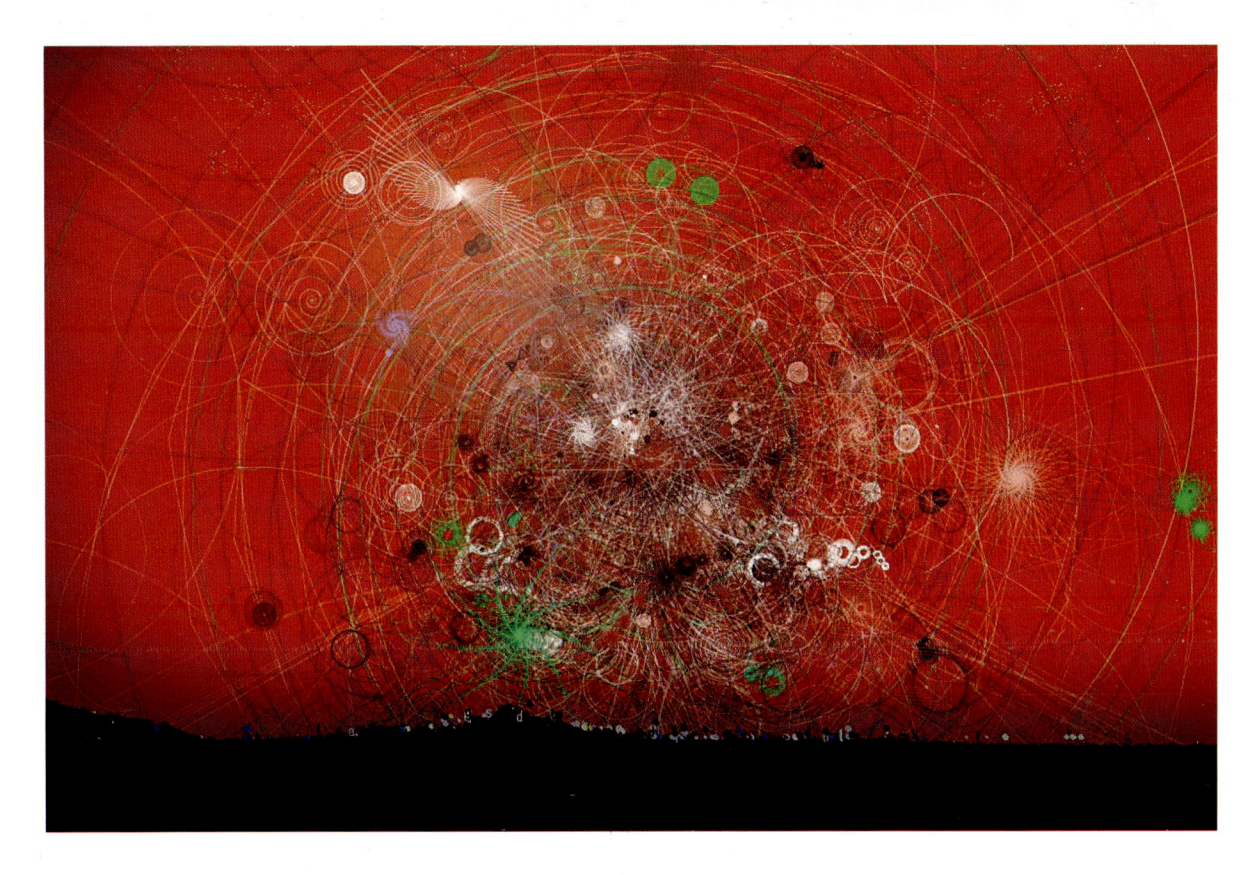

Surrounding the Sky

How do you sell a car when there is no car? Build the experience, first. This innovative project from Goodby Silverstein & Partners conveyed the dichotomy of inside/outside under one fascinating dome: a car's intimate details are x-rayed while clouds roll above head; visitors feel like they're driving with the top down, when they are actually surrounded by a canopy of technology.

AWARD:
GOLD
CATEGORY:
Other Digital Media:
Business To Consumer
AGENCY:
Goodby, Silverstein & Partners /
San Francisco
CLIENT:
Saturn
WRITERS:
Toria Emery, Aaron Griffiths
PRODUCTION COMPANIES:
Speedshape, Obscura Digital
CREATIVE DIRECTORS:
Toria Emery, Keith Anderson
Will McGinness
CONTENT STRATEGISTS:
Maury Boswell, Brit Charlebois
Mike Geiger
ANNUAL ID:
06050N
URL:
http://www.goodbysilverstein.com
/awards/oneshow_2006/sky_dome/

This was the first projection mapping done on a car. How did you come to approach the brief by doing something that's never been done before, on a car that wasn't yet in existence, from a brand not particularly known for performance vehicles? Early on, research showed that the best way to get people interested in buying a roadster was to get them to drive a roadster. That feeling of freedom that comes with putting the top down can't be explained in words—it has to be experienced. The problem for us was, the SKY wasn't in production yet, so test-drives weren't a possibility. Our goal was to re-create the experience of driving a roadster as much as we could.

As for the projection mapping, Saturn also wanted to show people that the SKY is a well-engineered and well-equipped car—it's not just a piece of fluff with a nice exterior design. That was important, given that the price point was quite low—people needed to be convinced that they wouldn't be compromising their driving experience. The projection mapping did a great job of screaming "technical" while still being interesting and accessible. We worked closely with Obscura Digital, who had been working on the mapping technology, and was waiting for an opportunity to put it to the test.

Kiosks surrounding the car allowed users to choose one of six projection/animation sequences, each of which focused on a different system of the car: Engine, Transmission, Vehicle Dynamics, Suspension, Safety/Security and Driving Comfort. We talked to a number of people after they experienced the Dome, and their comments were exactly what we'd hoped for: they had positive feelings about the car and about Saturn were impressed by the car's technology learned a lot more about the car's features than they would have in a typical display and they spent a lot of time interacting with the Saturn brand.

Pencil Winners
127

128   GOLD WINNER // GOODBY, SILVERSTEIN & PARTNERS

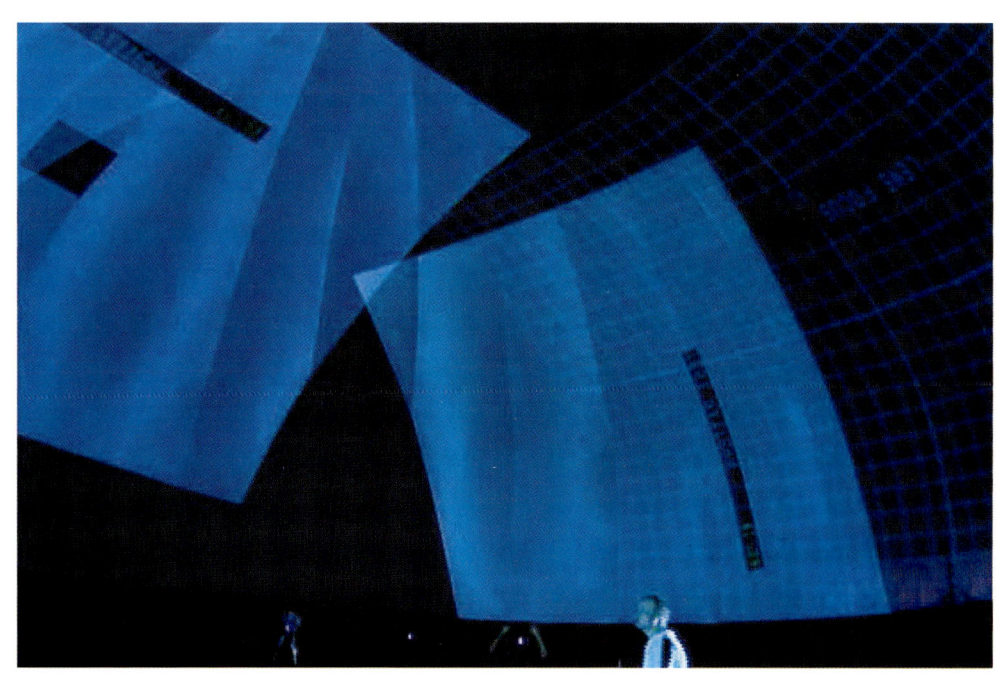

Pencil Winners
129

Welcome to the Holodeck

The shoe responds to the surface it treads on; kinesthetic knowledge is transferred away from the body down to the sole. Mediated by a microchip embedded in layers of rubber, the first intelligent shoes by adidas are a pair you can wear everywhere, except, probably, the airport. The Australian outfit OneDigital set to create an interactive store that responded likewise, with playful and prescient installations that moved to your motion.

Walk us through the different interactive elements that made up the store.
There are 3 key interactive components to the environment:

1. An interactive window.
With the lenticular window, what you see on the window changes depending on the angle from which the window is viewed. There is also a massive LED video wall in another window. This video wall screens the curious "Hello Tomorrow" TVC for the shoe by acclaimed director Spike Jonze.

To complement the interactive and window components, OneDigital developed a series of prints mounted on back-lit window displays and internal gondolas. These print pieces highlighted the shoes featured in high detail. As the shoe itself responded to the surface on which the wearer was moving, the print work also illustrated the range of different surface textures that the shoes would respond to—turf, the road and the track.

2. An interactive floor.
In another first, OneDigital partnered with US firm Reatrix to create an interactive "in-store-on-floor." Imagine this as a massive computer screen projected downwards onto the

AWARD:
SILVER
CATEGORY:
Other Digital Media:
Business To Consumer
AGENCY:
OneDigital / Sydney
CLIENT:
adidas
ART DIRECTOR:
Liz Sivell
PROGRAMMERS:
Ian Tilley, Terabyte
CREATIVE DIRECTOR:
Liz Sivel
CONTENT STRATEGISTS:
Sarah Barry, Keith Pinney
ANNUAL ID:
06051N
URL:
http://clientpreview.
onedigital.com.au/adidas_1

store floor—a screen where the customer's body works as the mouse. With the Reatrix "in-store-on-floor", the ground itself appears to change in response to the customer's movement. This was achieved through a combination of projection and infra-red motion sensing—you can even play virtual soccer on it using your body motion to kick a virtual ball across virtual turf.

3. Touch screen plasma kiosk.
OneDigital also drew on the international resources of its global network, re-purposing the content from the international campaign for use on a huge touch plasma-screen kiosk inside the store. This plasma screen kiosk allowed the customer to explore the unique attributes of the shoe. It's a combination of information, entertainment and pure art.

Some of the technology used already existed, but not for everything that you wanted to do. Which features did you have to innovate yourself? The project was ambitious. We took a lot of cutting edge elements and used them together. It was possibly the first time in the world that three key technologies were combined to create a total environment—a completely immersive interactive experience.

OneDigital innovated some of this technology and actually created a whole program for the external interactive window, which to our knowledge hadn't been done in Australia before.

The window, a combination of rear projection and motion tracking technology tracked body movements of people outside the window. Move your head, hands or body and the motion is captured by the technology which then changes the images projected on the screen in response. As you move, different images and aspects of the shoe are revealed.

132   SILVER WINNER // ONE DIGITAL

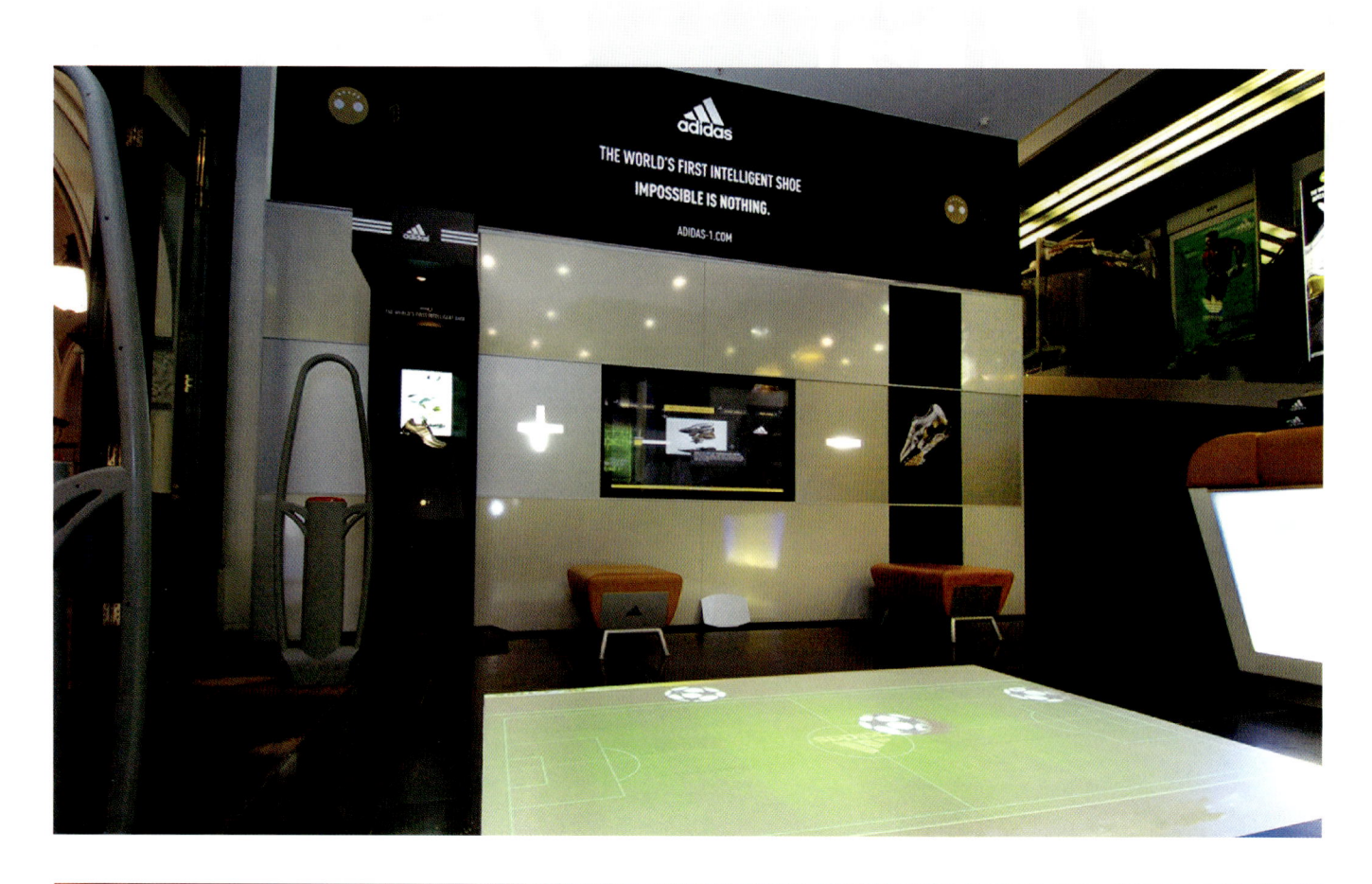

Pencil Winners
133

Hallucinatory Drive-by

Team One's holographic creation lets users interact with a car-approximating projection via a touchscreen interface. They can spin it, change its colors, and even send the car kicking up virtual dust in an imagined landscape. With gas prices as such, the next step is, obviously, teleportation.

AWARD:
BRONZE
CATEGORY:
Other Digital Media:
Business To Consumer
AGENCY:
Team One / El Segundo
CLIENT:
Lexus
ART DIRECTOR:
Brian Doyl
WRITER:
Edward Mun
DIGITAL ARTISTS/MULTIMEDIA:
Vizoo, Imaginary Forces
CREATIVE DIRECTORS:
Gabrielle Mayeur, Dawn DeKeyser
Chris Graves
ANNUAL ID:
06052N
URL:
http://archive.teamone-usa.com/ishologram/

WHY LIVE IN ONE DIMENSION?

Pencil Winners
135

The Energizing Boony

Cricket can seem like an interminable sport to those who've never fallen under the banner of the Empire. But for those cricket mad, a talking plastic figurine with the nuggety resemblance of a sporting legend is a boon indeed. Turn up the telly and break open the stubbies!

How did you initially come up with the idea of a commentating figurine? Did you foresee it would become a cult collector's item? David Boon played cricket for Australia in the '80s. He is short. He is round. He has a moustache and importantly, he loves a beer. When one of our promo guys returned from the States with this interactive broadcast technology, the Talking Boony seemed to be the perfect fit for a VB/Cricket cross promotion.

Please explain how the audio triggers worked. Would the Boony talk in other countries as long as the cricket was on? There is no on/off switch for Boony. An internal timing device would "power-up" Boony for the duration of live cricket broadcasts, and electronic pip signals sent through the broadcast would make Boony talk. He would automatically say "Get me a beer—the cricket is about to start!" when he powered up and "When are we going to the

AWARD:
SILVER
CATEGORY:
Other Digital Media:
Promotional Advertising
AGENCY:
George Patterson Y&R / Melbourne
CLIENT:
VB
ART DIRECTOR:
Ben Coulson
WRITER:
Josh Stephens
CREATIVE DIRECTOR:
James McGrath
ANNUAL ID:
06053N

pub?" before powering down. Boony was also programmed to make a random comment once every hour like "Got any Nachos...I love Nachos" throughout the duration of the match. This is why he would still talk in other countries (usually at 4am in the morning).

I read that a number of boonies mysteriously "resurrected" long after the VB cricket series was over, disturbing people early in the morning and inviting them for a few beers even though they've been packed away. How do you think this has happened?
There are lots of stories but the real reason is pretty boring. The batteries had a longer life than expected...and Boony decided to pipe up again for a few final comments.

Through a Mirror, Infinitely

Nissan Infiniti commissioned a digital installation for the 2006 auto show season, and they were given the future of interactivity. With mirrors instead of monitors, visitors engaged with content in an organic way that yet required no contact—sensors anticipated one's next move and need. The images that appear are integrated with the viewer's reflection, for an experience that, while immersive, also demanded the act of self-contemplation.

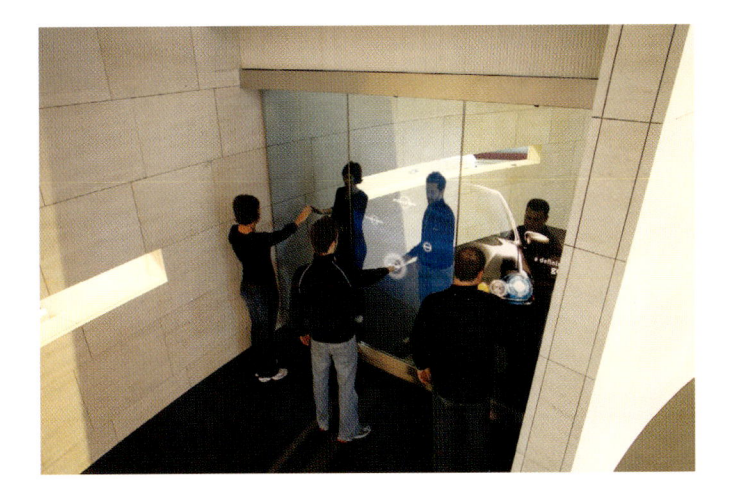

AWARD:
BRONZE
CATEGORY:
Other Digital Media: Promotional Advertising
AGENCY:
Mindflood / Santa Ana
CLIENT:
Infiniti Division,
Nissan North America
ART DIRECTOR:
Noah Huber (The Designory)
WRITER:
Jon King (The Designory)
PROGRAMMERS:
Phil van Allen (Commotion)
Chris Kief (Mindflood)
DIGITAL ARTIST/MULTIMEDIA:
John Mastri (Mindflood)
PRODUCTION COMPANY:
The George P. Johnson Company
INFORMATION ARCHITECTS:
Noah Costello (Mindflood)
Katy MacQuoid (The Designory)
CREATIVE DIRECTORS:
Chris Lund (Mindflood)
Chad Weiss (The Designory)
Steve Davis (The Designory)
Nikolai Cornell (The George P. Johnson Company)
CONTENT STRATEGIST:
Joel McCall (The George P. Johnson Company)
ANNUAL ID:
06054N
URL:
http://www.interactivemirror.net

The Techniques of Nature

The answers are with us, all along, and all around. The UK Pavilion in Japan's Aichi Expo 05 was an exploratory forest of new technologies, presented as unique installations that replicated the natural phenomena they were based on. Created by Land Design Studio, the pavilion achieved a level of spirituality that comes when technology unobtrusively taps into the genius of nature.

AWARD:
GOLD
CATEGORY:
Other Digital Media:
Public Service/Non-Profit/Educational
AGENCY:
Land Design Studio / London
CLIENT:
UK Government, Foreign & Commonwealth Office
ART DIRECTOR:
Robin Clark
WRITER:
Katie Edwards
DIGITAL ARTISTS/MULTIMEDIA:
Paul Maguire, Anthony Pearson
CREATIVE DIRECTORS:
Shirley Walker, Peter Higgins
ANNUAL ID:
06055N

The theme of the Expo was "Nature's Wisdom." How do the installations embody this theme, and how do visitors engage with them? Each interactive installation showcases a UK technological innovation that has been inspired by remarkable natural phenomenon.

"Swim like a Shark" interactive – inspired by sharkskin.
Innovation: Sharkskin feels rough when you touch it. This is because it is covered with tiny V-shaped scales, which reduce the friction, or drag, through the water as the shark swims. The qualities of sharkskin have been used to develop the fastest swimsuit in the world.

The Fastsuit FSII has ridges along the fabric imitating the sharkskin's scales. These grooves help to channel water around the body as the swimmer moves forwards. Different fabrics are used for different parts of the swimsuit to vary the amount of drag reduction over the body.

Scientists from the Speedo Aqualab, CyberFX and the Natural History Museum developed the Fastsuit FSII.

Interactive: A stainless steel shark model is embedded into a flat glass surface. The shark's shadow is projected onto a sandy floor beneath. As the user waves their hand behind the shark, the projected shadow is animated and appears to swim around the seafloor and past other marine animals.

"Hanging by a Hair" interactive – inspired by geckos climbing upside down.
Innovation: Have you ever wondered how geckos walk up windows and across ceilings? It's all down to their hairy toes. The sole of a gecko's foot is covered with branched hairs. This ensures that when the foot touches a surface, millions of hairs come into contact with it.

A weak molecular attraction occurs between each hair and the surface. The weak forces of all the hairs add together to produce a gravity-defying sticking power. This effect has been mimicked in developing a new adhesive tape. Only a small sample has been made so far but in the future gecko tape could have many uses from easy-peel bandages to rock-climbing.

Scientists at Manchester University developed the gecko tape concept.

Interactive: A gecko puppet is moved by a rocker handle, which then activates a large screen animation projected in front of the user. On the screen an outline of 'gecko man' is seen through a window of a tall building (Swiss Re building) to be scaling the outside of the building. As he moves, visitors see a constantly changing London skyline on the screen, showing well-known landmarks, such as Piccadilly Circus, the London Eye, Tate Modern, Tower Bridge, etc.

142 GOLD WINNER // LAND DESIGN STUDIO

Pencil Winners
143

The Method in Madness

Designed for the San Francisco Museum of Modern Art, these interactive kiosks are meant to bring the full experience of modern art—incomprehensible, abstract, but potentially glorious—to regular people. Through a sorting system based on meticulous user research, the sprawling movements of modern art have been vitally categorized and cross-referenced, opening up avenues of exploration and exposing the nodes of connection.

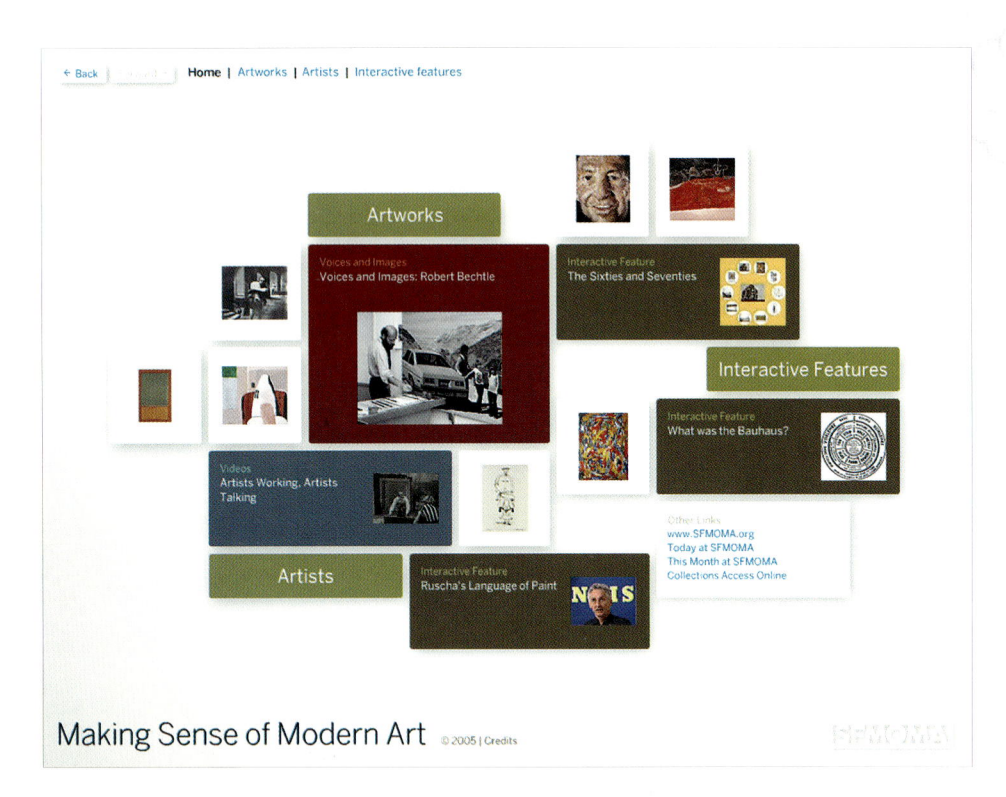

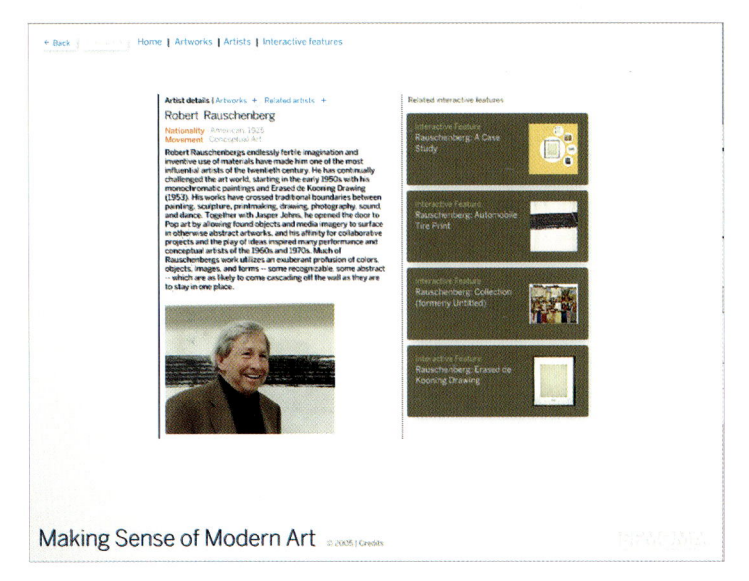

AWARD:
BRONZE
CATEGORY:
Other Digital Media:
Public Service / Non-Profit / Educational
AGENCY:
Method / San Francisco
CLIENT:
San Francisco Museum of Modern Art
WRITERS:
Stephanie Pau, Kathleen Maloney
DESIGNERS:
Bruce Bell, Baykal Askar
PROGRAMMERS:
Manny Tan, Guillermo Torres Troconis
David Nelson
PRODUCTION COMPANY:
Alex Kaplinsky
INFORMATION ARCHITECTS:
Tana Johnson, Tim Svenonius
CREATIVE DIRECTORS:
Michael Lemme, Kevin Farnham
Patrick Newbery, Peter Samis
ANNUAL ID:
06056N

144 BRONZE WINNER // METHOD

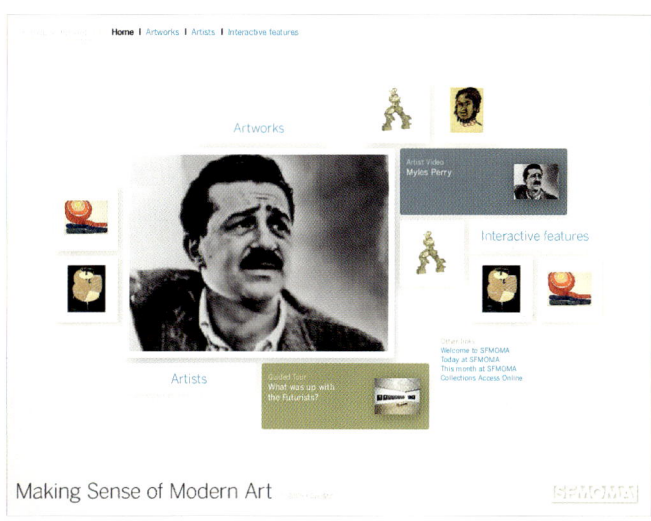

Presenting the connections between artists and movements can be a potentially never-ending endeavor. How did you manage all the information? Please describe the interface. The connections between artist-movement-artist are one of the key aspects of the UI. Initial user interviews told us that people search either by artist or by movement, and once they have initial results, they begin to explore more randomly. That is why we decided that to make both artist and movement key navigation categories. Once you have specified a choice in one category, it is easy for the system to use that choice to connect you to other information that is directly or indirectly of interest. For instance, if you choose an artist, in addition to details about the artist and their works, the system can tell you which movements they are associated with, and that can be used to find more artists or more artworks. The challenge is to make sure that the underlying database and meta-data are accurate and kept up to date as new material is added. This is an area in which the team at SFMoMA really excels.

In your user research with museum visitors, staff and guides, what did you learn about how people view art and what kind of information they're looking for? How did you implement that in the kiosk? We learned two important points that helped form the design of the kiosk UI. The first point was that people think visually. They may want to learn about a piece they had seen elsewhere in the museum, but didn't remember the name or the artist. To serve this need, we made sure that the UI has a visual representation of the artwork that is easily filtered, to allow the users to "visually" search for the artwork they want to learn more about.

The second point was that we learned that the docents created themes that they used to help people understand modern art, because modern art is as much about intent as it is technique. The docents felt that people became more engaged with the artwork if you gave them a context from which to consider art. We wanted to make sure that the system and the UI would allow for these kinds of themes. In fact, themes are really the third leg that connects to artists and movements, that creates the endless possibilities for exploring artists and artwork in this system.

The title "Making sense of modern art" —was it meant to appeal to a wider range of people who might be put off or intimidated by modern art? Actually the name pre-existed. It was the title of a large amount of interactive content, prepared by the SFMoMA interactive group, that the kiosk was going to display. We recommended that from a branding perspective this name now made more sense as applied to the entire UI system and contents. They agreed.

The Counterfeit Coup

Fake-spotting has become a necessary skill among the devoted consumers of luxury brands. In the tradition of Prana bags and Nuke sneakers that are shiftily hawked on the sidewalk, the MINI Counterfeit campaign knocks off its own black market trend with the creation of the CCC, the Counter Counterfeit Commission. Forge ahead!

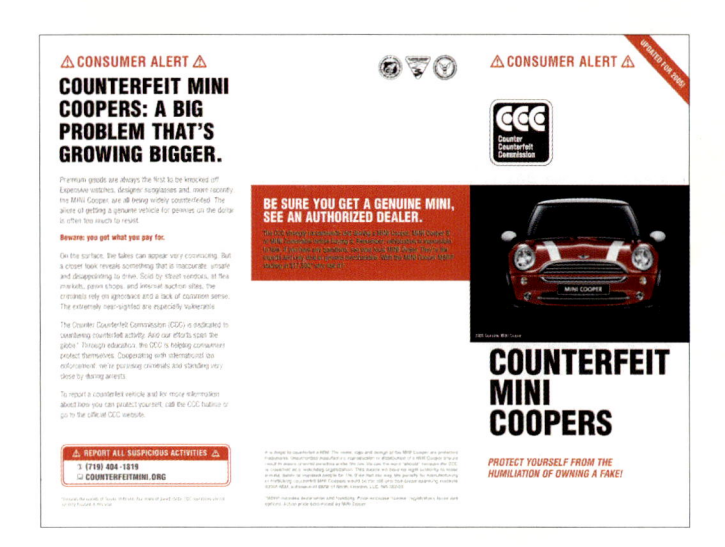

How was the Counterfeit idea conceived? Of all the things that we've done, that's an idea that I think really represents what this agency is all about. It was a lot of people coming together and brainstorming and then something like Counterfeit happening. There were so many creatives involved, and it was built on a strategy. You have a lot of other small cars coming to the market and there are a lot that are starting to use the iconic elements of the MINI, like the roof and the graphics and things. So this was a fun way of making sure that people knew the MINI was the car that owned all those elements.

You had all of these creatives coming together like Andrew Keller, Frank Tipton, Alex Bogusky, etc. They all came up with the whole campaign and then we worked with them and figured out some interactive elements that go along with it in the form of the site and the eBay auction site. It's pretty weird because there were some things that happened that we had nothing to do with, like someone really auctioned off a counterfeit car on eBay. That's pretty spectacular when you have an idea that's so good that people are really participating in it. It's a sign that it has found its way into pop culture and is really connecting with people.

AWARD:
GOLD
CATEGORY:
Integrated
Branding Campaign
AGENCY:
Crispin Porter + Bogusky / Miami
CLIENT:
MINI
ART DIRECTORS:
Paul Stechschulte
Tiffany Kosel
WRITERS:
Franklin Tipton
Rob Reilly, Steve O'Connell
DESIGNERS:
Rahul Panchal
Mike Ferrare
PHOTOGRAPHER:
Sebastian Gray
PROGRAMMER:
Luis Santi
AGENCY PRODUCERS:
David Niblick
Julieana Stechschulte
Paul Sutton, Amy Bonin
Rupert Samuel
David Rolfe, Matt Bonin
Bill Meadows
PRODUCTION COMPANIES:
Exopolis, iChameleon
Hungry Man, Jodaf/Mixer
Outpost Digital
DIRECTOR:
Brian Buckley
CREATIVE DIRECTORS:
Alex Bogusky, Andrew Keller
Jeff Benjamin
ANNUAL ID:
06057N
URL:
http://www.cpbgroup.com/awards/
counterfeit_intinter.html

After "Subservient Chicken" was it a hard act to follow? I don't think there was a ton of pressure after that. We've always seen "Subservient Chicken" as a phenomenon. I don't know if we'll ever do something like that again, because it was a great campaign, but it was also during a time in our industry when no one else was doing anything like that. It's kind of a different time right now.

Going into MINI, we wanted to do great work for our client. We wanted it to be well thought out and make sure there was something to talk about. We added elements into it like, "Slap Some Sense Into a Victim," the Tough Love thing. That took about two months to perfect to make it look really good. And then people were creating counterfeits on their own and submitting it to the site. There were all these elements where people get behind the cause. At the end of the day it worked because it was good fun.

Who else on the outside are you working with in terms of building the sites? The Tough Love and MINIs for auction were done in-house. The website for counterfeit.org (except the Tough Love part) was done by Exopolis. We designed it but they programmed it, and they did a really great job.

The only hard thing in terms of programming was the Tough Love part. You don't realize it, but there was a lot of technology and programming involved with it. One thing that worked for us is that things are successful when you can't tell how much technology and innovation went into it. We used a lot of stuff that was already out there, so it wasn't that complicated in terms of the technology, but it was difficult bringing it all together in a great idea. The "Slap Some Sense" part used Flash-based technology and there's video, but in order to get it really right and have it be reactive, that was where the work was.

TIP: A MINI TENDS TO BE SMALL.

COUNTERFEITMINI.ORG

YOU'RE BUSTED

SUSPICIOUS ACTIVITY HAS BEEN DETECTED.

SEARCHNG FOR COUNTERFEIT CONTENT ON YOUR COMPUTER. DO NOT SHUT DOWN.

Scan complete.
Despite finding some questionable jpegs on your hard drive, no counterfeit materials were uncovered at this time. So, consider this a warning. The CCC will be monitoring you. Behave yourself.

COUNTERFEITMINI.ORG

Pencil Winners
149

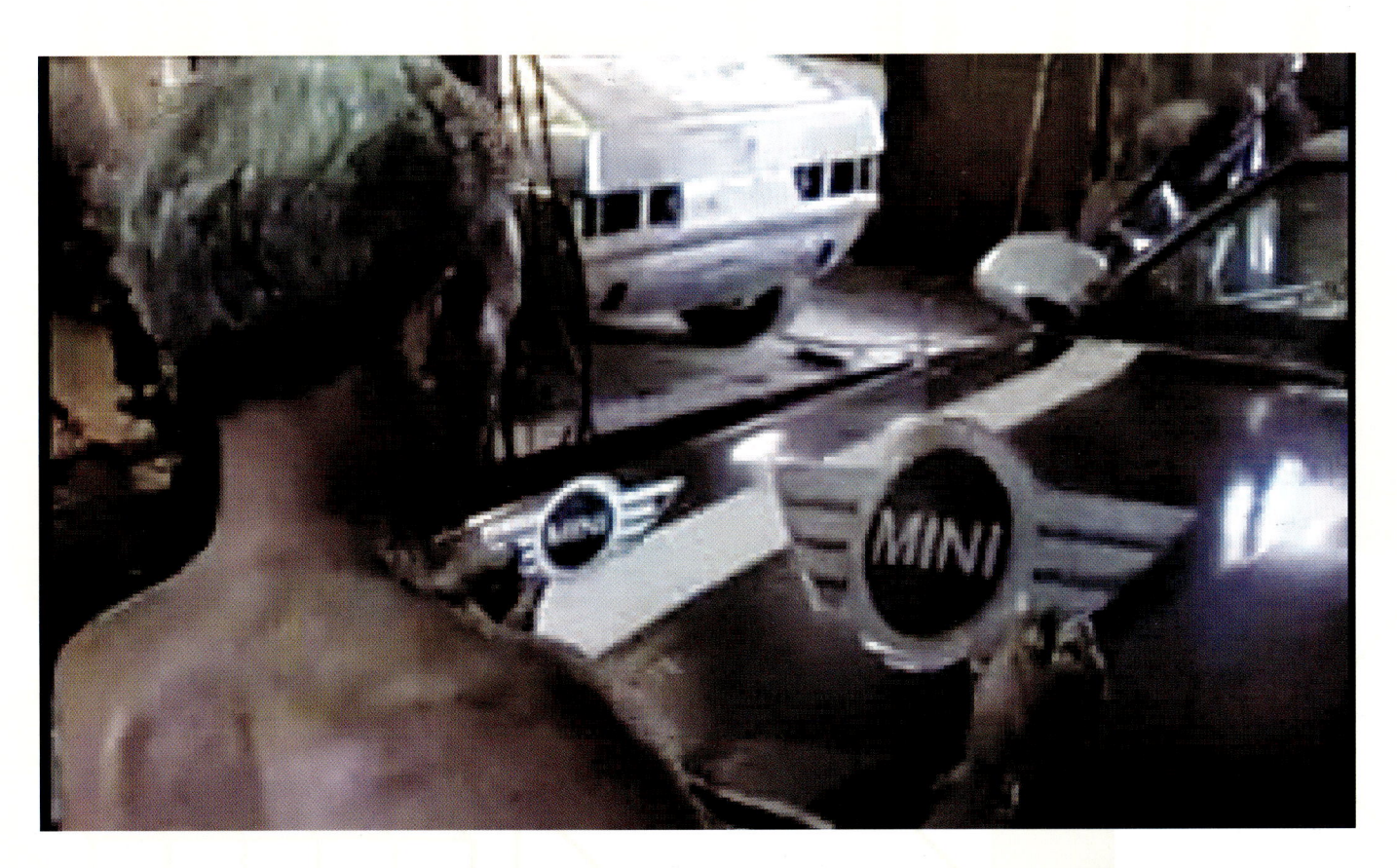

London is the Course

The Run London campaign encouraged more people to pound the pavement by getting them to promise it in writing, and then publicly reminding them of their pledges on a giant plasma screen. Nike helped the Run London community engage fully with the event through digital routefinders, SMS alerts, and naturally, a lot of fancy footgear.

AWARD:
SILVER
CATEGORY:
Integrated
Branding Campaign
AGENCY:
AKQA / London
CLIENT:
Nike
ART DIRECTOR:
Duan Evans
WRITER:
Nick Bailey
DESIGNER:
Masaya Nakade
PROGRAMMERS:
Tim Noll, Matthew Elwin
Miriam Healy, Steve Smith
Gareth Rowlands, Jeremy Brewster
AGENCY PRODUCERS:
Matthew Lodder, Jasel Mehta
James Jenkins
CONTENT STRATEGIST:
Simon Jefferson
ANNUAL ID:
06058N
URL:
http://awards.akqa.com/awards/nike/runlondon_integrated/index.html

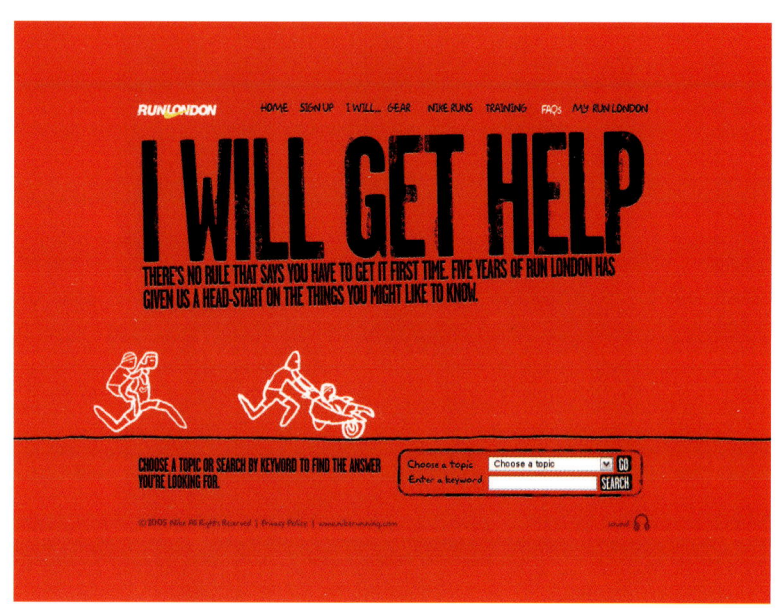

150 SILVER WINNER // AKQA

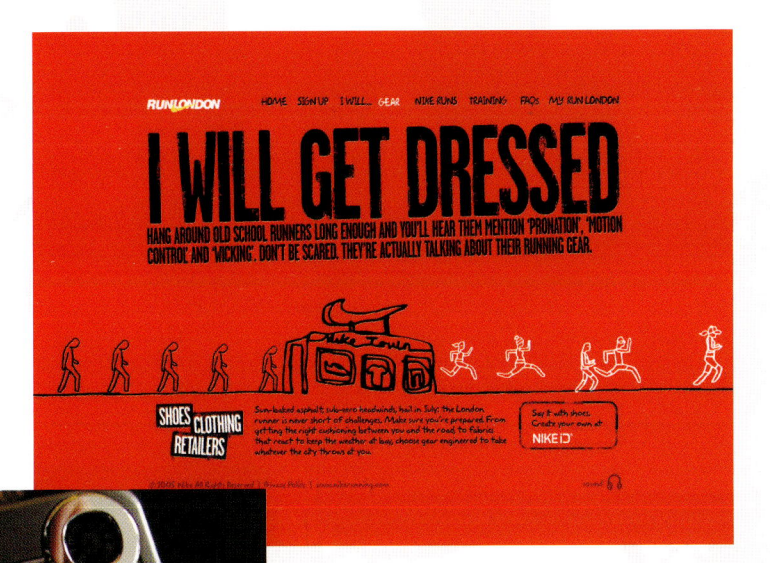

What was the campaign all about? The theme of this year's Run London campaign was "I will run a year," based on the insight that Londoners are more likely to do something if they not only set themselves a goal but, more importantly, they tell someone else about it; they make a pledge.

The campaign objectives were to recruit 32,000 runners to that year's Run London, and to build a deeper relationship/engage with the Run London community to help them live up to their pledge of running a year.

How was interactivity integrated with the very physical event of running? The digital components of the Run London campaign enabled Nike to build an engaging customer experience throughout the duration of the campaign and encompassed Web, email, mobile (SMS and 3G), in-store T-shirt collection system, digital chips, Nike Training Run attendance system using chip scanners and digitized filming of the Nike 10K finish time.

The highlights of this year's work included customized pledges made by runners on the website post-registration. Using the PledgeMaker™, motivational messages like "I will not think about the pee word" were broadcast on a giant plasma screen in the main window of NikeTown London.

"Mash-ups" with Google Maps enabled runners to easily find retailers that stocked Nike products, and to create their own running routes around London.

A CRM program consisting of over 25 outbound emails was implemented, triggered by behavioral information collected digitally at Nike Training Runs and performance at Nike events via the scanning of runners' personal digital chips.

Individual video clips of runners crossing the Nike 10K finish line were sent to runners equipped with 3G mobile phones, and SMS' containing accurate race times were sent to all runners within 24 hours.

Pencil Winners
151

Car Booty

With novelty products like the Hey Horn and the G-Whiz! G-Force Indicator, MOTORmate is an automotive aftermarket company that was created to "enhance the motoring experience," or rather trick your car out with witty gewgaws of dubious usefulness. And these are in no way counterfeit: A fully functional online shop lets motorists order and receive the manufactured goods within days.

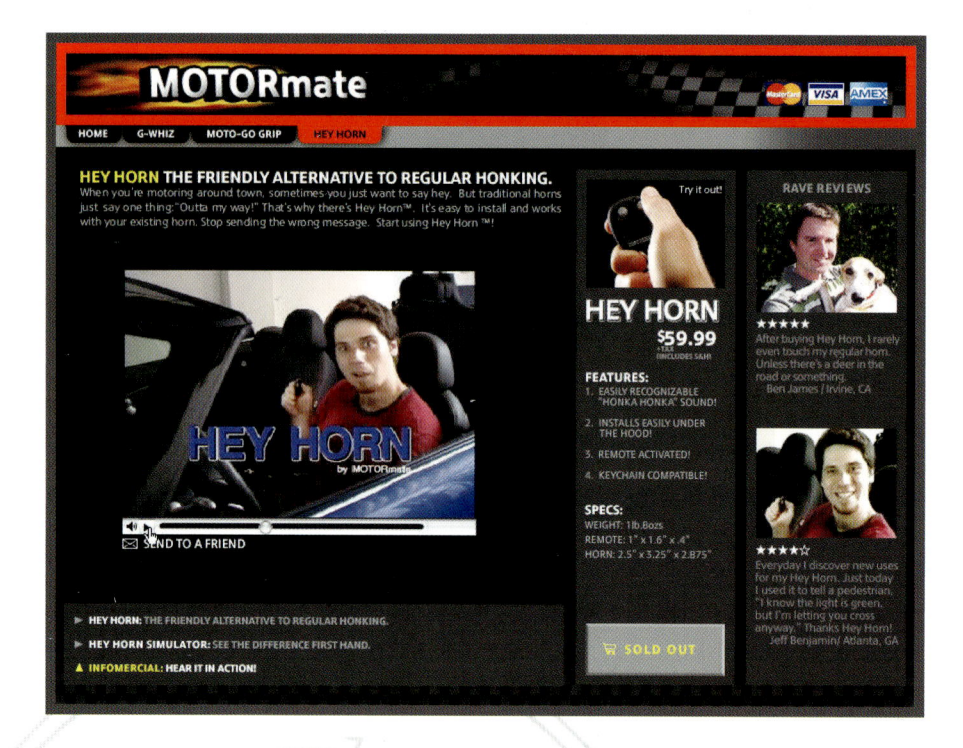

AWARD:
BRONZE
CATEGORY:
Integrated Branding Campaign
AGENCY:
Crispin Porter + Bogusky / Miami
CLIENT:
MINI
ART DIRECTORS:
Jason Ambrose
Paul Stechschulte
Jed Grossman
WRITERS:
Dustin Ballard, Franklin Tipton
Larry Corwin
DESIGNER:
Rahul Panchal
PROGRAMMER:
Fuel Industries
DIGITAL ARTISTS/MULTIMEDIA:
Spontaneous Combustion,
David Elkins, Amir Qureshi
AGENCY PRODUCERS:
Shawna Lopez, Rupert Samuel, David Rolfe
Matthew Bonin, Bill Meadows
PRODUCTION COMPANIES:
Hungry Man, 2150 Editorial
Beacon Street Music
DIRECTOR:
Bryan Buckley
CREATIVE DIRECTORS:
Alex Bogusky, Andrew Keller
Jeff Benjamin, Steve O'Connell
ANNUAL ID:
06059N
URL:
http://www.cpbgroup.com/awards/motormateintegrated.html

G-Whiz
by MOTORmate

$29.99 + Sales Tax includes S&H

NOT AVAILABLE IN STORES

MOTORmate
P.O. BOX 415
WHITE PLAINS, NY 10603

To Order Visit:
www.MOTORmate.com

New!

Moto-*Go* Grip
by MOTORmate

Order Now!
www.MOTORmate.com

Pencil Winners
153

Where the Candy is Sour, and the Pain, Sweet

Sir Gerald Pines, quintessential pasty-skinned anthropologist, "discovers" the lost island of Altoidia and gives us the grand tour via diorama recreations and BBC-style documentaries. We meet Altoidia's curious and curiouser indigenous tribes, people made immune to pain through their birthright exposure to the Strong Sour Taste. Fertile grounds for the retrograde pleasure of seeing Pines attacked by giant swooping bats and getting kicked in the balls.

AWARD:
BRONZE
CATEGORY:
Integrated Branding Campaign
AGENCY:
Leo Burnett / Chicago
CLIENT:
Altoids
ART DIRECTOR:
Adrien Bindi
WRITER:
Nick Cade
PHOTOGRAPHER:
Tony D'Orio
AGENCY PRODUCER:
Vincent Geraghty
DIRECTOR:
Craig Gillespie
CREATIVE DIRECTORS:
Noel Haan, G. Andrew Meyer
ANNUAL ID:
06060N
URL:
http://www.altoidia.com

Your mother smells like monkey butt.

An important outcome of the campaign launch was that the films were picked up spread virally on the Internet. Why did you choose to launch initially in cinema? The campaign was engineered to create a full spectrum of contact, from print, to cinema, to television, to online. We love cinema advertising; the nature of the medium gives us a uniquely captive audience. And it seemed to us that the idea and the film documentary style could be fully realized in this medium.

Increasingly, viewers are providing feedback and posting their reactions on blogs. Do you monitor these comments and take them into consideration? We unofficially monitored the viral spread of the campaign online, but we had enough faith in the material that we were confident letting the conversation happen organically.

Sir Gerald Pines—what was the inspiration behind this character? We first crafted the notion of the place that became Altoidia, and then built the character who would be a natural narrator to lead people through the exploration. Gerald is very much someone who could have sprung forth from one of our many print executions; he is fascinatingly flawed and a charming bumbler who feels the effects of curious strength.

The campaign was very successful and appreciated humorously, but there was a thin line where the anthropological element could have been taken as being colonialist or racially stereotyped. How was this avoided? Altoids is an "equal opportunity offender"— we poke fun at everything and everybody, including ourselves. We've always been willing to throw caution to the wind, and always will. Also, there is an intentional subtext to the campaign, in that Gerald represents colonial meddling with cultures that are better left alone. It's no coincidence that Gerald is repeatedly punished for being in a place where he doesn't belong.

Pencil Winners
155

Grand Theft Audi

It started, simply enough, with a stolen car. But rabid bloggers, car aficionados, conspiracy theorists, and the media all played their part into turning the H3ist into a full blown immersive reality that smudged the lines between fact and fiction, advertising and entertainment. The campaign took it into overdrive, involving a fake game inventor, a fake stolen-art recoverer, and fake "missing" signs all over the city.

What was your favorite part of the campaign? How far did you want to take it? From the beginning of this campaign, we knew we faced a very unique challenge: Reach a target demographic that was adept at filtering out traditional advertising. We realized early on that we would have to do something bold and highly distinctive if we were going to get them to take notice of Audi's newest car model, the A3. With that hurdle in mind, we decided to invite this community to participate in a real-life spy drama about a stolen car and plans for the largest art heist in history. We knew that if we engaged them on their terms and made the reward for participating enticing enough, the target would make their way to our story in a traditional example of pull vs. push advertising.

From the beginning, we knew we had something very unique that the audience was enjoying. It took on a life of its own, driven by the interest from the exact community we wanted to reach. Within hours of the car being "stolen" from the Park Avenue dealership, blogs all over the world were reporting the "theft" of the A3 and debating whether it was real or not. Within the first few weeks, 10 fan sites devoted to following the development of the campaign had been created. We received calls from Audi A3 owners who had actually been flagged down by participants in the campaign to ask if their car was the "stolen" A3.

As the campaign progressed, participants themselves kept pushing the line between fact and fiction by actually becoming characters in the story themselves. In fact, the more we made the campaign and story seem real, the more the participants responded by getting others to join the story, by participating in live events with the characters and even suggesting

AWARD:
BRONZE
CATEGORY:
Integrated
Branding Campaign
AGENCY:
McKinney / Durham
CLIENT:
Audi of America, Inc
ART DIRECTOR:
Jason Musante
WRITERS:
Matt Fischvogt, Brian Cain
Jim Gunshanon, Ernie Larsen
Gregg Hale
DESIGNERS:
Justin Smith, Dave Szulborski
AGENCY PRODUCER:
Regina Brizzolara
PRODUCTION COMPANY:
Chelsea Pictures/campfire
DIRECTORS:
Ben Rock, Mike Monello
CREATIVE DIRECTORS:
Dave Cook, David Baldwin
Jonathan Cude, Brian Clark
ANNUAL ID:
06061N

alternative endings and subplots. In the end, 500,000 participants felt they had been apart of something very big and different, especially coming from a major automotive manufacturer.

The campaign was entertaining but, moreover, experiential. Were there any particular films, books, TV shows or characters that inspired the development of the story? As we were developing the campaign, we kept reading news stories about art theft in Europe becoming increasingly common. The interesting thing that linked many of these real-life heists together was the fact that Audi seemed to be the brand of choice for the getaway vehicle. We felt like we could capitalize on this reality to make our story seem more real and further blur the lines between fact and fiction. So we took this thread and wove it together with other classic spy novel motifs; blackmail, murder, lovers betrayed, scandal, and above all a roller-coaster ride where, up until the end, you were never sure who was the good guy and who was the bad guy.

The H3ist is a classic example of a hoax-based integrated branding. Why do you think it worked as well as it did at that time? One of the amazing results of The Art of the H3ist had to do with the level of consumer involvement. The facts are clear: Consumers are willing to spend a considerable amount of time deeply engaging and participating in your brand if you provide them with an experience rich enough to reward that time. The more we pushed the lines of fact and fiction, the more the audience responded. The more we hid the seams of production and made everything seem as if it were real and happening in real time, the more the audience encouraged others to join in an adventure that seemed to be more real than any movie or novel.

The largest influx of active participants occurred when we reached into the mainstream with our message, specifically with a national television spot, which was purposefully awkward and rushed. With technology working both for and against advertising, new avenues to reach consumers in new and entertaining ways will continue to emerge. We are always looking for ways to have interesting and engaging conversations with consumers and The H3ist was an exciting evolution in a process that continues to evolve.

The Customized is Always Right

For some, Nike is a religion. For those who insist on tailor-made details, NIKE iD is their church. And for a month in 2005, the 23-story Reuters sign in New York City was its steeple: Sneaker freaks and the buy-curious on Times Square texted their pair of paint-by-number Nikes to the sign, communing in the world's first interactive billboard experience.

Describe the relaunch of NIKE iD. What was new about it? (And can consumers still have customized words on their shoe, or did that prove too troublesome?) There were a ton of new features added to the relaunch of nikeid.com.

We re-structured the navigation of the site and added a better filtering and breadcrumbing system so consumers were able to move around the site with better ease. We created sport category landing pages to allow Nike to briefly tell stories for their sport categories like Basketball, Running, Soccer, etc. An iD Exclusives section was also added to allow Nike to tell larger collection stories for big brand initiatives like Air Max Classics, World Soccer 2006, Nike Free, and Rihanna.

Product description pages (PDP) were added into the purchase path for every product to give consumers product background information. Additionally, from the PDP, consumers were given inspirational design starting points so they could jump right into a design build with pre-selected choices. The shoe builder was also given a facelift that included a wider interface, better sound design, and subtle interaction cues to help guide the user through the design process.

Consumers can still have customized words on their shoe. That is huge part of the personalization offering that NIKE iD provides.

AWARD:
BRONZE
CATEGORY:
Integrated
Branding Campaign
AGENCY:
R/GA / New York
CLIENT:
Nike
ART DIRECTOR:
Marlon Hernandez
WRITERS:
Josh Bletterman, Scott Tufts
DESIGNERS:
Matt Walsh, Ian Brewer
David Hyung, Michelle Zassenhaus
Lara Horner, Andrew Thompson
John James, Takafumi Yamaguchi
Brian Votaw, Troy Kooper
PROGRAMMERS:
Scott Prindle, Sean Lyons
Stan Wiechers, Chuck Genco
Martin Legowiecki, August Yang
Todd Kovner, Michele Roman
CREATIVE DIRECTOR:
Richard Ting
CONTENT STRATEGISTS:
Erica Millado, Briggs Davidson
ANNUAL ID:
06062N
URL:
http://rga.com/nikeid.html

How was the website promoted online? Nikeid.com was promoted through a massive online media buy on Yahoo and UGO. All of the online banners that were created allowed users to design their shoes via a mini NIKE iD builder. We also created an AIM expression that featured a mini-NIKE iD builder. A blog contest was also conducted on the top 20 sneaker blogs to raise awareness of nikeid.com within the sneakerhead community. Each of the top 20 sneaker blogs were allowed to design a shoe and post to the nikeid.com site. The creator of the top rated shoe was awarded the grand prize of 50 free nikeid.com shoes.

The highlight of the campaign was the Times Square billboard event, which was controlled by cell-phone. Please explain a little about how the whole thing worked.
To help promote the relaunch of nikeid.com, Nike enthusiasts and Times Square passers-by were invited to participate in the world's first cellphone-controlled, commerce-enabled interactive billboard experience. Set in the heart of Times Square, the challenge called for pedestrians to design the Nike Free 5.0 shoe live on the 23-story Reuters sign. Participants use their wireless phone (unrestricted by carrier) to call an 800-number featured on the sign. After making the call, users are placed in a queue or prompted to begin the design session. They have up to 60 seconds to create a design from a modified palette of five base colors. Users navigate color changes with their cellphone keypad.

After they finish their design, an SMS message is sent to their mobile phone that includes a link to a mobile site, where users can directly download a "one size fits all" mobile wallpaper of their newly created shoe. The SMS message also contains a unique code and a text link to nyc.nikeid.com. By entering the unique code the participants will be able to retrieve their Times Square creation and add to cart for purchase.

Miles Away

Miami Ad School shows that the hybrid vehicle is the runaway choice for driving past the competition with more miles per gallon. Designed to be placed on car guide websites, the hybrid rolls across the screen, above and beyond a slew of other car ads.

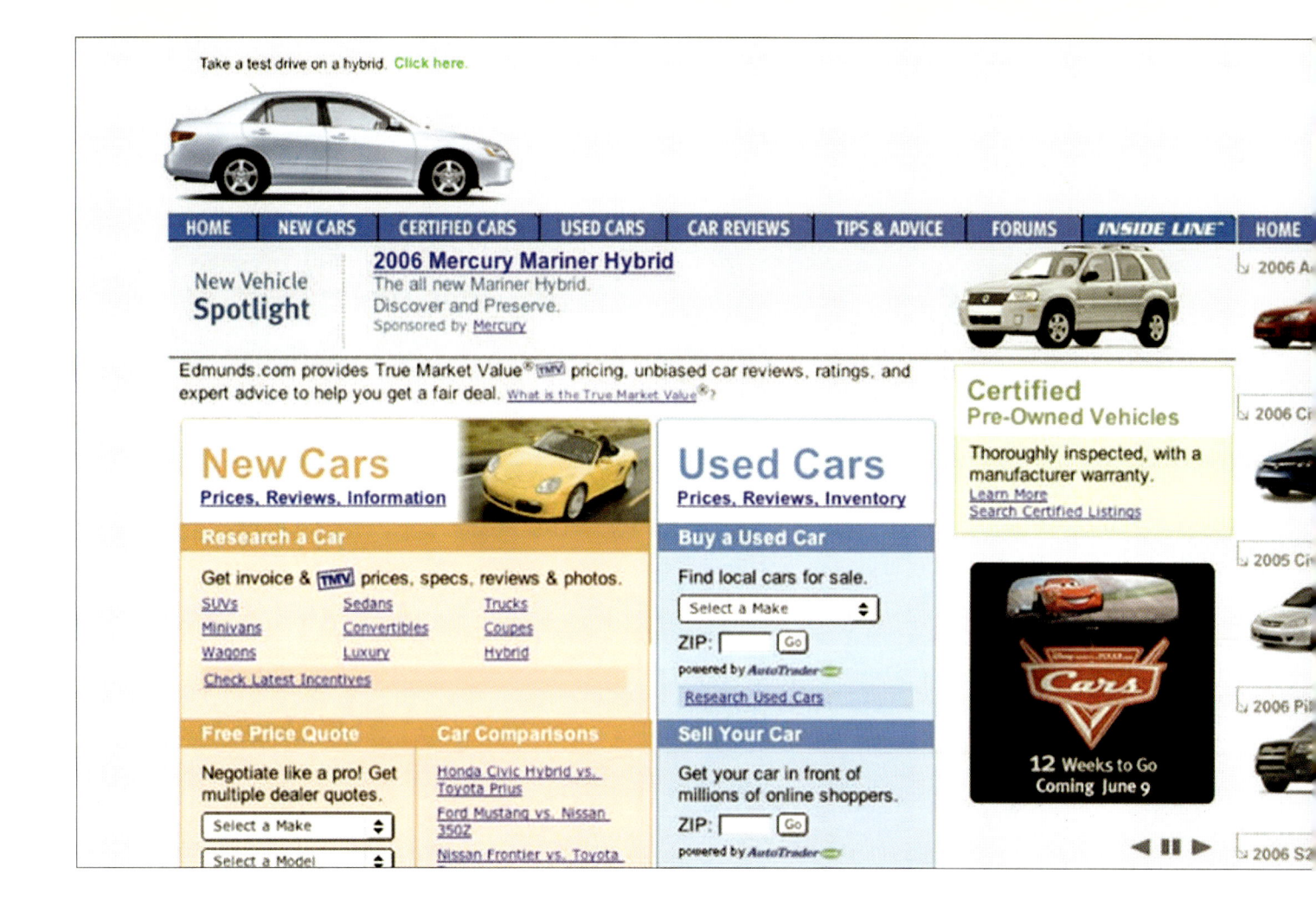

AWARD:
GOLD
CATEGORY:
Interactive:
Single / Campaign
SCHOOL:
Miami Ad School / Miami Beach
ART DIRECTOR:
Moyeenul Alam
WRITER:
Juan Guzman
CLIENT:
Hybridcenter.org
ANNUAL ID:
CCI001
URL:
http://geocities.com/
hybridbanner

The Exhaustive Truth

Pollution, lung disease—and oh, lower sperm count—what more needs to be said?

Car pollution damages sperm.
*Read article on WebMD

Car pollution damages sperm.
*Read article on WebMD

nokers
d smoke.

Even non-smokers cause second hand smoke.

To learn more about hybrid car engines visit

Hybrid center.org

Relax, take a deep breath.

AWARD:
SILVER
CATEGORY:
Interactive:
Single . Campaign
SCHOOL:
School of Visual Arts /
New York
ART DIRECTOR:
Ben Bartholomew
CLIENT:
Hybridcenter.org
ANNUAL ID:
CCI002
URL:
http://www.benbart.com/oneclub

Pencil Winners
163

SUVersive

Skinny-dipping and frolicking unclothed on the grass are apt celebrations of the hybrid's benefits to nature. The Academy of Art took tree-hugging to its freaky limits with their fantasyland of happy nudists and snarky turtles who make fun of traditional SUV drivers.

AWARD:
BRONZE
CATEGORY:
Interactive:
Single . Campaign
SCHOOL:
Academy of Art University / San Francisco
ART DIRECTORS:
Lisa Doman
Nicolle Correa
CLIENT:
Hybridcenter.org
ANNUAL ID:
CCI003
URL:
http://nudes4hybrids.org

natural people for a better world

rollover car for more information

home
skinny dip
hybrid school
naked hybrid

Hybridcenter.org
a project of the Union of Concerned Scientists

merit winners

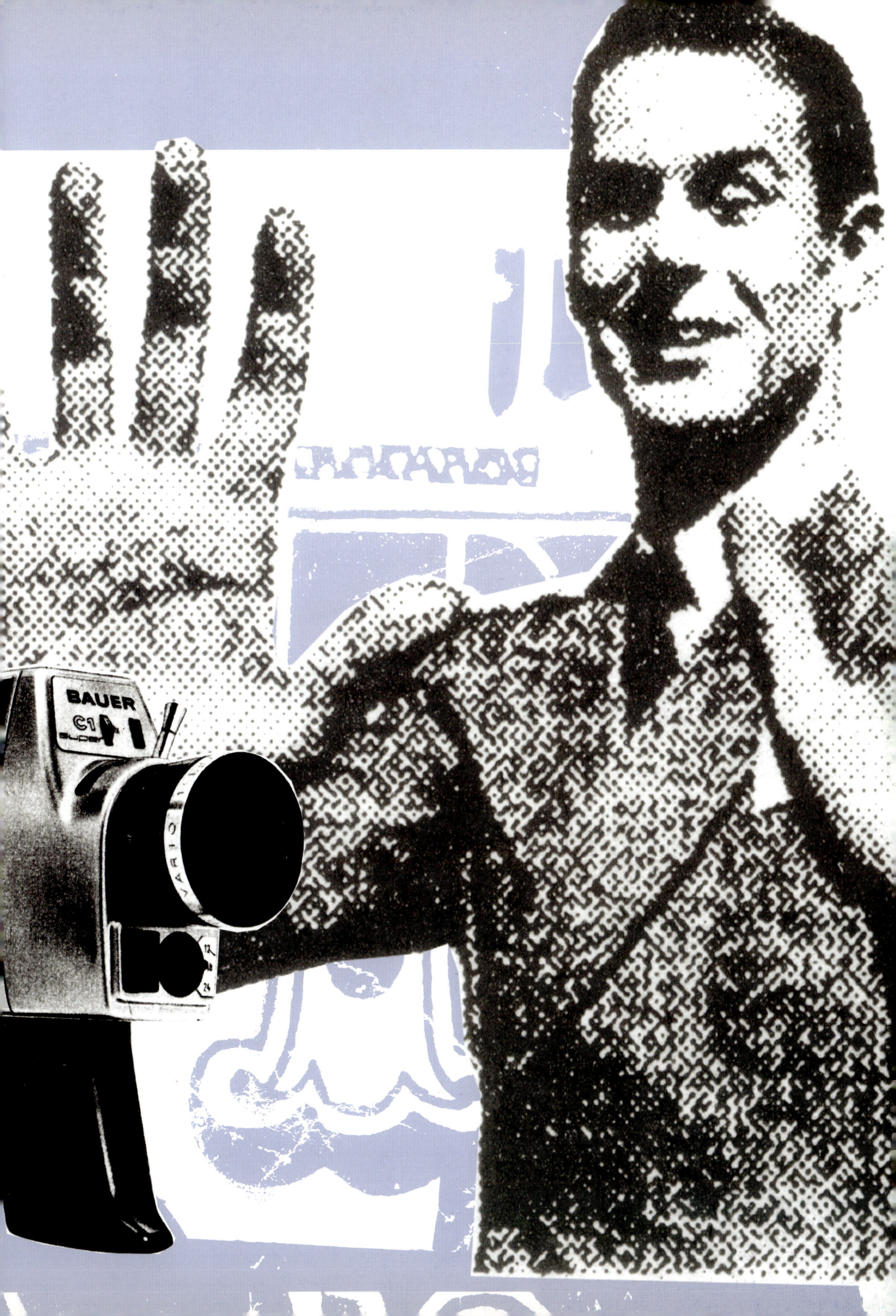
BAUER
C1

BANNERS . FIXED SPACE:
BUSINESS TO CONSUMER . SINGLE

AGENCY
AgênciaClick / São Paulo
CLIENT
The Coca-Cola Company

ART DIRECTORS:
Fred Siqueira
Vicente da Silva e Silva
WRITERS:
Ricardo Figueira
Jones Krahl Junior
DESIGNERS:
César Augusto Marchetti
Henrique Lima
CREATIVE DIRECTOR:
Ricardo Figueira
ANNUAL ID:
06063N
URL:
http://www.virtualsofa.net
/2006/cocacola/upsidedown/en

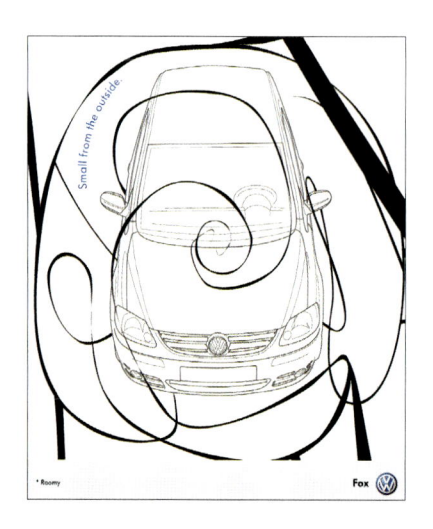

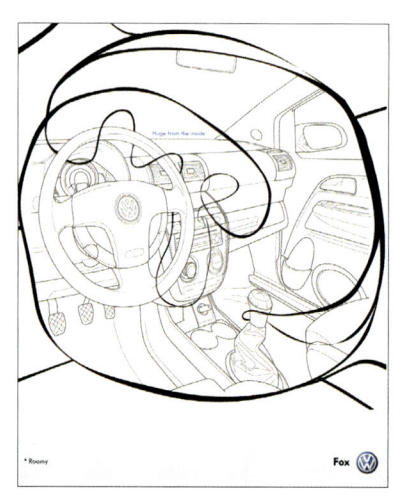

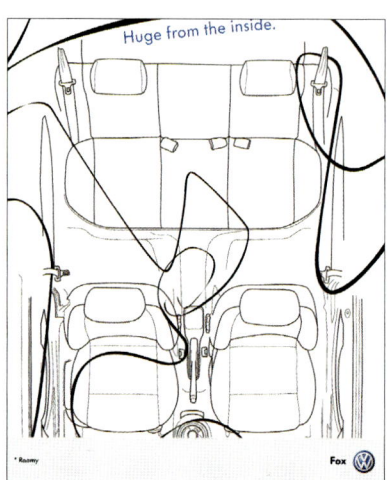

BANNERS . FIXED SPACE:
BUSINESS TO CONSUMER . SINGLE

AGENCY
AlmapBBDO / São Paulo
CLIENT
Volkswagen

ART DIRECTOR:
Sergio Mugnaini
WRITER:
Luciana Haguiara
DESIGNER:
Carmelo di Lorenzo
PROGRAMMER:
Flávio Ramos
CREATIVE DIRECTOR:
Sergio Mugnaini
ANNUAL ID:
06064N
URL:
http://www.almapbbdo.com.br
/awards/2006/vw/fractal

168   MERIT WINNERS // AGÊNCIACLICK // ALMAPBBDO // CRISPIN PORTER + BOGUSKY

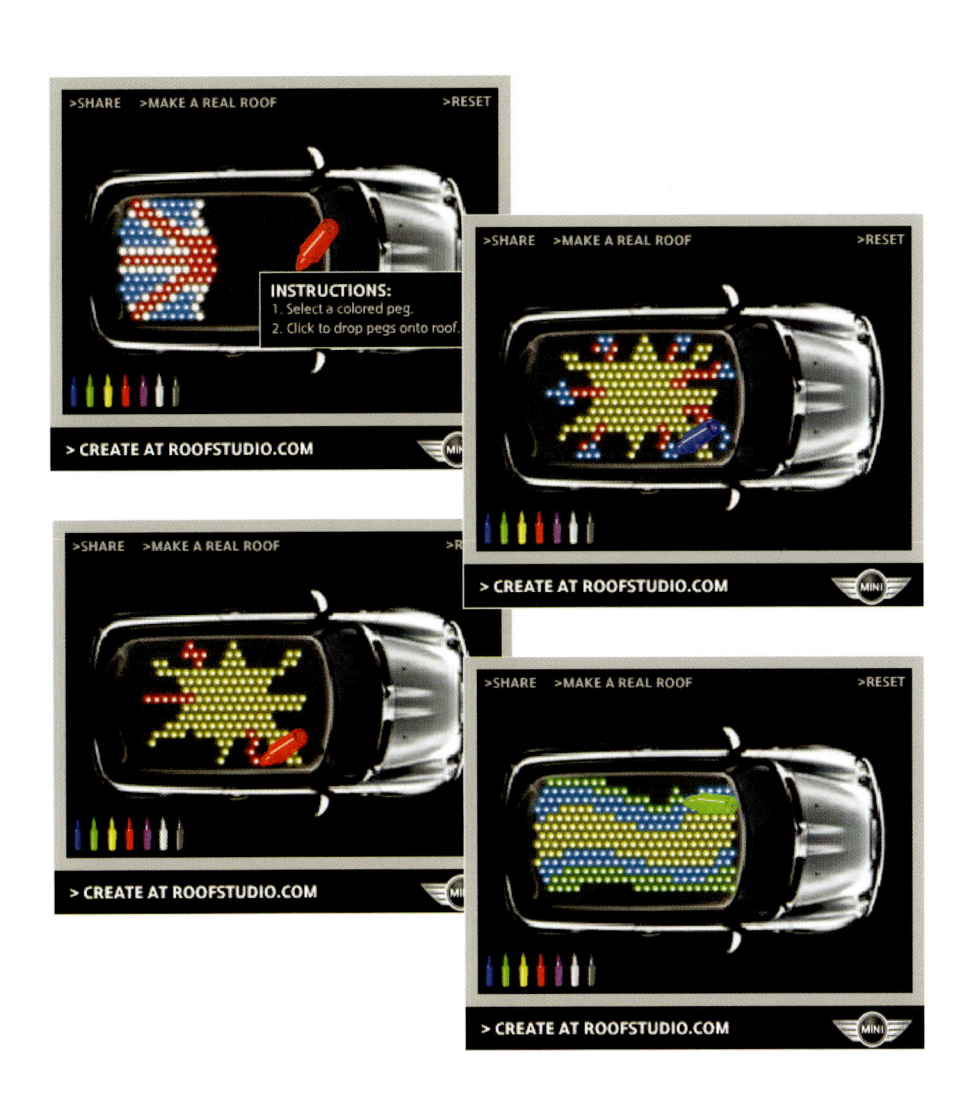

BANNERS . FIXED SPACE:
BUSINESS TO CONSUMER . SINGLE

AGENCY
Crispin Porter + Bogusky / Miami
CLIENT
MINI

ART DIRECTOR:
Rahul Panchal
WRITER:
Brian Tierney
DESIGNER:
Chean Wei Law
PRODUCTION COMPANY:
Dev Impact
CREATIVE DIRECTORS:
Andrew Keller, Rob Strasberg
Jeff Benjamin, Alex Bogusky
ANNUAL ID:
06065N
URL:
http://www.cpbgroup.com
/awards/peg.html

BANNERS . FIXED SPACE:
BUSINESS TO CONSUMER . SINGLE

AGENCY
Crispin Porter + Bogusky / Miami
CLIENT
PINK

ART DIRECTOR:
Tiffany Kosel
WRITER:
Scott Linnen
DESIGNERS:
Mike Ferrare, Cybele
PROGRAMMER:
Milky Elephant
CREATIVE DIRECTORS:
Alex Bogusky, Scott Linnen
Jeff Benjamin
ANNUAL ID:
06066N
URL:
http://www.cpbgroup.com
/awards/personality.html

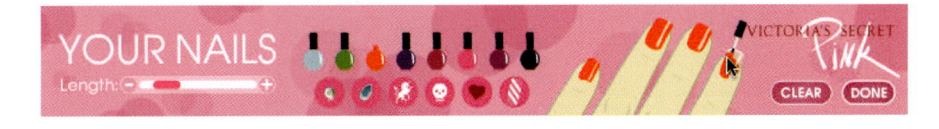

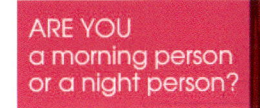

Merit Winners
169

BANNERS . FIXED SPACE:
BUSINESS TO CONSUMER . SINGLE

AGENCY
DoubleYou / Barcelona

CLIENT
American Nike

DESIGNER:
Nacho Guijarro

DIGITAL ARTIST/MULTIMEDIA:
Nacho Guijarro

CREATIVE DIRECTORS:
Edu Pou
Joakim Borgström

CONTENT STRATEGIST:
Jordi Pont

ANNUAL ID:
06067N

URL:
http://festivals.doubleyou.com
/2006/nikerunning/oneshow.html

BANNERS . FIXED SPACE:
BUSINESS TO CONSUMER . SINGLE

AGENCY
Freestyle Interactive / San Francisco

CLIENT
Dolby

ART DIRECTOR:
Hiro Mori

WRITER:
Chris Gatewood

DESIGNER:
Franz Gabriel

PROGRAMMER:
Joshua Hart

CREATIVE DIRECTORS:
Andrew Schmeling
Chris Gatewood

ANNUAL ID:
06068N

URL:
http://www.freestyleinteractive.com
/submissions/storm/

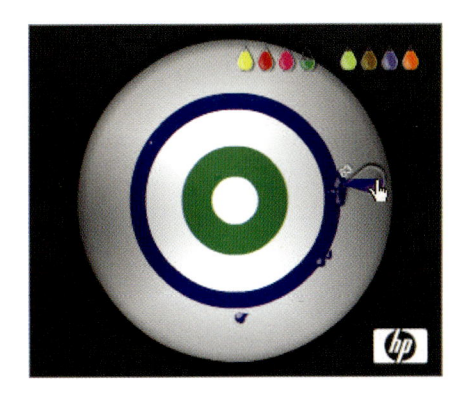

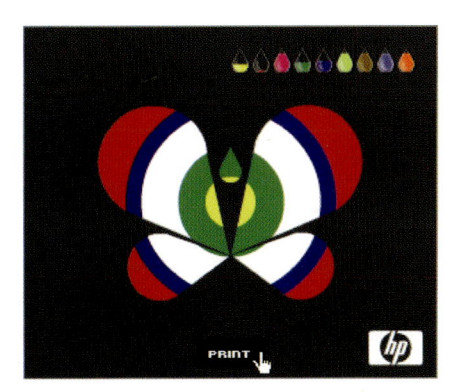

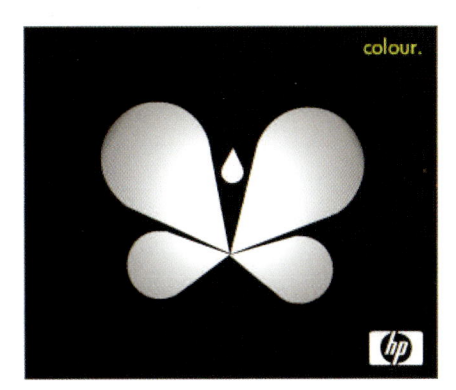

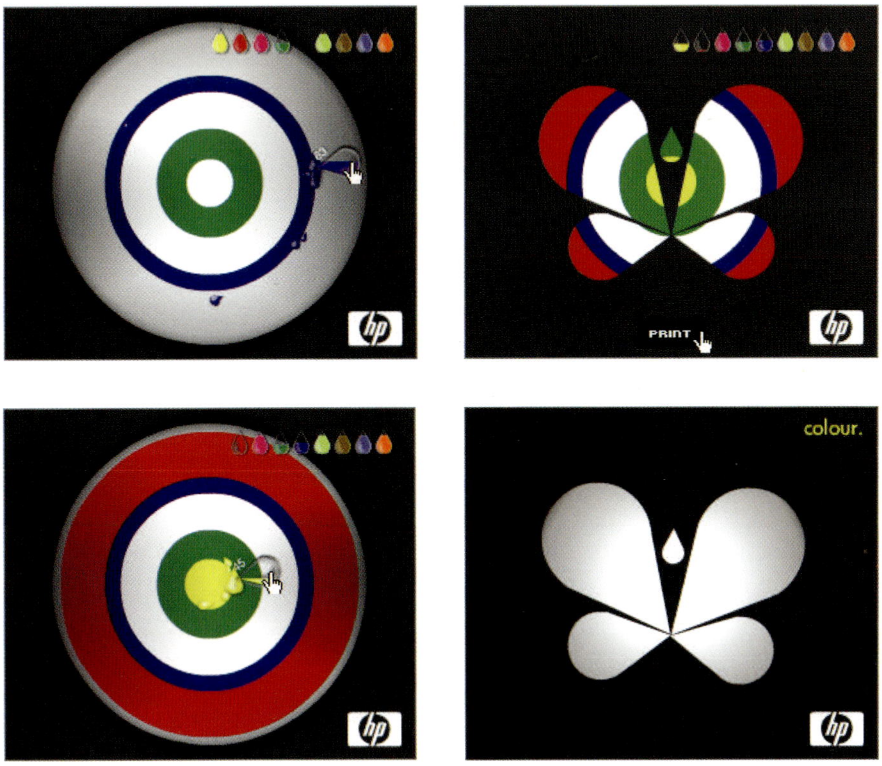

BANNERS . FIXED SPACE:
BUSINESS TO CONSUMER . SINGLE

AGENCY
Goodby, Silverstein & Partners /
San Francisco
CLIENT
Hewlett-Packard

ART DIRECTOR:
Kevin Hughes
WRITER:
Todd Lemmon
PRODUCTION COMPANY:
Natzke Design
CONTENT STRATEGISTS:
Amanda Kelso
Mike Geiger
CREATIVE DIRECTORS:
Steve Simpson, John Matejczyk
Will McGinness, Keith Anderson
ANNUAL ID:
06069N
URL:
http://www.goodbysilverstein.com/awards/oneshow_2006/hp_butterfly/

BANNERS . FIXED SPACE:
BUSINESS TO CONSUMER . SINGLE

AGENCY
Goodby, Silverstein & Partners /
San Francisco
CLIENT
Saturn

ART DIRECTOR:
Aaron Dietz
WRITER:
Mandy Dietz
PRODUCTION COMPANY:
The Barbarian Group
CONTENT STRATEGISTS:
Brit Charlebois
Mike Geiger
CREATIVE DIRECTORS:
Will McGinness
Keith Anderson
ANNUAL ID:
06070N
URL:
http://www.goodbysilverstein.com/awards/oneshow_2006/sky_sounds/

Merit Winners
171

BANNERS . FIXED SPACE:
BUSINESS TO CONSUMER . SINGLE

AGENCY
Nordpol+ Hamburg / Hamburg

CLIENT
Renault Germany

ART DIRECTORS:
Dominik Anweiler
Gunther Schreiber
WRITER:
Ingmar Bartels
DESIGNER:
Mark Höfler
PROGRAMMER:
Mark Höfler
PRODUCTION COMPANY:
Element E
CREATIVE DIRECTOR:
Ingo Fritz
ANNUAL ID:
06071N
URL:
http://www.nordpol.com/2005/renault/unfall/en/

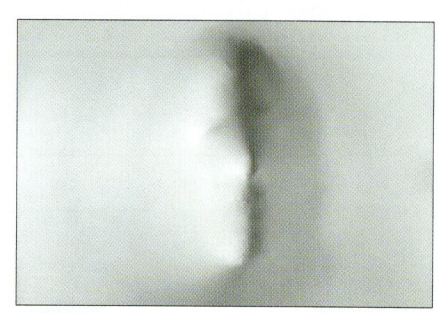

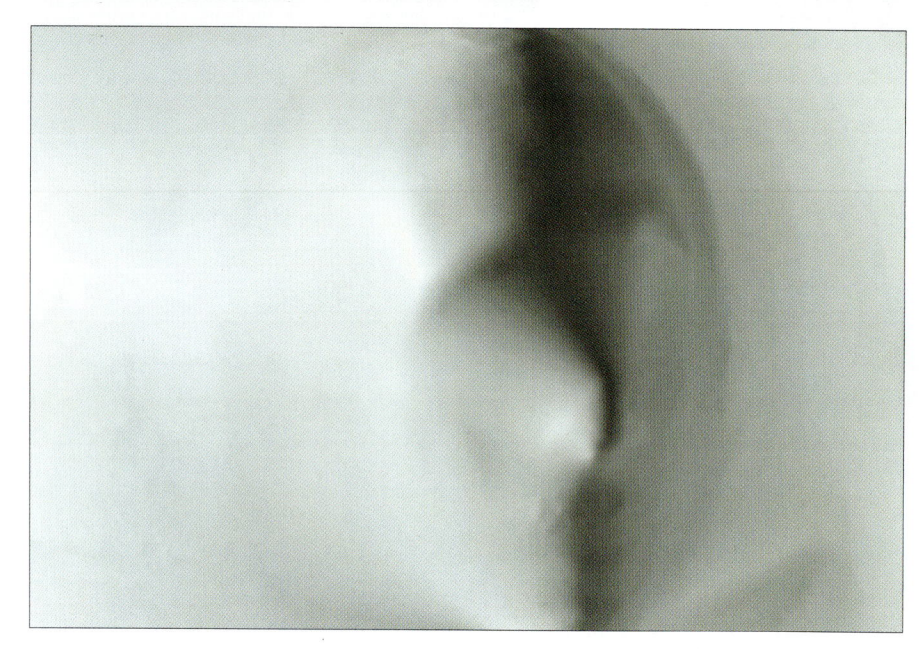

BANNERS . FIXED SPACE:
BUSINESS TO CONSUMER . SINGLE

AGENCY
OgilvyOne / Beijing

CLIENT
Audi

ART DIRECTOR:
Yanyan Yang
WRITER:
Meng Wan
DESIGNER:
Jimmy Wang
DIGITAL ARTIST/MULTIMEDIA:
Ryan Liu
CREATIVE DIRECTOR:
Dirk Eschenbacher
ANNUAL ID:
06072N
URL:
http://www.our-work.org/work/audi/autoshow2/index.html

172   MERIT WINNERS // NORDPOL+ HAMBURG // OGILVYONE // SAATCHI & SAATCHI // AGENCY REPUBLIC

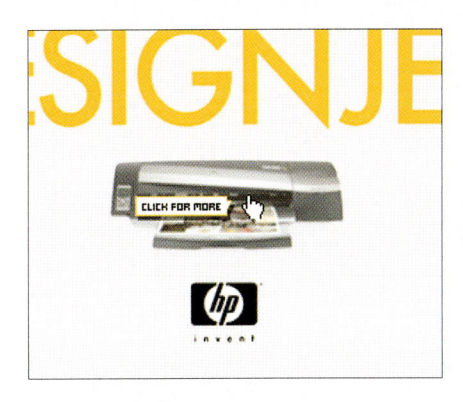

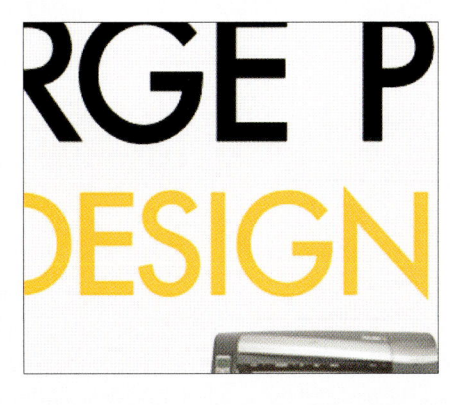

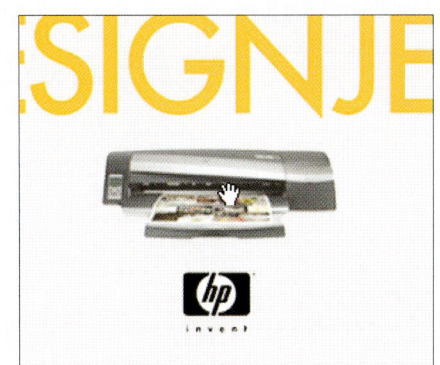

BANNERS . FIXED SPACE:
BUSINESS TO CONSUMER . SINGLE

AGENCY
Saatchi & Saatchi / Singapore
CLIENT
HP Asia Pacific

ART DIRECTOR:
Robin Tan
WRITERS:
Justine Lee
Roger Makak
DESIGNER:
Robin Tan
PROGRAMMER:
Robin Tan
CREATIVE DIRECTOR:
Bruce Watt
ANNUAL ID:
06073N
URL:
http://www.the-ideas.com
/hp_designjet130/

BANNERS . FIXED SPACE:
BUSINESS TO CONSUMER . CAMPAIGN

AGENCY
Agency Republic / London
CLIENT
BBC World Service

ART DIRECTOR:
Russ Tucker
WRITER:
Chirs Bayliss
INFORMATION ARCHITECT:
Adam Johnston
CREATIVE DIRECTOR:
Andy Sandoz
ANNUAL ID:
06074N
URL:
http://agencyrepublic.net/awards
/bbc_creatives/contents.php

Merit Winners
173

BANNERS . FIXED SPACE:
BUSINESS TO CONSUMER . CAMPAIGN

AGENCY
Goodby, Silverstein & Partners /
San Francisco
CLIENT
Discover Card

ART DIRECTOR:
Aaron Dietz
WRITER:
Mandy Dietz
PRODUCTION COMPANY:
unit9.creative.production
CREATIVE DIRECTORS:
Keith Anderson
Will McGinness
CONTENT STRATEGISTS:
Dora Lee, Mike Geiger
ANNUAL ID:
06075N
URL:
http://www.goodbysilverstein.com
/awards/oneshow_2006/discover_elf/

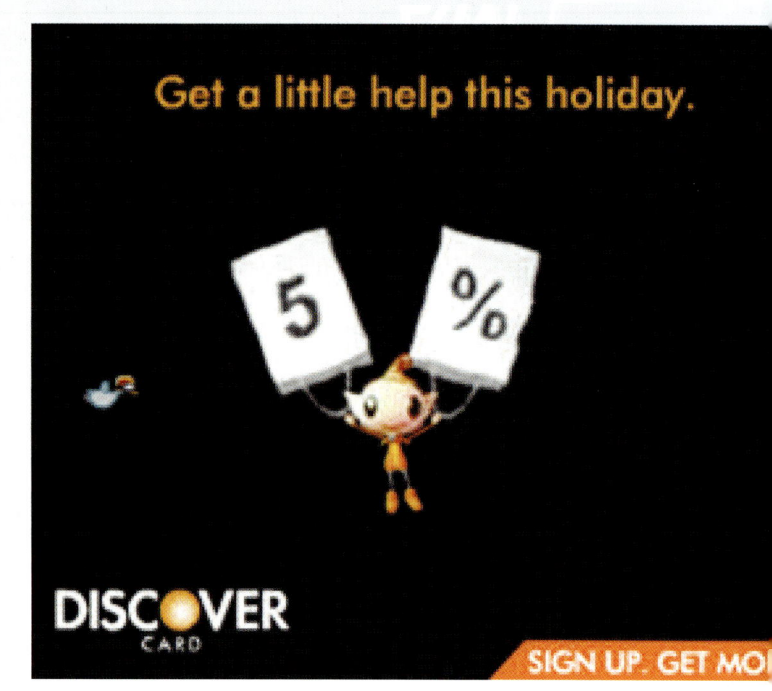

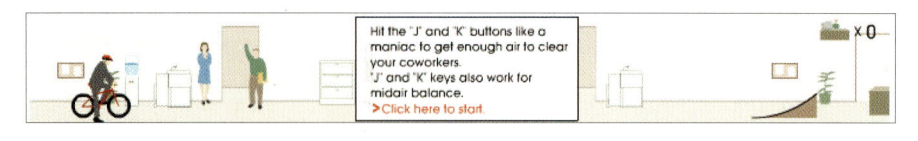

BANNERS . FIXED SPACE:
PROMOTIONAL ADVERTISING . SINGLE

AGENCY
Crispin Porter + Bogusky / Miami
CLIENT
Shimano

ART DIRECTOR:
Tom Zukoski
WRITER:
Ryan Kutscher
DESIGNER:
Rahul Panchal
PROGRAMMER:
Milky Elephant
CREATIVE DIRECTORS:
Alex Bogusky, Scott Linnen
Jeff Benjamin
ANNUAL ID:
06076N
URL:
http://www.cpbgroup.com/awards
/biketowork.html

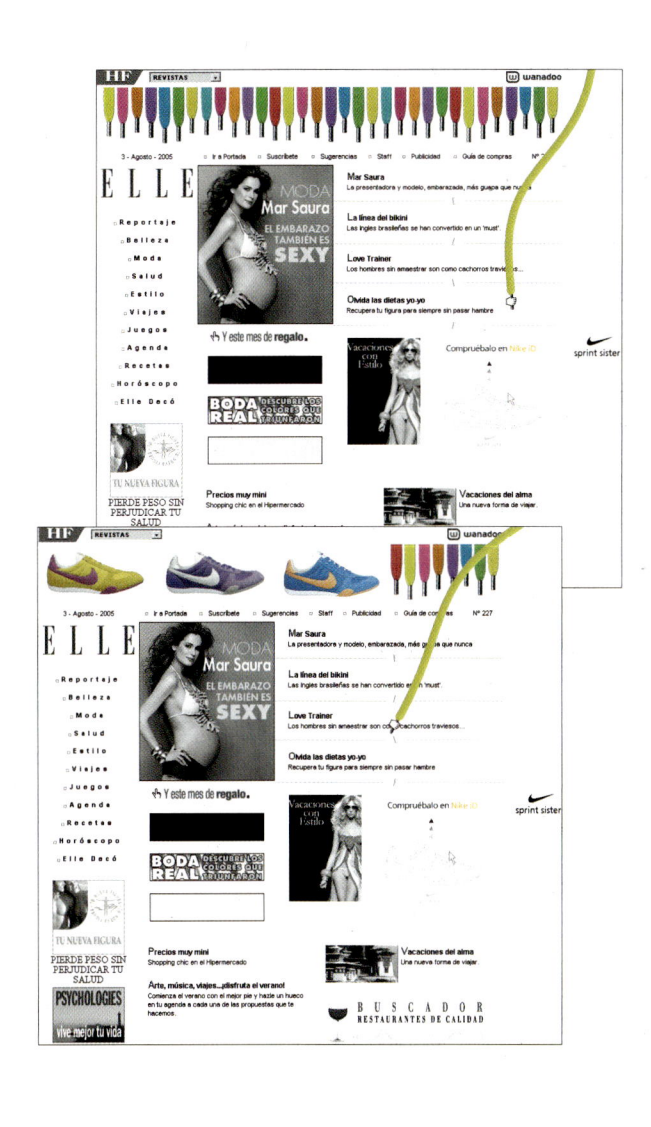

BANNERS . FIXED SPACE: PROMOTIONAL
ADVERTISING . CAMPAIGN

AGENCY
DoubleYou / Barcelona
CLIENT
Nike

ART DIRECTOR:
Blanca Piera
WRITER:
Esther Pino
DESIGNER:
Natalie Long
PROGRAMMER:
Joakim Borgström
DIGITAL ARTIST/MULTIMEDIA:
Nacho Guijarro
CONTENT STRATEGIST:
Jordi Pont
CREATIVE DIRECTORS:
Edu Pou
Joakim Borgström
ANNUAL ID:
06077N
URL:
http://festivals.doubleyou.com/2006/nikesprintsister/oneshow.html

---

BANNERS . FIXED SPACE: PUBLIC SERVICE
/NON-PROFIT/ EDUCATIONAL . SINGLE

AGENCY
AlmapBBDO / São Paulo
CLIENT
Greenpeace

ART DIRECTOR:
Rodrigo Buim
WRITER:
Luciana Haguiara
PROGRAMMER:
Raphael Hamzagic
DIGITAL ARTIST/MULTIMEDIA:
Z Quatro Animação
CREATIVE DIRECTOR:
Sergio Mugnaini
ANNUAL ID:
06078N
URL:
http://www.almapbbdo.com.br/awards/2006/greenpeace/clock

Merit Winners
175

BANNERS . FIXED SPACE:
PUBLIC SERVICE/NON-PROFIT/
EDUCATIONAL . SINGLE

AGENCY
glue / London
CLIENT
COI Royal Navy

ART DIRECTORS:
glue creatives
WRITERS:
glue creatives
DESIGNERS:
Matt Verity, Leon Ostle
CREATIVE DIRECTOR:
Seb Royce
ANNUAL ID:
06079N
URL:
http://www.gluelondon.com
/awards/oneshow/

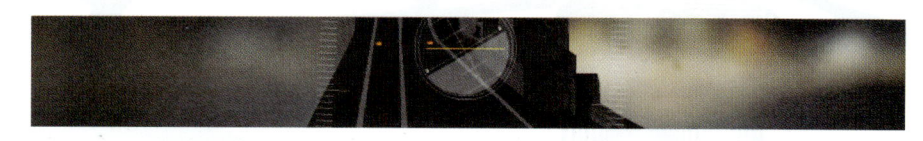

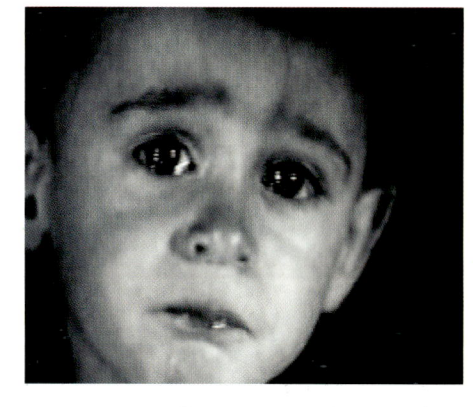

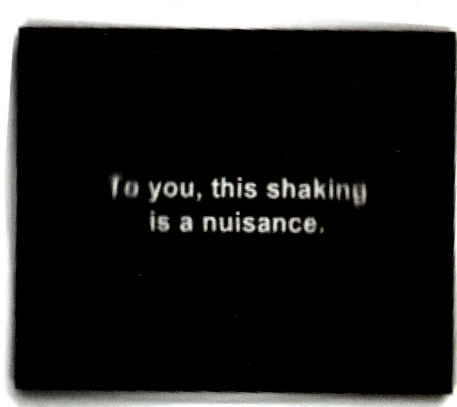

BANNERS . FIXED SPACE:
PUBLIC SERVICE/NON-PROFIT/
EDUCATIONAL . CAMPAIGN

AGENCY
Agency.com / London
CLIENT
NSPCC

ART DIRECTOR:
Scott Bedford
WRITER:
Jon Mackness
DESIGNERS:
Wil Bevan, Rob Mills
Paul Collins
CREATIVE DIRECTOR:
Paul Banham
ANNUAL ID:
06080N
URL:
http://awards.london.agency.com
/nspcc/july_05/

BANNERS . DYNAMIC:
BUSINESS TO CONSUMER . SINGLE

AGENCY
BEAM Interactive / Boston
CLIENT
MINI USA

ART DIRECTOR:
Jamie Bakum
PROGRAMMERS:
Sam Roach, Keith Peters
DIGITAL ARTIST/MULTIMEDIA:
James Cho
CREATIVE DIRECTORS:
Birch Norton, Jeff Benjamin
ANNUAL ID:
06081N
URL:
http://stage.beamland.com/
award_shows/mini/coneman_demo/
coneman_cardomain.html

BANNERS . DYNAMIC:
BUSINESS TO CONSUMER . SINGLE

AGENCY
Dentsu / Tokyo
CLIENT
Fumakilla Co.

ART DIRECTOR:
Masayoshi Niwa
WRITER:
Masayoshi Niwa
DESIGNER:
Hiroki Nakamura
PROGRAMMER:
Masumi Oobuchi
DIGITAL ARTISTS/MULTIMEDIA:
Hiroki Nakamura
Masayoshi Niwa
CREATIVE DIRECTOR:
Masayoshi Niwa
CONTENT STRATEGIST:
Masayoshi Niwa
ANNUAL ID:
06082N
URL:
http://www.interactive-salaryman.com
/pieces/fuma_super_e/

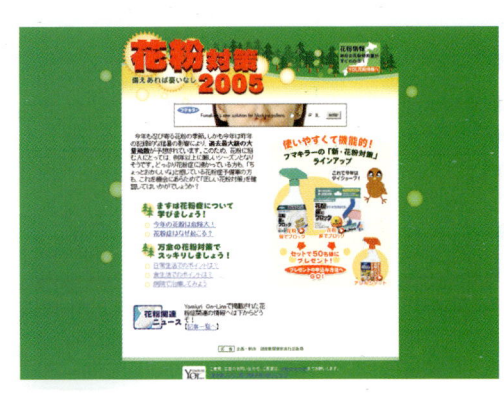

Merit Winners
177

BANNERS . DYNAMIC:
BUSINESS TO CONSUMER . SINGLE

AGENCY
DoubleYou / Barcelona

CLIENT
Diageo

ART DIRECTORS:
Blanca Piera, Ana Delgado
WRITERS:
Emma Pueyo, Paco Conde
DESIGNERS:
Nacho Guijarro, Lisi Badía
PROGRAMMERS:
Xavi Caparrós, Joakim Borgström
DIGITAL ARTISTS/MULTIMEDIA:
Nacho Guijarro, Daniel González
Davis Lisboa, Xavi Caparrós
Quique Alcatena
CREATIVE DIRECTORS:
Daniel Solana, Joakim Borgström
Marta Rico, Judith Francisco
CONTENT STRATEGISTS:
Sascha Kraft
Álvaro Olalquiaga
ANNUAL ID:
06083N
URL:
http://festivals.doubleyou.com/2006
/caciquecampaign/oneshow.html

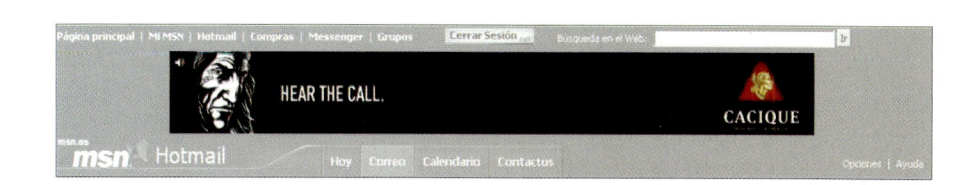

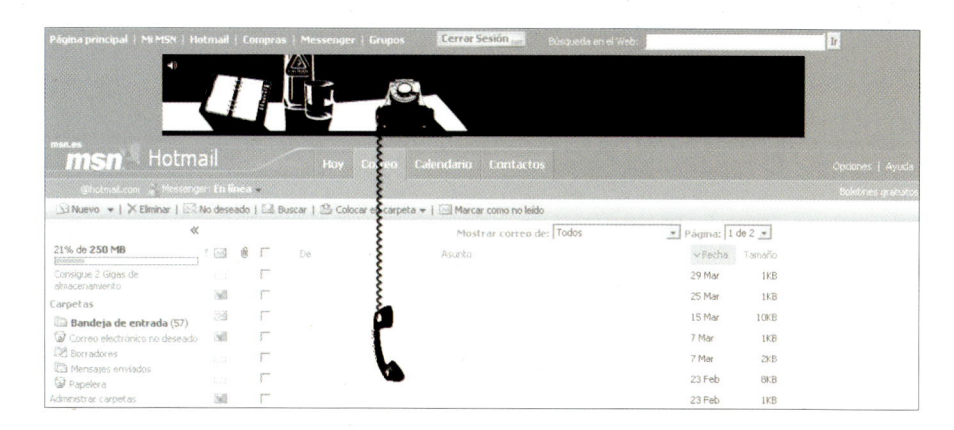

BANNERS . DYNAMIC:
BUSINESS TO CONSUMER . SINGLE

AGENCY
Euro RSCG 4D / São Paulo

CLIENT
Reckitt Benckiser

ART DIRECTOR:
Valter Klug
WRITER:
Fábio Pierro
DESIGNER:
Euro RSCG 4D
PROGRAMMER:
Euro RSCG 4D
CREATIVE DIRECTORS:
Alon Sochaczewski
Marcio Paiva
ANNUAL ID:
06084N
URL:
http://www.itsrainingagain.com
/english/13

BANNERS . DYNAMIC:
BUSINESS TO CONSUMER . SINGLE

AGENCY
Lean Mean Fighting
Machine / London
CLIENT
Too Far Publishing

DESIGNERS:
Mark Beacock
Jonas Persson
Jessica Pillings
PROGRAMMER:
Dave Cox
CONTENT STRATEGIST:
Tom Bazeley
CREATIVE DIRECTORS:
Sam Ball
Dave Bedwood
ANNUAL ID:
06085N
URL:
http://www.leanmean
fightingmachine.co.uk/
wildanimus/pillings

BANNERS . DYNAMIC:
BUSINESS TO CONSUMER . SINGLE

AGENCY
McKinney / Durham
CLIENT
Audi of America

ART DIRECTOR:
Jason Musante
WRITERS:
Matt Fischvogt, Brian Cain
Gregg Hale, Jim Gunshanon
Ernie Larsen
DESIGNER:
Justin Smith
PRODUCTION COMPANY:
Chelsea Pictures/campfire
CREATIVE DIRECTORS:
Dave Cook, Jonathan Cude
David Baldwin, Brian Clark
ANNUAL ID:
06086N
URL:
http://www.awardshowsubmissions.com
/06oneshow/

Merit Winners
179

BANNERS . DYNAMIC:
BUSINESS TO CONSUMER . SINGLE

AGENCY
Proximity / Singapore

CLIENT
WD-40

ART DIRECTOR:
Kun

WRITER:
Juliana Koh

CREATIVE DIRECTOR:
Jon Pye

ANNUAL ID:
06087N

URL:
http://202.157.162.188/web
/awards/wd40/smooth.htm

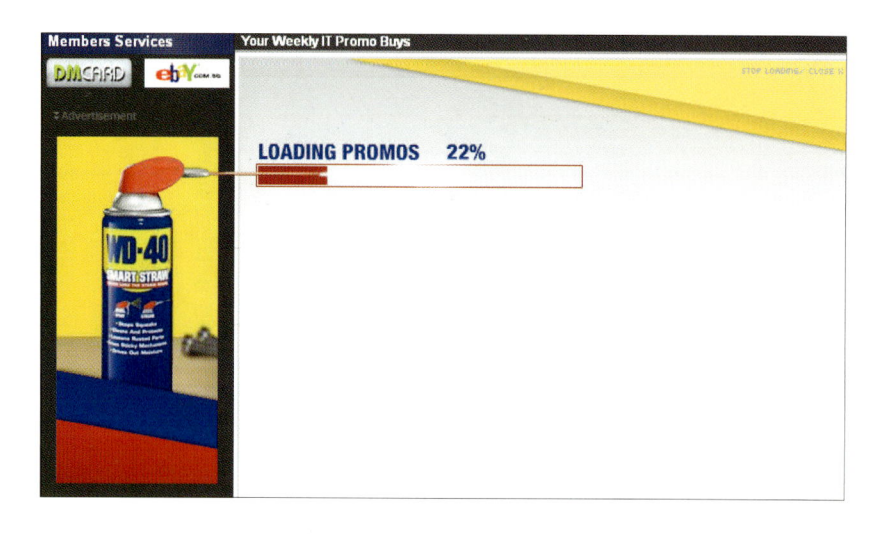

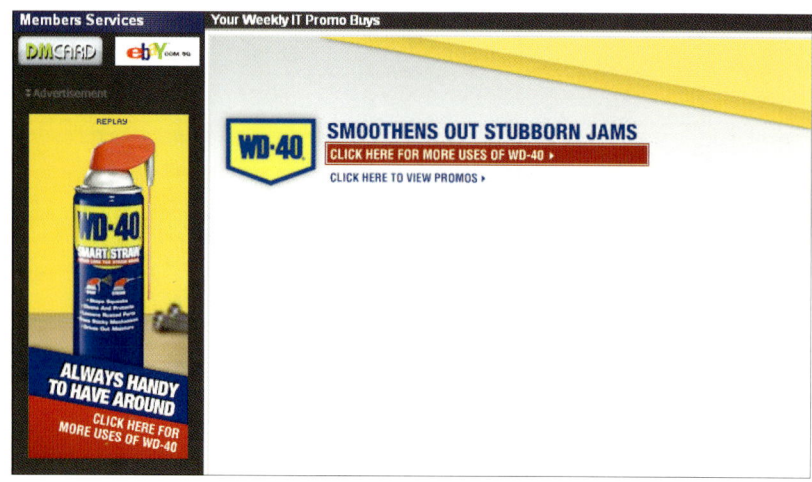

BANNERS . DYNAMIC:
BUSINESS TO CONSUMER . SINGLE

AGENCY
Tribal DDB / New York

CLIENT
Philips

ART DIRECTOR:
Gabrielle DiClemente

WRITER:
Cedric Devitt

DIGITAL ARTIST/MULTIMEDIA:
Benjamin Weisman

CREATIVE DIRECTORS:
Duncan Mitchell
Steve Nesle

ANNUAL ID:
06088N

URL:
http://www.tribalddb.com/ny
/awards/norelco/index.html

180 MERIT WINNERS // PROXIMITY // TRIBAL DDB // VCCP // AGÊNCIACLICK

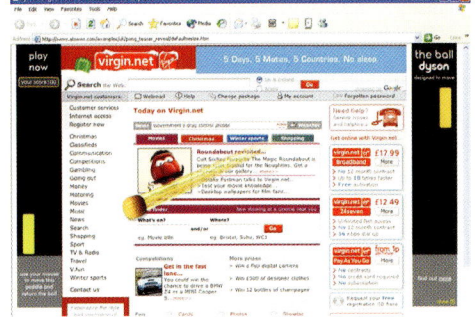

BANNERS . DYNAMIC:
BUSINESS TO CONSUMER . SINGLE

AGENCY
vccp / London
CLIENT
Dyson

ART DIRECTOR:
Steve Vranakis
DESIGNER:
@www
PROGRAMMER:
@www
CREATIVE DIRECTOR:
Steve Vranakis
ANNUAL ID:
06089N
URL:
http://www.atwww.com/
examples/uk/pong_
teaser_reveal/defaultresize.htm

BANNERS . DYNAMIC:
BUSINESS TO CONSUMER . CAMPAIGN

AGENCY
AgênciaClick / São Paulo
CLIENT
Fiat Automóveis

ART DIRECTORS:
Domênico Massareto
Cesar Augusto Marchetti
Diego Cardoso
WRITERS:
Tatiane Bernardi
Domênico Massareto
DESIGNER:
João Luis da Silva Lopes
CREATIVE DIRECTOR:
Ricardo Figueira
ANNUAL ID:
06090N
URL:
http://www.virtualsofa.net
/2006/fiatidea/campanhatestdrive/en

Merit Winners
181

BANNERS . DYNAMIC: BUSINESS TO
CONSUMER . CAMPAIGN

AGENCY
Arnold Worldwide / Boston and
Crispin Porter + Bogusky / Miami
CLIENT
American Legacy Foundation

ART DIRECTOR:
Meghan Siegal
WRITER:
Marc Einhorn
DESIGNER:
Meghan Siegal
PROGRAMMERS:
Andrew McNutt, John Policano
CREATIVE DIRECTORS:
Ron Lawner, Pete Favat
Alex Bogusky, John Kearse, Tom Adams
ANNUAL ID:
06091N
URL:
http://awards.arn.com/2005/awards
/hatch/Truth/Seek/banners.html

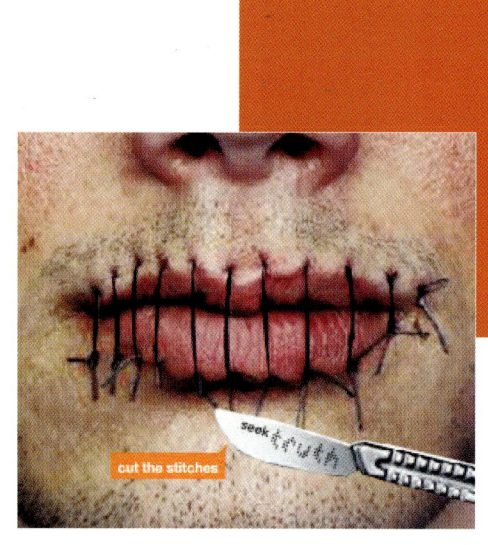

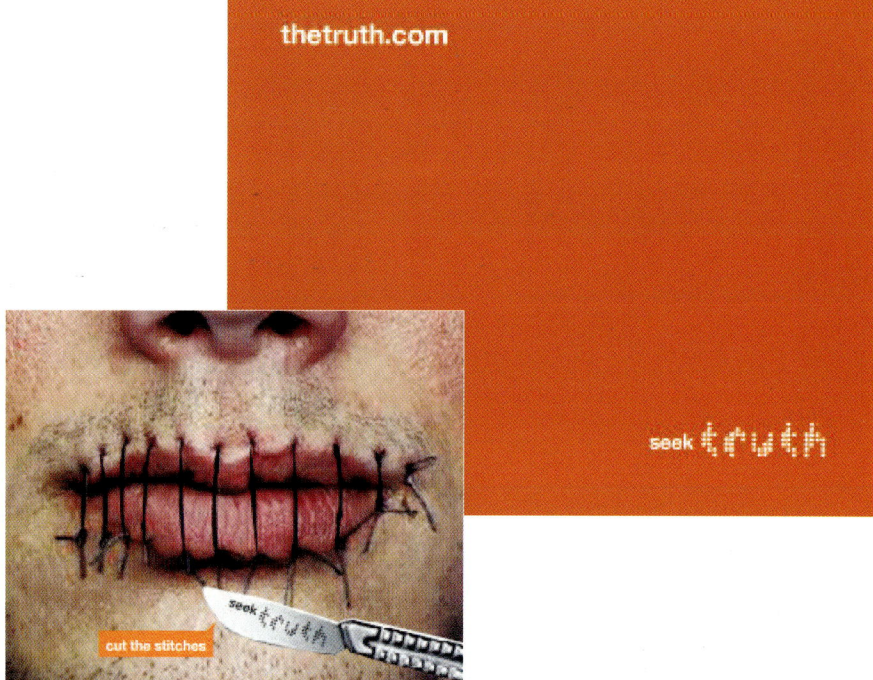

BANNERS . DYNAMIC:
BUSINESS TO CONSUMER . CAMPAIGN

AGENCY
Lowe Tesch / Stockholm
CLIENT
Saab Automobile

ART DIRECTOR:
Patrik Westerdahl
WRITER:
Cissi Högkvist
DIGITAL ARTISTS/MULTIMEDIA:
Tobias Löfgren, Peter Eneroth
CREATIVE DIRECTOR:
Niklas Wallberg
ANNUAL ID:
06092N
URL:
http://www.lowetesch.com/showroom
/saab/93caution/

182 MERIT WINNERS // ARNOLD WORLDWIDE / CRISPIN PORTER + BOGUSKY // LOWE TESCH // DOMANI STUDIOS // JWT HAMBURG

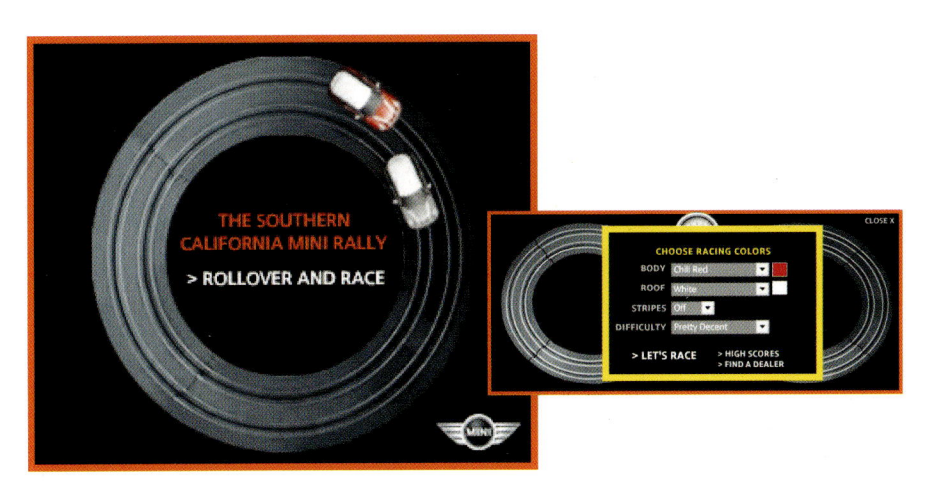

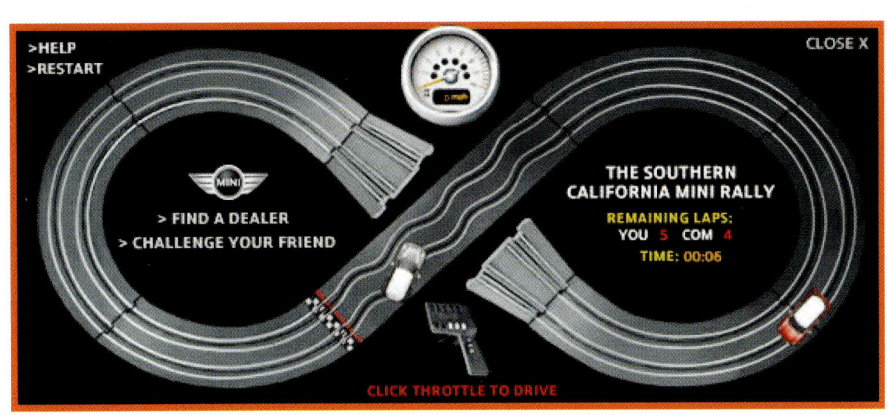

BANNERS . DYNAMIC:
PROMOTIONAL ADVERTISING . SINGLE

AGENCY
Domani Studios / Brooklyn
CLIENT
MINI

DIGITAL ARTIST/MULTIMEDIA:
Domani Studios
CREATIVE DIRECTOR:
Crispin Porter + Bogusky
ANNUAL ID:
06093N
URL:
http://domanistudios.com
/samples/mini/

BANNERS . DYNAMIC:
SELF-PROMOTION . SINGLE

AGENCY
JWT / Hamburg
CLIENT
Heide Park Soltau

ART DIRECTOR:
Jens Pantzke
WRITER:
Oliver von Kempen
DESIGNER:
Davies Meyer
PROGRAMMER:
Davies Meyer
CREATIVE DIRECTOR:
Torsten Rieken
ANNUAL ID:
06094N
URL:
http://banner.daviesmeyer.de
/heidepark/index_english.html

Merit Winners
183

BANNERS . DYNAMIC:
PUBLIC SERVICE/NON-PROFIT /
EDUCATIONAL . SINGLE

AGENCY
Tribal DDB / Dallas

CLIENT
happytaxday.com

ART DIRECTORS:
Eric Snodgrass
Jordan Kretchmer

WRITER:
Geoff Owens

DIGITAL ARTIST/MULTIMEDIA:
Justin Kipner

CREATIVE DIRECTORS:
Scott Johnson, Travis Stout
Braden Bickle

ANNUAL ID:
06095N

URL:
http://www.happytaxday.com
/unclesam/index.html

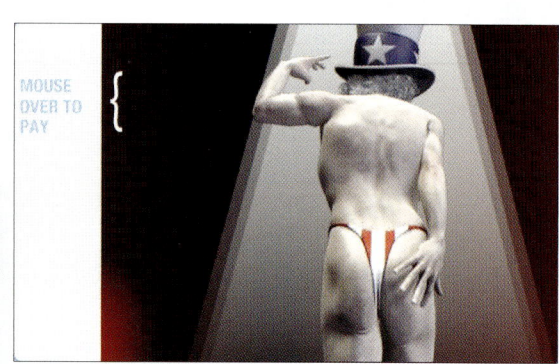

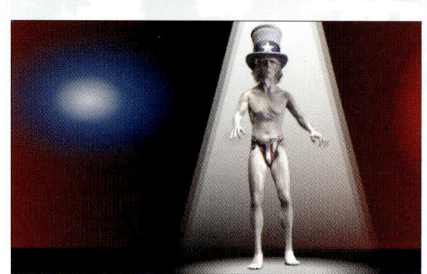

BEYOND THE BANNER:
BUSINESS TO CONSUMER . SINGLE

AGENCY
Agency Republic / London

CLIENT
Egg

ART DIRECTOR:
Andy Sandoz

WRITER:
Chris Bayliss

DESIGNER:
Russ Tucker

ANNUAL ID:
06096N

URL:
http://agencyrepublic.net
/awards/egg_creatives

184   MERIT WINNERS // TRIBAL DDB DALLAS // AGENCY REPUBLIC // AGÊNCIACLICK // ALMAPBBDO

BEYOND THE BANNER:
BUSINESS TO CONSUMER . SINGLE

AGENCY
AgênciaClick/ São Paulo
CLIENT
The Coca-Cola Company

ART DIRECTOR:
Fred Siqueira
DESIGNER:
Haydee Uekubo
CREATIVE DIRECTOR:
Ricardo Figueira
ANNUAL ID:
06097N
URL:
http://www.virtualsofa.net/2006/cocacola/brincadeiradecrianca/en

BEYOND THE BANNER:
BUSINESS TO CONSUMER . SINGLE

AGENCY
AlmapBBDO / São Paulo
CLIENT
Bauducco

ART DIRECTOR:
Caetano Carvalho
WRITER:
Luciana Haguiara
DESIGNER:
Carmelo di Lorenzo
PROGRAMMER:
Flávio Ramos
DIGITAL ARTIST/MULTIMEDIA:
Ricardo Martins
CREATIVE DIRECTOR:
Sergio Mugnaini
ANNUAL ID:
06098N
URL:
http://www.almapbbdo.com.br/awards/2006/bauducco/boy

Merit Winners
185

BEYOND THE BANNER:
BUSINESS TO CONSUMER . SINGLE

AGENCY
Arnold Worldwide / Boston

CLIENT
Volkswagen

ART DIRECTORS:
Dmitri Cavander
Gabriel Jeffrey
Jen Wells
WRITERS:
Sy Ingoglia
Kerry Lynch
DESIGNERS:
Sean Conrad
Raoul Kim
PROGRAMMERS:
WDDG
Roy Wetherbee
INFORMATION ARCHITECT:
Dave Cumberbatch
CREATIVE DIRECTORS:
Ron Lawner, Alan Pafenbach
Dave Weist, Chris Bradley
ANNUAL ID:
06099N
URL:
http://www.forceofgood.com

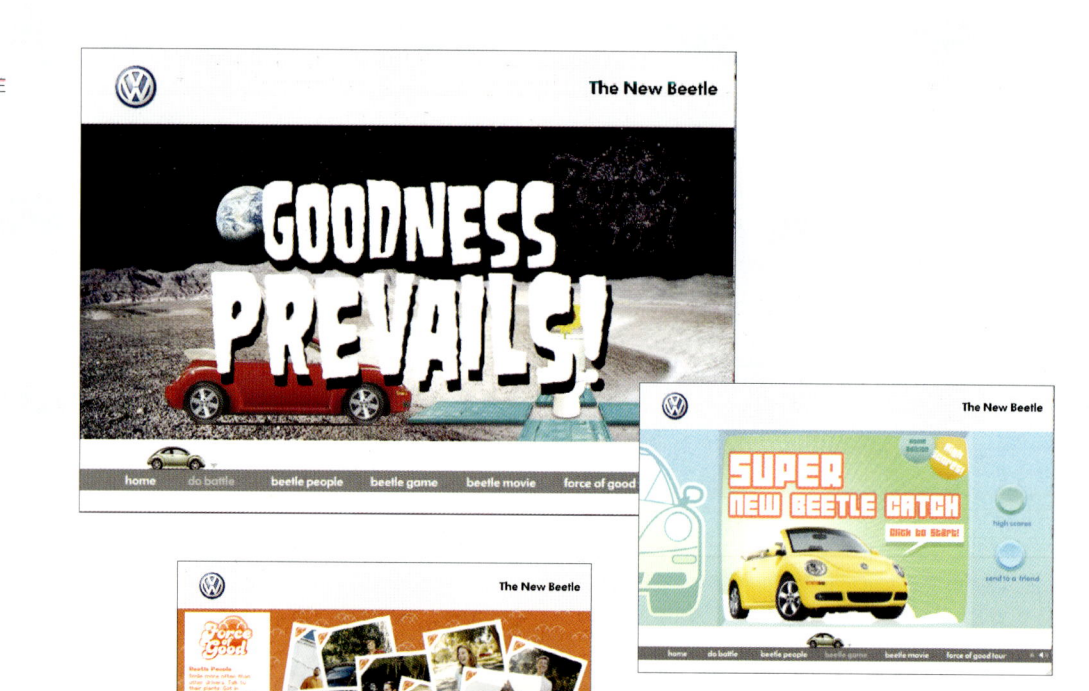

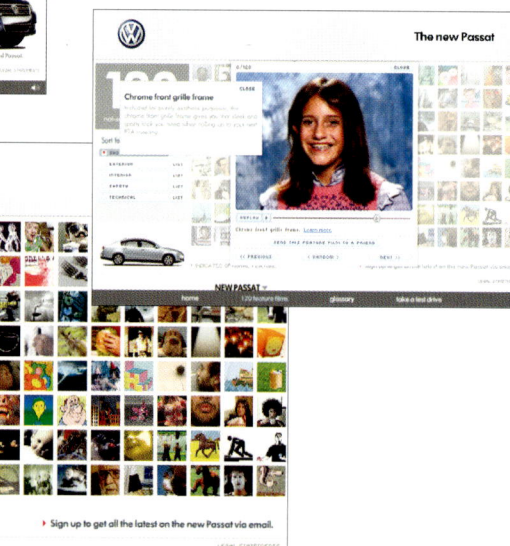

BEYOND THE BANNER: BUSINESS TO CONSUMER . SINGLE

AGENCY
Arnold Worldwide / Boston

CLIENT
Volkswagen

ART DIRECTORS:
Colin Jefferey, Phillip Squier
Paulo Lopez, Paul Lee
WRITERS:
Dave Weist
Chris Carl
PROGRAMMERS:
Roy Wetherbee
The Barbarian Group
INFORMATION ARCHITECT:
Dave Cumberbatch
CREATIVE DIRECTORS:
Ron Lawner, Alan Pafenbach
Chris Carl, Chris Bradley
ANNUAL ID:
06100N
URL:
http://awards.arn.com/2005/shared/vw/minisites/Passat_120/index.html

186   MERIT WINNERS // ARNOLD WORLDWIDE // CRISPIN PORTER + BOGUSKY // DADDY

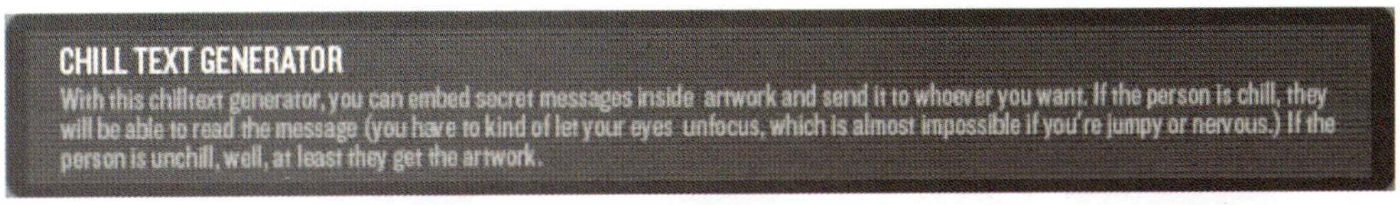

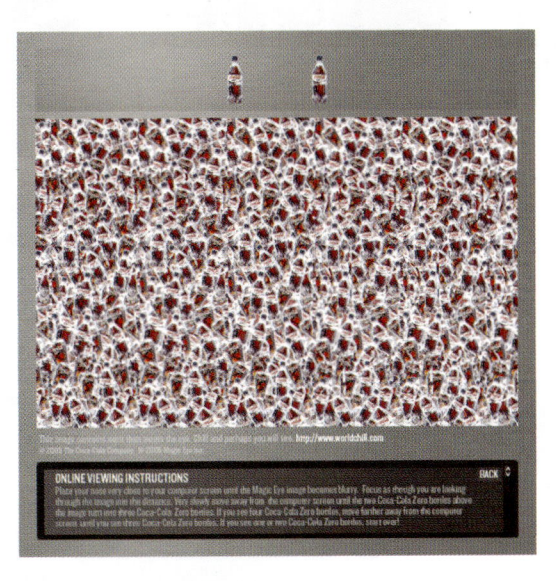

CHILL TEXT GENERATOR
With this chilltext generator, you can embed secret messages inside artwork and send it to whoever you want. If the person is chill, they will be able to read the message (you have to kind of let your eyes unfocus, which is almost impossible if you're jumpy or nervous.) If the person is unchill, well, at least they get the artwork.

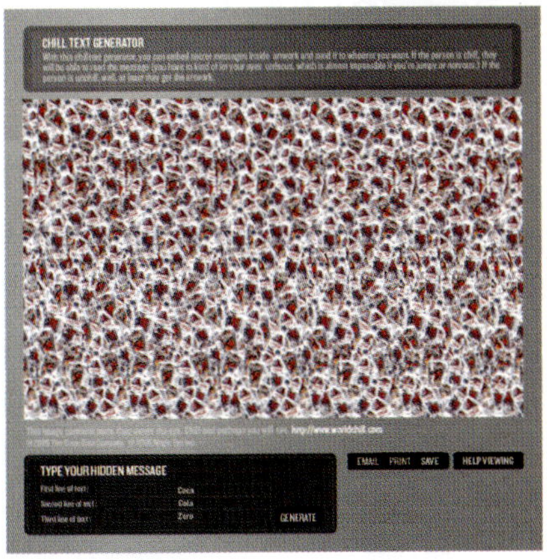

BEYOND THE BANNER:
BUSINESS TO CONSUMER . SINGLE

AGENCY
Crispin Porter + Bogusky / Miami

CLIENT
Coke Zero

PRODUCTION COMPANY:
Magic Eye

CREATIVE DIRECTORS:
Andrew Keller, Dave Schiff
Jeff Benjamin, Alex Bogusky

ANNUAL ID:
06101N

URL:
http://www.cpbgroup.com/awards/chilltext.html

BEYOND THE BANNER:
BUSINESS TO CONSUMER . SINGLE

AGENCY
Daddy / Gothenburg

CLIENT
Carlsberg Sverige

ART DIRECTOR:
Christian Knutsson

WRITER:
Johan Kruse

DESIGNER:
Tommy Carlsson

PROGRAMMERS:
Marcus Åslund
Daniel Pilsetnek

DIGITAL ARTIST/MULTIMEDIA:
Erik Sterner

CONTENT STRATEGISTS:
Gustav Martner
Robert Waern

CREATIVE DIRECTOR:
Björn Höglund

ANNUAL ID:
06102N

URL:
http://www.daddy.se/oneshow2006/falcon_bestseats/

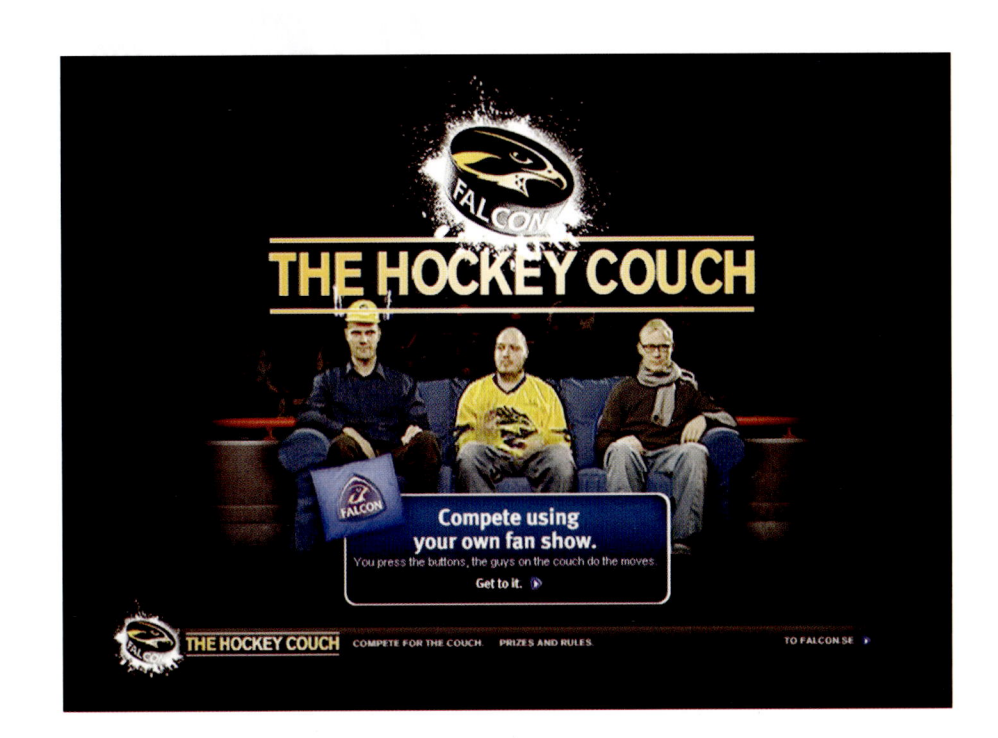

Merit Winners
187

BEYOND THE BANNER:
BUSINESS TO CONSUMER . SINGLE

AGENCY
Daddy / Gothenburg

CLIENT
Carlsberg Sverige

ART DIRECTOR:
Christian Knutsson

WRITER:
Johan Kruse

PROGRAMMERS:
Marcus Åslund
Per Rundgren

DIGITAL ARTISTS/MULTIMEDIA:
Erik Sterner
Tommy Carlsson

CONTENT STRATEGISTS:
Gustav Martner, Robert Waern
Robert German

CREATIVE DIRECTOR:
Björn Höglund

ANNUAL ID:
06103N

URL:
http://www.daddy.se/oneshow2006/falcon_theduel/

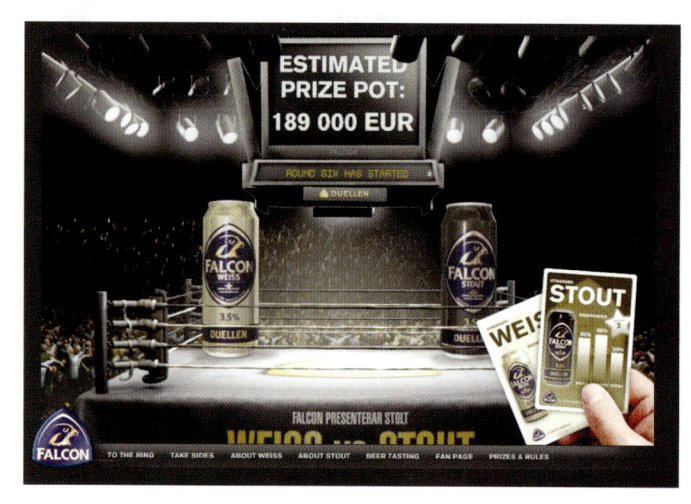

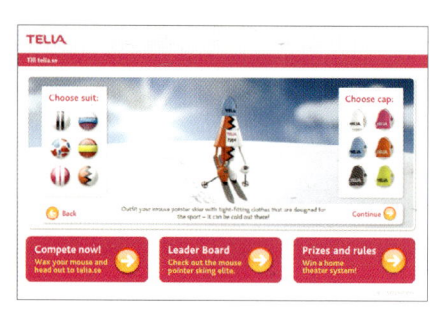

BEYOND THE BANNER:
BUSINESS TO CONSUMER . SINGLE

AGENCY
Daddy / Gothenburg

CLIENT
TeliaSonera

WRITER:
Johan Kruse

DESIGNERS:
Albert Isaksson,
Robert Melander

PROGRAMMERS:
Daniel Pilsetnek
Marcus Åslund

CONTENT STRATEGIST:
Gustav Martner

CREATIVE DIRECTOR:
Björn Höglund

ANNUAL ID:
06104N

URL:
http://www.daddy.se/oneshow2006/telia_crosscountry/

188 MERIT WINNERS // DADDY

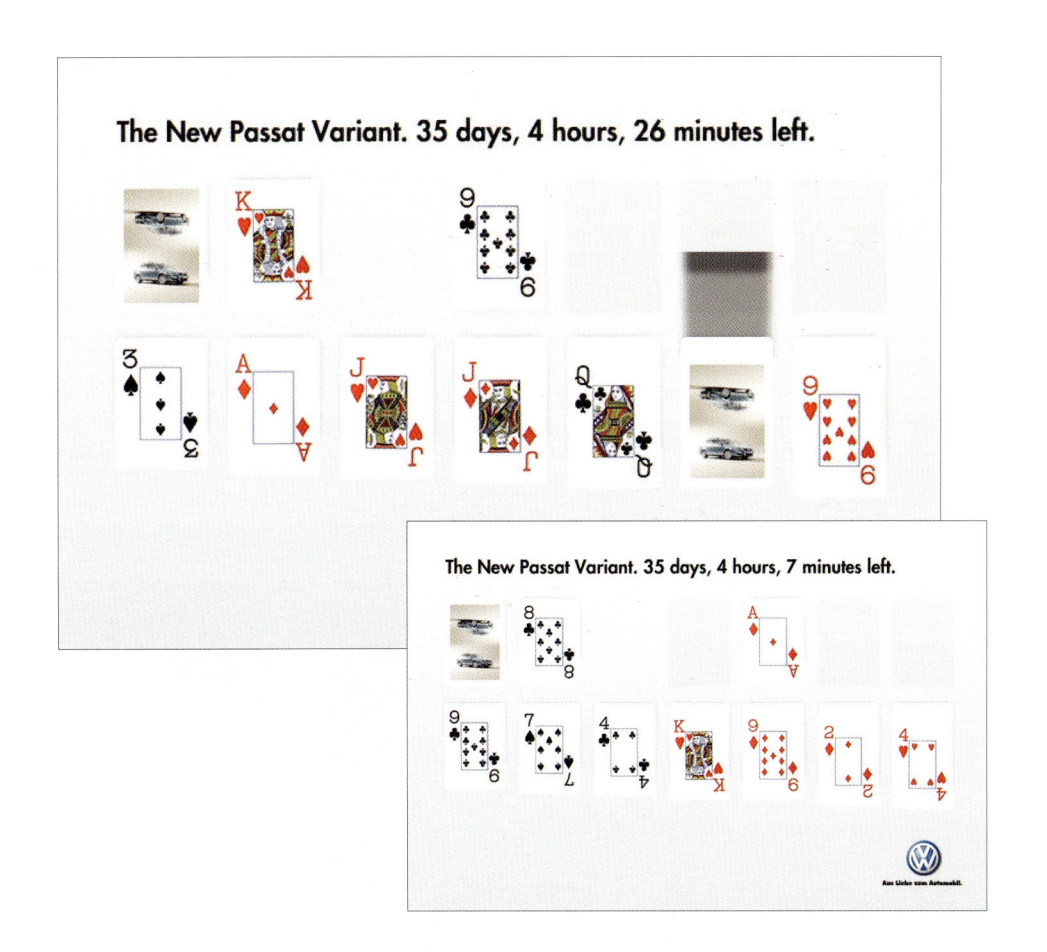

BEYOND THE BANNER: BUSINESS TO
CONSUMER . SINGLE

AGENCY
Daddy / Gothenburg
CLIENT
Volksvagen Sverige

ART DIRECTOR:
Björn Höglund
WRITER:
Johan Kruse
PROGRAMMER:
Daniel Pilsetnek
DIGITAL ARTIST/MULTIMEDIA:
Erik Sterner
CONTENT STRATEGIST:
Gustav Martner
CREATIVE DIRECTOR:
Björn Höglund
ANNUAL ID:
06105N
URL:
http://www.daddy.se/oneshow2006/passat_variantteaser/

BEYOND THE BANNER:
BUSINESS TO CONSUMER . SINGLE

AGENCY
Daddy / Gothenburg
CLIENT
Volkswagen Sverige

ART DIRECTOR:
Björn Höglund
WRITER:
Johan Kruse
PROGRAMMERS:
Daniel Pilsetnek, Per Rundgren
DIGITAL ARTIST/MULTIMEDIA:
Erik Sterner
CONTENT STRATEGIST:
Gustav Martner
CREATIVE DIRECTOR:
Björn Höglund
ANNUAL ID:
06106N
URL:
http://www.daddy.se/oneshow2006/passat_launchsite/

Merit Winners
189

BEYOND THE BANNER:
BUSINESS TO CONSUMER . SINGLE

AGENCY
DDB Brasil / São Paulo
CLIENT
Tok&Stok

ART DIRECTORS:
Mauricio Mazzariol
Alexandre D'Albergaria
WRITER:
Keke Toledo
PRODUCTION COMPANIES:
Roberta Padilla, Renata Oliveira
Sandra Zimb, Helena Bordon
INFORMATION ARCHITECT:
Heloisa Lima
CREATIVE DIRECTORS:
Sergio Valente, Miguel Bemfica
Mariana Sa, Fernanda Romano
ANNUAL ID:
06107N
URL:
http://www.dm9ddb.com.br/awards/oneshow/kamasutra.html

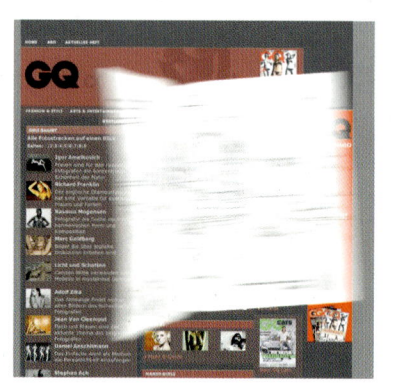

BEYOND THE BANNER:
BUSINESS TO CONSUMER . SINGLE

AGENCY
DDB Germany / Berlin
CLIENT
Volkswagen

ART DIRECTOR:
Sandra Schilling
WRITER:
Ulrich Lützenkirchen
DIGITAL ARTISTS/MULTIMEDIA:
Clemens Mahler, Mathias Persch
Daniel Rothaug
PRODUCTION COMPANY:
Robert Wauer
CREATIVE DIRECTORS:
Wolfgang Schneider
Mathias Stiller
CONTENT STRATEGIST:
Malte Sudendorf
ANNUAL ID:
06108N
URL:
www.azionare.de/awards/gti

190   MERIT WINNERS // DDB BRASIL // DDB GERMANY // FORSMAN & BODENFORS

BEYOND THE BANNER:
BUSINESS TO CONSUMER . SINGLE

AGENCY
DDB Germany / Berlin
CLIENT
Volkswagen

WRITER:
Andrea Geiter
PROGRAMMERS:
Werner Goldbach
Christian Rudolph
DIGITAL ARTISTS/MULTIMEDIA:
Matthias Persch, Daniel Rothaug
PRODUCTION COMPANY:
Robert Wauer
CREATIVE DIRECTOR:
Mathias Stiller
CONTENT STRATEGISTS:
Wiebke Dreyer, Malte Sudendorf
Michael Betz
ANNUAL ID:
06109N
URL:
http://www.de.ddb.com/online-cases
/fox/english/index.html

BEYOND THE BANNER: BUSINESS TO
CONSUMER - SINGLE

AGENCY
Forsman & Bodenfors /
Gothenburg
CLIENT
Abba Seafood

ART DIRECTORS:
Martin Cedergren
Joakim Blondell
WRITERS:
Martin Ringqvist
Jacob Nelson
PRODUCTION COMPANIES:
B-Reel , Swiss
ANNUAL ID:
06110N
URL:
http://demo.fb.se/e
/abba/designtube/

Merit Winners
191

BEYOND THE BANNER:
BUSINESS TO CONSUMER . SINGLE

AGENCY
Genex / Los Angeles

CLIENT
Acura

ART DIRECTOR:
Wilson Yin
WRITER:
Adair Seldon
DESIGNERS:
Wilson Yin, Daniel Alegria
PROGRAMMER:
Jon Ruppel
INFORMATION ARCHITECTS:
Wilson Yin, Sara Gallivan
CREATIVE DIRECTOR:
David Glaze
ANNUAL ID:
06111N
URL:
http://www.acura.com/index.aspx?initPath=RL_Explore_InteractiveShowroom_intro

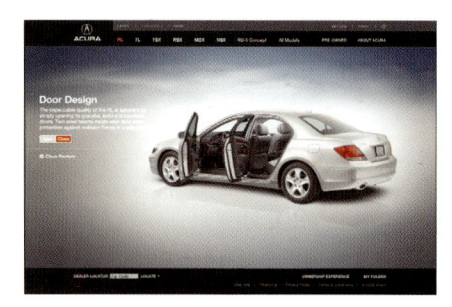

BEYOND THE BANNER:
BUSINESS TO CONSUMER . SINGLE

AGENCY
Genex / Los Angeles
CLIENT
Acura

ART DIRECTORS:
Michael Takeashita
Eric Wergerbauer
WRITERS:
Adair Seldon
George Langworthy
DESIGNERS:
Benny Campa
Michael Takeashita
PROGRAMMER:
Patrick Mullady
INFORMATION ARCHITECT:
Sara Gallivan
CREATIVE DIRECTOR:
David Glaze
ANNUAL ID:
06112N
URL:
http://www.acura.com/index.aspx?initPath=RSX_Explore_ExperiencetheRSX

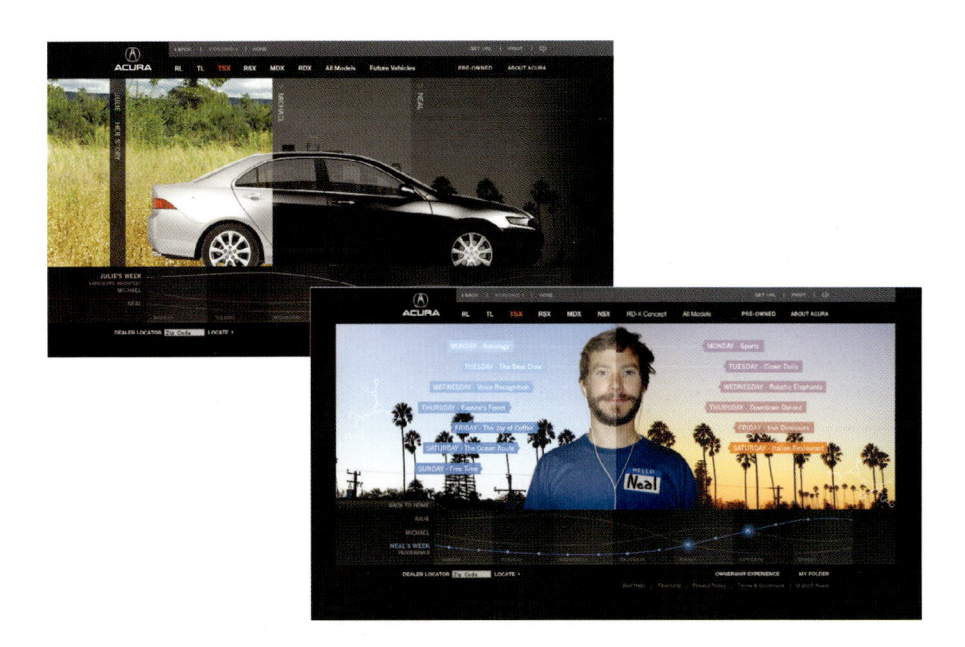

BEYOND THE BANNER:
BUSINESS TO CONSUMER . SINGLE

AGENCY
Genex / Los Angeles
CLIENT
Acura

ART DIRECTORS:
Eric Wergerbauer, Simona Lo
Kelly Kliebe
WRITER:
George Langworthy
DESIGNERS:
Simona Lo, Crispin Bixler
Ryan Conlin
DIGITAL ARTISTS/MULTIMEDIA:
Alex Bunin, Rebecca Cabbage
Simona Lo, Ryan Conlin
Crispin Bixler, Vinny Pacheco
INFORMATION ARCHITECT:
Sara Gallivan
CREATIVE DIRECTORS:
David Glaze
Eric Wergerbauer
ANNUAL ID:
06113N
URL:
http://www.acura.com/index.aspx?initPath=TSX_Explore_ExperiencetheTSX

BEYOND THE BANNER:
BUSINESS TO CONSUMER . SINGLE

AGENCY
NetX / Sydney
CLIENT
Virgin Atlantic Airways

ART DIRECTOR:
Sean Ganann
WRITER:
Sean Ganann
DESIGNER:
Yas Nakano
PROGRAMMER:
Yas Nakano
CREATIVE DIRECTOR:
Sean Ganann
ANNUAL ID:
06114N
URL:
http://staging.dataport.com.au/Awards/virginatlantic_phobias/

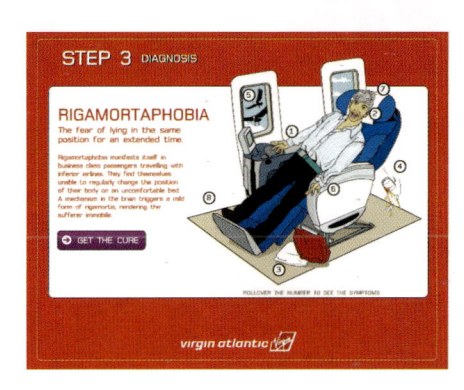

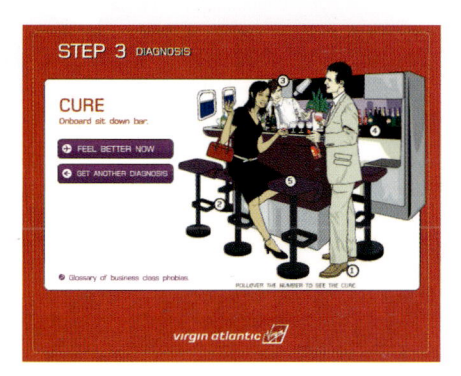

Merit Winners
193

BEYOND THE BANNER:
BUSINESS TO CONSUMER . SINGLE

AGENCY
North Kingdom / Skellefteå

CLIENT
Toyota Sweden

ART DIRECTORS:
Bjarne Melin
Andreas Hellström

WRITER:
Anders Lidzell

DESIGNERS:
Staffan Lamm
Mattias Möller

PROGRAMMER:
Isak Wiström

PRODUCTION COMPANIES:
Rebekah Kvart, Roger Stighäll

ANNUAL ID:
06115N

URL:
http://www.northkingdom.com/competition/aygo/en/

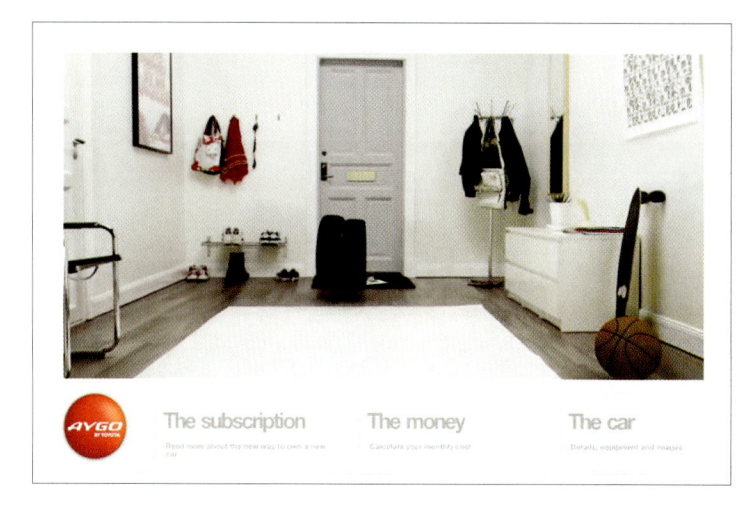

BEYOND THE BANNER:
BUSINESS TO CONSUMER . SINGLE

AGENCY
Organic / San Francisco

CLIENT
Sprint

WRITER:
Ben Citron

DIGITAL ARTIST/MULTIMEDIA:
Aaron Clinger

DESIGNER:
Maria Tyomkina

PRODUCTION COMPANY:
V3@ Anonymous Content

CREATIVE DIRECTORS:
Christian Haas, Roger Wong
Ben Citron

ANNUAL ID:
06116N

URL:
http://awards.organic.com/entertain

194   MERIT WINNERS // NORTH KINGDOM // ORGANIC // POKE // PUBLICIS & HAL RINEY

BEYOND THE BANNER:
BUSINESS TO CONSUMER . SINGLE

AGENCY
POKE / London
CLIENT
Penguin Books

ART DIRECTOR:
Emil Lanne
DESIGNER:
Emil Lanne
PRODUCTION COMPANY:
POKE London
CREATIVE DIRECTOR:
Tom Hostler
ANNUAL ID:
06117N
URL:
http://www.happybirthday
penguin.com

BEYOND THE BANNER:
BUSINESS TO CONSUMER . SINGLE

AGENCY
Publicis & Hal Riney / San Francisco
CLIENT
Peter Kim Jewelry

ART DIRECTORS:
Colin Kim
Dominic Goldman
WRITERS:
Mike Danko
Jesse Dillow
PRODUCTION COMPANY:
Rocket Society
INFORMATION ARCHITECT:
Jim Vaughan
CREATIVE DIRECTORS:
Jae Goodman, Jon Soto
Dominic Goldman
ANNUAL ID:
06118N
URL:
www.hrp.com/peterkim/valentine

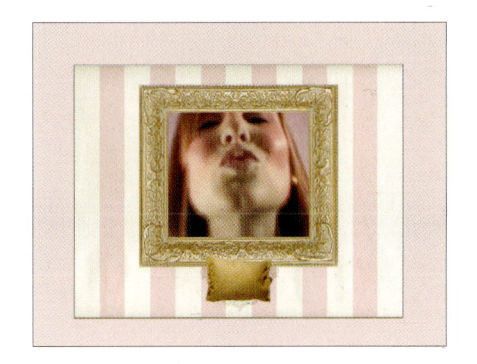

Merit Winners
195

BEYOND THE BANNER:
BUSINESS TO CONSUMER . SINGLE

AGENCY
R/GA / New York

CLIENT
Nike

ART DIRECTOR:
Marlon Hernandez

WRITERS:
Steve Caputo
Omid Fatemi

DESIGNERS:
Shu Zheng Li
Joseph Cartman
Yu-Ming Wu
Mike Reger

PROGRAMMERS:
Charles Duncan
Todd Kovner
Michele Roman

CREATIVE DIRECTOR:
Richard Ting

ANNUAL ID:
06119N

URL:
awards.web.rga.com
/2005/family.html

BEYOND THE BANNER:
BUSINESS TO CONSUMER . SINGLE

AGENCY
StrawberryFrog / Amsterdam

CLIENT
Asics: Onitsuka Tiger

ART DIRECTOR:
Erik Holmdahl

WRITERS:
Mark Chalmers
David Smith, Ute Geisler
Roos Smit

DESIGNERS:
Paul Hutcheson
Peppin from SaltedHerring
Kalle Thyselius

PRODUCTION COMPANIES:
Gavin Elder
Takaya Tomoko

CREATIVE DIRECTOR:
Mark Chalmers

ANNUAL ID:
06120N

URL:
http://onitsukatiger.com/lovely
football/index.html

196 MERIT WINNERS // R/GA // STRAWBERRYFROG // TAXI

BEYOND THE BANNER:
BUSINESS TO CONSUMER . SINGLE

AGENCY
TAXI / Toronto
CLIENT
MINI Canada

ART DIRECTOR:
Stephanie Yung
WRITER:
Jason McCann
DESIGNER:
Stephanie Yung
PROGRAMMER:
pixelpusher.ca
DIGITAL ARTIST/MULTIMEDIA:
Meld Media
INFORMATION ARCHITECT:
Amy Miranda
CREATIVE DIRECTORS:
Jason McCann
Steve Mykolyn
ANNUAL ID:
06121N
URL:
http://www.neverinneutral.com/dominatrix

BEYOND THE BANNER:
BUSINESS TO CONSUMER . SINGLE

AGENCY
TAXI / Toronto
CLIENT
MINI Canada

ART DIRECTOR:
Nuno Ferreira
WRITER:
Jason McCann
DESIGNER:
Nuno Ferreira
PRODUCTION COMPANY:
pixelpusher.ca
CREATIVE DIRECTORS:
Jason McCann
Steve Mykolyn
ANNUAL ID:
06122N
URL:
http://www.mini.ca/simulator

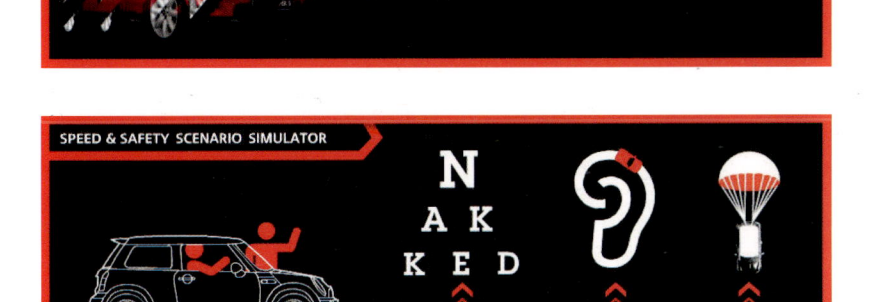

Merit Winners
197

BEYOND THE BANNER:
BUSINESS TO CONSUMER . SINGLE

AGENCY
Tribal DDB / New York

CLIENT
Jose Cuervo

ART DIRECTOR:
Shane Watson

WRITER:
Mike Condrick

DESIGNER:
Erick Vogel

PRODUCTION COMPANY:
Code & Theory

CREATIVE DIRECTORS:
Duncan Mitchelll
Steve Nesle

ANNUAL ID:
06123N

URL:
http://www.tribalddb.com/ny/awards/cuervo3/index.html

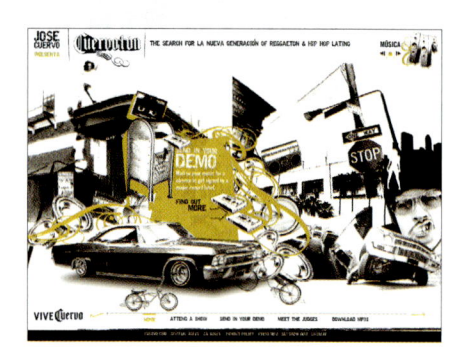

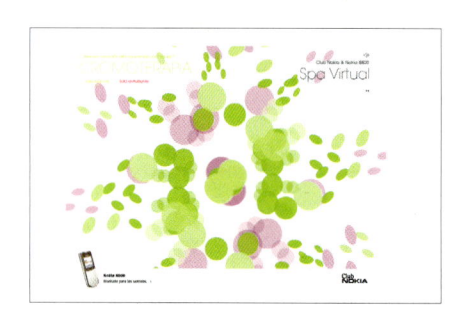

BEYOND THE BANNER:
BUSINESS TO CONSUMER . SINGLE

AGENCY
Wysiwyg Comunicación Interactiva / Madrid

CLIENT
Nokia

ART DIRECTOR:
Adolfo González

WRITER:
Nuria Martínez

PROGRAMMER:
Jordi Martínez

CONTENT STRATEGIST:
Ignacio Álvarez-Borrás

CREATIVE DIRECTORS:
Adolfo González, Nuria Martínez

ANNUAL ID:
06124N

URL:
www.wysiwyg.net/fests06/oneshow/index.html

198 MERIT WINNERS // TRIBAL DDB // WYSIWYG COMUNICACIÓN INTERACTIVA // DDB BRASIL // DOUBLEYOU

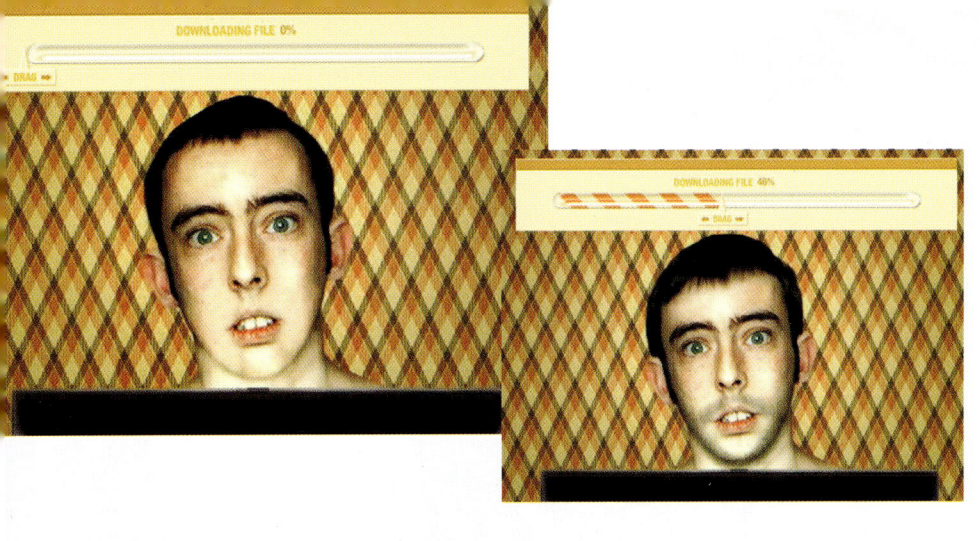

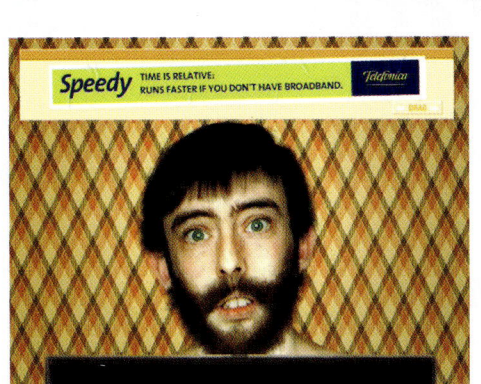

BEYOND THE BANNER:
BUSINESS TO CONSUMER . CAMPAIGN

AGENCY
DDB Brasil / São Paulo
CLIENT
Telefonica

ART DIRECTOR:
Mauricio Mazzariol
WRITER:
Keke Toledo
PRODUCTION COMPANIES:
Heloisa Lima, Roberta Padilla
Renata Oliveira, Sandra Zimb
Helena Bordon
CREATIVE DIRECTORS:
Sergio Valente, Marcos Medeiros
Wilson Mateos, Fernanda Romano
ANNUAL ID:
06125N
URL:
http://www.dm9ddb.com.br
/awards/oneshow/down
loads01.html

BEYOND THE BANNER:
PROMOTIONAL ADVERTISING . SINGLE

AGENCY
DoubleYou / Barcelona
CLIENT
Coca-Cola France

ART DIRECTOR:
Blanca Piera
WRITERS:
Emma Pueyo
Trini Rodríguez
DESIGNER:
Natalie Long
PROGRAMMER:
Jordi Martínez
DIGITAL ARTIST/MULTIMEDIA:
Jordi Martínez, Joakim Borgström
CONTENT STRATEGIST:
Jordi Pont
CREATIVE DIRECTORS:
Joakim Borgström
Frédéric Sanz
ANNUAL ID:
06126N
URL:
http://festivals.doubleyou.com/2006/
cokeblak/oneshow.html

Merit Winners
199

BEYOND THE BANNER:
PROMOTIONAL ADVERTISING . SINGLE

AGENCY
Goodby, Silverstein & Partners /
San Francisco
CLIENT
Saturn

ART DIRECTOR:
Will McGinness
WRITER:
Aaron Griffiths
PRODUCTION COMPANY:
exopolis
CONTENT STRATEGISTS:
Guy Overfelt, Mike Geiger
CREATIVE DIRECTORS:
Keith Anderson, Will McGinness
Jamie Barrett
ANNUAL ID:
06127N
URL:
http://www.goodbysilverstein.com/awards/oneshow_2006/saturn_sky_microsite/

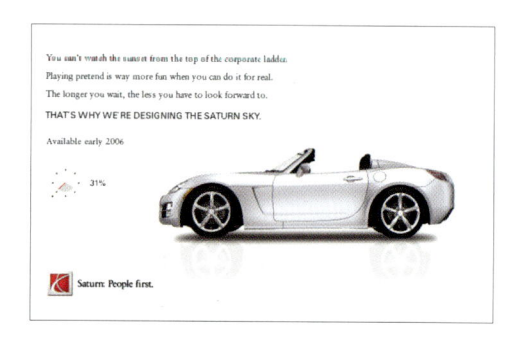

BEYOND THE BANNER:
PROMOTIONAL ADVERTISING . SINGLE

AGENCY
VIEW. / Cascais
CLIENT
Montepio Geral Bank

ART DIRECTOR:
Carlos Guedes
DESIGNERS:
Daniel Teixeira
Jean Pierre
PROGRAMMERS:
Andre Assalino
Rute Franca
CREATIVE DIRECTOR:
Joao Fernandes
ANNUAL ID:
06128N
URL:
www.e-ja-a-seguir.com

200   MERIT WINNERS-// GOODBY, SILVERSTEIN & PARTNERS // VIEW. // AKQA // FORSMAN & BODENFORS

BEYOND THE BANNER:
BUSINESS TO BUSINESS . SINGLE

AGENCY
AKQA / London
CLIENT
3M Corporate
ART DIRECTORS:
Miles Unwin, Kevin Russell
CREATIVE DIRECTOR:
Daniel Bonner
ANNUAL ID:
06129N
URL:
http://awards.akqa.com
/awards/3m/everywhere
/index.html

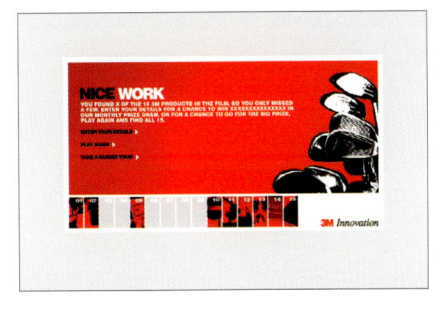

BEYOND THE BANNER:
BUSINESS TO BUSINESS . SINGLE

AGENCY
Forsman & Bodenfors / Gothenburg
CLIENT
Ministry of Health and Social Affairs

ART DIRECTORS:
Martin Cedergren
Silla Öberg
WRITER:
Jacob Nelson
DESIGNERS:
Lars Jansson
Viktor Larsson
PRODUCTION COMPANY:
Itiden
ANNUAL ID:
06130N
URL:
http://demo.fb.se/e/girlpower/retouch/

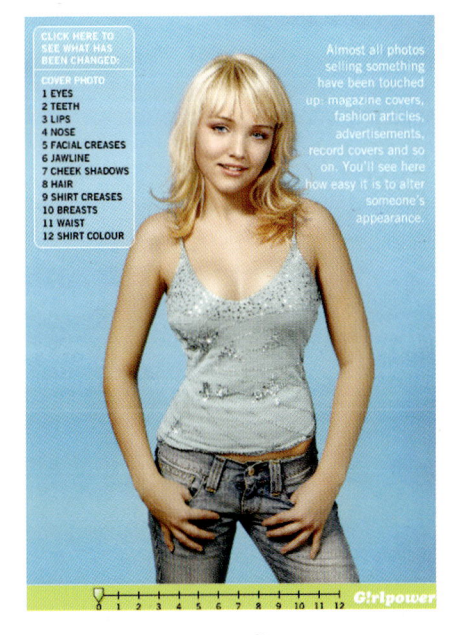

Merit Winners
201

BEYOND THE BANNER:
BUSINESS TO BUSINESS . SINGLE

AGENCY
OgilvyOne / New York
CLIENT
IBM

ART DIRECTOR:
Amy Hodgins
WRITERS:
Simon Foster
Krista Khun
PROGRAMMERS:
Ernie Parada
Filips Baumanis
Pharanai Suwannatat
Grant Janes
CREATIVE DIRECTORS:
Jan Leth
Greg Kaplan
Susan Westre
ANNUAL ID:
06131N
URL:
http://www.wwpl.net/ibm/helpdesk/helpdesk_microsite.html

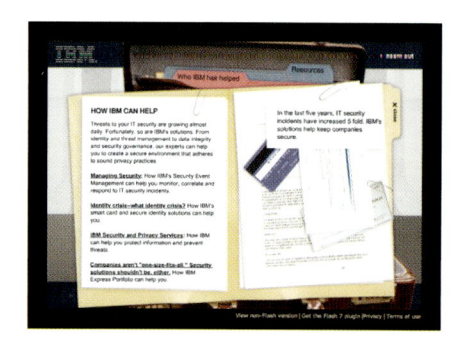

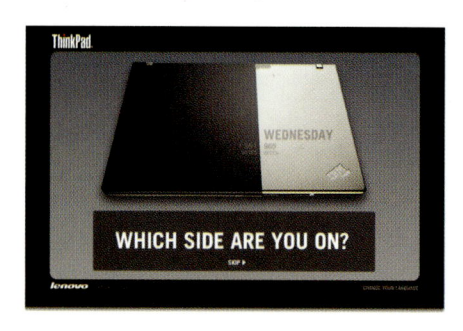

BEYOND THE BANNER:
BUSINESS TO BUSINESS . SINGLE

AGENCY
OgilvyOne / New York
CLIENT
Lenovo

ART DIRECTOR:
Alastair Green
WRITERS:
Simon Foster
Tristan Kincaid
PROGRAMMERS:
Jon Rubino
Irwin Horowitz
CREATIVE DIRECTORS:
Jan Leth, Andy Bernt
Jeff Curry
ANNUAL ID:
06132N
URL:
http://www.wwpl.net/lenovo/whichside.html

202 MERIT WINNERS // OGILVYONE // ARC WORLDWIDE / LEO BURNETT // OGILVYINTERACTIVE

BEYOND THE BANNER: PUBLIC SERVICE/
NON-PROFIT / EDUCATIONAL . SINGLE

AGENCY
Leo Burnett and Arc Worldwide /
Kuala Lumpur

CLIENT
Women's Aid Organization

ART DIRECTORS:
Theresa Tsang
Kien Eng Tan

WRITER:
Valerie Chen

DESIGNER:
Nurazlinn Fariss

PROGRAMMER:
Joo Wah Wong

CREATIVE DIRECTOR:
Kien Eng Tan

ANNUAL ID:
06133N

URL:
http://www.wao.org.my/flash/speakup.swf

BEYOND THE BANNER: PUBLIC SERVICE/
NON-PROFIT / EDUCATIONAL . SINGLE

AGENCY
OgilvyInteractive / Madrid

CLIENT
Acción Contra el hambre

ART DIRECTOR:
Diego Gonzalez

CREATIVE DIRECTORS:
Jesús Rasines, Miguel Martin

ANNUAL ID:
06134N

URL:
http://212.101.74.50/web/premios/html/index.asp?id_premio=oneshow06&id_campanya=14

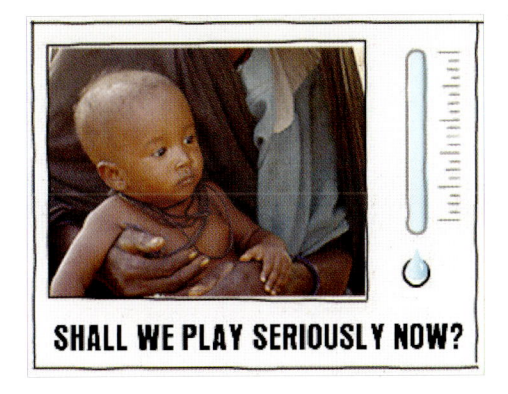

Merit Winners
203

BEYOND THE BANNER: PUBLIC SERVICE/
NON-PROFIT / EDUCATIONAL . CAMPAIGN

AGENCY
Netthink / Madrid

CLIENT
Anesvad

ART DIRECTORS:
Javier Galiana
Ruben Mártinez
David Mirete

PROGRAMMERS:
David Lopez Mesas
Iván Gajate

CREATIVE DIRECTOR:
Mario Sánchez del Real

ANNUAL ID:
06135N

URL:
http://extranet.netthink.es
/festivales/one_show2005/

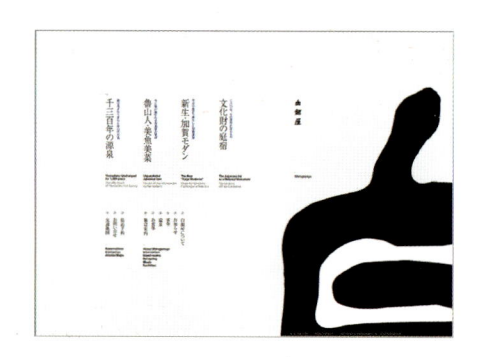

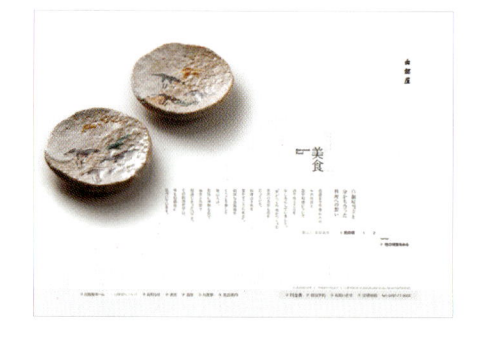

WEB SITES: BUSINESS TO CONSUMER

AGENCY
7779 / Tokyo

CLIENT
Hoshino Resort

ART DIRECTOR:
Jeong-ho Im

WRITER:
Ayumi Muro

DESIGNER:
Jeong-ho Im

PROGRAMMER:
Takeshiro Umetsu

DIGITAL ARTISTS/MULTIMEDIA:
Norie Miyahara, Isao Yamazaki
Takeshiro Umetsu, Yasushi Nakai
Masaharu Okita

CREATIVE DIRECTOR:
Jeong-ho Im

CONTENT STRATEGIST:
Mitsunori Yoshimura

ANNUAL ID:
06136N

URL:
http://7779.net/award/2005
/shiroganeya.html

204 MERIT WINNERS // NETTHINK // 7779 // ÅKESTAM.HOLST // ALMAPBBDO

WEB SITES: BUSINESS TO CONSUMER

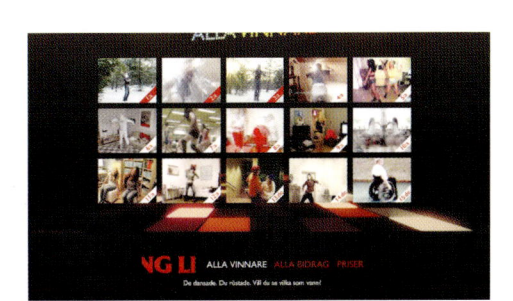

AGENCY
Åkestam.Holst/ Stockholm
CLIENT
Viking Line

ART DIRECTORS:
Fredrik Josefsson
Olle Mattson
WRITER:
Calle Lewenhaupt
PRODUCTION COMPANY:
B-Reel
INFORMATION ARCHITECT:
Kjell Månsson
CONTENT STRATEGIST:
Jessica Söder
ANNUAL ID:
06137N
URL:
http://www.b-reel.com/submit/oneshow06/viking

WEB SITES: BUSINESS TO CONSUMER

AGENCY
AlmapBBDO / São Paulo
CLIENT
Havaianas

ART DIRECTOR:
Adhemas Batista
WRITER:
Luciana Haguiara
PROGRAMMERS:
Fabrizio Zuardi
Flavio Ramos
Raphael Hamzagic
DIGITAL ARTIST/MULTIMEDIA:
Ricardo Martins
MUSIC AND SOUND:
Lua Web
CREATIVE DIRECTORS:
Marcello Serpa, Sergio Mugnaini
ANNUAL ID:
06138N
URL:
http://www.havaianas.com.br

Merit Winners
205

WEB SITES: BUSINESS TO CONSUMER

AGENCY
Atmosphere BBDO / New York

CLIENT
GE

ART DIRECTOR:
Ron Lent
WRITER:
John Heath
DESIGNER:
Peggy Pi-Yu Chuang
CREATIVE DIRECTORS:
Andreas Combuechen
Arturo Aranda
ANNUAL ID:
06139N
URL:
www.atmospherebbdo.com
/awards/2005/ge/seed/

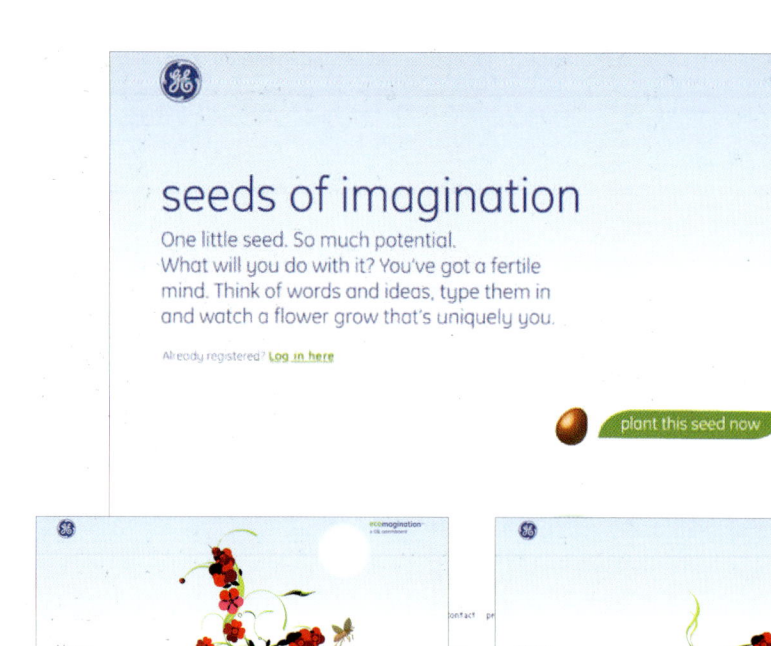

WEB SITES: BUSINESS TO CONSUMER

AGENCY
Atmosphere BBDO / New York

CLIENT
Masterfoods USA

ART DIRECTORS:
Aaron Adler, Richard Ardito
Melissa Haworth, Scott Kaplan
Vina Lam, Jerome Marucci
Jonathan Mackler, Jamie Overkamp
Elena Fridman, Ron Lent
Brett Simon
WRITERS:
Scott Cooney, Tom Christmann
Tina Divino, Adam Kanzer
Jim Lemaitre, Steve McElligott
Grant Smith, Ari Weiss
Dan Kelleher, John Heath
DESIGNER:
Donovan Goodly
PROGRAMMERS:
Henry Cho, Cesar Muñoz
Fatima Osman, Katy Walker
CREATIVE DIRECTOR:
Arturo Aranda
ANNUAL ID:
06140N
URL:
www.atmospherebbdo.com/awards
/2005/snickers/snickers.html

206   MERIT WINNERS // ATMOSPHERE BBDO // BIG SPACESHIP

WEB SITES: BUSINESS TO CONSUMER

AGENCY
Big Spaceship / Brooklyn

CLIENT
Sony Pictures

ART DIRECTOR:
Jens Karlsson

WRITER:
Karen Dahlstrom

DESIGNERS:
Joel Syzmanski, Jens Karlsson
Tyson Damman, Joel Syzmanski

PROGRAMMER:
Jamie Kosoy

DIGITAL ARTISTS/MULTIMEDIA:
Tyson Damman, Joel Syzmanski
Zander Brimijoin, Bjorn Fagerholm
Jens Karlsson

CREATIVE DIRECTOR:
Michael Lebowitz

ANNUAL ID:
06141N

URL:
www.entertheunderworld.com

WEB SITES: BUSINESS TO CONSUMER

AGENCY
Big Spaceship / Brooklyn

CLIENT
TBS

PRODUCTION COMPANIES:
Mother, Big Spaceship

ANNUAL ID:
06142N

URL:
www.tbshumorstudy.com

Merit Winners
207

WEB SITES: BUSINESS TO CONSUMER

AGENCY
Blast Radius / Vancouver

CLIENT
Jordan Brand

ART DIRECTOR:
Francis Chan

PROGRAMMERS:
Steve Bond
Bruce Pomeroy

DIGITAL ARTIST/MULTIMEDIA:
Mitsuaki Yajima

PRODUCTION COMPANY:
Blast Radius

CREATIVE DIRECTOR:
Marcus Ericsson

CONTENT STRATEGIST:
Greg Liburd

ANNUAL ID:
06143N

URL:
www.nike.com/jumpman23

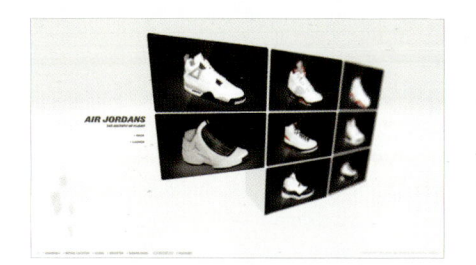

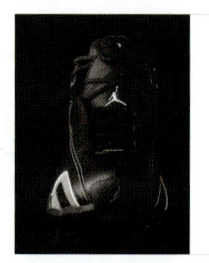

WEB SITES: BUSINESS TO CONSUMER

AGENCY
BLITZ / Beverly Hills

CLIENT
Warner Bros.

ART DIRECTORS:
Josh Esguia, Paul Hikiji

WRITER:
Chris Shellen

DESIGNERS:
Mark Chosak
Jon Dobrowolski
Dathan Dedman

PROGRAMMERS:
Mark Carolin, Mark Gardner
Jason Seigler, John Grden
Tim Brady, Justin Bastedo
Ivan Todorov, Bobbi McClellan

DIGITAL ARTISTS/MULTIMEDIA:
Brian Sanchez, Andru Phoenix
Phiyen Nguyen

INFORMATION ARCHITECT:
Mark Sloan

CREATIVE DIRECTORS:
Ken Martin, Mark Cohn
Anna Baxter

ANNUAL ID:
06144N

URL:
www.corpsebridemovie.com

WEB SITES: BUSINESS TO CONSUMER

AGENCY
Butler, Shine, Stern & Partners / Sausalito

CLIENT
nick(it)

WRITER:
Charlie Gschwend

DESIGNER:
Andreas Tagger

PROGRAMMERS:
Joseph Piro
Joshua Brewer

DIGITAL ARTIST/MULTIMEDIA:
Andreas Tagger

CREATIVE DIRECTORS:
John Butler
Neil Sobral Caetano da Silva

ANNUAL ID:
06145N

URL:
http://staging.bssp.com/awardshow_2006/nickit/index2.htm

WEB SITES: BUSINESS TO CONSUMER

AGENCY
Crispin Porter + Bogusky / Miami

CLIENT
MINI

ART DIRECTORS:
Paul Stechschulte, Tiffany Kosel
Rahul Panchal, Mike Ferrare

WRITERS:
Steve O'Connell
Franklin Tipton
Rob Reilly

PROGRAMMER:
Luis Santi

PRODUCTION COMPANIES:
Exopolis, iChameleon
Hungry Man, Jodef/Mixer
Outpost Digital

CREATIVE DIRECTORS:
Alex Bogusky, Andrew Keller
Jeff Benjamin

ANNUAL ID:
06146N

URL:
http://www.cpbgroup.com/awards/counterfeit_intinter.html

Merit Winners
209

WEB SITES: BUSINESS TO CONSUMER

AGENCY
de-construct / London

CLIENT
adidas

ART DIRECTOR:
Fred Flade
DESIGNER:
Tom Kershaw
DIGITAL ARTIST/MULTIMEDIA:
Rory MacDonald
INFORMATION ARCHITECT:
Ben Hindmarch
CREATIVE DIRECTOR:
Alex Griffin
ANNUAL ID:
06147N
URL:
http://www.adidas.com/1

WEB SITES: BUSINESS TO CONSUMER

AGENCY
Dentsu / Tokyo

CLIENT
Mitsui Fudosan Co.

ART DIRECTORS:
Hirozumi Takakusaki
Takehide Kunii
WRITERS:
Yasuharu Sasaki
Tetsuhiko Kato
DESIGNERS:
Ikuko Kawa, Momoko Kobayashi
Seiko Ushiki
CREATIVE DIRECTORS:
Hirozumi Takakusaki
Yasuharu Sasaki
ANNUAL ID:
06148N
URL:
http://www.interactive-salaryman.com/pieces/shibaura_e/

210 MERIT WINNERS // DE-CONSTRUCT // DENTSU // EURO RSCG 4D INTERACTIVE // EVB

WEB SITES: BUSINESS TO CONSUMER

AGENCY
Euro RSCG 4D
Interactive / London

CLIENT
Diesel

WRITER:
Patrick Baglee

DESIGNERS:
Chloe George
Peter Aston

PROGRAMMERS:
James Rowley
Mike Smith
Alex Sayle

PRODUCTION COMPANIES:
Doug Allan, Bob Mitchell
Mark Dawber, Tom Saunders
John Hatfield

INFORMATION ARCHITECT:
Natasha Allen

CONTENT STRATEGIST:
St John Lewis

CREATIVE DIRECTOR:
Trevor Chambers

ANNUAL ID:
06149N

URL:
http://www.awards-entry.co.uk/2006/dreams/

WEB SITES: BUSINESS TO CONSUMER

AGENCY
EVB / San Francisco

CLIENT
adidas

ART DIRECTORS:
Eddy Tofslie
Todd Bois

WRITER:
Paul Charney

PROGRAMMER:
Josh Sullivan

DIGITAL ARTIST/MULTIMEDIA:
Chris Kelley

CONTENT STRATEGIST:
Justin Acuff

CREATIVE DIRECTOR:
Jason Zada

ANNUAL ID:
06150N

URL:
http://www.evb.com/enter_2006/adidas.html

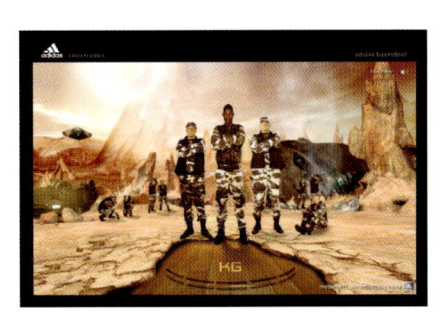

Merit Winners
211

WEB SITES: BUSINESS TO CONSUMER

AGENCY
EVB / San Francisco

CLIENT
LeapFrog

ART DIRECTOR:
Todd Bois
WRITER:
Alexandra Tyler
DESIGNERS:
Jessica Sexton
Eddy Tofslie
DIGITAL ARTISTS/MULTIMEDIA:
Gregor Roberts, Dan Smith
CREATIVE DIRECTOR:
Jason Zada
CONTENT STRATEGIST:
Ryan Toland
ANNUAL ID:
06151N
URL:
http://www.evb.com/enter_2006/leapfrog_fly.html

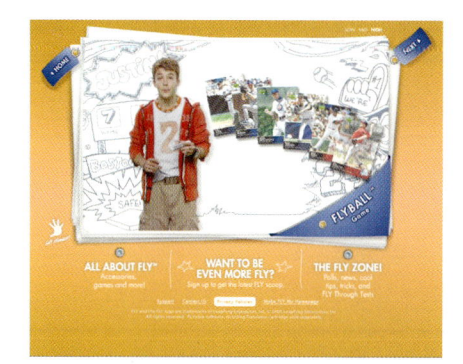

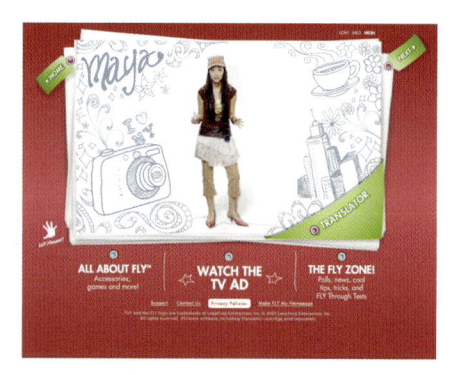

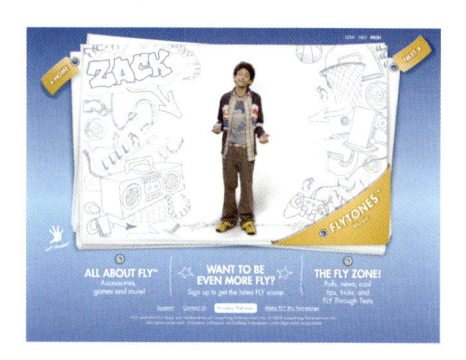

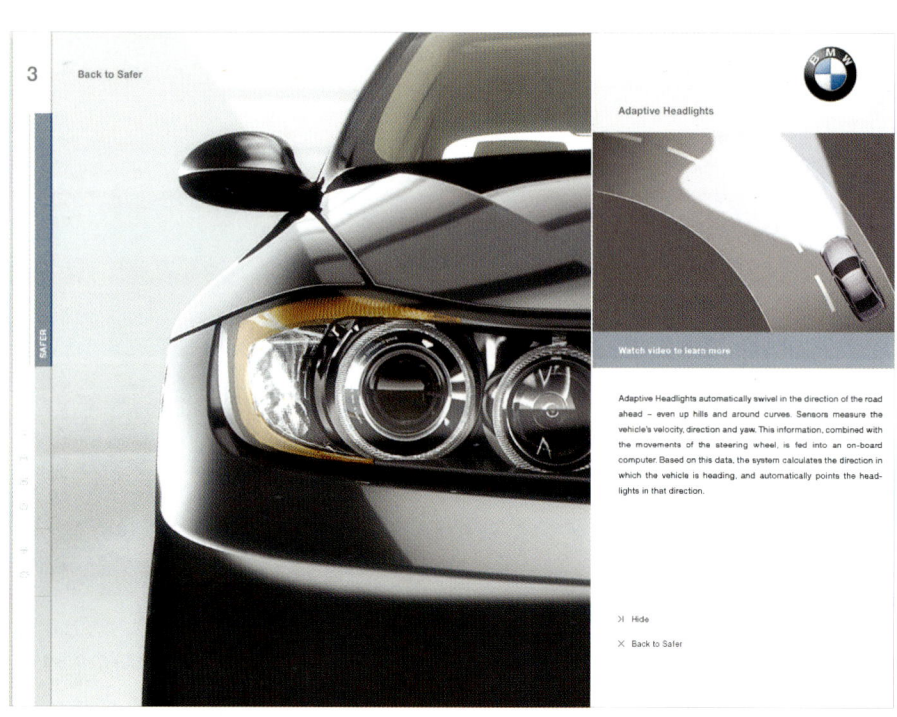

WEB SITES: BUSINESS TO CONSUMER

AGENCY
Fallon / Minneapolis

CLIENT
BMW

ART DIRECTOR:
Andy Gugel
WRITER:
Rich Black
DESIGNER:
Andy Gugel
PROGRAMMER:
Andy Gugel
CREATIVE DIRECTOR:
Kevin Flatt
ANNUAL ID:
06152N
URL:
http://interactive.fallon.com/05/bmw3/

212   MERIT WINNERS // EVB // FALLON // FARFAR // FITZGERALD+CO

WEB SITES: BUSINESS TO CONSUMER

AGENCY
Farfar / Stockholm
CLIENT
Heineken

ART DIRECTOR:
Jakob Swedenborg
WRITER:
Henrik Berglof
PROGRAMMER:
Bo Gustafsson
DIGITAL ARTIST/MULTIMEDIA:
Erik Norin
CREATIVE DIRECTOR:
Nicke Bergstrom
CONTENT STRATEGISTS:
Jonas Andersson
Matias Palm-Jensen
ANNUAL ID:
06153N
URL:
http://www.farfar.se/oneshow
2006/heineken

WEB SITES: BUSINESS TO CONSUMER

AGENCY
Fitzgerald+CO / Atlanta
CLIENT
Durex

ART DIRECTOR:
David MacCarroll
WRITER:
Evan Levy
DESIGNER:
Josh Murphy
DIGITAL ARTISTS/MULTIMEDIA:
Paula Voorhies, Mike Jones
CREATIVE DIRECTOR:
Eddie Snyder
ANNUAL ID:
06154N
URL:
http://www.durexdickorations.com

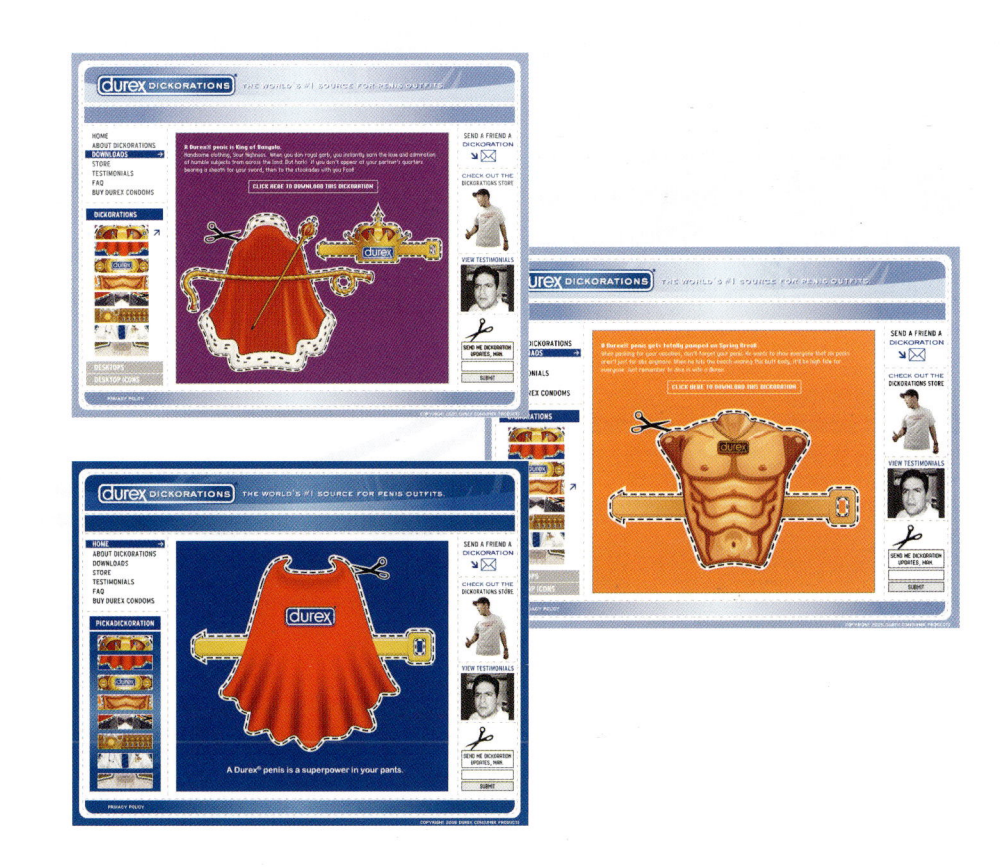

Merit Winners
213

WEB SITES: BUSINESS TO CONSUMER

AGENCY
Framfab / Copenhagen

CLIENT
Nike

ART DIRECTORS:
Kamilla Blæsbjerg
Peter Ringtved

WRITER:
Rhiannon Davies

PROGRAMMERS:
Kim Jensen
Philip Louderback

CREATIVE DIRECTOR:
Lars Cortsen

CONTENT STRATEGIST:
Martin Kristensen

ANNUAL ID:
06155N

URL:
http://www.nikewomen.com/integrated/

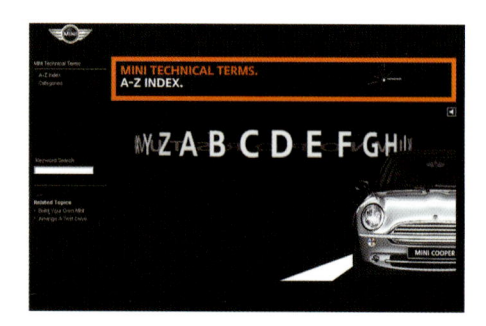

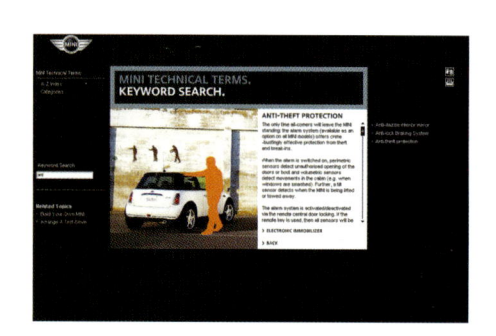

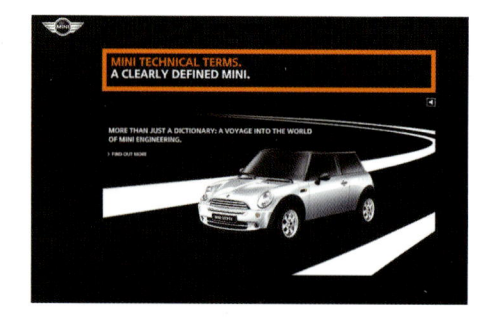

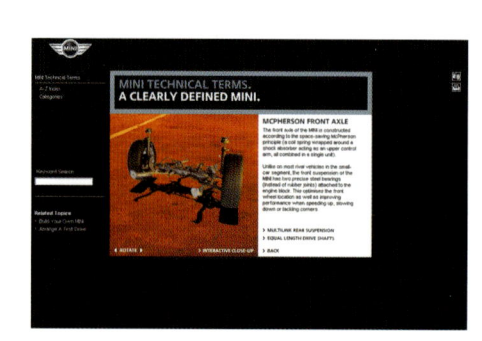

WEB SITES: BUSINESS TO CONSUMER

AGENCY
Interone Worldwide / Hamburg

CLIENT
MINI

ART DIRECTOR:
Alexandra Titius

WRITERS:
Jan Matullat, Stephen James

DESIGNER:
Tanja Fröhlich

PROGRAMMER:
Rico Marquardt

DIGITAL ARTIST/MULTIMEDIA:
Michael Ploj

INFORMATION ARCHITECT:
David Athey

CONTENT STRATEGIST:
Anke Schliedermann

CREATIVE DIRECTOR:
Martin Gassner

ANNUAL ID:
06156N

URL:
http://www.mini.com/technical-terms

WEB SITES: BUSINESS TO CONSUMER

AGENCY
juxt interactive / Newport Beach

CLIENT
Coca-Cola Company

ART DIRECTOR:
Jorge Calleja

WRITER:
Joe Shepter

DESIGNERS:
Kenneth Macy
Justin Bernard

PROGRAMMERS:
Victor Allen
Christian Ayotte

CREATIVE DIRECTOR:
Todd Purgason

CONTENT STRATEGIST:
Kristen Myers

ANNUAL ID:
06157N

URL:
http://www.nesteaice.com

WEB SITES: BUSINESS TO CONSUMER

AGENCY
juxt interactive / Newport Beach

CLIENT
Fuse TV

ART DIRECTOR:
Brian Miller

DESIGNERS:
Justin Bernard
Alex Mustacich

PROGRAMMER:
Casey Corcoran

DIGITAL ARTIST/MULTIMEDIA:
Miguel Castro

CONTENT STRATEGIST:
Sean Gibson

CREATIVE DIRECTOR:
Todd Purgason

ANNUAL ID:
06158N

URL:
http://www.justforthefofit.com/index.asp

Merit Winners
215

VIRAL AND EMAIL:
BUSINESS TO CONSUMER

AGENCY
Atmosphere BBDO / New York

CLIENT
Masterfoods

ART DIRECTORS:
Aaron Adler, Richard Ardito
Melissa Haworth, Scott Kaplan
Vina Lam, Jerome Marucci
Jonathan Mackler, Jamie Overkamp
Elena Fridman, Ron Lent, Brett Simon

WRITERS:
Scott Cooney, Tom Christmann
Adam Kanzer, Jim Lemaitre
Steve McElligott, Grant Smith
Ari Weiss, Dan Kelleher

DESIGNER:
Donovan Goodly

PROGRAMMERS:
Katy Walker, Fatima Osman
Cesar Munoz, Henry Cho

CREATIVE DIRECTOR:
Arturo Aranda

ANNUAL ID:
06215N

URL:
http://www.atmospherebbdo.com/awards/2005/snickers/snickers.html

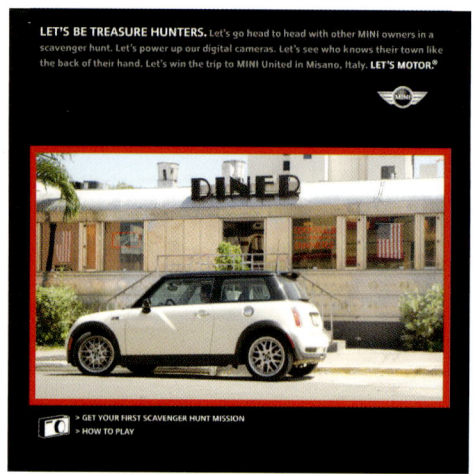

VIRAL AND EMAIL:
BUSINESS TO CONSUMER

AGENCY
Crispin Porter + Bogusky / Miami

CLIENT
MINI

ART DIRECTOR:
Rahul Panchal

WRITERS:
Rob Strasberg, Jackie Guerra

PRODUCTION COMPANY:
Beam Interactive

CREATIVE DIRECTORS:
Alex Bogusky, Andrew Keller
Jeff Benjamin

ANNUAL ID:
06218N

URL:
http://www.cpbgroup.com/awards/scavenger.html

216   MERIT WINNERS // ATMOSPHERE BBDO // CRISPIN PORTER + BOGUSKY // NEUE DIGITALE // PRISACOM

WEB SITES: BUSINESS TO CONSUMER

AGENCY
NEUE DIGITALE / Frankfurt
CLIENT
Olympus

ART DIRECTOR:
Rolf Borcherding
DESIGNER:
André Bourguignon
PROGRAMMER:
Heiko Schweickhardt
CREATIVE DIRECTOR:
Olaf Czeschner
ANNUAL ID:
06161N
URL:
http://www.neue-digitale.de/projects/olympus_brandcampaign_2005

WEB SITES: BUSINESS TO CONSUMER

AGENCY
Prisacom / Madrid
CLIENT
Prisacom

ART DIRECTOR:
Antonio Pasagali
DESIGNERS:
Carlos Cruz
Francisco Merino
ANNUAL ID:
06162N
URL:
http://www.elpais.es/comunes/2005/resumen/

Merit Winners
217

WEB SITES: BUSINESS TO CONSUMER

AGENCY
Publicis & Hal Riney / San Francisco

CLIENT
Peter Kim Jewelry

ART DIRECTORS:
Colin Kim
Dominic Goldman

WRITERS:
Jesse Dillow
Mike Danko

DESIGNER:
Michael Kern

PRODUCTION COMPANY:
Struck Design

INFORMATION ARCHITECT:
Sosia Bert

CREATIVE DIRECTORS:
Jae Goodman, Jon Soto
Dominic Goldman

ANNUAL ID:
06163N

URL:
http://www.flossyogrill.com

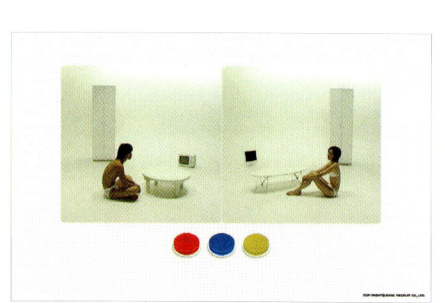

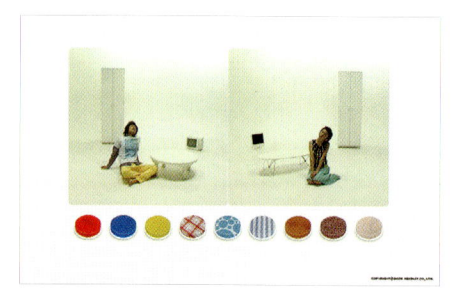

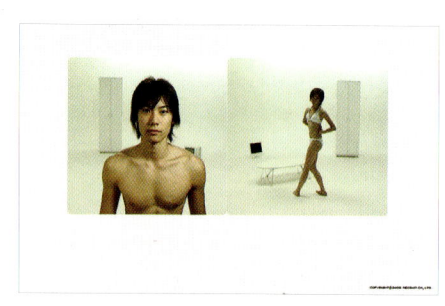

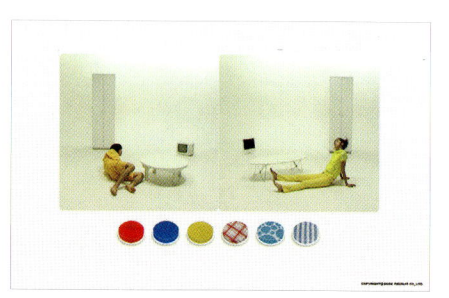

WEB SITES: BUSINESS TO CONSUMER

AGENCY
Recruit Media Communications / Nagoya

CLIENT
Takisada-Nagoya

ART DIRECTOR:
Takanori Yamada

WRITERS:
Takayuki Hino
Ryoko Yamagiwa

DESIGNER:
Takanori Yamada

CREATIVE DIRECTOR:
Takayuki Hino

ANNUAL ID:
06164N

URL:
http://www.a-n-t.jp/06awards/takisada_e/index.html

WEB SITES: BUSINESS TO CONSUMER

AGENCY
Scholz & Volkmer / Wiesbaden
CLIENT
Mercedes-Benz

ART DIRECTORS:
Katja Rickert
Philipp Bareiss
WRITER:
Andreas Henke
PROGRAMMERS:
Dennis Baum, Philippe Just
Peter Reichard
PRODUCTION COMPANY:
Macke Vision
CREATIVE DIRECTOR:
Heike Brockmann
ANNUAL ID:
06165N
URL:
www.s-v.de/projects/r-klasse

WEB SITES: BUSINESS TO CONSUMER

AGENCY
Tribal DDB / Vancouver
CLIENT
BC Dairy Foundation

ART DIRECTOR:
Alex Beim
WRITER:
Kevin Shortt
PROGRAMMER:
James Marshall
PRODUCER:
Zerlina Chan
CREATIVE DIRECTOR:
Bruce Sinclair
ANNUAL ID:
06166N
URL:
http://www.drinkmilk.ca

Merit Winners
219

WEB SITES: BUSINESS TO CONSUMER

AGENCY
Zugara / Los Angeles

CLIENT
Reebok

ANNUAL ID:
06167N

URL:
http://www.rbk.com/us/answer9

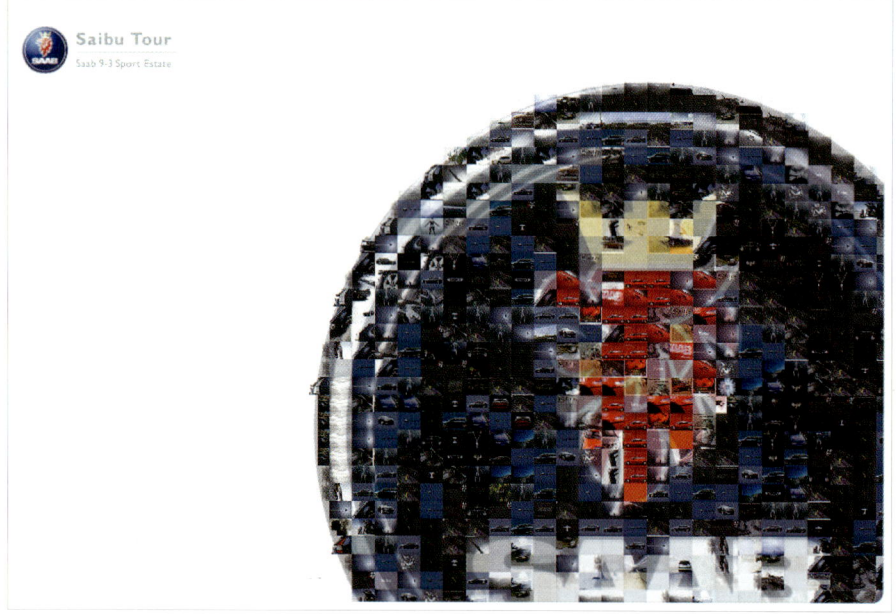

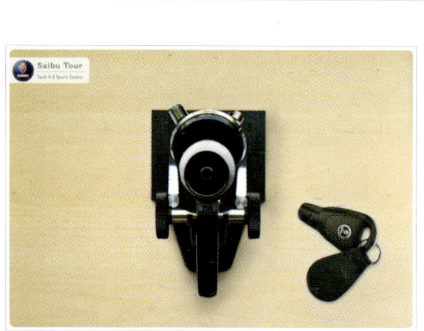

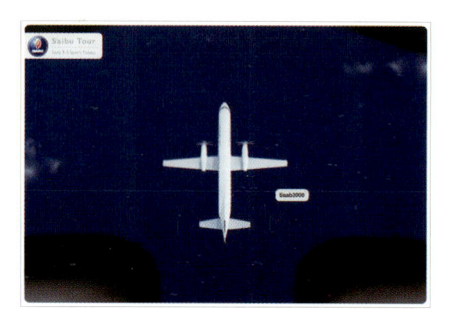

WEB SITES: PROMOTIONAL ADVERTISING

AGENCY
ADK / Tokyo

CLIENT
General Motors

ART DIRECTOR:
Naoki Ito

WRITERS:
Shinji Tao, Naoki Ito
Mamiko Koike

DESIGNERS:
Yusuke Kitani
Yuko Tomioka

CREATIVE DIRECTOR:
Jiro Kanahara

ANNUAL ID:
06168N

URL:
http://www.bascule.co.jp/saab/en/

WEB SITES: PROMOTIONAL ADVERTISING

AGENCY
AKQA / London
CLIENT
Nike

ART DIRECTOR:
Duan Evans
WRITER:
Kerry Finlay
DESIGNER:
Masaya Nakade
PROGRAMMERS:
Rick Williams
Matthew Elwin
DIGITAL ARTIST/MULTIMEDIA:
Andy Foulds
INFORMATION ARCHITECT:
Laura Grant
CONTENT STRATEGISTS:
Simon Jefferson
James Jenkins
ANNUAL ID:
06169N
URL:
http://awards.akqa.com/awards/nike/free/index.html

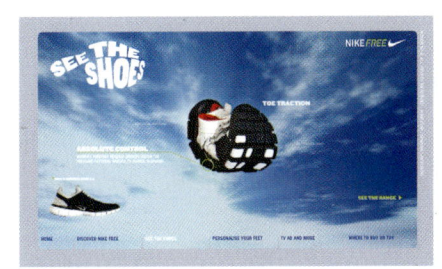

WEB SITES: PROMOTIONAL ADVERTISING

AGENCY
AKQA / San Francisco
CLIENT
Xbox

ART DIRECTOR:
David Lee
WRITER:
Steve Tornello
DESIGNER:
Matthew Law
DIGITAL ARTISTS/MULTIMEDIA:
Hoj Jomehri, Sam Bouguerra
Guillermo Torres
CREATIVE DIRECTORS:
Mauro Alencar, Rei Inamoto
PJ Pereira
ANNUAL ID:
06170N
URL:
http://awards.sf.akqa.com/creative/pgr3/index.html

Merit Winners
221

WEB SITES: PROMOTIONAL ADVERTISING

AGENCY
Aoi Advertising Promotion / Tokyo
CLIENT
Adobe

ART DIRECTOR:
Koji Nishida
WRITERS:
Jun , Yosuke Kurita
DESIGNER:
Tarout
PROGRAMMERS:
Hisayuki Takagi
Takeshiro Umetsu
Shin Matsumura
DIGITAL ARTIST/MULTIMEDIA:
Minoru Tanaka
PRODUCTION COMPANIES:
Hikaru Seto, Tadanobu Sudo
Maiko Miyagawa
CREATIVE DIRECTOR:
Yujiro Kaizawa
ANNUAL ID:
06171N
URL:
http://aoi-award.com/eight8/

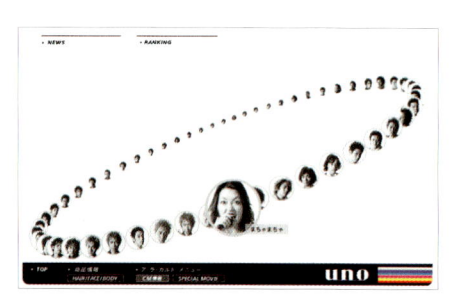

WEB SITES: PROMOTIONAL ADVERTISING

AGENCY
Dentsu / Tokyo
CLIENT
Shiseido

ART DIRECTORS:
Hiroki Nakamura, Yusuke Kitani
Kei Marubashi
WRITER:
Hiroaki Murasawa
PROGRAMMER:
Synthetic-leather Koike
DIGITAL ARTIST/MULTIMEDIA:
Emperor Nakamura
INFORMATION ARCHITECT:
Koichi Hanyu
CONTENT STRATEGISTS:
Hiroaki Murasawa
Yasushi Okuwa
Takehiko Okoshi
CREATIVE DIRECTORS:
Koji Yamamoto
Michihiko Yanai
ANNUAL ID:
06172N
URL:
http://www.181cm75kg.jp/uno_e/

WEB SITES: PROMOTIONAL ADVERTISING

AGENCY
Forsman & Bodenfors / Gothenburg

CLIENT
IF

ART DIRECTORS:
Martin Cedergren
Lotta Ågerup

WRITER:
Oscar Askelöf

DESIGNER:
Jonas Sjövall

PRODUCTION COMPANY:
B-Reel

ANNUAL ID:
06173N

URL:
http://demo.fb.se/e/if/badluck/

WEB SITES: PROMOTIONAL ADVERTISING

AGENCY
Grupo W / Saltillo

CLIENT
Nike

ART DIRECTORS:
Francisco Romanh
Cesar Moreno

WRITER:
Ivan Gonzalez

PROGRAMMERS:
Homero Sousa, Raul Uranga

DIGITAL ARTISTS/MULTIMEDIA:
Jezreel Gutierrez, Roberto Espero
Sebastian Mariscal, Sara Davila
Fernando Valdes, Marcela de la Cruz

CREATIVE DIRECTORS:
Ulises Valencia
Miguel Calderon

ANNUAL ID:
06174N

URL:
http://www.grupow.com/nike10/festivales

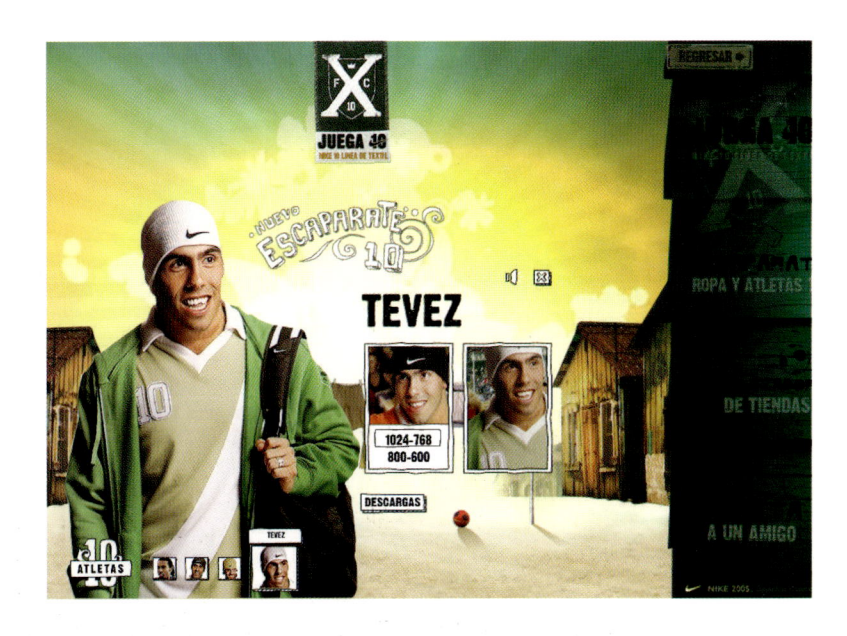

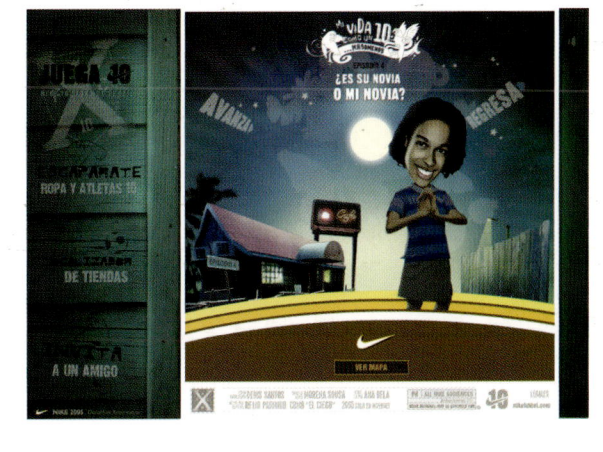

Merit Winners
223

WEB SITES: PROMOTIONAL ADVERTISING

AGENCY
Hi-ReS! / London

CLIENT
Beck/Interscope US

ART DIRECTOR:
Florian Schmitt

DESIGNERS:
Carl Burgess
Thomas Eberwein

PRODUCTION COMPANY:
Hi-ReS!

CREATIVE DIRECTOR:
Florian Schmitt

ANNUAL ID:
06175N

URL:
http://www.beck.com

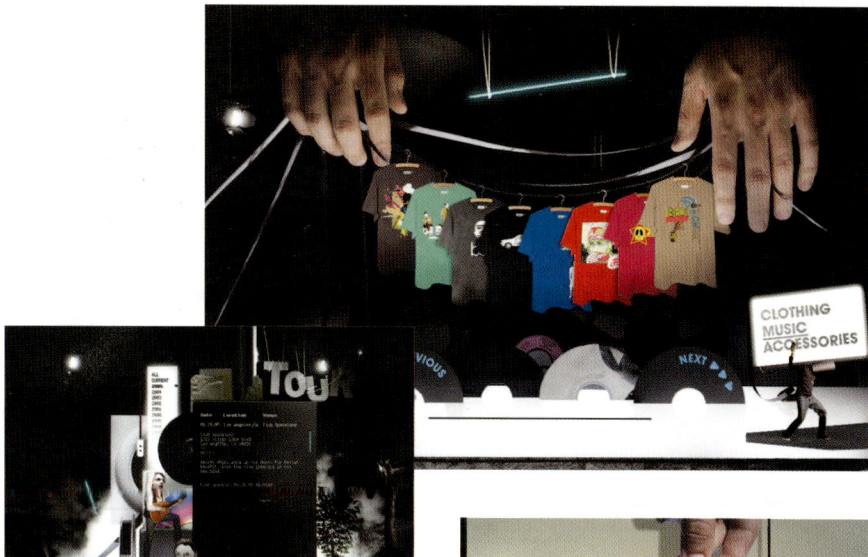

WEB SITES: PROMOTIONAL ADVERTISING

AGENCY
Hi-ReS! / London

CLIENT
Channel4 UK

ART DIRECTOR:
Florian Schmitt

DESIGNERS:
Carl Burgess
Thomas Eberwein
Florian Schmitt

PRODUCTION COMPANY:
Hi-ReS!

CREATIVE DIRECTOR:
Florian Schmitt

ANNUAL ID:
06176N

URL:
http://www.channel4.com/lostuntold

WEB SITES: PROMOTIONAL ADVERTISING

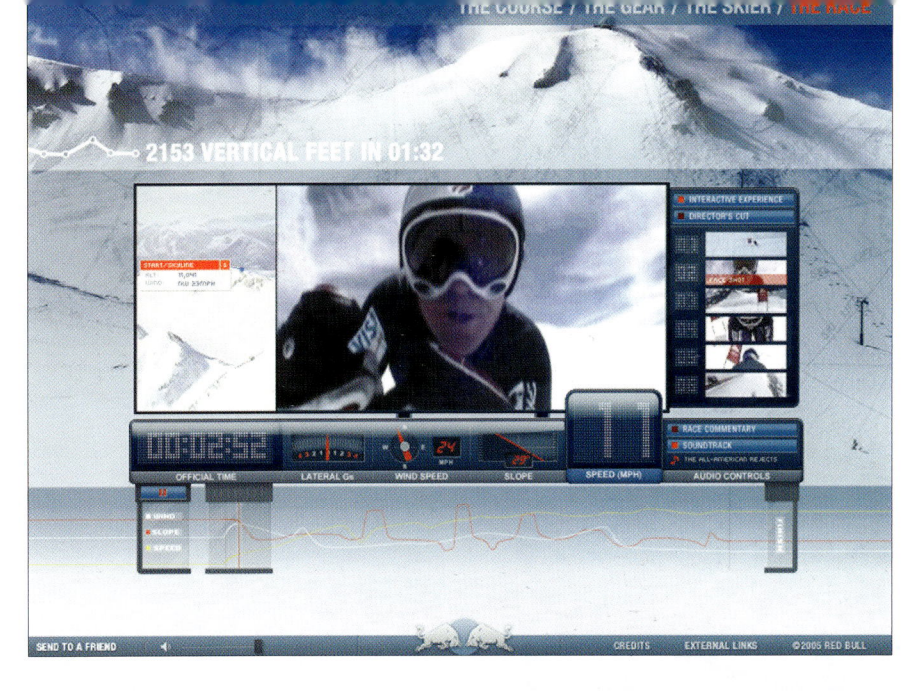

AGENCY
Odopod / San Francisco

CLIENT
Red Bull

ART DIRECTOR:
Micheal E. Cole

WRITER:
Tim Barber

DESIGNERS:
Steve Mason
Ammon Haggerty

PROGRAMMERS:
Ammon Haggerty
Michelangelo Capraro

DIGITAL ARTISTS/MULTIMEDIA:
Steve Mason, Gino Nave
Scott Runcorn

CREATIVE DIRECTORS:
Tim Barber, Jacquie Moss
David Bliss

ANNUAL ID:
06177N

URL:
http://www.redbullcopilot.com

WEB SITES: PROMOTIONAL ADVERTISING

AGENCY
OgilvyOne Worldwide/
Singapore

CLIENT
Levi Strauss Asia

ART DIRECTOR:
Robert Davies

WRITER:
Sridhar Gopalratnam

DESIGNER:
Shawn Loo

PROGRAMMERS:
Nicholas Ng, TV Raju
Colin Foo

CREATIVE DIRECTOR:
Peter Moss

ANNUAL ID:
06178N

URL:
http://www.ap.levi.com/squarecut/

Merit Winners
225

WEB SITES: PROMOTIONAL ADVERTISING

AGENCY
One Sky / Tokyo

CLIENT
Fuji Heavy Industries

ART DIRECTOR:
Ryuta Modeki
WRITERS:
Nobuhito Inoue, Koshi Uchiyama
DESIGNERS:
Yohei Iwaki, Naoto Tanaka
PROGRAMMERS:
Minoru Sako, Kojiro Futamura
Makoto Watanabe
DIGITAL ARTISTS/MULTIMEDIA:
Taiyo Kikaku, Masaomi Kurihara
PRODUCTION COMPANIES:
One Sky, Business Architects
CREATIVE DIRECTOR:
Koshi Uchiyama
CONTENT STRATEGISTS:
Koshi Uchiyama, Yasuhisa Kudo
Hirofum Azuma
ANNUAL ID:
06179n
URL:
http://www.subaru.co.jp/legacy/300sp/

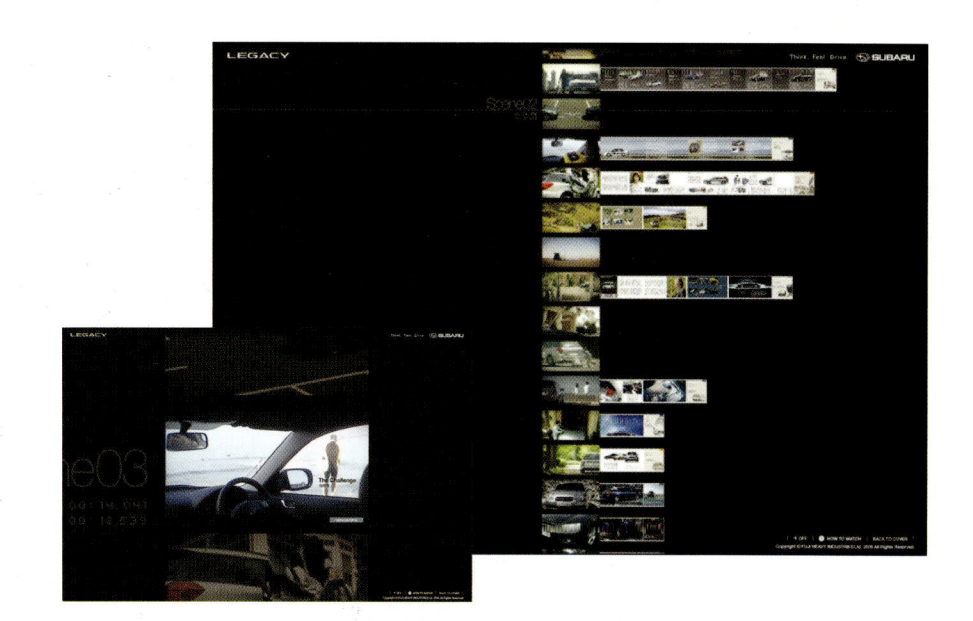

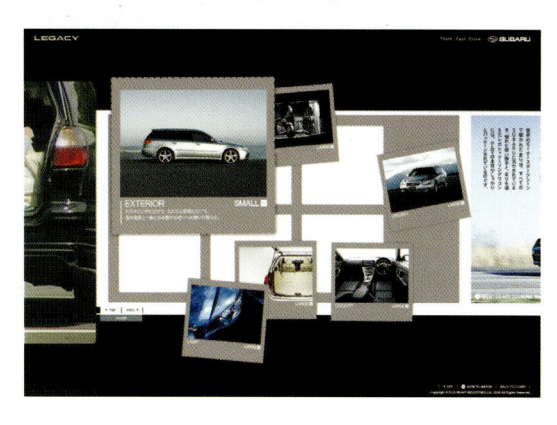

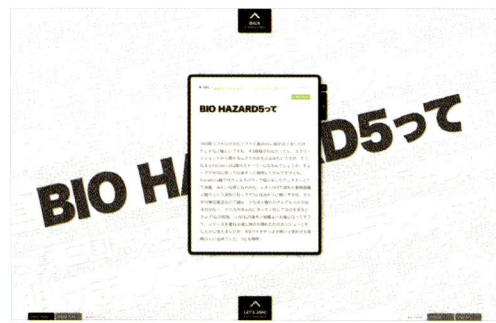

WEB SITES: PROMOTIONAL ADVERTISING

AGENCY
One Sky / Tokyo

CLIENT
Microsoft Corporation Japan

ART DIRECTOR:
Yugo Nakamura
WRITER:
Koshi Uchiyama
DESIGNERS:
Yugo Nakamura
Takayuki Fukatsu
PROGRAMMER:
Keita Kitamura
DIGITAL ARTIST/MULTIMEDIA:
Suguru Yamaguchi
PRODUCTION COMPANIES:
One Sky, Tha
CREATIVE DIRECTOR:
Yugo Nakamura
CONTENT STRATEGIST:
Koshi Uchiyama
ANNUAL ID:
06180N
URL:
http://Jump-In.P.Tha.Jp

226 MERIT WINNERS // ONE SKY // EURO RSCG 4D INTERACTIVE // FIRSTBORN

WEB SITES: BUSINESS TO BUSINESS

AGENCY
Euro RSCG 4D Interactive / London

CLIENT
Intel

ART DIRECTOR:
Ross Elliott
WRITER:
Mike Watson
DESIGNER:
Sean Howard
PROGRAMMERS:
Matthew Muller
Matthew Lawrence
Tom Saunders
PRODUCTION COMPANIES:
Alex Turner (Viral Factory)
Ed Robinson (Viral Factory)
Jess Hunter, Ingo Auer
Giles Phelps
CREATIVE DIRECTORS:
Scott Ex Rodgers
Sean Chambers
CONTENT STRATEGIST:
Ryan Murphy
ANNUAL ID:
06181N
URL:
http://www.awards-entry.co.uk/2006/crimescene/

WEB SITES: BUSINESS TO BUSINESS

AGENCY
Firstborn / New York

CLIENT
Kohn Pedersen Fox Architects

PROGRAMMERS:
Joon Yong Park, Gicheol Lee
CREATIVE DIRECTOR:
Vas Sloutchevsky
CONTENT STRATEGIST:
Jeremy Berg
ANNUAL ID:
06182N
URL:
http://www.kpf.com

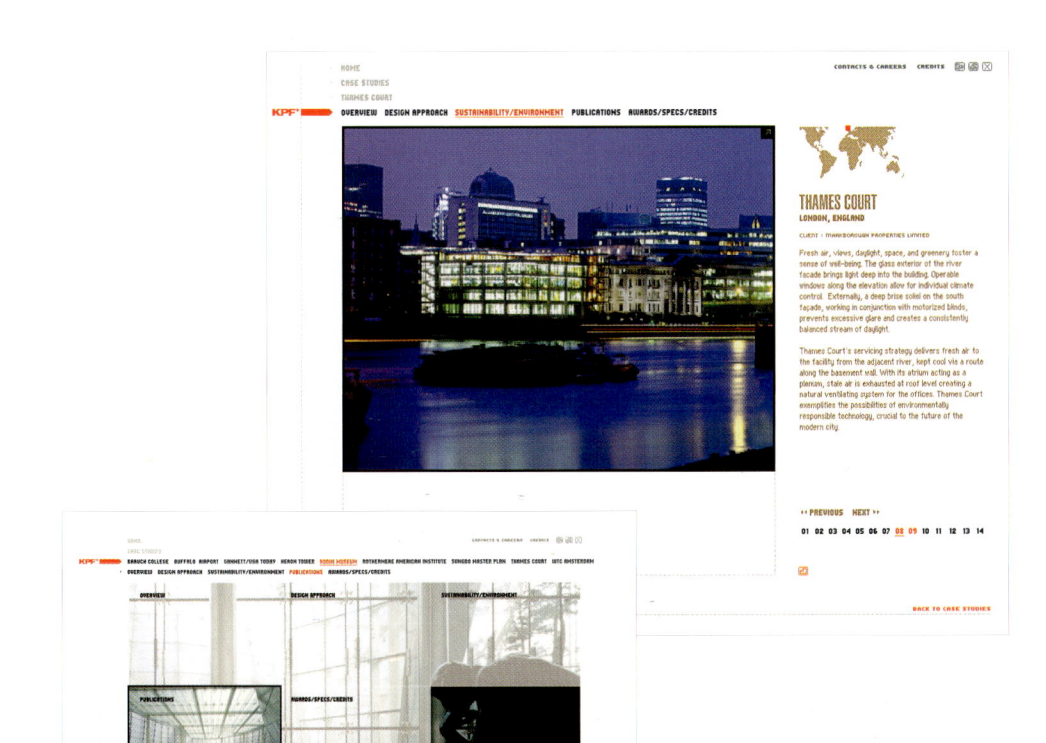

Merit Winners
227

WEB SITES: E-COMMERCE

AGENCY
777interactive / Tokyo
CLIENT
Sony Family Club

ART DIRECTOR:
Yosuke Abe
DESIGNERS:
Mayumi Hayashi
Yosuke Abe
PROGRAMMERS:
Sohei Ibe, Daisuke Murase
Toshimitsu Matsuzawa
PRODUCTION COMPANY:
Kayac
CREATIVE DIRECTORS:
Toshiya Fukuda
Daisuke Yanagisawa
Koichiro Tanaka
CONTENT STRATEGIST:
Hroo Suzuki
ANNUAL ID:
06183N
URL:
http://beyes.jp/

WEB SITES: E-COMMERCE

AGENCY
BEAM Interactive / Boston
CLIENT
Puma

ART DIRECTOR:
Carlos Lunetta
DESIGNER:
Chris Jansma
PROGRAMMER:
Carlos Lunetta
CREATIVE DIRECTOR:
Dave Batista
ANNUAL ID:
06184N
URL:
http://www.pumafootball.com

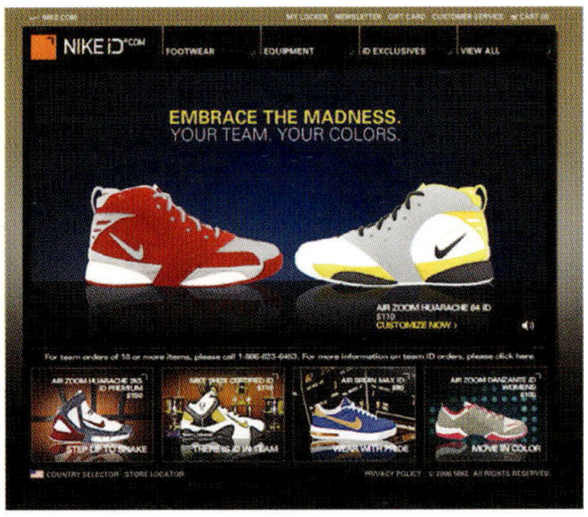

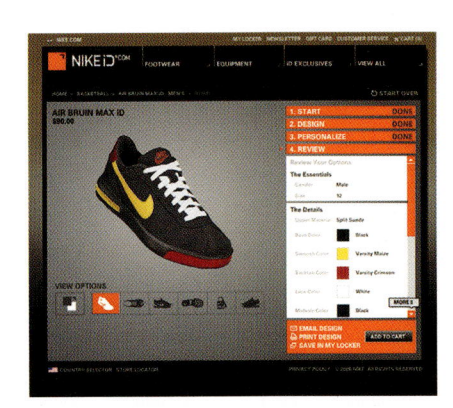

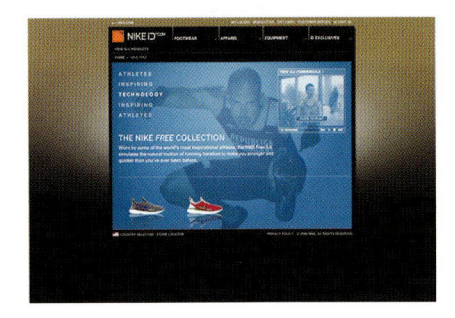

WEB SITES: E-COMMERCE

AGENCY
R/GA / New York

CLIENT
Nike

ART DIRECTOR:
Marlon Hernandez

WRITERS:
John Bletterman, Scott Tufts

DESIGNERS:
Matt Walsh, Ian Brewer
David Hyung, Michelle Zassenhaus
Lara Horner, Andrew Thompson
John James, Takafumi Yamaguchi
Brian Votaw

PROGRAMMERS:
Scott Prindle, Sean Lyons
Chuck Genco, Stan Wiechers
Martin Legowiecki, Todd Kovner
Michele Roman, August Yang

CREATIVE DIRECTOR:
Richard Ting

ANNUAL ID:
06185N

URL:
http://awards.web.rga.com
/2005/nike_id.html

WEB SITES: E-COMMERCE

AGENCY
Wysiwyg Comunicación
Interactiva / Madrid

CLIENT
Camper

ART DIRECTOR:
Max Turi

WRITER:
Daniel Molinillo

PROGRAMMER:
Filippo de la Casa

CREATIVE DIRECTORS:
Adolfo González
Nuria Martínez

CONTENT STRATEGIST:
Ignacio Álvarez-Borrás

ANNUAL ID:
06186N

URL:
www.wysiwyg.net/fests06
/oneshow/index.html

Merit Winners
229

WEB SITES: SELF-PROMOTION

AGENCY
Bascule / Tokyo
CLIENT
Bascule

ART DIRECTOR:
Mitsuhiro Oga
WRITERS:
Masayoshi Boku, Yutaka Kodama
DESIGNERS:
Mitsuhiro Oga, Mayo Tobita
PROGRAMMERS:
Go Kameda, Nobuo Hara
Kampei Baba, Haruyuki Imai
Kazuki Nakata, Akira Ohtsuka
DIGITAL ARTISTS/MULTIMEDIA:
Kampei Baba, Nobuo Hara
Shojiro Nakaoka, Iwao Noritomi
INFORMATION ARCHITECTS:
Go Kameda, Kampei Baba
CREATIVE DIRECTORS:
Masayoshi Boku, Mitsuhiro Oga
CONTENT STRATEGISTS:
Masayoshi Boku, Nobuo Hara
ANNUAL ID:
06187N
URL:
http://www.bascule.co.jp/

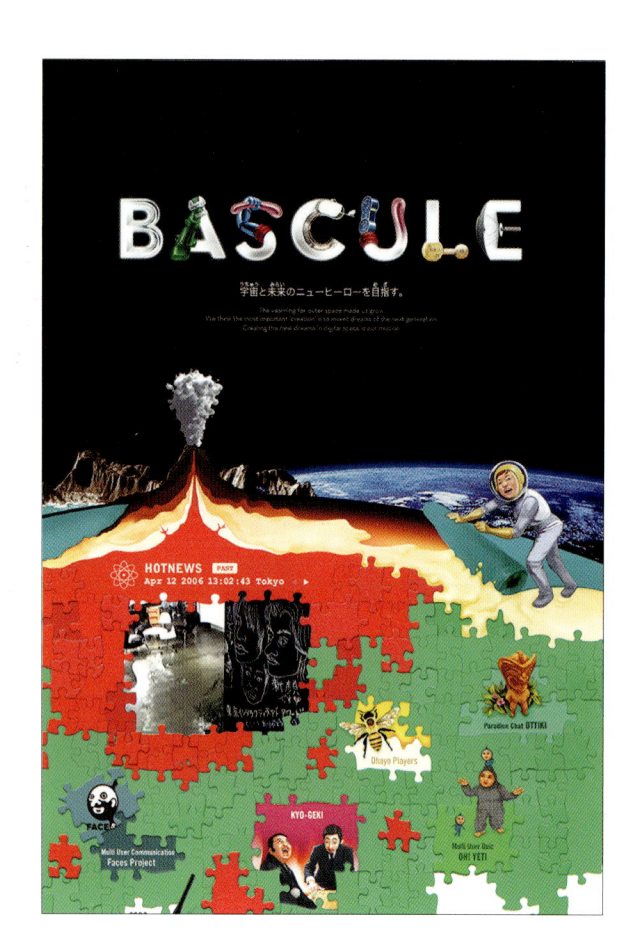

WEB SITES: SELF-PROMOTION

AGENCY
boone/oakley advertising / Charlotte
CLIENT
boone/oakley advertising

DESIGNER:
Logan Watts
PROGRAMMER:
Jeremy Walker
DIGITAL ARTIST/MULTIMEDIA:
Logan Watts
PRODUCTION COMPANY:
BigNoise
CREATIVE DIRECTORS:
David Oakley, John Boone
CONTENT STRATEGIST:
Phil Smith
ANNUAL ID:
06188N
URL:
www.booneoakley.com

230   MERIT WINNERS // BASCULE // BOONE/OAKLEY // F/NAZCA SAATCHI & SAATCHI // HAKUHODO I-STUDIO

WEB SITES: SELF-PROMOTION

AGENCY
F/Nazca Saatchi & Saatchi / São Paulo
CLIENT
Campana Brothers

ART DIRECTORS:
Mariana Bukvic
Lucio Rufo
WRITER:
Christiane Gribel
DESIGNER:
William Queen
PROGRAMMERS:
Paulo Pacheco, Leonardo Barbosa
DIGITAL ARTIST/MULTIMEDIA:
André Abujamra
PRODUCTION COMPANY:
F/Nazca Saatchi & Saatchi
INFORMATION ARCHITECT:
Paula Yuri Obata
CREATIVE DIRECTORS:
Fabio Fernandes, Fabio Simoes
CONTENT STRATEGIST:
Ana Carolina Ramos
ANNUAL ID:
06189N
URL:
http://www.campanas.com.br

WEB SITES: SELF-PROMOTION

AGENCY
Hakuhodo i-studio / Tokyo
CLIENT
Shu Akashi

ART DIRECTOR:
Katsuhiko Sano
DESIGNER:
Katsuhiko Sano
PROGRAMMER:
Katsuhiko Sano
DIGITAL ARTIST/MULTIMEDIA:
Takashi Morio
ANNUAL ID:
06190N
URL:
http://award.i-studio.co.jp/2005_shuakashi/

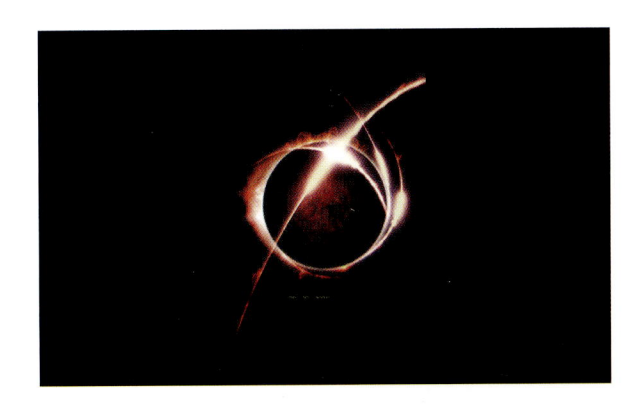

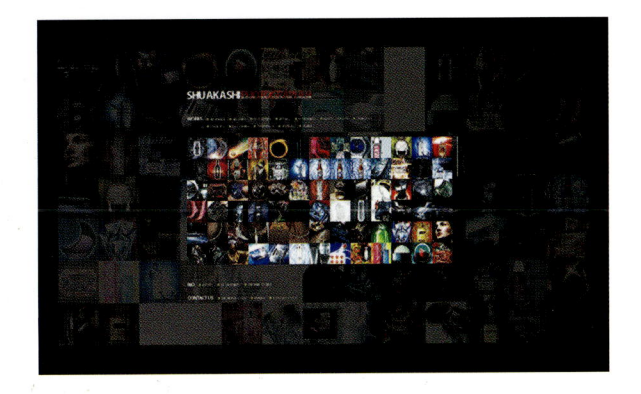

Merit Winners
231

WEB SITES: SELF-PROMOTION

AGENCY
Jung von Matt / Stuttgart
CLIENT
Jung von Matt Group

ART DIRECTORS:
Michael Zoelch, Marcus Widmann
WRITER:
Philipp Mayer
DESIGNER:
Dominik Kentner
PROGRAMMER:
Stefanie Hezinger
DIGITAL ARTIST/MULTIMEDIA:
Fabian Buergy
CREATIVE DIRECTORS:
Stefan Walz, Till Hohmann
Tobias Eichinger, Peter Waibel
ANNUAL ID:
06191N
URL:
http://www.jvm.de/weihnachtsmarkt2005/oneshow

WEB SITES: SELF-PROMOTION

AGENCY
Kinetic / Singapore
CLIENT
Kinetic / Singapore

ART DIRECTOR:
Sean Lam
WRITER:
Alex Goh
PROGRAMMER:
Sean Lam
DIGITAL ARTIST/MULTIMEDIA:
Sean Lam
CREATIVE DIRECTOR:
Sean Lam
ANNUAL ID:
06192N
URL:
http://www.kinetic.com.sg

232   MERIT WINNERS // JUNG VON MATT // KINETIC SINGAPORE // MAKINE STUDIOS // MCKINNEY

WEB SITES: SELF-PROMOTION

AGENCY
Makine Studios / Venice

CLIENT
Makine Studios

ART DIRECTOR:
Pierre-Etienne Poulin
DESIGNER:
Hugues Morin
PROGRAMMER:
Stef Funaro
PRODUCTION COMPANY:
Mecano
CREATIVE DIRECTORS:
Pierre-Etienne Poulin
Eduardo Garcia
ANNUAL ID:
06193N
URL:
http://www.makinestudios.com

WEB SITES: SELF-PROMOTION

AGENCY
McKinney / Durham

CLIENT
McKinney

ART DIRECTOR:
Jason Musante
WRITER:
Matt Fischvogt
DESIGNER:
Justin Smith
PROGRAMMER:
Clive Sweeney
CREATIVE DIRECTORS:
Dave Cook, David Baldwin
Jonathan Cude
ANNUAL ID:
06194N
URL:
http://awardshowsubmissions.com/06oneshow

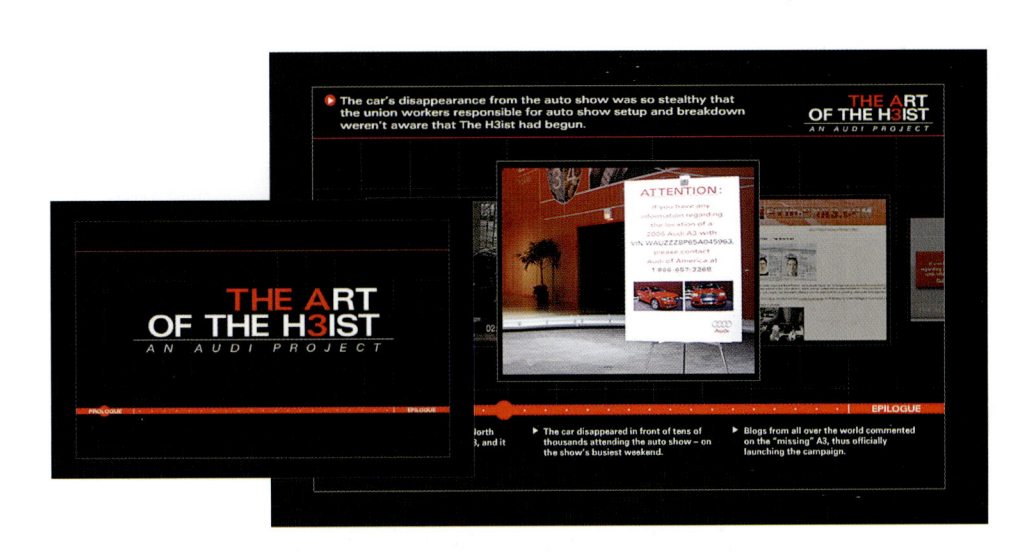

Merit Winners
233

WEB SITES: SELF-PROMOTION

AGENCY
POKE / London
CLIENT
Mother

ART DIRECTOR:
Kim Gehrig
WRITER:
Erik Enberg
DESIGNER:
Nico Nuzzaci
PROGRAMMER:
Simon Kallgard
PRODUCTION COMPANY:
POKE London
CREATIVE DIRECTOR:
Simon Waterfall
CONTENT STRATEGIST:
Tom Hostler
ANNUAL ID:
06195N
URL:
http://www.motherlondon.com

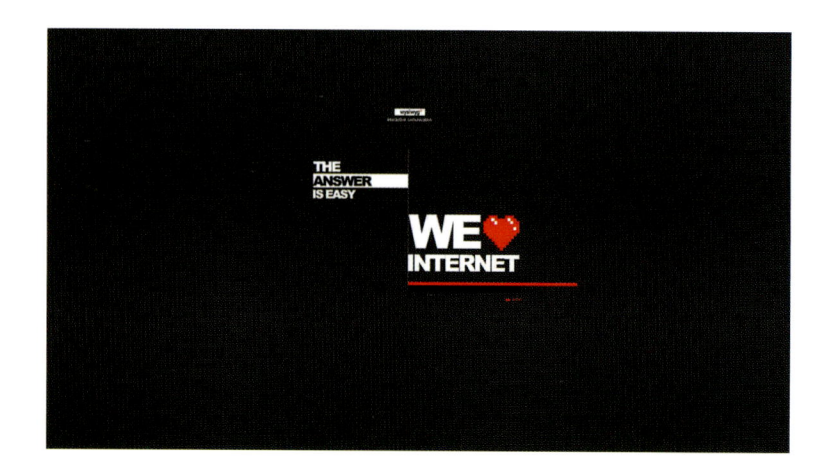

WEB SITES: SELF-PROMOTION

AGENCY
Wysiwyg Comunicación Interactiva / Madrid
CLIENT
Wysiwyg

ART DIRECTOR:
Marga Castaño
WRITERS:
Esther de la Rosa
Daniel Molinillo
PROGRAMMER:
Filippo de la Casa
DIGITAL ARTIST/MULTIMEDIA:
Charly Rodríguez
CREATIVE DIRECTORS:
Adolfo González, Nuria Martínez
CONTENT STRATEGIST:
Ignacio Álvarez-Borrás
ANNUAL ID:
06196N
URL:
http://www.wysiwyg.net/fests06/oneshow/index.html

WEB SITES: PUBLIC SERVICE/NON-PROFIT
/ EDUCATIONAL

AGENCY
Anderson DDB Health &
Lifestyle / Toronto
CLIENT
Wyeth Canada

ART DIRECTOR:
Monica Broekhoven
WRITER:
Abraham Zachariah
DESIGNER:
Brendyn Zachary
PROGRAMMER:
Brendyn Zachary
DIGITAL ARTIST/MULTIMEDIA:
Brendyn Zachary
CREATIVE DIRECTOR:
Ron Hudson
ANNUAL ID:
06197N
URL:
http://www.alesse.ca

WEB SITES: PUBLIC SERVICE/NON-PROFIT
/ EDUCATIONAL

AGENCY
BlueMars - Gesellschaft für digitale
Kommunikation / Frankfurt
CLIENT
Hessischer Rundfunk

ART DIRECTOR:
Nicole Holzenkamp
WRITERS:
Thomas Schernbeck
Volker Denkel
DIGITAL ARTIST/MULTIMEDIA:
Karsten Gerigk
INFORMATION ARCHITECT:
Stephan Grofl
CREATIVE DIRECTOR:
Layla Keramat
CONTENT STRATEGISTS:
Dr. Anja Rau, Tobias Kirchhofer
ANNUAL ID:
06198N
URL:
http://award.bluemars.net/2006/one-show/ende-des-schweigens/

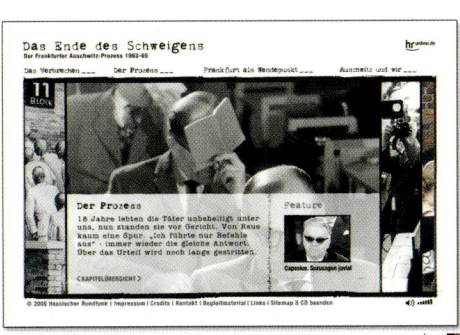

Merit Winners
235

WEB SITES: PUBLIC SERVICE/NON-PROFIT
/ EDUCATIONAL

AGENCY
Grupo W / Saltillo
CLIENT
Museo del Desierto

ART DIRECTORS:
Francisco Romanh
Cesar Moreno
PROGRAMMERS:
Homero Sousa, Raul Uranga
DIGITAL ARTISTS/MULTIMEDIA:
Jezreel Gutierrez, Roberto Espero
Sebastian Mariscal, Sara Davila
Fernando Valdes, Marcela de la Cruz
CREATIVE DIRECTORS:
Ulises Valencia, Miguel Calderon
ANNUAL ID:
06199N
URL:
http://www.grupow.com/museode

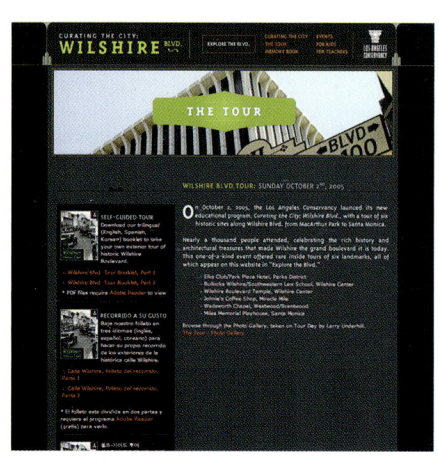

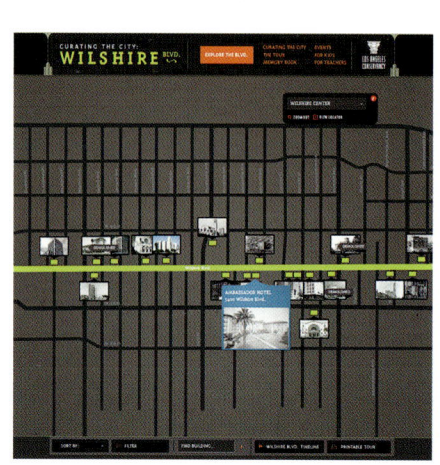

WEB SITES: PUBLIC SERVICE/NON-PROFIT
/EDUCATIONAL

AGENCY
Hello Design / Culver City
CLIENT
Los Angeles Conservancy

ART DIRECTOR:
Casey Sheehan
PROGRAMMERS:
Hugo Zhu, Jason Taylor
Jon Lorenz
CREATIVE DIRECTORS:
David Lai, Hiro Niwa
CONTENT STRATEGISTS:
Anna Simonse, Szu Ann Chen
Morgan Weatherford
ANNUAL ID:
06200N
URL:
http://www.curatingthecity.org

236 MERIT WINNERS // GRUPO W // HELLO DESIGN // SEDGWICK RD // TRIBAL DDB

WEB SITES: PUBLIC SERVICE/NON-PROFIT
/ EDUCATIONAL

AGENCY
Sedgwick Rd. / Seattle

CLIENT
Washington State
Department of Health

ART DIRECTOR:
Mishy Cass

WRITER:
Scott Stripling

DIGITAL ARTIST/MULTIMEDIA:
Seven2

CREATIVE DIRECTOR:
Zach Hitner

ANNUAL ID:
06201N

URL:
http://www.ashtraymouth.com

WEB SITES: PUBLIC SERVICE/NON-PROFIT
/ EDUCATIONAL

AGENCY
Tribal DDB / Vancouver

CLIENT
Fraser Health Authority

ART DIRECTOR:
Kelly Hale

WRITER:
Kevin Shortt

PROGRAMMER:
Dana Brousseau

CREATIVE DIRECTOR:
Bruce Sinclair

ANNUAL ID:
06202N

URL:
http://www.exhale.ca/

Merit Winners
237

BRAND GAMING: BUSINESS TO CONSUMER

AGENCY
Big Spaceship / Brooklyn
CLIENT
Sony Pictures

ART DIRECTOR:
David Chau
WRITERS:
David Chau, Jeanne McCabe
Karen Dahlstrom
DESIGNERS:
David Chau, Michael Dillingham
Zander Brimijoin, Jesse Greenberg
Tyson Damman, Staffan Estberg
Carl Nyman
PROGRAMMERS:
Joshua Hirsch, Tai U
DIGITAL ARTISTS/MULTIMEDIA:
David Chau, David Hill, Zander Brimijoin
Michael Dillingham, Bjorn Fagerholm
Christian Johansson
INFORMATION ARCHITECT:
Joshua Hirsch
CREATIVE DIRECTOR:
Michael Lebowitz
ANNUAL ID:
06203N
URL:
www.entertheunderworld.com/game/

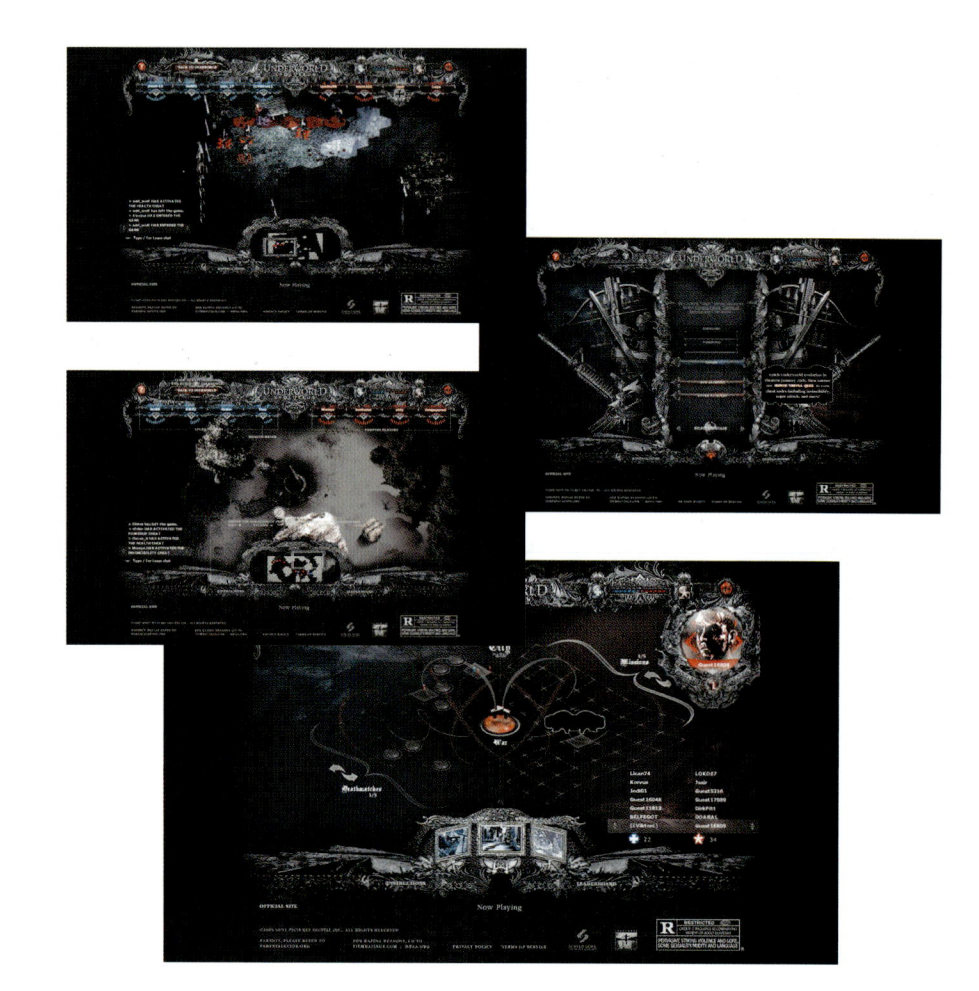

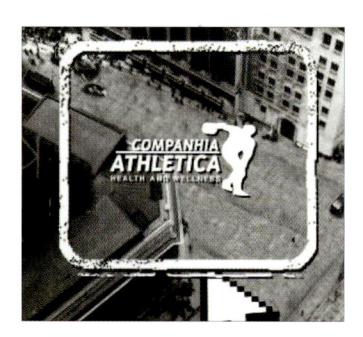

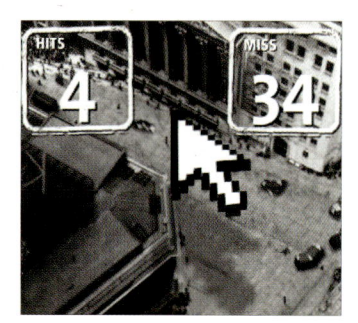

BRAND GAMING: BUSINESS TO CONSUMER

AGENCY
DDB Brasil / São Paulo
CLIENT
Companhia Athletica

ART DIRECTOR:
Mauricio Mazzariol
WRITER:
Mauricio Mazzariol
PRODUCTION COMPANIES:
Heloisa Lima, Roberta Padilla
Renata Oliveira, Sandra Zimb
Helena Bordon
CREATIVE DIRECTORS:
Sergio Valente, Ricardo Chester
Felipe Cama, Fernanda Romano
ANNUAL ID:
06204N
URL:
http://www.dm9ddb.com.br/awards
/oneshow/run01.html

238 MERIT WINNERS // BIG SPACESHIP // DDB BRASIL // EURO RSCG 4D // MAX WEBER

BRAND GAMING: BUSINESS TO CONSUMER

AGENCY
Euro RSCG 4D / Amstelveen
CLIENT
Nokia

ART DIRECTOR:
Martijn Sengers
WRITER:
Bram de Rooij
DESIGNERS:
Roland Lamers, Feike Kloostra
Antonio Costa, Rijk-Jan van Silfhout
Andrew Crawford
PRODUCTION COMPANY:
hazazaH
INFORMATION ARCHITECTS:
Tanya Hayes, Bob Elbersen
CREATIVE DIRECTORS:
Martijn Sengers
Bram de Rooij
CONTENT STRATEGIST:
Sicco Beerda
ANNUAL ID:
06205N
URL:
www.prize-entry.com/nokia/oneshow

BRAND GAMING: BUSINESS TO CONSUMER

AGENCY
Max Weber / Warsaw
CLIENT
Sanitec Kolo

ART DIRECTOR:
Piotr Tracki
DESIGNERS:
Bartosz Witulski
Andrzej Kryszpiniuk
PROGRAMMER:
Piotr Tracki
DIGITAL ARTIST/MULTIMEDIA:
Mieszko Saktura
CREATIVE DIRECTORS:
Marcin Talarek
Grzegorz Mogilewski
Krzysztof Dykas
ANNUAL ID:
06206N
URL:
http://www.saniteckolo.com/reflex

Merit Winners
239

BRAND GAMING: BUSINESS TO CONSUMER

AGENCY
RMG Connect / Sydney
CLIENT
Samsung

ART DIRECTOR:
Hazim Abdul-Hamid
WRITER:
Josh Bryer
PRODUCTION COMPANY:
Soap Creative
PHOTOGRAPHER:
Dean Wilmont
CREATIVE DIRECTOR:
Ashadi Hopper
CONTENT STRATEGISTS:
Hema Civil, Liz Smith
ANNUAL ID:
06207N
URL:
http://www.rmgconnect.com.au
/oneshow/samsung/

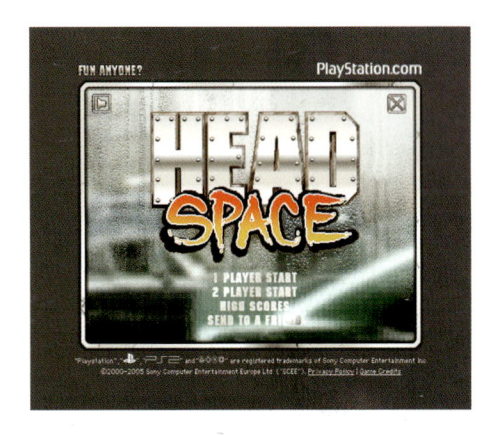

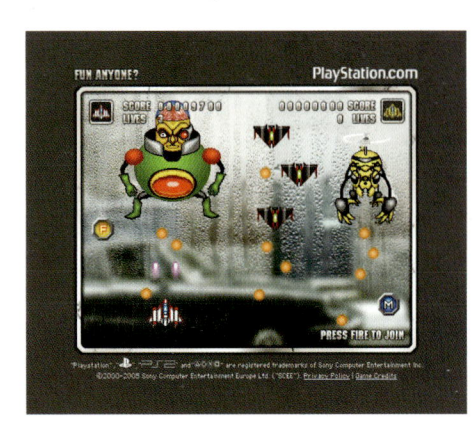

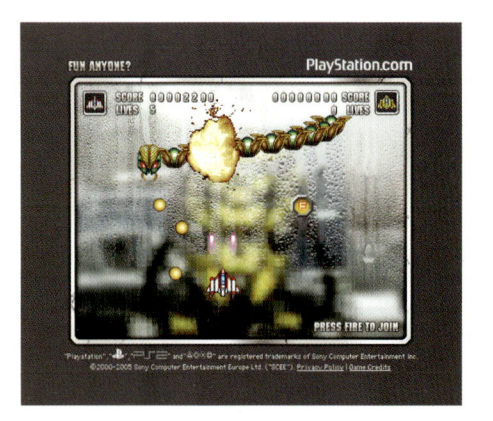

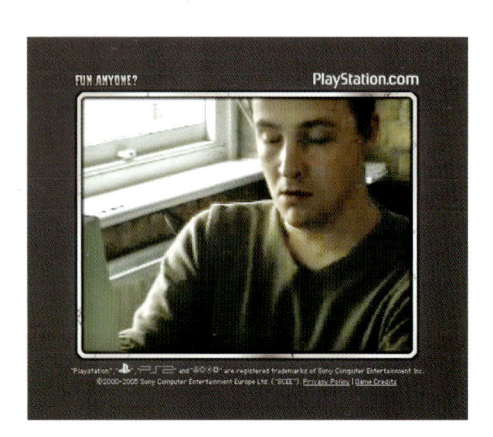

BRAND GAMING:
PROMOTIONAL ADVERTISING

AGENCY
Bloc Media / London
CLIENT
Sony Computer
Entertainment Europe

ART DIRECTOR:
Rick Palmer
DESIGNER:
Tom Jennings
PROGRAMMER:
Iain Lobb
CREATIVE DIRECTOR:
John Denton
ANNUAL ID:
06208N
URL:
http://portfolio.blocmedia.com
/mindgames/

240   MERIT WINNERS // RMG CONNECT // BLOC MEDIA // FORSMAN & BODENFORS // POP&CO

BRAND GAMING:
PROMOTIONAL ADVERTISING

AGENCY
Forsman & Bodenfors / Gothenburg
CLIENT
Abba Seafood

DESIGNER:
Jonas Sjövall
ART DIRECTORS:
Martin Cedergren
Joakim Blondell
Mathias Appelblad
WRITERS:
Martin Ringqvist
Jacob Nelson
PRODUCTION COMPANY:
Daddy
ANNUAL ID:
06209N
URL:
http://demo.fb.se/e/abba/kallesjumbo/

BRAND GAMING:
PROMOTIONAL ADVERTISING

AGENCY
Pop&Co. / New York
CLIENT
Cartoon Network

ART DIRECTOR:
Scott Gursky
DESIGNER:
Will Hall
PROGRAMMER:
Mike Szabo
PRODUCTION COMPANY:
Pop&Co.
INFORMATION ARCHITECT:
Chris Lamb
CREATIVE DIRECTOR:
Vincent Lacava
CONTENT STRATEGIST:
Fergus Galligan
ANNUAL ID:
06210N
URL:
http://www.popandco.com/archive/ben10/ben10.html

Merit Winners
241

BRAND GAMING: SELF-PROMOTION

AGENCY
Bloc Media / London
CLIENT
Bloc Media

ART DIRECTOR:
Rick Palmer
DESIGNERS:
Tom Jennings
Lee Pennington
PROGRAMMERS:
Iain Lobb, Steve Hayes
CREATIVE DIRECTOR:
John Denton
ANNUAL ID:
06211N
URL:
http://www.stackopolis.com/

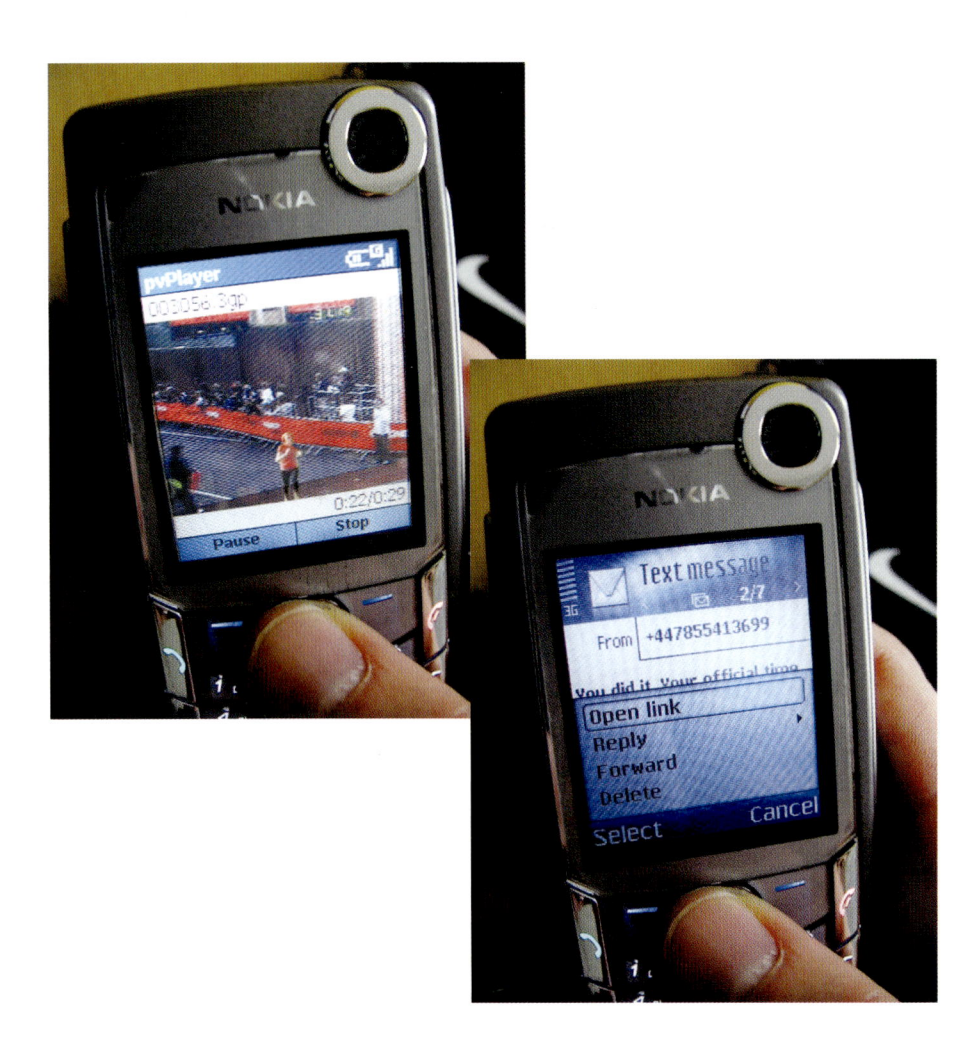

WIRELESS: BUSINESS TO CONSUMER

AGENCY
AKQA / London
CLIENT
Nike

WRITER:
Nick Bailey
PROGRAMMERS:
Gareth Rowlands
Matthew Elwin
CONTENT STRATEGIST:
Simon Jefferson
ANNUAL ID:
06212N
URL:
http://awards.akqa.com/awards/nike/free/index.html

242 MERIT WINNERS // BLOC MEDIA // AKQA // LATERAL NET // ARNOLD

WIRELESS: BUSINESS TO CONSUMER

AGENCY
Lateral Net / London
CLIENT
Levi Strauss and Co. Europe

ART DIRECTOR:
Simon Crabtree
WRITER:
David Jones
DESIGNERS:
Ted Hunt, Karl Andersson
PROGRAMMER:
Karsten Schmidt
INFORMATION ARCHITECT:
Daniel Jordan-Bambach
ANNUAL ID:
06213N
URL:
http://eu.levi.com/max

VIRAL AND EMAIL:
BUSINESS TO CONSUMER

AGENCY
Arnold / McLean
CLIENT
McDonald's

WRITERS:
Elizabeth Phillips
Don Corrigan
PROGRAMMER:
Chris Davis
CREATIVE DIRECTORS:
Ron Lawner
Woody Kay
Jeff McWeeny
ANNUAL ID:
06214N
URL:
http://bboybattle.com

Merit Winners
243

VIRAL AND EMAIL:
BUSINESS TO CONSUMER

AGENCY
Crispin Porter + Bogusky / Miami
CLIENT
Virgin Atlantic Airways

ART DIRECTOR:
Geordie Stephens
WRITER:
Franklin Tipton
PROGRAMMER:
Luis Santi
PRODUCTION COMPANY:
Varitalk
CREATIVE DIRECTORS:
Alex Bogusky, Bill Wright
Jeff Benjamin
ANNUAL ID:
06219N
URL:
http://www.cpbgroup.com/awards
/ringmerichard.html

VIRAL AND EMAIL:
BUSINESS TO CONSUMER

AGENCY
glue / London
CLIENT
Virgin Trains

ART DIRECTORS:
Christine Turner
Simon Lloyd
WRITERS:
Christine Turner
Simon Lloyd
DESIGNERS:
Tomboy Virals
Adam Lee
PRODUCTION COMPANY:
Tomboy Virals
CREATIVE DIRECTOR:
Seb Royce
ANNUAL ID:
06220N
URL:
http://www.gluelondon.com
/awards/oneshow/

244   MERIT WINNERS // CRISPIN PORTER + BOGUSKY // GLUE LONDON // GROUND ZERO ADVERTISING // LEO BURNETT

VIRAL AND EMAIL:
BUSINESS TO CONSUMER

AGENCY
Ground Zero Advertising

CLIENT
Virgin Digital

ART DIRECTOR:
Rodrigo Butori
WRITER:
Kristina Slade
PRODUCTION COMPANY:
National Television
CREATIVE DIRECTOR:
Court Crandall
ANNUAL ID:
06221N
URL:
http://virgindigital.com/index_us.html?target=video

VIRAL AND EMAIL:
BUSINESS TO CONSUMER

AGENCY
Leo Burnett / Frankfurt

CLIENT
Revell

ART DIRECTOR:
Klaus Trapp
WRITER:
Mathias Henkel
CREATIVE DIRECTORS:
Peter Steger, Andreas Heinzel
ANNUAL ID:
06222N
URL:
http://home.arcor.de/mhenkel/revellviralspots.html

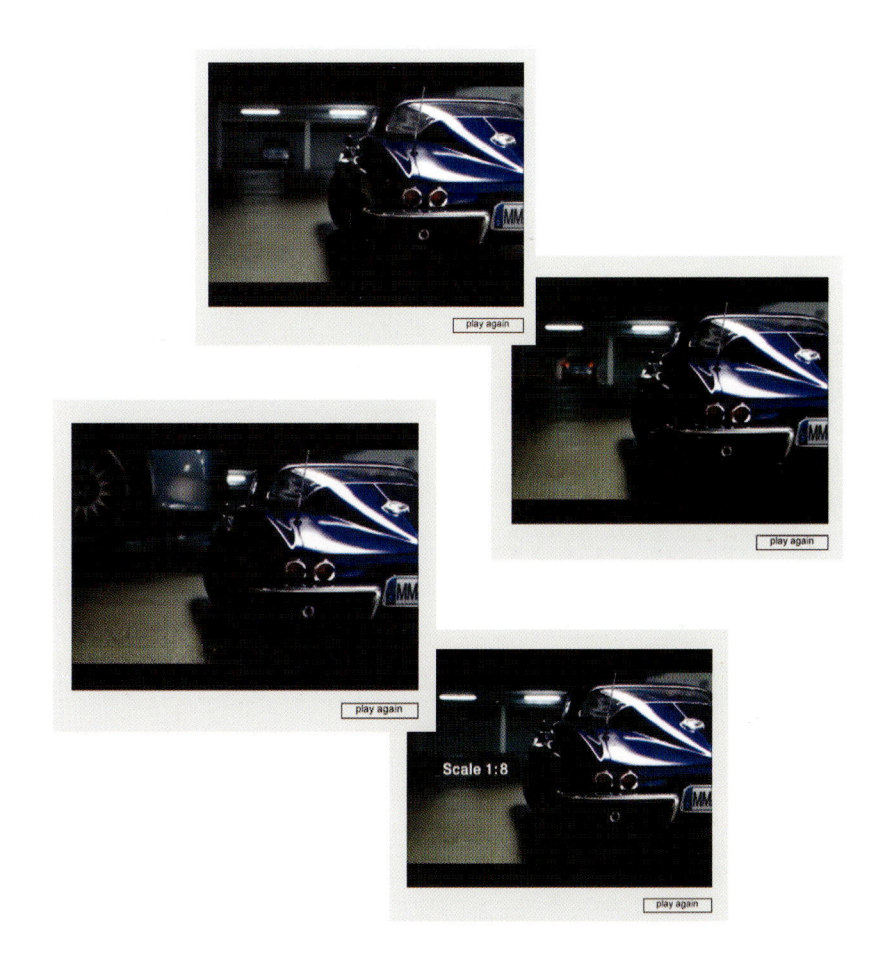

Merit Winners
245

VIRAL AND EMAIL:
BUSINESS TO CONSUMER

AGENCY
McKinney / Durham
CLIENT
Audi of America

ART DIRECTOR:
Jason Musante
WRITERS:
Matt Fischvogt, Gregg Hale
Ernie Larsen, Brian Cain
Jim Gunshanon
AGENCY PRODUCER:
Regina Brizzolara
PRODUCTION COMPANY:
Chelsea Pictures/campfire
CREATIVE DIRECTORS:
Dave Cook, David Baldwin
Jonathan Cude, Brian Clark
ANNUAL ID:
06223N
URL:
http://www.awardshowsubmissions.com
/06oneshow/

VIRAL AND EMAIL:
BUSINESS TO CONSUMER

AGENCY
Mekanism / San Francisco
CLIENT
SEGA

ART DIRECTOR:
Ian Kovalik
DESIGNER:
Ian Kovalik
PRODUCTION COMPANY:
Mekanism
CREATIVE DIRECTOR:
Tommy Means
ANNUAL ID:
06224N
URL:
http://www.segalabs.com

VIRAL AND EMAIL:
BUSINESS TO CONSUMER

AGENCY
Nordpol+ Hamburg
CLIENT
Renault Germany

ART DIRECTOR:
Gunther Schreiber
WRITER:
Ingmar Bartels
DESIGNERS:
Christoph Bielefeldt
Philipp Dörner
Bertrand Kirschenhofer
PRODUCTION COMPANY:
Element E
DIRECTOR:
Silvio Helbig
CREATIVE DIRECTOR:
Lars Rühmann
ANNUAL ID:
06225N
URL:
http://www.nordpol.com/2005/renault/crashtest/en/

VIRAL AND EMAIL:
BUSINESS TO CONSUMER

AGENCY
Organic / San Francisco
CLIENT
Sprint

WRITER:
Ben Citron
DESIGNER:
Maria Tyomkina
DIGITAL ARTIST/MULTIMEDIA:
Aaron Clinger
PRODUCTION COMPANY:
V3@ Anonymous Content
CREATIVE DIRECTORS:
Christian Haas, Roger Wong
Ben Citron
ANNUAL ID:
06226N
URL:
http://awards.organic.com/entertain

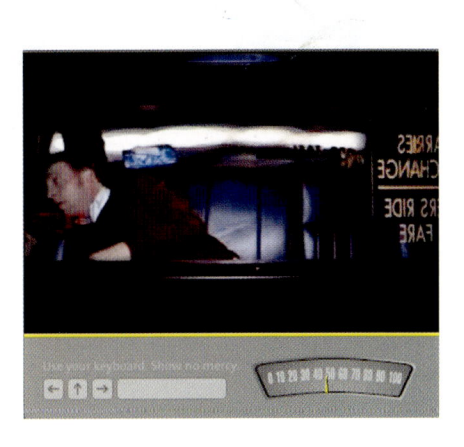

Merit Winners
247

VIRAL AND EMAIL:
BUSINESS TO CONSUMER

AGENCY
POKE / London
CLIENT
SAB Miller

PROGRAMMER:
Andrew Knott
DIGITAL ARTISTS/MULTIMEDIA:
Mr Bingo, Kenneth Tinkin Hun
Han Hoogerbrugge, Joel Veitch
Natalie Ballard, Rafael Rosendaal
Steve Scott, Nick Ryan
PRODUCTION COMPANY:
POKE London
CREATIVE DIRECTOR:
Nicolas Roope
CONTENT STRATEGIST:
Kate Theakston
ANNUAL ID:
06227N
URL:
http://secure.pokelondon.com/awards/OneShow/miller_revue

VIRAL AND EMAIL:
BUSINESS TO CONSUMER

AGENCY
Publicis & Hal Riney /
San Francisco
CLIENT
Peter Kim Jewelry

ART DIRECTORS:
Colin Kim
Dominic Goldman
WRITERS:
Jesse Dillow
Mike Danko
DESIGNER:
Michael Kern
PRODUCTION COMPANY:
Struck Design
INFORMATION ARCHITECT:
Sosia Bert
CREATIVE DIRECTORS:
Jae Goodman, Jon Soto
Dominic Goldman
ANNUAL ID:
06228N
URL:
http://www.flossyogrill.com

248 MERIT WINNERS // POKE // PUBLICIS & HAL RINEY // DENTSU WEST

Now give her some flowers.

VIRAL AND EMAIL:
BUSINESS TO CONSUMER

AGENCY
Publicis & Hal Riney /
San Francisco
CLIENT
Peter Kim Jewelry

ART DIRECTORS:
Colin Kim
Dominic Goldman
WRITERS:
Mike Danko
Jesse Dillow
PRODUCTION COMPANY:
Rocket Society
INFORMATION ARCHITECT:
Jim Vaughan
CREATIVE DIRECTORS:
Jae Goodman, Jon Soto
Dominic Goldman
ANNUAL ID:
06229N
URL:
http://www.hrp.com/peterkim/valentine

VIRAL AND EMAIL:
PROMOTIONAL ADVERTISING

AGENCY
Dentsu West /
Hiroshima
CLIENT
Ui-Bellmony

ART DIRECTOR:
Kazuhiko Nakajima
WRITER:
Yukari Kusaka
PROGRAMMER:
Mr. Y
DIGITAL ARTIST/MULTIMEDIA:
Masaru Yamamoto
PRODUCTION COMPANIES:
Agreed , Plan Do Production
Aflog Design Unit
CREATIVE DIRECTOR:
Kaoru Doi
CONTENT STRATEGISTS:
Wataru Hirose
Hirokazu Makinouchi
ANNUAL ID:
06230n
URL:
http://www.w-story.jp

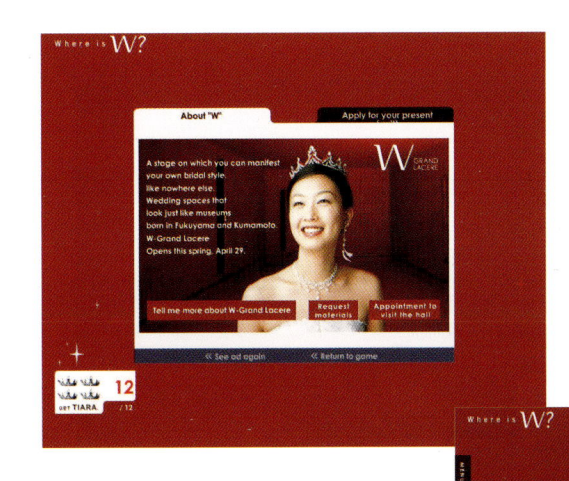

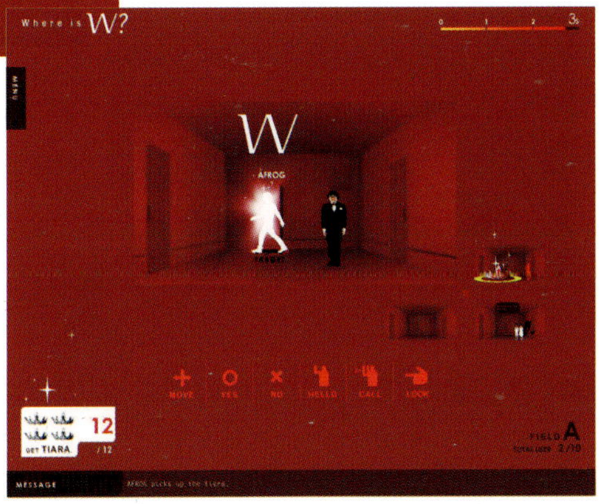

Merit Winners
249

ONLINE MOVIES: BUSINESS TO CONSUMER

AGENCY
Johnson Cowan Hanrahan / Portland

CLIENT
Brooks Sports

ART DIRECTOR:
Brent Anderson
WRITER:
Eric Samsel
DIGITAL ARTIST/MULTIMEDIA:
Matt Clark
PRODUCTION COMPANY:
Manbaby
CREATIVE DIRECTOR:
Tim Hanrahan
MUSIC & SOUND:
Chris Ballew
ANNUAL ID:
06237N
URL:
http://brooksrunning.com/life

VIRAL AND EMAIL: SELF-PROMOTION

AGENCY
Euro RSCG 4D / Amstelveen

CLIENT
Nokia

DESIGNERS:
Antonio Costa, Roland Lamers
Feike Kloostra, Rijk-Jan van Silfhout
Andrew Crawford
ART DIRECTOR:
Martijn Sengers
WRITER:
Bram de Rooij
PRODUCTION COMPANY:
hazazaH
INFORMATION ARCHITECTS:
Tanya Hayes, Bob Elbersen
CREATIVE DIRECTORS:
Bram de Rooij, Martijn Sengers
CONTENT STRATEGIST:
Sicco Beerda
ANNUAL ID:
06232N
URL:
http://www.prize-entry.com/nokia/oneshow

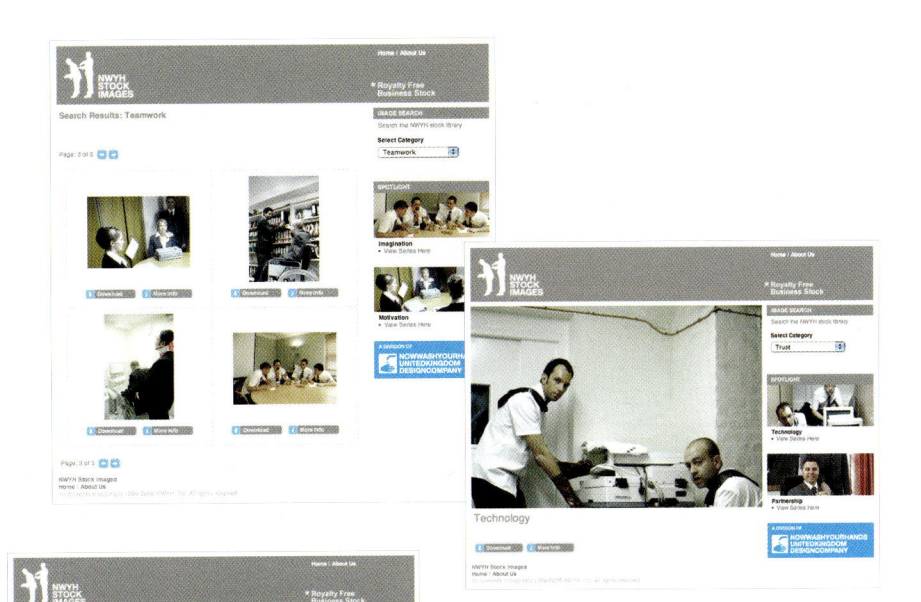

VIRAL AND EMAIL: SELF-PROMOTION

AGENCY
NOWWASHYOURHANDS /
London
CLIENT
NOWWASHYOURHANDS

DESIGNERS:
Alex Amelines
Kevin Coffey
PROGRAMMERS:
Jamie Warren, Jake Collins
PRODUCTION COMPANIES:
Neil Jeffries, Lise Mesztig
CREATIVE DIRECTOR:
Angus Mackinnon
CONTENT STRATEGIST:
Bob Silver
ANNUAL ID:
06233N
URL:
http://www.nwyhstockimages.com

VIRAL AND EMAIL: SELF-PROMOTION

AGENCY
TAXI / Toronto
CLIENT
Ihaveanidea

ART DIRECTOR:
Guybrush Taylor
WRITER:
Ryan Wagman
PRODUCTION COMPANY:
UNTITLED
DIRECTOR:
Michael Downing
CREATIVE DIRECTOR:
Zak Mroueh
ANNUAL ID:
06234N
URL:
http://www.neverinneutral.com/ihaveanidea

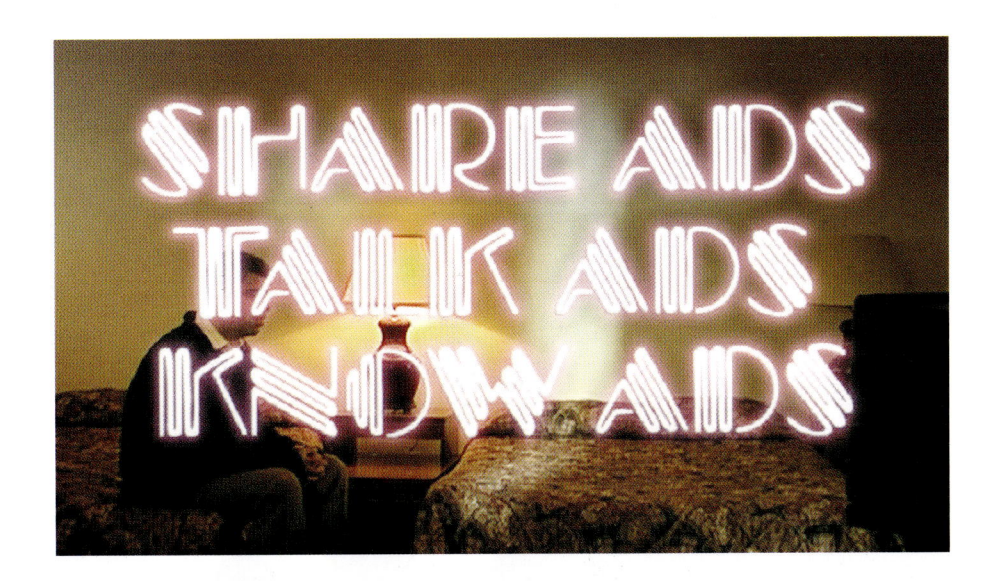

Merit Winners
251

VIRAL AND EMAIL: PUBLIC SERVICE
/NON-PROFIT/ EDUCATIONAL

AGENCY
Leo Burnett / London

CLIENT
Department for Transport
Teen Road Safety

ART DIRECTOR:
Angus Macadam

WRITER:
Paul Jordan

CREATIVE DIRECTOR:
Jim Thornton

ANNUAL ID:
06235N

URL:
http://www.notlooking.co.uk

ALSO AWARDED:
MERIT Online Movies: Business to Consumer
MERIT Other Digital Media: Public Service /
Non-Profit / Educational

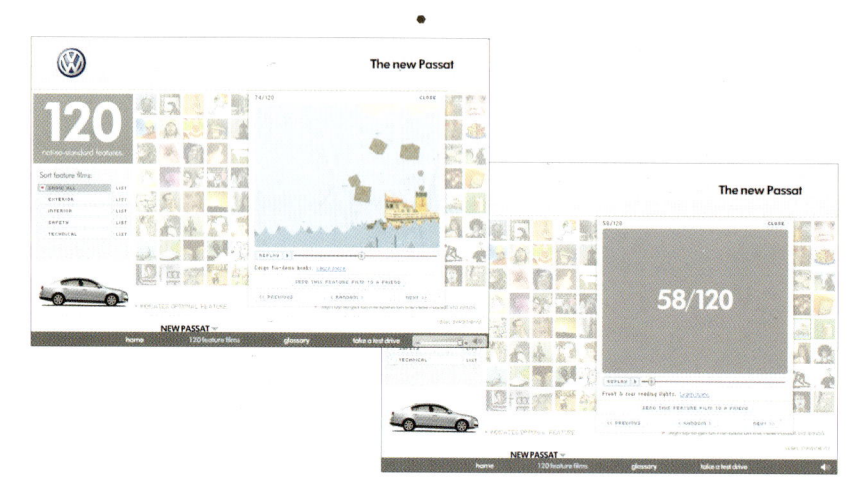

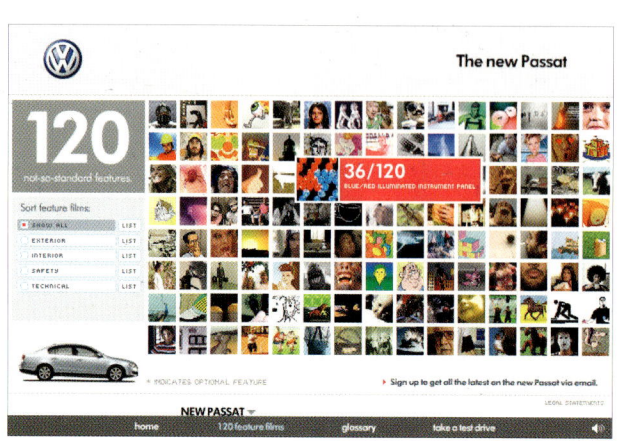

ONLINE MOVIES: BUSINESS TO CONSUMER

AGENCY
Arnold Worldwide / Boston

CLIENT
Volkswagen

ART DIRECTORS:
Colin Jeffery
Phillip Squier

WRITER:
Dave Weist

PRODUCTION COMPANIES:
Tomato, Lifelong Friendship Society
V3 @ Anonymous

CREATIVE DIRECTORS:
Ron Lawner, Alan Pafenbach
Dave Weist, Colin Jeffery

ANNUAL ID:
06236N

URL:
http://awards.arn.com/2005/shared/vw/minisites/Passat_120/campaign1.html

252 MERIT WINNERS // LEO BURNETT // ARNOLD WORLDWIDE // JUXT INTERACTIVE // TEAM ONE

OTHER DIGITAL MEDIA:
BUSINESS TO CONSUMER

AGENCY
juxt interactive / Newport Beach

CLIENT
Target Corporation

ART DIRECTOR:
Joe Stewart
WRITER:
Joe Shepter
DESIGNERS:
Justin Bernard
Brian Miller
PROGRAMMERS:
Casey Corcoran
Victor Allen, Erik Bianchi
CREATIVE DIRECTOR:
Todd Purgason
CONTENT STRATEGIST:
Bryan Booy
ANNUAL ID:
06251N
URL:
http://www.juxtinteractive.com
/up2d8/index.html

OTHER DIGITAL MEDIA:
PROMOTIONAL ADVERTISING

AGENCY
Team One / El Segundo

CLIENT
Lexus

ART DIRECTORS:
Gabrielle Mayeur
Nels Dielman
WRITER:
Dawn DeKeyser
DIGITAL ARTIST/MULTIMEDIA:
Dondi Fusco
PRODUCTION COMPANY:
Dave Jennsen
CREATIVE DIRECTORS:
Gabrielle Mayeur
Dawn DeKeyser
Chris Graves
ANNUAL ID:
06252N
URL:
http://archive.teamone-usa.com
/ismosaic/

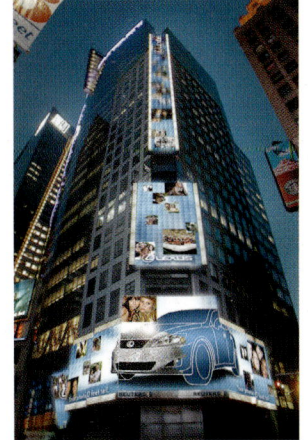

Merit Winners
253

ONLINE MOVIES: BUSINESS TO CONSUMER

AGENCY
Young & Rubicam / Chicago
CLIENT
Miller Brewing Company

ART DIRECTORS:
Mark Figliulo, Corey Ciszek
WRITERS:
Ken Erke, Pete Figel
PROGRAMMER:
Michael Brumm
DIGITAL ARTIST/MULTIMEDIA:
Chris Von Ende
PRODUCTION COMPANY:
MJZ
DIRECTOR:
Spike Jonze
CREATIVE DIRECTORS:
Dave Loew, Jon Wyville
Mark Figliulo
MUSIC & SOUND:
Tyrell LLC
ANNUAL ID:
06239N
URL:
http://www.millerauditions.com/penguin.php

ONLINE MOVIES:
PROMOTIONAL ADVERTISING

AGENCY
Red Tettemer / Philadelphia
CLIENT
Pennsylvania Tourism

ART DIRECTORS:
Erik Silverson, Tom Carr
WRITERS:
Erik Silverson, Tom Carr
DIGITAL ARTIST/MULTIMEDIA:
Ripple Effects
DIRECTORS:
Tom Carr, Erik Silverson
CREATIVE DIRECTORS:
Steve Red, Ken Cills
MUSIC & SOUND:
Patrick de Caumette
ANNUAL ID:
06240N
URL:
http://www.groundhog202.com/

254 MERIT WINNERS // YOUNG & RUBICAM // RED TETTEMER // DENTSU // DDB BRASIL

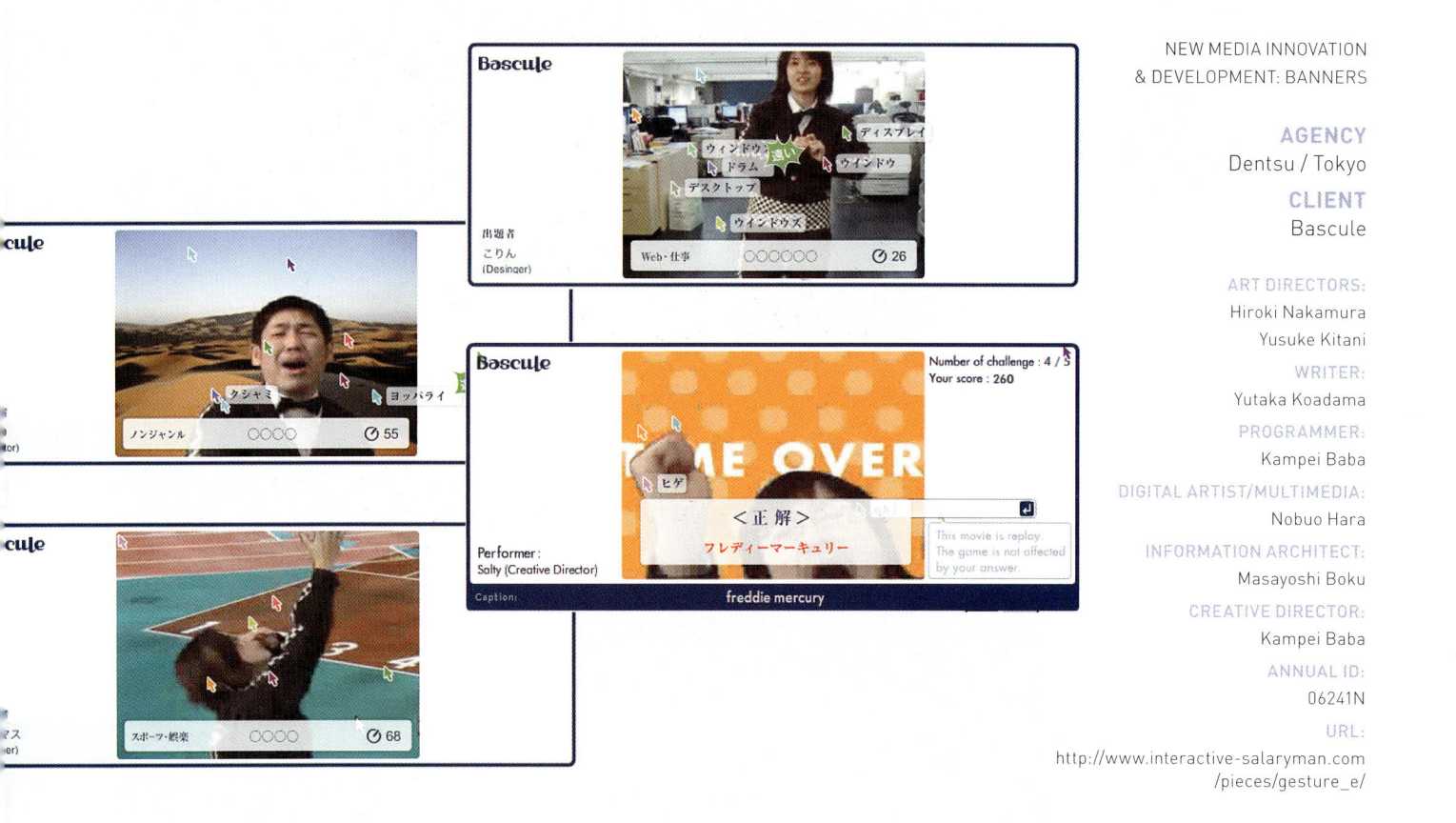

NEW MEDIA INNOVATION
& DEVELOPMENT: BANNERS

AGENCY
Dentsu / Tokyo

CLIENT
Bascule

ART DIRECTORS:
Hiroki Nakamura
Yusuke Kitani

WRITER:
Yutaka Koadama

PROGRAMMER:
Kampei Baba

DIGITAL ARTIST/MULTIMEDIA:
Nobuo Hara

INFORMATION ARCHITECT:
Masayoshi Boku

CREATIVE DIRECTOR:
Kampei Baba

ANNUAL ID:
06241N

URL:
http://www.interactive-salaryman.com/pieces/gesture_e/

NEW MEDIA INNOVATION
& DEVELOPMENT: WEB SITES

AGENCY
DDB Brasil / São Paulo

CLIENT
Henkel

ART DIRECTORS:
Cris Santoro, Pedro Gravena
Mauricio Mazzariol
Alexandre D'albergaria

WRITER:
Keke Toledo

PRODUCTION COMPANIES:
Heloisa Lima, Roberta Padilla
Renata Oliveira, Helena Bordon
Sandra Zimb

CREATIVE DIRECTORS:
Sergio Valente, Wilson Mateo
Marcos Medeiros, Fernanda Romano

ANNUAL ID:
06242N

URL:
http://www.dm9ddb.com.br/awards/oneshow/reality.html

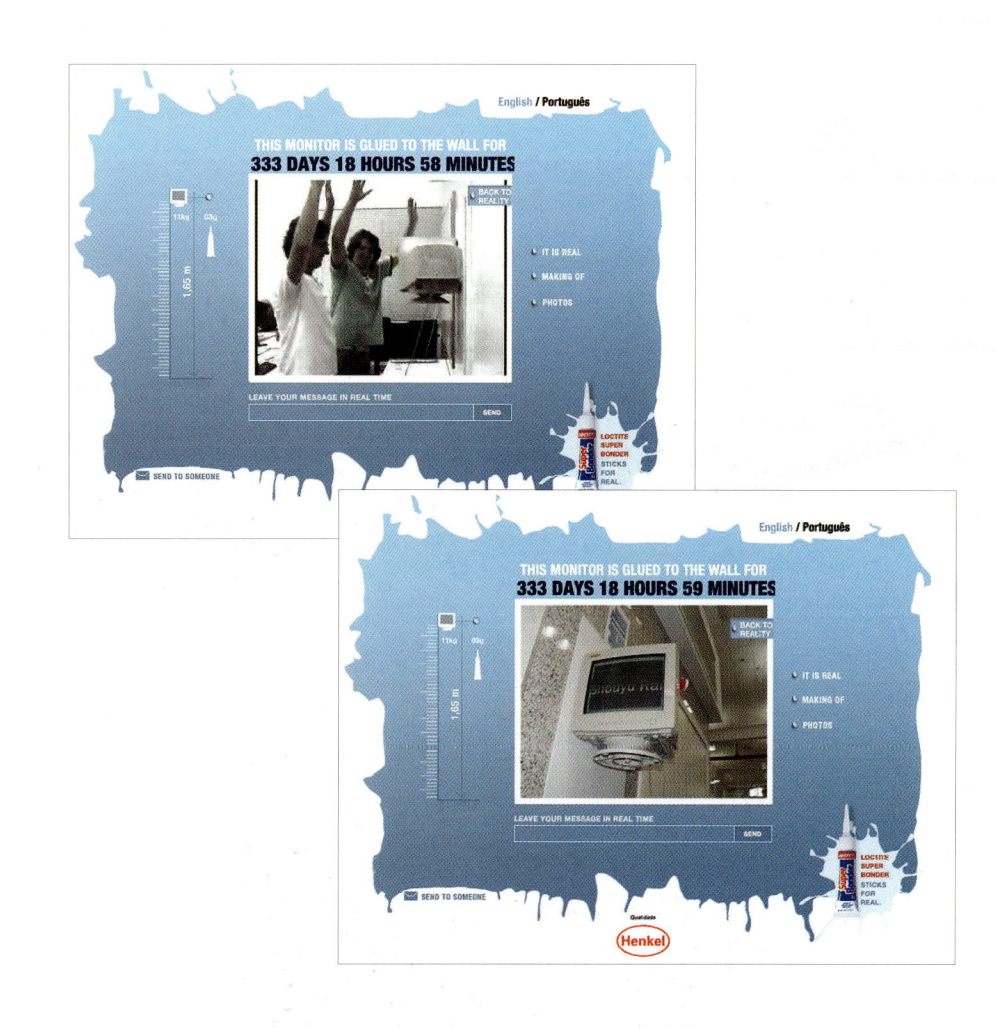

Merit Winners
255

NEW MEDIA INNOVATION
& DEVELOPMENT: WEB SITES

AGENCY
Dentsu / Tokyo
CLIENT
Dentsu

ART DIRECTOR:
Hirozumi Takakusaki
WRITER:
Yasuharu Sasaki
DESIGNER:
Yusuke Kitani
PROGRAMMERS:
Kampei Baba, Shintaro Kanega
DIGITAL ARTIST/MULTIMEDIA:
Hiroki Nakamura
CREATIVE DIRECTORS:
Hirozumi Takakusaki
Yasuharu Sasaki
ANNUAL ID:
06243N
URL:
http://www.interactive-salaryman.com
/pieces/crjuku2005_e/oneshow.html

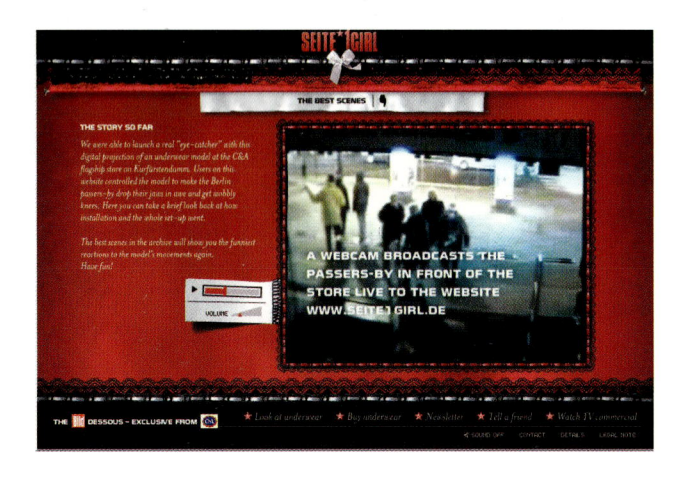

NEW MEDIA INNOVATION
& DEVELOPMENT: WEB SITES

AGENCY
Jung von Matt / Hamburg
CLIENT
Axel Springer

ART DIRECTOR:
Sven Loskill
WRITER:
Robert Ehlers
PROGRAMMERS:
Benjamin Herholz
Jan M. Studt
PRODUCTION COMPANY:
Fata Morgana
CREATIVE DIRECTOR:
Bernd Kraemer
ANNUAL ID:
06244N
URL:
http://award.jvm.de/en/seite1girl/

256 MERIT WINNERS // DENTSU // JUNG VON MATT // SCHOLZ & VOLKMER // TRIBAL DDB

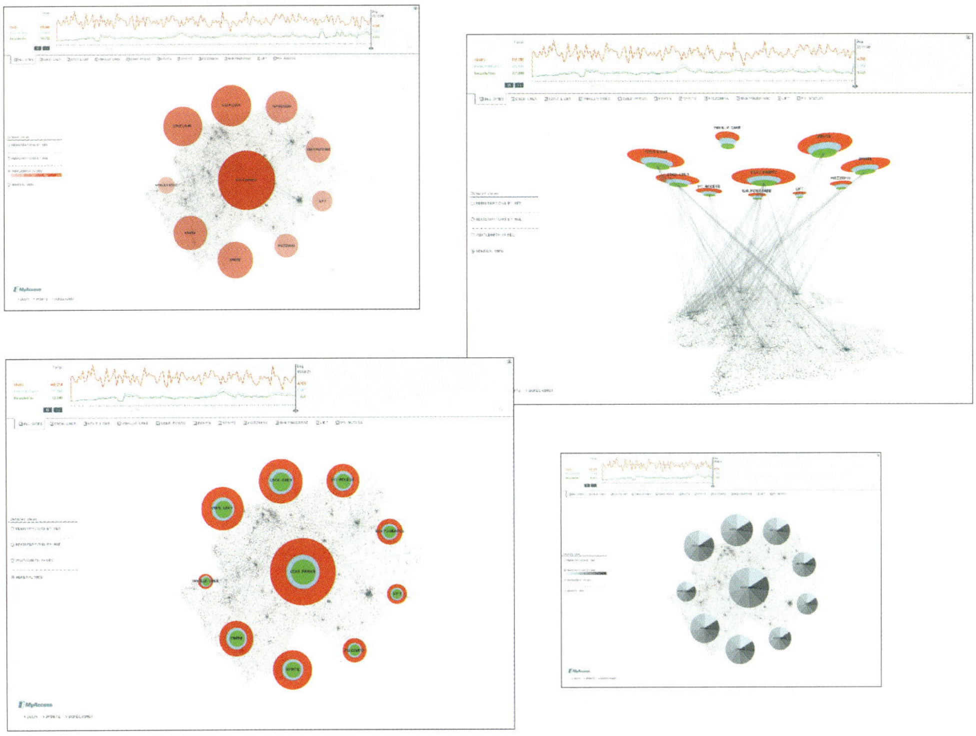

OTHER DIGITAL MEDIA:
BUSINESS TO BUSINESS

AGENCY
Scholz & Volkmer /
Wiesbaden
CLIENT
Coca-Cola

PROGRAMMER:
Manfred Kraft
CREATIVE DIRECTOR:
Heike Brockmann
CONTENT STRATEGISTS:
Manfred Kraft, Peter Reichard
BjörnSternsdorf, Clemens Dopjans
ANNUAL ID:
06253N
URL:
http://www.s-v.de/projects/coke
-visualisierung

NEW MEDIA INNOVATION
& DEVELOPMENT: WEB SITES

AGENCY
Tribal DDB / Sydney
CLIENT
McDonald's Australia

ART DIRECTOR:
Mark Cracknell
DESIGNERS:
Ivan Yip, Sojung Lee
PROGRAMMER:
Mitchell Death
CREATIVE DIRECTOR:
Aaron Turk
CONTENT STRATEGIST:
Aaron Michie
ANNUAL ID:
06246N
URL:
http://www.tribalddb.com.au/oneshow2006

Merit Winners
257

NEW MEDIA INNOVATION
& DEVELOPMENT: GAMES

AGENCY
Bernstein-Rein / Kansas City

CLIENT
Ruby Tuesday

ART DIRECTORS:
Anthony Magliano
Bart Ashford

WRITER:
Eric Knittel

DIGITAL ARTISTS/MULTIMEDIA:
Travis Beckham, Derek Badsky

PRODUCTION COMPANY:
Janet Bacus

CREATIVE DIRECTORS:
Bob Morrow, Arlo Oviatt

ANNUAL ID:
06247N

URL:
http://www.chompchamp.com/

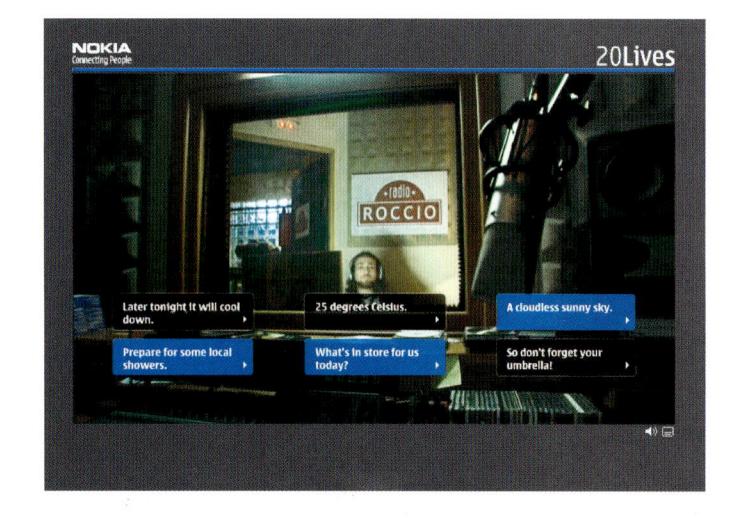

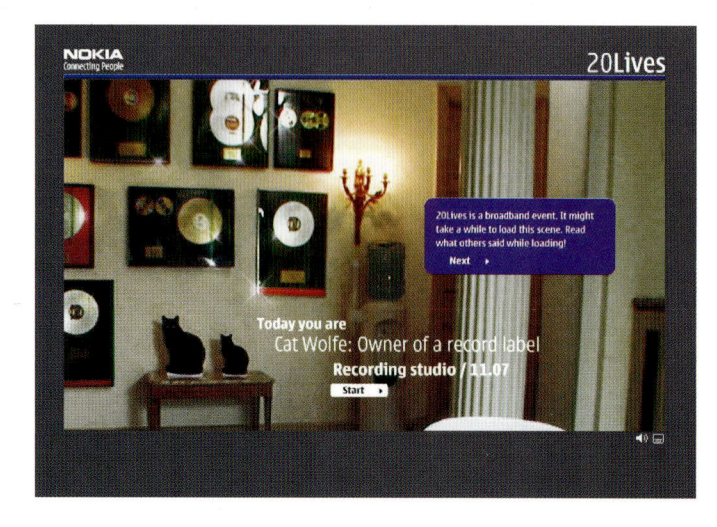

NEW MEDIA INNOVATION
& DEVELOPMENT: GAMES

AGENCY
Euro RSCG 4D / Amstelveen

CLIENT
Nokia

ART DIRECTOR:
Martijn Sengers

WRITER:
Bram de Rooij

DESIGNERS:
Antonio Costa, Roland Lamers
Feike Kloostra, Andrew Crawford
Rijk-Jan van Silfhout

PRODUCTION COMPANY:
hazazaH

INFORMATION ARCHITECTS:
Tanya Hayes, Bob Elbersen

CREATIVE DIRECTORS:
Bram de Rooij, Martijn Sengers

CONTENT STRATEGIST:
Sicco Beerda

ANNUAL ID:
06248N

URL:
http://www.prize-entry.com/nokia/oneshow

NEW MEDIA INNOVATION
& DEVELOPMENT: ANIMATION

AGENCY
Forsman & Bodenfors / Gothenburg
CLIENT
Volvo Cars Corporation

ART DIRECTORS:
Martin Cedergren
Andreas Malm
WRITERS:
Jacob Nelson, Filip Nilsson
DESIGNERS:
Mikko Timonen, Lars Jansson
Viktor Larsson, Jerry Wass
PRODUCTION COMPANIES:
B-Reel, Itiden, Paradise
ANNUAL ID:
06249N
URL:
http://demo.fb.se/e/volvo/xsea/3d

NEW MEDIA INNOVATION
& DEVELOPMENT: MOVIES

AGENCY
MargeotesFertittaPowell / New York
CLIENT
Samsung

WRITERS:
Josh Rogers, Neil Powell
Dan Shefelman, Jenny Lee
DESIGNERS:
The Barbarian Group, Mark Sloan
PRODUCTION COMPANIES:
The Barbarian Group
Berwyn, Outside Editorial
CREATIVE DIRECTORS:
Neil Powell, Chris Bradley
Josh Rogers, Morihiro Harano
CONTENT STRATEGIST:
Morihiro Harano
ANNUAL ID:
06250N
URL:
http://www.anyfilms.net

Merit Winners
259

INTEGRATED BRANDING:
INTEGRATED BRANDING CAMPAIGN

AGENCY
Dentsu / Tokyo
CLIENT
Toyota Motor Corporation

ART DIRECTORS:
Florian Schmitt
Kaori Mochizuki
WRITER:
Takaharu Mamiya
DESIGNER:
Tetsuya Yamada
PROGRAMMERS:
Naoto Oiwa, Tetsuji Oshita
John Cowen, Takeshiro Umezu
AGENCY PRODUCER:
Tomohiko Sugiura
PRODUCTION COMPANIES:
Aoi Digital Creation
Aoi Promotion
DIRECTORS:
Makoto Teramoto
Yasushi Arikawa
CREATIVE DIRECTORS:
Naoto Oiwa, Keita Yamada
ANNUAL ID:
06259N
URL:
http://www.aoi-dc.com/classix/bb/en/

INTEGRATED BRANDING:
INTEGRATED BRANDING CAMPAIGN

AGENCY
Crispin Porter + Bogusky / Miami
CLIENT
Burger King

ART DIRECTORS:
Mark Taylor, Kevin Koller
Anja Duering
WRITERS:
Bob Cianfrone
Carl Corbitt
DESIGNERS:
Stan Winston Studios
PROGRAMMER:
Luis Santi
AGENCY PRODUCERS:
Eva Dimick, Neil D'Amico
Brian McMillen, Darren Himebrook
Julieana Stechschulte
CREATIVE DIRECTORS:
Alex Bogusky, Andrew Keller
Rob Reilly, Jeff Benjamin
ANNUAL ID:
06256N
URL:
http://www.cpbgroup.com/awards/bkkingintegrated.html

260 MERIT WINNERS // DENTSU // CRISPIN PORTER + BOGUSKY

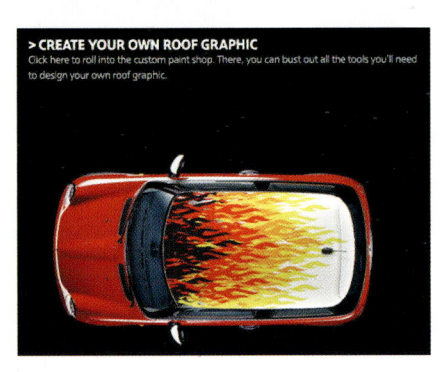

INTEGRATED BRANDING:
INTEGRATED BRANDING CAMPAIGN

AGENCY
Crispin Porter + Bogusky / Miami
CLIENT
MINI

ART DIRECTORS:
Ben James
Rahul Panchal
Trisha Ting
WRITERS:
Brian Tierney
Jackie Hathiramani
DESIGNER:
Chean Wei Law
PHOTOGRAPHERS:
Sebastian Gray
Daniel Hartz
AGENCY PRODUCERS:
Stephanie McKinney
Marcelino Alvarez
Rebekah Mateu
PRODUCTION COMPANIES:
EVB, Dev Impact, Beam Interactive
CREATIVE DIRECTORS:
Alex Bogusky, Andrew Keller
Jeff Benjamin, Rob Strasberg
ANNUAL ID:
06258N

AGENCY
Crispin Porter + Bogusky / Miami
CLIENT
Maxim

ART DIRECTORS:
Alex Burnard, Geordie Stephens
Mike Del Marmol
WRITERS:
David Schiff, David Gonzalez
DESIGNERS:
Alex Burnard, Rahul Panchal
Oscar Rivas, JJ Sedelmaier
ILLUSTRATOR:
Mike del Marmol
PROGRAMMER:
Andrew Reale
DIGITAL ARTISTS/MULTIMEDIA:
Rob Fielack, Mike Nonelle
AGENCY PRODUCERS:
Paul Sutton, Cindy Pérez, Sheri Radel
Rupert Samuel, David Rolfe
Dan Ruth, Eddie Alonso
PRODUCTION COMPANIES:
JJ Sedelmaier Productions
Nutmeg Audio Post, 2150 Editorial
Beaconstreet Studios
DIRECTOR:
JJ Sedelmaier
CREATIVE DIRECTORS:
Alex Bogusky, Jeff Benjamin
David Schiff, Alex Burnard
ANNUAL ID:
06257N
URL:
http://www.cpbgroup.com/awards
/mantropyintegrated.html

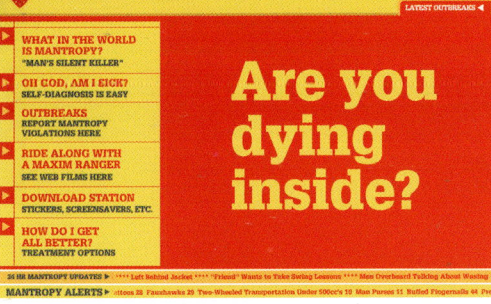

Merit Winners
261

INTEGRATED BRANDING:
INTEGRATED BRANDING CAMPAIGN

AGENCY
Crispin Porter + Bogusky / Miami
CLIENT
Burger King

ART DIRECTORS:
Tom Zukoski, James Dawson-Hollis
Geordie Stephens, Tom Zukoski
James Dawson-Hollis
Geordie Stephens
WRITERS:
Ryan Kutscher
Rob Strasberg, Jeff Gillette
DESIGNERS:
Chean Wei Law, DJ Neff
PROGRAMMER:
Milky Elephant
DIGITAL ARTISTS/MULTIMEDIA:
X-1, Los Angeles, Mark Larranaga
Jon Jacobsen, Jeff Payne
AGENCY PRODUCERS:
Julieana Stechschulte, Natalie Gora
David Rolfe, Rupert Samuel
Amanda Ormerod, Bill Meadows
Julieana Stechschulte, Natalie Gora
Paul Sutton
PRODUCTION COMPANIES:
Milky Elephant, HSI Los Angeles
Radke Film Group, Cosmo Street
DIRECTOR:
Paul Hunter
CREATIVE DIRECTORS:
Alex Bogusky, Andrew Keller
Jeff Benjamin, Rob Reilly
ANNUAL ID:
06255N
URL:
http://www.cpbgroup.com/awards/coqroqintegrated.html

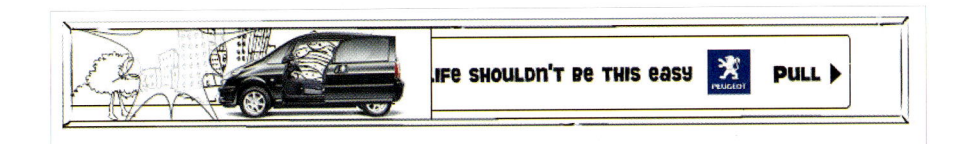

INTEGRATED BRANDING:
INTEGRATED BRANDING CAMPAIGN

AGENCY
Euro RSCG 4D Interactive / London

CLIENT
Peugeot

ART DIRECTORS:
David Brown
Ross Elliott

WRITER:
Mike Watson

DESIGNERS:
Fan Li, Teo Ardoy
Lee Carrotte

PROGRAMMERS:
Gregory Roekens, Matthew Muller
Matthew Lawrence, Tony Burbage

CONTENT STRATEGISTS:
Anne Davis, Kristin Berg

AGENCY PRODUCERS:
John Batholomew, Duncan Hamilton

PRODUCTION COMPANIES:
Dylan Inns, Special Moves

CREATIVE DIRECTOR:
Scott Ex Rodgers

ANNUAL ID:
06260N

URL:
http://www.awards-entry.co.uk/2006
/1007INT/

INTEGRATED BRANDING:
INTEGRATED BRANDING CAMPAIGN

AGENCY
McKinney / Durham

CLIENT
GroundWorks Dancetheater

ART DIRECTOR:
Jason Musante

WRITER:
Lisa Shimotakahara

DESIGNER:
Justin Smith

AGENCY PRODUCER:
Maria Cippichio

CREATIVE DIRECTORS:
David Baldwin
Lisa Shimotakahara

ANNUAL ID:
06261N

Merit Winners
263

INTERACTIVE: SINGLE . CAMPAIGN

AGENCY
Academy of Art University / San Francisco

CLIENT
Hybridcenter.org

ART DIRECTOR:
Mike Brenner

WRITER:
Inseeyah Barma

DESIGNER:
Brent Pocker

ANNUAL ID:
CCI005

URL:
http://www.killconventionalcars.com

INTERACTIVE: SINGLE . CAMPAIGN

AGENCY
Academy of Art University / San Francisco

CLIENT
Hybridcenter.org

ART DIRECTOR:
Trevor Hubbard

ANNUAL ID:
CCI004

URL:
http://www.gonashar.com

264   MERIT WINNERS // ACADEMY OF ART // COLLEGE FOR CREATIVE STUDIES // MIAMI AD SCHOOL

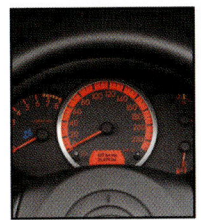

INTERACTIVE: SINGLE . CAMPAIGN

AGENCY
College for Creative
Studies / Detroit
CLIENT
Hybridcenter.org

ART DIRECTORS:
Bob Basiewicz
Tia Harper
WRITERS:
Bob Basiewicz
Tia Harper
PHOTOGRAPHER:
Rob Dawson
ANNUAL ID:
CCI006

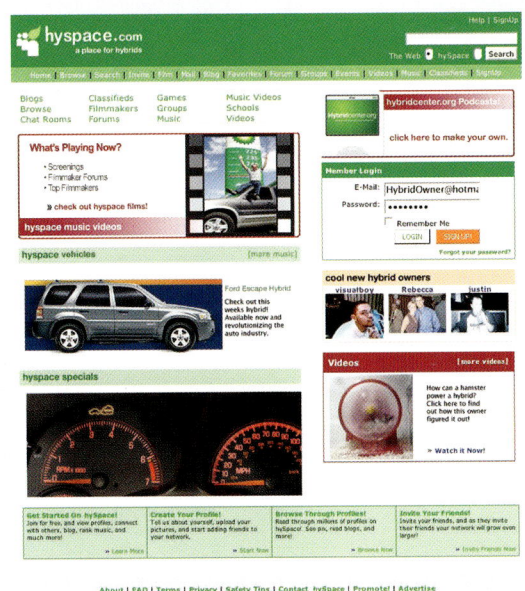

INTERACTIVE: SINGLE . CAMPAIGN

AGENCY
Miami Ad School / Minneapolis
CLIENT
Hybridcenter.org

ART DIRECTOR:
Drew Shamen
WRITER:
John Paquette
ANNUAL ID:
CCI007
URL:
http://www.filthington.org

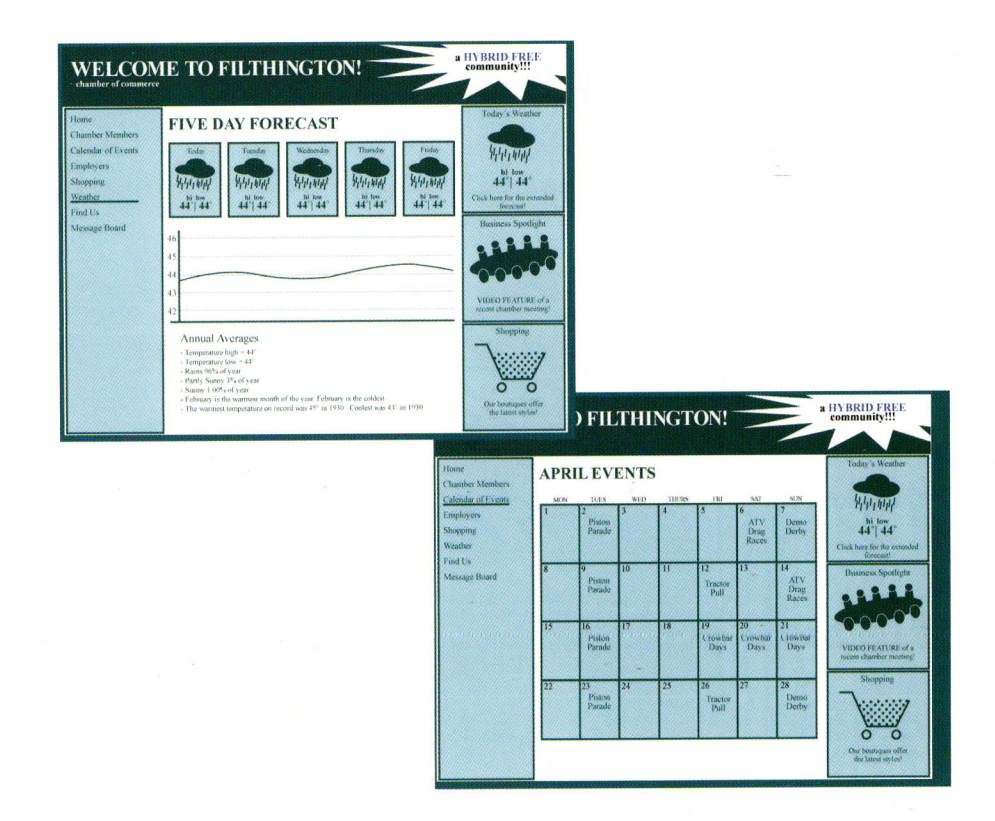

Merit Winners
265

index

AGENCY

7779 204
777interactive 228

A
ADK. 220
AgênciaClick 168, 181, 185
Agency Republic: 82, 94, 173, 184
Agency.com 34, 176
Åkestam.Holst 66, 205
AKQA / San Francisco 106, 120, 221
AKQA / London 150, 201, 221, 242
AlmapBBDO 168, 175, 185, 205
Anderson DDB Health & Lifestyle 235
Ant 26
Aoi Advertising Promotion 222
Arnold / McLean 243
Arnold / Boston. 182, 186, 252
Atmosphere BBDO 206, 206, 215

B
Bascule 230
BEAM Interactive 177, 228
Bernstein-Rein 258
Big Spaceship 207, 238
Blast Radius 208
BLITZ 208
Bloc Media 240, 242
BlueMars 235
Boone/Oakley 230
Butler, Shine, Stern & Partners 209

C, D
Crispin Porter + Bogusky . .32, 36, 48, 68, 70, 96, 102,
. . 146, 152, 169, 174, 187, 209, 215, 244, 260, 261, 262
Daddy. 187, 188, 189
DDB Brasil. 24, 30, 190, 199, 238, 255
DDB Germany 190, 191
De-Construct 210
Dentsu 177, 210, 222, 255, 256, 260, 44
Dentsu West 249
Domani Studios. 183
DoubleYou 42, 170, 175, 178, 199

E, F
Euro RSCG 4D /São Paulo 178
Euro RSCG 4D /Amstelveen. 239, 250, 258
Euro RSCG 4D Interactive 211, 227, 263
EVB. 211, 212
F/Nazca Saatchi & Saatchi 231
Fallon 212
Farfar 213
Firstborn 227
Fitzgerald+CO 213
Forsman & Bodenfors . . .74, 191, 201, 223, 241, 259
Framfab 28, 114, 214
Freestyle Interactive 170

G, H
Genex 192, 193
George Patterson Y&R 136
The George P. Johnson Company 138
Glue London 176, 244
Goodby, Silverstein & Partners: . . .50, 52, 108, 126,
. . . . 171, 174, 200
Great Works .56
Ground Zero 245
Grupo W 223, 236
Hakuhodo I-Studio 92, 231
Hello Design 236
Hi-ReS! 224

I-J
Interone Worldwide 214
Johnson Cowan Hanrahan 250
Jung von Matt / Stuttgart 122, 134, 232
Jung von Matt / Hamburg 256
Juxt Interactive 215, 253
JWT 183

K, L
Kinetic Singapore 232
Land Design Studio 140
Lateral Net 243
Lean Mean Fighting Machine 54, 179
Leo Burnett / Chicago 154, 252
Leo Burnett / Frankfurt 245
Leo Burnett and Arc Worldwide / Kuala Lumpur . 204
Leo Burnett and Arc Worldwide / Toronto 88
Lowe Tesch 72, 182

M, N
Makine Studios 233
MargeotesFertittaPowell 110, 259
Max Weber 239
McKinney 156, 179, 233, 246, 263
Mekanism 100, 246
Method 144
Mindflood 138
Mother 78
Netthink 204
NetX 193
Neue Digitale 60, 64, 217
Nordpol+ Hamburg 98, 172, 247
North Kingdom 194
NOWWASHYOURHANDS 251

O, P
Odopod 225
OgilvyInteractive / Madrid 203
OgilvyInteractive / Frankfurt 40
OgilvyOne / New York 202
OgilvyOne / Beijing 172
OgilvyOne / Singapore 225
One Sky 226
OneDigital 130

Organic 194, 247
POKE London 195, 234, 248
Pop&Co 241
Prisacom 217
Proximity Singapore 38, 180
Publicis & Hal Riney 195, 218, 248, 249

R, S
R/GA 86, 158, 196, 229
Recruit Media Communications 218
Red Tettemer 254
RMG Connect 240
Saatchi & Saatchi / Frankfurt 118
Saatchi & Saatchi / Singapore 173
Scholz & Volkmer 219, 257
Sedgwick Rd 237
StrawberryFrog 196

T
TAXI 46, 197, 197, 251
Team One 134, 253
TEQUILA 104
Tha Ltd 84
Tribal DDB / Dallas 184
Tribal DDB / New York 180, 198
Tribal DDB / Sydney 257
Tribal DDB / Vancouver 219, 237

V-Z
VCCP 181
VIEW 200
The Viral Factory 116
Wysiwyg Comunicación Interactiva . . 198, 229, 234
Young & Rubicam 112, 254
Zugara 220

AGENCY PRODUCER
A-D
Allen, Jennifer 86
Alonso, Eddie 261
Alvarez, Marcelino 261
Bartholomew, John 263
Bonin, Amy 146
Bonin, Matthew 146, 152
Brizzolara, Regina 156, 246
Cippichio, Maria 263
D'Amico, Neil 260
Dimick, Eva 260

G-J
Geraghty, Vincent 154
Gora, Natalie 262, 262
Hamilton, Duncan 263
Himebrook, Darren 260
Jenkins, James 150

L, M
Lodder, Matthew 150
Lopez, Shawna 152
Mateu, Rebekah 261

McKinney, Stephanie 261
McMillen, Brian 260
Meadows, Bill 146, 152, 262
Mehta, Jasel 150

N-S
Niblick, David 146
Ormerod, Amanda 262
Pérez, Cindy 261
Radel, Sheri 261
Rolfe, David 146, 152, 261, 262
Ruth, Dan 261
Samuel, Rupert 146, 152, 261, 262
Stechschulte, Julieana 146, 260, 262, 262
Sugiura, Tomohiko 260
Sutton, Paul 146, 261, 262

ART DIRECTOR
A
Ågerup, Lotta 223
Abdul-Hamid, Hazim 240
Abe, Yosuke 84, 228
Adler, Aaron 206, 215
Ambrose, Jason 152
Anderson, Brent 250
Anweiler, Dominik 98, 172
Appelblad, Mathias 74, 241
Ardito, Richard 206, 215
Ashford, Bart 258
Austria, Jerome 86

B
Bakum, Jamie 177
Bareiss, Philipp 219
Batista, Adhemas 205
Bedford, Scott 34, 176
Beim, Alex 219
Bergdahl, John 74
Bindi, Adrien 154
Blæsbjerg, Kamilla 214
Blondell, Joakim 191, 241
Bois, Todd 211, 212
Borcherding, Rolf 217
Bott, Melanie 40
Broekhoven, Monica 235
Brown, David 263
Buim, Rodrigo 175
Bukvic, Mariana 231
Burnard, Alex 261
Butler, Gemma 82, 94
Butori, Rodrigo 245

C
Calleja, Jorge 215
Cardoso, Diego 181
Carr, Tom 254
Carvalho, Caetano 185
Cass, Mishy 237

Index 269

Castaño, Marga 234
Cavander, Dmitri 186
Cedergren, Martin 191, 201, 223, 241, 259
Chan, Francis 208
Chau, David 238
Christine Turner and Simon Lloyd 244
Ciszek, Corey. 112, 254
Clark, Robin 140
Cole, Micheal E 225
Cornell, Nikolai 138
Coulson, Ben 136
Crabtree, Simon 243
Cracknell, Mark 257

D
D'albergaria, Alexandre 190, 255
Da Silva e Silva, Vicente 168
Davies, Robert 225
Davis, Steve 138
Dawson-Hollis, James 262
Delgado, Ana 178
Del Marmol, Mike 261
Diaz, Israel 88
DiClemente, Gabrielle 180
Dielman, Nels 253
Dietz, Aaron 50, 52, 171, 174
Doyle, Brian 134
Duering, Anja 260

E, F
Eklind, Anders 74
Elliott, Ross 227, 263
Esguia, Josh 208
Evans, Duan 150, 221
Ferrare, Mike 209
Ferreira, Nuno 197
Figliulo, Mark 112, 254
Flade, Fred 210
Frandsen, Rasmus 114
Fridman, Elena 206, 215
Frisell, Karin 74

G
Galiana, Javier 204
Ganann, Sean 193
Garnett, Alison 46
Gehrig, Kim 234
Goldman, Dominic 195, 218, 248, 249
Gomes, Peter 88
González, Adolfo 198
González, Diego 203
Gordon-Rogers, Gavin 82, 94
Gravena, Pedro 24, 255
Green, Alastair 202
Groezinger, Nicole 118
Grossman, Jed 152
Guedes, Carlos 200
Gugel, Andy 212

Gursky, Scott 241

H
Höglund, Björn 189
Hale, Kelly 237
Hanrahan, Rory 78
Haworth, Melissa 206, 215
Hellström, Andreas 194
Hernandez, Marlon 158, 196, 229
Hikiji, Paul 208
Hodgins, Amy 202
Holmdahl, Erik 196
Holzenkamp, Nicole 235
Huber, Noah 138
Hughes, Kevin 171

I, J
Im, Jeong-ho 204
Ito, Naoki 220
James, Ben 261
Jeffery, Colin 186, 252
Jeffery, Gabriel 186
Josefsson, Fredrik 66, 205

K
Kaplan, Scott 206, 215
Karlsson, Jens 207
Kay, Ian 88
Kim, Colin 195, 218, 248, 249
Kitani, Yusuke 44, 222, 255
Kliebe, Kelly 193
Klug, Valter 178
Knutsson, Christian 187, 188
Koller, Kevin 260
Kosel, Tiffany 48, 96146, 169, 209,
Kovalik, Ian 246
Kretchmer, Jordan 184
Kun 180, 38
Kunii, Takehide 210

L
Lam, Sean 232
Lam, Vina 206, 215
Lanne, Emil 195
Larsson Von Reybekiel, Max 56
Lee, David 120, 221
Lee, Paul 186
Lent, Ron 206, 215
Lo, Simona 193
Lopez, Paulo 186
Loskill, Sven 256
Lund, Chris 138
Lunetta, Carlos 228

M
Mártinez, Ruben 204
Macadam, Angus 252
MacCarroll, David 213
Mackler, Jonathan 206, 215
Magliano, Anthony 258

Malm, Andreas 74, 259
Marchetti, Cesar Augusto 181
Marubashi, Kei 222
Marucci, Jerome 206, 215
Massareto, Domnico 181
Mattson, Olle 205
Mayeur, Gabrielle 253
Mazzariol, Mauricio 30, 190, 199, 238, 255
McGinness, Will 108, 200
Melin, Bjarne 194
Miller, Brian 215
Mirete, David 204
Miyasato, Mako 104
Mochizuki, Kaori 260
Modeki, Ryuta 226
Moreno, Cesar 223, 236
Mori, Hiro 170
Mugnaini, Sergio 168
Muñoz, Nick 102
Musante, Jason 156, 179, 233, 246, 263

N, O
Nakajima, Kazuhiko 249
Nakamura, Hiroki 44, 222, 255
Nakamura, Yugo 226
Nishida Koji 222
Niwa, Masayoshi 177
Öberg, Silla 201
Oga, Mitsuhiro 230
Overkamp, Jamie 206, 215

P, R
Palmer, Rick 240, 242
Panchal, Rahul . . 32, 48, 70, 169, 209, 215, 244, 261,
Pantzke, Jens 183
Pasagali, Antonio 217
Piera, Blanca 42, 175, 178, 199
Poulin, Pierre-Etienne 233
Rickert, Katja 219
Ringtved, Peter 214
Romanh, Francisco 223, 236
Rufo, Lucio 231
Russell, Kevin 201

S
Sandoz, Andy 184
Sano, Katsuhiko 92, 231
Santoro, Cris 255
Scheibel, Tim 72
Schilling, Sandra 190
Schmitt, Florian 224, 260
Schreiber, Gunther 98, 172, 247
Selimi, Bejadin 60
Sengers, Martijn 239, 250, 258
Sheehan, Casey 236
Siegal, Meghan 182
Silverson, Erik 254
Simon, Brett 206, 215

Siqueira, Fred 168, 185
Sivell, Liz 130
Snodgrass, Eric 184
Squier, Phillip 186, 252
Stechschulte, Paul 48, 146, 152, 209
Stephens, Geordie 244, 261, 262
Stewart, Joe 253
Swedenborg, Jakob 213

T
Takakusaki, Hirozumi 210, 256
Takeashita, Michael 192
Tan, Kien Eng 203
Tan, Robin 173
Taylor, Guybrush 251
Taylor, Mark 260
Tesch, Johan 72
Ting, Trisha 70, 261
Titius, Alexandra 214
Tofslie, Eddy 211
Tracki, Piotr 239
Trapp, Klaus 245
Tsang, Theresa 203
Tsuchiya, Hironobu 92
Tucker, Russ 173
Turi, Max 229

U, V, W
Unwin, Miles 201
Voigt, Thorsten 40
Vranakis, Steve 181
Waldschütz, Jörg 64
Watson, Shane 198
Weiss, Chad 138
Wells, Jen 186
Wergerbauer, Eric 192, 193
Westerdahl, Patrik 182
Widmann, Marcus 232

Y, Z
Yamada, Takanori 26, 218
Yamashita, Norikazu 26
Yang, Yanyan 172
Yin, Wilson 192
Yung, Stephanie 197
Zanato, Thiago 106
Zoelch, Michael 232
Zukoski, Tom 174, 262

CLIENT
3M Corporate 201

A
A.R.T. Studios 118
Abba Seafood 191, 241
Acción Contra el Hambre 203
Acura 192, 193
Adidas 60, 64, 130, 210, 211
Adobe Systems 222

Altoids	154
Amana	84
American Legacy Foundation	182
Anesvad	204
Asics: Onitsuka Tiger	196
Audi	172
Audi of America	156, 179, 246
Axel Springer	256

B

Bascule	230, 255
Bauducco	185
BBC World Service	173
BC Dairy Foundation	219
Beck/Interscope	224
Bloc Media	242
BMW	212
Boone/Oakley	230
Brooks Sports	250
Burger King	68, 260, 262

C

Campana Brothers	231
Camper	229
Carlsberg Sverige	187, 188
Cartoon Network	241
Channel4 UK	224
Coca-Cola	168, 185, 199, 215, 257
COI Royal Navy	176
Coke Zero	187
Comcast	108
Comic Relief	94
Companhia Athletica	30, 238
Crispin Porter + Bogusky	183

D, E

Dentsu	256
Department for Transport-Teen Road Safety	252
Diageo	178
Diesel	211
Discover Card	50, 174
Dolby	170
Durex	213
Dyson	181
Egg	184
EnBW	122, 134

F, G

Fedex	24
Fiat Automóveis	181
Fraser Health Authority	237
Fuji Heavy Industries	226
Fumakilla	177
Fuse TV	215
GAP	102
GE	206
General Motors	220
Greenpeace	175
GroundWorks Dancetheater	263

H, I

Hakuhodo	92
Happytaxday.com	184
Havaianas	205
Heide Park Soltau	183
Heineken	213
Henkel	255
Hessischer Rundfunk	235
Hewlett-Packard	171
Hoshino Resort	204
HP Asia Pacific	173
IBM	202
IF	223
Ihaveanidea	251
IKEA	74
Intel	227

J, K, L

Japan Advertising Council	44
Jordan Brand	208
Jose Cuervo	198
Jung von Matt	232
Kinetic Singapore	232
Kohn Pedersen Fox Architects	227
Lean Mean Fighting Machine	54
LeapFrog	212
Lenovo	202
Leo Burnett	88
Levi Strauss and Co. Europe	243
Levi Strauss Asia Pacific	225
Lexus	134, 253
Los Angeles Conservancy	236
Lovely Pop	26

M

Makine Studios	233
Masterfoods	206, 215
Maxim	261
McDonald's	243
McDonald's Australia	257
McKinney	233
Mercedes-Benz	82, 219
Microsoft Corporation Japan	226
Miller Brewing Company	112, 254
MINI	32, 36, 48, 70, 146, 152, 169, 177, 209, 214, 215, 244, 261
MINI Canada	46, 197
Ministry of Health and Social Affairs	201
Mitsui Fudosan	210
Montepio Geral Bank	200
Mother	207, 234
Museo del Desierto	236

N, O

Nick(it)	209
Nike	114, 150, 158, 196, 214, 221, 223, 229, 242, 28, 86, 42, 170, 175

Nokia 198, 239, 250, 258
NOWWASHYOURHANDS 251
NSPCC 34, 176
Olympus 217
P
Penguin Books 195
Pennsylvania Tourism 254
Peter Kim Jewelry 195, 218, 248, 249
Peugeot 263
Philips 180
PINK 96, 169
PlayStation Portable 40
Posten 66
Prisacom 217
Puma 228
R
Reckitt Benckiser 178
Red Bull 225
Reebok 220
Renault Germany 98, 172, 247
Revell 245
Ruby Tuesday 258
S
Saab Automobile 72, 182
SAB Miller International 248
Samsung 110, 240, 259
San Francisco Museum of Modern Art 144
Sanitec Kolo 239
Saturn 126, 171, 200
Sega 100, 246
Shimano 174
Shiseido 222
Shu Akashi 231
Sony Computer Entertainment Europe 240
Sony Family Club 228
Sony Pictures 207, 238
Sony PlayStation 104
Specialized 52
Sprint 194, 247
T
Takisada-Nagoya 218
Target Corporation 253
TBS 207
Telefonica 199
TeliaSonera 188
Tok&Stok 190
Too Far Publishing 179
Toyota Motor Corporation 260
Toyota Sweden 194
Turner Broadcasting System 78
U, V
UI-Bellmony 249
UK Government, Foreign & Commonwealth Office 140
Unilever 116
V&S ABSOLUT Spirits 56

VB 136
Viking Line 205
Virgin Atlantic Airways 193, 244
Virgin Digital 245
Virgin Trains 244
Volkswagen Sverige 189
Volkswagen 168, 186, 190, 191, 252
Volkswagen Sverige 189
Volvo 259
W, X
Warner Bros 208
Washington State Department of Health . . . 237
WD-40 . . . . 38, 180
Women's Aid Organisation 203
Wyeth Canada 235
Wysiwyg 234
Xbox 106, 120, 221

CONTENT STRATEGIST
A, B
Álvarez-Borrás, Ignacio 198, 229, 234
Acuff, Justin 211
Andersson, Jonas 213
Azuma, Hirofumi 226
Barry, Sarah 130
Bazeley, Tom 54, 179
Beerda, Sicco 239, 250, 258
Bendixen, Caroline 114
Berg, Jeremy 227
Berg, Kristin 263
Betz, Michael 191
Boku, Masayoshi 230
Booy, Bryan 253
Boswell, Maury 126
C, D
Charlebois, Brit 126, 171
Chen, Szu Ann 236
Civil, Hema 240
Davidson, Briggs 158
Davis, Anne 263
Dopjans, Clemens 257
Dreyer, Wiebke 191
G, H
Galligan, Fergus 241
Geiger, Mike 50, 52, 108, 126, 171, 174, 200
German, Robert 188
Gibson, Sean 215
Hara, Nobuo 230
Harano, Morihiro 110, 259
Head, Carey 52
Hirose, Wataru 249
Hostler, Tom 234
J, K
Jefferson, Simon 150, 221, 242
Jenkins, James 221

Kelso, Amanda 108, 171
Kirchhofer, Tobias. 235
Kochi, Kyoko 92
Kraft, Manfred 257
Kraft, Sascha. 178
Kristensen, Martin 28, 214
Kudo, Yasuhisa 226
L, M
Lee, Dora 50, 108, 174
Lewis, St John 211
Liburd, Greg 208
Makinouchi, Hirokazu 249
Martner, Gustav. 187, 188, 189
Michie, Aaron. 257
Millado, Erica 158
Murasawa, Hiroaki 92, 222
Murphy, Ryan. 227
Myers, Kristen 215
N, O, P
Niwa, Masayoshi 177
Okoshi, Takehiko 222
Okuwa, Yasushi. 222
Olalquiaga, Álvaro. 178
Overfelt, Guy 200
Palm-Jensen, Matias 213
Persson, Patrik. 56
Pinney, Keith 130
Pont, Jordi 42, 170, 175, 199
R, S
Ramos, Ana Carolina 231
Rau, Anja 235
Reichard, Peter. 257
Söder, Jessica 205
Schliedermann, Anke 214
Silver, Bob 251
Simonse, Anna 236
Smith, Liz 240
Smith, Phil 230
Sternsdorf, Björn 257
Sudendorf, Malte 190, 191
Suzuki, Hroo 228
T, U
Theakston, Kate 248
Toland, Ryan 212
Tomikawa, Teruaki 92
Uchiyama, Koshi 226
W, Y
Wålsten, Magnus 56
Waern, Robert 187, 188
Weatherford, Morgan 236
Yoshimura, Mitsunori 204

CREATIVE DIRECTOR
A
Adams, Tom 182

Alencar, Mauro 106, 120, 221
Anderson, Keith . . . 50, 52, 108, 126, 171,174, 200
Aranda, Arturo 206, 206, 215
B
Baba, Kampei 255
Baldwin, David 156, 179, 233, 246, 263
Ball, Sam 54, 179
Banham, Paul 34, 176
Barber, Tim 225
Barrett, Jamie 200
Batista, Dave. 228
Baxter, Anna 208
Bedwood, Dave 54, 179
Bemfica, Miguel 190
Benjamin, Jeff 32, 36, 48, 68, 70, 96, 102, 146,
. . 152, 169, 174, 177, 187, 209, 215, 244, 260, 261, 262
Bergstrom, Nicke 213
Bernt, Andy 202
Bickle, Braden 184
Bliss, David 225
Bogusky, Alex 32, 36, 48, 68, 70, 96, 102, 146, 152, 169,
. . . . 174, 182, 187, 209, 215, 244, 260, 261, 261, 262
Boku, Masayoshi 230
Bonner, Daniel 201
Boone, John 230
Borgström, Joakim 42, 170, 175, 178, 199
Bradley, Chris 110, 186, 259
Brockmann, Heike 219, 257
Burnard, Alex 261
Butler, John 209
C
Calderon, Miguel 223, 236
Cama, Felipe 30, 238
Carl, Chris. 186
Chalmers, Mark 196
Chambers, Sean 227
Chambers, Trevor. 211
Chester, Ricardo 30, 238
Cills, Ken 254
Citron, Ben. 194, 247
Clark, Brian 156, 179, 246
Cohn, Mark 208
Combuechen, Andreas. 206
Cook, Dave. 156, 179, 233, 246
Cortsen, Lars 28, 114, 214
Crandall, Court. 245
Crispin Porter + Bogusky. 183
Cude, Jonathan 156, 179, 233, 246
Curry, Jeff 202
Czeschner, Olaf. 60, 64, 217
D, E
Davidge, Nick. 104
DeKeyser, Dawn 134, 253
Denton, John 240, 242
De Rooij, Bram 239, 250, 258

Doi, Kaoru	249
Dykas, Krzysztof	239
Eichinger, Tobias	232
Emery, Toria	108, 126
Ericsson, Marcus	208
Eschenbacher, Dirk	172

F

Farnham, Kevin	144
Favat, Pete	182
Fernandes, Fabio	231
Fernandes, Joao	200
Figliulo, Mark	112, 254
Figueira, Ricardo	168, 181, 185
Flatt, Kevin	212
Fleig, Paul	122, 134
Francisco, Judith	178
Fritz, Ingo	98, 172
Fukuda, Toshiya	228

G

Ganann, Sean	193
Garcia, Eduardo	233
Gassner, Martin	214
Gatewood, Chris	170
Gentile, Gerry	104
Glaze, David	192, 193
Goldman, Dominic	195, 218, 248, 249
González, Adolfo	198, 229, 234
Goodman, Jae	195, 218, 248, 249
Graves, Chris	134, 253
Griffin, Alex	210

H

Höglund, Björn	187, 188, 189
Haan, Noel	154
Haas, Christian	194, 247
Hackstock, Nathan	104
Hanrahan, Tim	250
Harano, Morihiro	110, 259
Heinzel, Andreas	245
Higgins, Peter	140
Hino, Takayuki	26, 218
Hitner, Zach	237
Hohmann, Till	232
Hopper, Ashadi	240
Hostler, Tom	195
Hudson, Ron	235

I, J

Im, Jeong-ho	204
Inamoto, Rei	106, 120, 221
Jeffery, Colin	252
John, Judy	88
Johnson, Scott	184

K

Kaizawa, Yujiro	222
Kanahara, Jiro	220
Kanofsky, Thomas	118
Kaplan, Greg	202
Karlsson, Linus	78
Kay, Woody	243
Kearse, John	182
Keller, Andrew	32, 36, 48, 68, 70, 102, 146, 152, 169, 187, 209, 215, 244, 260, 261, 262
Kelly, Albert	52
Keramat, Layla	235
Kirchhoff, Eberhard	118
Kovalik, Ian	100
Kraemer, Bernd	256
Kutschinski, Michael	40

L

Lacava, Vincent	241
Lai, David	236
Lam, Sean	232
Lawner, Ron	182, 186, 243, 252
Lebowitz, Michael	207, 238
Lemme, Michael	144
Leth, Jan	202
Linnen, Scott	96, 169, 174
Loew, Dave	112, 254

M

Mackinnon, Angus	251
Malmstrom, Paul	78
Mapp, Steve	52
Martínez, Nuria	198, 229, 234
Martin, Ken	208
Martin, Miguel	203
Matejczyk, John	171
Mateo, Wilson	255
Mateos, Wilson	199, 24
Mayeur, Gabrielle	134, 253
McCann, Jason	197
McGinness, Will	50, 108, 126, 171, 174, 200
McGrath, James	136
McWeeny, Jeff	243
Means, Tommy	100, 246
Medeiros, Marcos	24, 199, 255
Meyer, Andrew G	154
Mitchell, Duncan	180, 198
Mogilewski, Grzegorz	239
Morrow, Bob	258
Moss, Jacquie	225
Moss, Peter	225
Mroueh, Zak	251
Mugnaini, Sergio	168, 175, 185, 205
Mykolyn, Steve	46, 197

N, O

Nakajima, Satoshi	44
Nakamura, Yugo	84, 226
Nesle, Steve	180, 198
Newbery, Patrick	144
Niwa, Hiro	236
Niwa, Masayoshi	177

Norton, Birch. 177
O'Connell, Steve 152
Oakley, David. 230
Oga, Mitsuhiro 230
Oiwa, Naoto 260
Oviatt, Arlo. 258

P
Pafenbach, Alan 186, 252
Paiva, Marcio. 178
Pereira, PJ. 106, 120, 221
Persson, Ted 56
Pou, Edu. 42, 170, 175
Poulin, Pierre-Etienne. 233
Powell, Neil 110, 259
Purgason, Todd. 215, 253
Pye, Jon. 38, 180

R
Rühmann, Lars. 247
Rasines, Jess 203
Red, Steve 254
Reilly, Rob 68, 102, 260, 262
Rico, Marta 178
Rieken, Torsten. 183
Rodgers, Scott Ex 227, 263
Rogers, Josh 110, 259
Romano, Fernanda . . . 24, 30, 190, 199, 238, 255
Roope, Nicolas 248
Royce, Seb 176, 244

S
Sánchez del Real, Mario 204
Sa, Mariana 190
Samis, Peter 144
Sandoz, Andy. 82, 173
Sanz, Frédéric 199
Sasaki, Yasuharu 210, 256
Schiff, David 187, 261
Schmeling, Andrew 170
Schmitt, Florian 224
Schneider, Wolfgang. 190
Sengers, Martijn 239, 250, 258
Serpa, Marcello. 205
Shimotakahara, Lisa 263
Simoes, Fabio 231
Simpson, Steve 171
Sinclair, Bruce 219, 237
Sivell, Liz 130
Sloutchevsky, Vas. 227
Snyder, Eddie. 213
Sobral Caetano da Silva, Nei 209
Sochaczewski, Alon 178
Solana, Daniel 178
Soto, Jon 195, 218, 248, 249
Speidel, Doug 104
Steger, Peter. 245
Stiller, Mathias 190, 191

Stout, Travis 184
Strasberg, Rob 32, 169, 261
Sugiyama, Yutaka 92

T, U, V
Takakusaki, Hirozumi 210, 256
Talarek, Marcin. 239
Tan, Kien Eng. 203
Tanaka, Koichiro 228
Thornton, Jim 252
Ting, Richard. 158, 196, 229
Turk, Aaron 257
Uchiyama, Koshi 226
Valencia, Ulises. 223, 236
Valente, Sergio 24, 30, 190, 199, 238, 255
Vranakis, Steve 181

W
Waibel, Peter. 232
Walker, Shirley 140
Wallberg, Niklas 72, 182
Walz, Stefan 122, 134, 232
Ward-Taggart, Shirley 88
Waterfall, Simon 234
Watt, Bruce 173
Weist, Dave 186, 252
Wergerbauer, Eric. 193
Westre, Susan 202
Wong, Roger 194, 247
Wright, Bill. 244
Wyville, Jon 112, 254

Y, Z
Yamada, Keita 260
Yamamoto, Koji 222
Yanagisawa, Daisuke 228
Yanai, Michihiko. 222
Zada, Jason 211, 212

DESIGNER

A
@www. 181
Abe, Yosuke 84, 228
Alegria, Daniel 192
Amelines, Alex 251
Andersson, Karl 243
Andersson, Nina 74
Ardoy, Teo 263
Arrom-Biboloni, Marga. 82
Askar, Baykal. 144
Aston, Peter 211
Augusto Marchetti, César 168

B
Badía, Lisi 178
The Barbarian Group 110, 259
Beacock, Mark. 54, 179
Bell, Bruce. 144
Bernard, Justin. 215, 253

Bevan, Wil .34, 176
Bielefeldt, Christoph 247
Bixler, Crsipin 193
Bourguignon, André. 64, 217
Brewer, Ian 158, 229
Brimijoin, Zander 238
Buergy, Fabian 122, 134
Burgess, Carl 224
Burnard, Alex 261

C
Campa, Benny 192
Carlsson, Tommy 187
Carrotte, Lee 263
Chau, David 238
Chosak, Mark 208
Coffey, Kevin 251
Collins, Paul 34, 176
Conlin, Ryan 193
Conrad, Sean 186
Costa, Antonio 239, 250, 258
Crawford, Andrew 239, 250, 258
Cruz, Carlos 217
Cybele 169

D
Dörner, Philipp 247
Damman, Tyson 207, 238
Danielsson, Patrik 28
Davies Meyer 183
Dedman, Dathan 208
Dillingham, Michael 238
Di Lorenzo, Carmelo 168, 185
Dobrowolski, Jon 208

E, F
Eberwein, Thomas 224
Eriksson, Jens 56
Estberg, Staffan 238
Fariss, Nurazlinn 203
Ferrare, Mike 146, 169
Ferreira, Nuno 197
Fröhlich, Tanja 214
Fukatsu, Takayuki 226

G
Gabriel, Franz 170
Garnett, Alison 46
George, Chloe 211
Gomes, Peter .88
Goodly, Donovan 206, 215
Greenberg, Jesse 238
Gugel, Andy 212
Guijarro, Nacho 170, 178

H
Höfler, Mark 172, 98
Haggerty, Ammon 225
Hall, Will 241
Hayashi, Mayumi 228

Horner, Lara 158, 229
Howard, Sean 227
Hunt, Ted 243
Hutcheson, Paul 196
Hyung, David 158, 229

I, J
Im, Jeong-ho 204
Isaksson, Albert 188
Iwaki, Yohei 226
James, John 158, 229
Jansma, Chris 228
Jansson, Lars 201, 259
Jennings, Tom 240, 242

K
Karlsson, Fredrik 56
Karlsson, Jens 207
Kawa, Ikuko 210
Kentner, Dominik 232
Kern, Michael 218, 248
Kershaw, Tom 210
Kim, Raoul 186
Kirsch, Peter .64
Kirschenhofer, Bertrand 247
Kitani, Yusuke 220, 256
Kloostra, Feike 239, 250, 258
Kobayashi, Momoko 210
Kooper, Troy 158
Korad, Thamrongphut 86
Kovalik, Ian 246
Kryszpiniuk, Andrzej 239

L
Lamers, Roland 239, 250, 258
Lamm, Staffan 194
Lanne, Emil 195
Larsson, Viktor 74, 201, 259
Laruelle, Oli 94
Law, Matthew 120, 221
Lee, Adam 244
Lee, Sojung 257
Li, Fan 263
Lima, Henrique 168
Lo, Simona 193
Long, Natalie 42, 175, 199
Loo, Shawn 225
Lopes, João Luis da Silva 181
Lubliner, Phil .86

M
Möller, Mattias 194
Macy, Kenneth 215
Mason, Steve 225
Mastri, John 138
Melander, Robert 188
Merino, Francisco 217
Miller, Brian 253
Mills, Rob .34, 176

Morin, Hugues 233
Murphy, Josh 213
Mustacich, Alex 215
N, O
Nakadai, Ryuhei 92
Nakade, Masaya 150, 221
Nakamura, Hiroki 177
Nakamura, Yugo 226
Nakano, Yas 193
Neff, DJ 262
Nuzzaci, Nico 234
Nyman, Carl 238
Oga, Mitsuhiro 230
Ooe, Tatsuro 92
Ostle, Leon 176
P, Q, R
Panchal, Rahul 68, 102, 146, 152, 174, 261
Pennington, Lee 242
Persson, Jonas 179
Pi-Yu Chuang, Peggy 206
Pierre, Jean 200
Pillings, Jessica 179
Queen, William 231
Reger, Mike 196
Rivas, Oscar 261
S
SaltedHerring 196
Sano, Katsuhiko 92, 231
Schmitt, Florian 224
Schuster, Stefan 64
Sedelmaier, JJ 261
Sexton, Jessica 212
Sharkey, Devin 108
Shimomura, Kenji 86
Siegal, Meghan 182
Sjövall, Jonas 223, 241
Sloan, Mark 110, 259
Smith, Justin 156, 179, 233, 263
Stan Winston Studios 260
Syzmanski, Joel 207
Szulborski, Dave 156
T
Tagger, Andreas 209
Takeashita, Michael 192
Tan, Robin 173
Tanaka, Naoto 226
Tarout 222
Teixeira, Daniel 200
Thompson, Andrew 158, 229
Thomsen, Antje 64
Thyselius, Kalle 196
Timonen, Mikko 74, 259
Tobita, Mayo 230
Tofslie, Eddy 212
Tomboy Virals 244

Tomioka, Yuko 220
Tucker, Russ 184
Tyomkina, Maria 194, 247
U, V, W
Uekubo, Haydee 185
Ushiki, Seiko 210
Van Silfhout, Rijk-Jan 239, 250, 258
Verity, Matt 176
Vogel, Erick 198
Votaw, Brian 158, 229
Walsh, Matt 158, 229
Wang, Jimmy 172
Wass, Jerry 74, 259
Watts, Logan 230
Wei Law, Chean 32, 36, 169, 261, 262
Witulski, Bartosz 239
Y, Z
Yamada, Takanori 218
Yamada, Tetsuya 260
Yamaguchi, Takafumi 158, 229
Yamashita, Norikazu 26
Yin, Wilson 192
Yip, Ivan 257
Yung, Stephanie 197
Zachary, Brendyn 235
Zassenhaus, Michelle 158, 229
Zheng Li, Shu 196

DIGITAL ARTIST/MULTIMEDIA
A, B
Abujamra, André 231
Alcatena, Quique 178
Baba, Kampei 230
Badsky, Derek 258
Ballard, Natalie 248
Beckham, Travis 258
Bixler, Crispin 193
Borgström, Joakim 199
Bouguerra, Sam 120, 221
Brimijoin, Zander 207, 238
Buergy, Fabian 232
Bunin, Alex 193
C
Cabbage, Rebecca 193
Caparrós, Xavi 178
Carlsson, Tommy 188
Cartman, Joseph 196
Castro, Miguel 215
Chau, David 238
Cho, James 177
Clark, Matt 250
Clinger, Aaron 194, 247
Conlin, Ryan 193
D, E
Damman, Tyson 207

Davila, Sara 223, 236
De la Cruz, Marcela 223, 236
Dillingham, Michael 238
Domani Studios 183
Drinkwater, Sean 108
Elkins, David 152
Eneroth, Peter 182
Espero, Roberto 223, 236
Ewen, Chris 108

F, G
Fagerholm, Bjorn 207, 238
Fielack, Rob 261
Foulds, Andy 221
Fusco, Dondi 253
Gatt, Jason 106
Gerigk, Karsten 235
González, Daniel 178
Guijarro, Nacho 42, 170, 175, 178
Gutierrez, Jezreel 223, 236

H, I, J
Hara, Nobuo 230, 255
Hill, David 238
Hoogerbrugge, Han 248
Imaginary Forces 134
Isaksson, Daniel 72
Jacobsen, Jon 262
Johannesdottir, Fura 86
Johansson, Christian 238
Jomehri, Hoj 120, 221
Jones, Mike 213

K, L
Karlsson, Jens 207
Kelley, Chris 211
Keytoon Animation Studio 108
Kipner, Justin 184
Kurihara, Masaomi 226
Löfgren, Tobias 182
Lam, Sean 232
Larranaga, Mark 262
Lisboa, Davis 178
Liu, Ryan 172
Lo, Simona 193

M
MacDonald, Rory 210
Maguire, Paul 140
Mahler, Clemens 190
Mariscal, Sebastian 223, 236
Martnez, Jordi 199
Martins, Ricardo 185, 205
Mason, Steve 225
Meld Media 197
Miyahara, Norie 204
Morio, Takashi 231
Mr Bingo 248

N
Nakai, Yasushi 204
Nakamura, Emperor 222
Nakamura, Hiroki 44, 177, 256
Nakaoka, Shojiro 230
Nave, Gino 108, 225
Nguyen, Phiyen 208
Niwa, Masayoshi 177
Nonelle, Mike 261
Norin, Erik 213
Noritomi, Iwao 230

O, P, Q
Okita, Masaharu 204
Pacheco, Vinny 193
Payne, Jeff 262
Pearson, Anthony 140
Persch, Mathias 190, 191
Phoenix, Andru 208
Ploj, Michael 214
Qureshi, Amir 152

R
Ripple Effects 254
Roberts, Gregor 212
Rodríguez, Charly 234
Rosendaal, Rafael 248
Roser, Fabian 122, 134
Rothaug, Daniel 190, 191
Runcorn, Scott 225
Ryan, Nick 248

S
Saktura, Mieszko 239
Sanchez, Brian 208
Sasae, Yukihiro 26
Scott, Steve 248
Seven2 237
Smith, Dan 212
Spontaneous Combustion 152
Sterner, Erik 187, 188, 189
Syzmanski, Joel 207

T, U, V
Tagger, Andreas 209
Taiyo Kikaku 226
Tanaka, Minoru 222
Taylor, Brian 108
Tinkin Hun, Kenneth 248
Torres, Guillermo 120, 221
Umetsu, Takeshiro 204
Valdes, Fernando 223, 236
Veitch, Joel 248
Vizoo 134
Von Ende, Chris 112, 254
Voorhies, Paula 213

W, X, Y, Z
Watts, Logan 230

Weisman, Benjamin 180
Williams, Garth 106
X-1 262
Yajima, Mitsuaki 208
Yamaguchi, Suguru 84, 226
Yamamoto, Masaru 249
Yamazaki, Isao 204
Z Quatro Animação 175
Zachary, Brendyn 235

DIRECTOR
Arikawa, Yasushi 260
Buckley, Bryan 146, 152
Carr, Tom 254
Downing, Michael 251
Feil, Alex 118
Gillespie, Craig 154
Helbig, Silvio 247
Hunter, Paul 262, 262
Jonze, Spike 112, 254
Lyngbye, Christian 114
Monello, Mike 156
Rock, Ben 156
Rouse, James 116
Sedelmaier, JJ 261
Silverson, Erik 254
Teramoto, Makoto 260

ILLUSTRATOR
Del Marmol, Mike 261

INFORMATION ARCHITECT
A-C
Allen, Natasha 211
Athey, David 214
Baba, Kampei 230
Bert, Sosia 218, 248
Boku, Masayoshi 255
Costello, Noah 138
Cumberbatch, Dale 186
E-H
Elbersen, Bob 239, 250, 258
Gallivan, Sara 192, 193
Grant, Laura 221
Groß, Stephan 235
Hamberg, Magnus 66
Hanyu, Koichi 222
Hayes, Tanya 239, 250, 258
Hindmarch, Ben 210
Hirsch, Joshua 238
J-M
Johnson, Tana 144
Johnston, Adam 173
Jordan-Bambach, Daniel 243
Kameda, Go 230

Lamb, Chris 241
Lima, Heloisa 190
MacQuoid, Katy 138
Månsson, Kjell 205
Miranda, Amy 197
O-Y
Obata, Paula Yuri 231
Sloan, Mark 208
Svenonius, Tim 144
Vaughan, Jim 195, 249
Yang, August 86
Yin, Wilson 192

MUSIC & SOUND
Ballew, Chris 250
Berwyn 110
De Caumette, Patrick 254
Lua Web 205
Tyrell LLC 112, 254

PHOTOGRAPHER
D'Orio, Tony 154
Gray, Sebastian 146, 261
Hartz, Daniel 261
Wilmont, Dean 240

PRODUCTION COMPANY
2150 Editorial 152, 261
3D-Production 219
20Q 68
A, B
Aflog Design Unit 249
Agreed 249
Allan, Doug 211
Aoi Digital Creation 260
Auer, Ingo 227
B-Reel 66, 191, 205, 223, 259
Bacus, Janet 258
The Barbarian Group 108, 110, 171, 259
Beacon Street Music 152
Beacon Street Studios 261
Beam Interactive 70, 215, 244
Berwyn 259
BigNoise 230
Big Spaceship 78, 207
Blast Radius 208
Bordon, Helena 24, 30, 190, 199, 238, 255
Business Architects 226
C, D
Chan, Zerlina 219
Chelsea Pictures/Campfire 156, 179, 246
Code & Theory 198
Commotion 138
Cosmo Street 262
Creative, Soap 240

Daddy 241
Dawber, Mark 211
The Designory 138
Dev Impact. 32, 169, 261

E, F, G
Elder, Gavin 196
Element E 172, 247
EVB 261
Enjoy Greener Grass 52
Exopolis 146, 200, 209
Fata Morgana 256
Firstborn Multimedia 68
The George P. Johnson Company 138

H, I
Hakuhodo i-studio 92
Hakuhodo 92
Hall, Branden 108
Hatfield, John 211
hazazaH 239, 250, 258
Hi-ReS! 224
HSI 262
Hungry Man 146, 152, 209
Hunter, Jess 227
iChameleon 146, 209
Idiotlamp 54
Inns, Dylan. 263
Itiden 201, 259

J, K, L
Jeffries, Neil 251
Jennsen, Dave 253
Jodaf/Mixer 146, 209
JJ Sedelmaier Productions 261
Kaka Entertainment 74
Kaplinsky, Alex 144
Kau, Niels 114
Kayac 228
Kvart, Rebekah 194
Lifelong Friendship Society 252
Lima, Heloisa 24, 30, 199, 238, 255

M
Magic Eye 187
Manbaby 250
Mecano 233
Mekanism 246
Mesztig, Lise 251
Mitchell, Bob 211
Milky Elephant 262
Miyagawa, Maiko 222
MJZ 112, 254
Mother 207

N, O
National Television 245
Natzke Design 108, 171
North Kingdom 96
Number 9 108

Nutmeg Audio Post 261
Obscura Digital 126
Oliveira, Renata 24, 30, 190, 199, 238, 255
One Sky 226
Outpost Digital 146, 209
Outside Editorial 110, 259

P
Padilla, Roberta 24, 30, 190, 199, 238, 255
Paradise 259
Phelps, Giles 227
Pixelpusher.ca 197
Plan Do 249
Pop & Company 241
Poke London 195, 234, 248

R, S
Radke Film Group 262
Robinson, Ed 227
Rocket Scoiety 195, 249
Sammarco Productions 74
Saunders, Tom 211
Seto, Hikaru 222
Schulten Film 118
Special Moves 263
Speedshape 126
Stighäll, Roger 194
Struck Design 218, 248
Sudo, Tadanobu: 222
Swiss 191

T, U
Tha Ltd 226
Tomato 252
Tomboy Virals 244
Tomoko, Takaya 196
Turner, Alex 227
Unit9.creative.production 50, 174
Untitled 251

V-Z
V3@Anonymous Content 194, 247, 252
Varitalk 244
The Viral Factory 116
Wauer, Robert 190, 191
Zimb, Sandra 24, 30, 190, 199, 238, 255

PROGRAMMER

A
Åslund, Marcus 187, 188
@www 181
Allen, Victor 215, 253
Assalino, Andre 200
Ayotte, Christian 215

B
Baba, Kampei 230, 255, 256
The Barbarian Group 186
Barbosa, Leonardo 231
Bastedo, Justin 208

Baum, Dennis 219
Baumanis, Filips 202
Bianchi, Erik 253
Billig, Noel 86
Bond, Steve 208
Borgström, Joakim 42, 175, 178
Brady, Tim 208
Brewer, Joshua 209
Brewster, Jeremy 150
Brousseau, Dana 237
Brumm, Michael 112, 254
Burbage, Tony 263

C
Caparrós, Xavi 178
Capraro, Michelangelo 225
Carolin, Mark 208
Cho, Henry 206, 215
Collins, Jake 251
Corcoran, Casey 215, 253
Cowen, John 260
Cox, Dave 54, 179

D, E
Davies Meyer 183
Davis, Chris 243
Death, Mitchell 257
De la Casa, Filippo 229, 234
DiTerlizzi, Joerg 122, 134
Domani Studios 36
Elwin, Matthew 150, 221, 242
EVB 70

F, G
Findlay, Mike 88
Foo, Colin 225
Franca, Rute 200
Fuel Industries 102, 152
Funaro, Stef 233
Futamura, Kojiro 226
Gajate, Iván 204
Gardner, Mark 208
Genco, Chuck 158, 229
Goldbach, Werner 191
Grden, John 208
Gugel, Andy 212
Gustafsson, Bo 213

H
Höfler, Mark 172
Haggerty, Ammon 225
Hamzagic, Raphael 175, 205
Hara, Nobuo 230
Hart, Joshua 170
Hayes, Steve 242
Healy, Miriam 150
Herholz, Benjamin 256
Hezinger, Stefanie 232
Hirsch, Joshua 238

Holland, Uwe 40
Hood, Andy 94
Horowitz, Irwin 202

I, J, K
Ibe, Sohei 228
Imai, Haruyuki 230
Janes, Grant 202
Jensen, Kim 214
Jones, Malik 104
Just, Philippe 219
Kallgard, Simon 234
Kameda, Go 230
Kanega, Shintaro 256
Karlsson, Fredrik 56
Kief, Chris 138
Kitamura, Keita 226
Knott, Andrew 248
Koike, Synthetic-leather 222
Kosoy, Jamie 207
Kovner, Todd 158, 229
Kraft, Manfred 257

L
Lam, Sean 232
Lawrence, Matthew 227, 263
Lee, Gicheol 227
Legowiecki, Martin 158, 229
Lobb, Iain 240, 242
Lopez Mesas, David 204
Lorenz, Jon 236
Louderback, Philip 214
Lunetta, Carlos 228
Lyons, Sean 158, 229

M
Marquardt, Rico 214
Marshall, James 219
Martínez, Jordi 198, 199
Matsumura, Shin 222
Matsuzawa, Toshimitsu 228
McClellan, Bobbi 208
McLoughlin, Michael 86
McNutt, Andrew 182
Milky Elephant 169, 174, 262
Mr.Y 249
Mullady, Patrick 192
Muller, Matthew 227, 263
Muñoz, Cesar 206, 215
Murase, Daisuke 228

N, O
Nakamura, Yugo 84
Nakano, Yas 193
Nakata, Kazuki 230
Nelson, David 144
Ng, Nicholas 225
Noll, Tim 150
North Kingdom 96

Ohtsuka, Akira 230
Oiwa, Naoto 260
Oobuchi, Masumi 177
Oshita, Tetsuji 260
Osman, Fatima 206, 215

P

Pacheco, Paulo 231
Parada, Ernie 202
Peters, Keith 177
Pilsetnek, Daniel 187, 188, 189
Piro, Joseph 209
Pixelpusher.ca 46, 197
Policano, John 182
Pomeroy, Bruce 208
Prindle, Scott 158, 229
Purdy, Dan 88

R

Raju, TV 225
Ramos, Flávio 168, 185, 205
Reale, Andrew 261
Resudek, Todd 104
Ritter, Marko 122, 134
Roach, Sam 177
Roekens, Gregory 263
Roman, Michele 158, 229
Rowlands, Gareth 150, 242
Rowley, James 211
Rubino, Jon 202
Rudolph, Christian 191
Rundgren, Per 188, 189
Ruppel, Jon 192

S

Sako, Minoru 226
Sano, Katsuhiko 231
Santi, Luis 48, 96, 146, 209, 244, 260
Saunders, Tom 227
Sayle, Alex 211
Schmidt, Karsten 243
Schweickhardt, Heiko 217
Seigler, Jason 208
Sjölén, Bengt 66
Smith, Mike 211
Smith, Steve 150
Sousa, Homero 223, 236
Steffen, Jens 60, 64
Studt, Jan M 256
Sullivan, Josh 211
Sundberg, Oskar 56
Suwannatat, Pharanai 202
Sweeney, Clive 233
Szabo, Mike 241

T

Takagi, Hisayuki 222
Tan, Manny 144
Tan, Robin 173

Taylor, Jason 236
Terabyte 130
Tilley, Ian 130
Todorov, Ivan 208
Tominaga, Kumi 86
Torres Troconis, Guillermo 144
Tracki, Piotr 239

U, V

U, Tai 238
Umetsu, Takeshiro 204, 222, 260
Uranga, Raul 223, 236
Van Allen, Phil 138
Voigt, Thorsten 40

W

Walker, Jeremy 230
Walker, Katy 206, 215
Warren, Jamie 251
Watanabe, Makoto 226
WDDG 186
Weiss, Jesper 28
Wetherbee, Roy 186
Wiechers, Stan 158, 229
Williams, Rick 221
Wissing, Jocke 56
Wiström, Isak 194
Wong, Joo Wah 203

Y, Z

Yang, August 158, 229
Yong Park, Joon 227
Zachary, Brendyn 235
Zhu, Hugo 236
Zuardi, Fabrizio 205

WRITER

A, B

Askelöf, Oscar 223
Baglee, Patrick 211
Bailey, Nick 150, 242
Ball, Sam 54
Ballard, Dustin 152
Barber, Tim 225
Bartels, Ingmar 98, 172, 247
Bayliss, Chris 173, 184
Bedwood, Dave 54
Berglof, Henrik 213
Bernardi, Tatiane 181
Black, Rich 212
Bletterman, Josh 158, 229
Boku, Masayoshi 230
Bryer, Josh 240
Butler, Gemma 82, 94

C

Cade, Nick 154
Cain, Brian 156, 179, 246
Caputo, Steve 196

Carl, Chris 186
Carr, Tom 254
Chalmers, Mark 196
Charney, Paul 211
Chau, David 238
Chen, Valerie 203
Christmann, Tom 206, 215
Cianfrone, Bob 260
Citron, Ben 194, 247
Clark, Dave 78
Conde, Paco 178
Condrick, Mike 198
Cooney, Scott 206, 215
Corbitt, Carl 260
Corrigan, Don 243
Corwin, Larry 68, 152
D
Dahlstrom, Karen 207, 238
Danko, Mike 195, 218, 248, 249
Davies, Rhiannon 214
DeKeyser, Dawn 253
De la Rosa, Esther 234
Denkel, Volker 235
De Rooij, Bram 239, 250, 258
Devitt, Cedric 180
Dietz, Mandy 50, 52, 171, 174
Dillow, Jesse 195, 218, 248, 249
Divino, Tina 206
E, F
Edwards, Katie 140
Ehlers, Robert 256
Einhorn, Marc 182
Emery, Toria 108, 126
Enberg, Erik 234
Erke, Ken 112, 254
Fatemi, Omid 196
Field-Smith, Jim 54
Figel, Pete 112, 254
Figueira, Ricardo 168
Finlay, Kerry 221
Fischvogt, Matt 156, 179, 233, 246
Fleig, Paul 122, 134
Foster, Simon 202
Frank, Kevin 100
G
Ganann, Sean 193
Gatewood, Chris 170
Geisler, Ute 196
Geiter, Andrea 191
Gillette, Jeff 262
Goh, Alex 232
Gonzalez, David 261
Gonzalez, Ivan 223
Gopalratnam, Sridhar 225
Gordon-Rogers, Gavin 82, 94

Gribel, Christiane 231
Griffiths, Aaron 126, 200
Gschwend, Charlie 209
Guerra, Jackie 215, 244
Gunshanon, Jim 156, 179, 246
H
Högkvist, Cissi 182
Haguiara, Luciana 168, 175, 185, 205
Hale, Gregg 156, 179, 246
Hathiramani, Jackie 70, 261
Haugen, Eric 104
Heath, John 206
Hegerfors, Anders 74
Henke, Andreas 219
Henkel, Mathias 245
Hino, Takayuki 26, 218
Howard, Mike 102
I, J
Ingall, Rob 104
Ingoglia, Sy 186
Inoue, Nobuhito 226
Ito, Naoki 220
James, Stephen 214
Jansson, Fredrik 74
Johnson, Paul 68
Jones, David 243
Jordan, Paul 252
Jun 222
K
Kanzer, Adam 206, 215
Kato, Tetsuhiko 210
Kelleher, Dan 206, 215
Khun, Krista 202
Kincaid, Tristan 202
King, Jon 138
Knittel, Eric 258
Kodama, Yutaka 230, 255
Koh, Juliana 180, 38
Koike, Mamiko 220
Krahl Junior, Jones 168
Kramm, Justin 106
Kruse, Johan 187, 188, 189
Kurita, Yosuke 222
Kusaka, Yukari 249
Kutscher, Ryan 174, 262
L
Lützenkirchen, Ulrich 190
Langworthy, George 192, 193
Larsen, Ernie 156, 179, 246
Lee, Jenny 110, 259
Lee, Justine 173
LeMaitre, Jim 206, 215
Lemmon, Todd 171
Levy, Evan 213
Lewenhaupt, Calle 205

Lidzell, Anders 194
Linnen, Scott 96, 169
Lloyd, Simon 244
Lynch, Kerry 186

M

Mackness, Jon 34, 176
Makak, Roger 173
Maloney, Kathleen 144
Mamiya, Takaharu 260
Martínez, Nuria 198
Massareto, Domênico 181
Matullat, Jan 214
Mayer, Philipp 232
Mazzariol, Mauricio 30, 238
McCabe, Jeanne 238
McCann, Jason 46, 197
McElligott, Steve 206, 215
Molinillo, Daniel 229, 234
Mun, Edward: 134
Murasawa, Hiroaki 222
Muro, Ayumi 204

N, O, P

Nakajima, Satoshi 44
Nelson, Jacob 191, 201, 241, 259
Nilsson, Filip 259
Niwa, Masayoshi 177
O'Connell, Steve 48, 146, 209
Ogata, Mariko 92
Owens, Geoff 184
Pau, Stephanie 144
Phillips, Elizabeth 243
Pierro, Fábio 178
Pino, Esther 42, 175
Povill, David 68
Powell, Neil 110, 259
Preskow, Len 88
Priebs-Macpherson, Alex 118
Pueyo, Emma 178, 199

R

Reilly, Rob 48, 146, 209
Ringqvist, Martin 191, 241
Rodríguez, Trini 199
Rogers, Josh 110, 259

S

Samsel, Eric 250
Sanders, Glenn 104
Sasaki, Yasuharu 210, 256
Schernbeck, Thomas 235
Schiff, David 261
Seldon, Adair 192
Shah, Arthur 88
Shefelman, Dan 110, 259
Shellen, Chris 208
Shepter, Joe 215, 253
Shimotakahara, Lisa 263
Shortt, Kevin 219, 237
Silverson, Erik 254
Slade, Kristina 245
Smit, Roos 196
Smith, David 196
Smith, Grant 206, 215
Stephens, Josh 136
Strasberg, Rob 215, 244, 262
Stripling, Scott 237

T

Tao, Shinji 220
Tierney, Brian 32, 36, 70, 169, 261
Tipton, Franklin 48, 146, 152, 209, 244
Toledo, Keke 24, 190, 199, 255
Tornello, Steve 120, 221
Triumf, Kristoffer 56
Tufts, Scott 158, 229
Turner, Christine 244
Tyler, Alexandra 212

U-Z

Uchiyama, Koshi 226
Von Kempen, Oliver 183
Wagman, Ryan 251
Wan, Meng 172
Watson, Mike 227, 263
Weiss, Ari 206, 215
Weist, Dave 186, 252
Whitlock, Stephen 72
Willbond, Ben 54
Yamagiwa, Ryoko 218
Zachariah, Abraham 235